OAKLAND COMMUNITY COLLEGE
3 2355 00249555 4

C0-ATG-495

The Nikon Manual

The

a Complete Handbook

Universal
Photo Books
New York, N. Y.

NIKON MANUAL

of 35mm Technique

by George B. Wright

Technical Assistance by

Joseph C. Abbott

Cora Wright

(Opposite) MORRIS JAFFE

Nikon S2, 35mm f/2.5 Nikkor
Tri-X, 1/30, f/4

First Edition

First Printing

Library of Congress Catalog Card Number: 57-10344

Printed in the United States of America

UNIVERSAL PHOTO BOOKS

67 West 44th Street New York 36, New York

Exclusive distributor to the photographic trade

AMPHOTO

33 West 60th Street New York 23, New York

Preface

THIS BOOK IS OFFERED as a manual of up-to-date, professionally tested, 35mm practices. It is intended to be thorough enough to serve as a guide for those seriously interested in photography as a hobby or as a future profession.

When a Nikon manual was first discussed, I visualized a guide to the equipment plus the necessary basics of 35mm camera use. The project, however, rapidly grew beyond these dimensions. Nikon equipment more than meets professional standards and could not be covered with a quick once-over "catalog" treatment. Quite as importantly, an extensive survey of the books in print on 35mm photography soon indicated that there was very little available which presented the methods of properly handling the present film emulsions or the contemporary approach to 35mm work.

The consequence has been a book larger in size than most "camera guides," and one which, it is hoped, is correspondingly more useful.

A project like this is not conducted in any literary ivory tower, and the list of those who rendered assistance is a long one. It must begin with my wife, Cora, who worked beside me, researching facts, retesting films and developers, criticizing the successive drafts of the manuscript phrase by phrase, holding up with patience and humor during the long, round-the-clock sessions of page lay-out when the jig-saw pieces of the book were assembled into final form. In addition, she took over the main responsibility for assembling and meticulously checking the endless details of the *Data and Formulas* section.

RAY SHORR

Nikon S2
35mm f/2.5 Nikkor
Plus-X, 1/60 f/8

Working with Nikon, Inc. proved to be very pleasant, indeed. Joseph Ehrenreich's cooperation from the inception of the idea, made the book possible in the first place. Joseph C. Abbott provided quantities of technical information, patiently checked manuscript and galleys and made very many valuable suggestions which improved the accuracy and usefulness of every chapter. E. Yamanaka of Nippon Kogaku, K. K., provided much valuable information on the Nikkor lenses and checked the galleys of Chapter 4 and the optical formulas of the *Data and Formulas* for accuracy. Len Silverman, also, went considerably out of his way to provide photographs of the equipment which supplemented those made especially for this book.

My special thanks must be extended to Seymour D. Uslan, President of Universal Photo Books, for cooperation above and beyond that normally expected from a publisher in allowing me a free hand in shaping the contents and physical form of the *Nikon Manual.*

It is impossible to name all of the others who were helpful. New equipment for the illustrations, for example, was loaned by Fred Simmon of Simmon Brothers, Inc., Robert P. Saunders of The Saunders Co., Jack Alberti of M. P. Manufacturing Co., George Winslow of Arel, Inc., George Ward of the Heiland Division, Minneapolis-Honeywell, Harry Parker of American Speedlight Corp., and others. Robert Brown and James Baxter of Eastman Kodak were, as always, helpful with information, as were Eugene Ostroff of Ilford, Inc. and Kenneth Johnson of Ansco and Arthur Kramer. My friend, Norman Rothschild, provided stereo information for Chapter 12.

It is probably needless to add that any errors of fact or interpretation which have crept in are the responsibility of the author.
New York, N. Y., October, 1957

GEORGE B. WRIGHT

(Above) GENE COOK
Ingrid Bergman visits New York

Nikon S2, 28mm f/3.5 Nikkor
Tri-X, 1/125, f/5.6

(Below) GENE COOK
Ingrid Bergman

Nikon S2, 50mm f/1.4 Nikkor
Tri-X, 1/30, f/4

Contents

1

35mm Photography Today

THE POPULARITY OF 35MM CAMERAS is a direct reflection of their ease of operation and general utility for advanced amateur and professional alike. The amateur finds a Nikon simple to operate, yet constantly challenging him to explore and control its further possibilities as a picture-making instrument. Professionals, who once considered anything smaller than 4x5-inch sheet film as "miniature," now find 35mm an indispensable tool, while photojournalism and editorial illustration as we know them would be impossible without equipment such as the Nikon and the Nikkor lenses.

The large-negative cameras certainly have a function, and it would be foolish to deny their utility, even though they have lost the general superiority they possessed a generation ago in the face of the development of 35mm cameras, lenses and available films. It is no exaggeration that these newer tools have opened a new photographic dimension and given us a fresh, new look at man and his world.

Photography serves two functions, that of recording and of interpreting the world around us, and every photograph is a merging of these two in some proportion. This double function has led to much wordy argument about photography's status as an "art." The recording function has blinded many critics to the camera's flexibility in reflecting the objective world in terms of the photographer's subjective reactions to what he sees through his viewfinder. The 35mm camera has piled up a mountain of evidence (to the large-film camera's less-frequent examples) of the creative possibilities of lens and film. It has pointed up the importance of personal selectivity of moment, angle and

---

1.1 GENE COOK — *Nikon S, 35mm f/3.5 Nikkor*
Harry Belafonte — *Two electronic flash units; Plus-X, f/11*

1.2 GERRY LOW — *Nikon S2, 50mm f/1.4 Nikkor*
Panatomic-X, 1/250, f/4

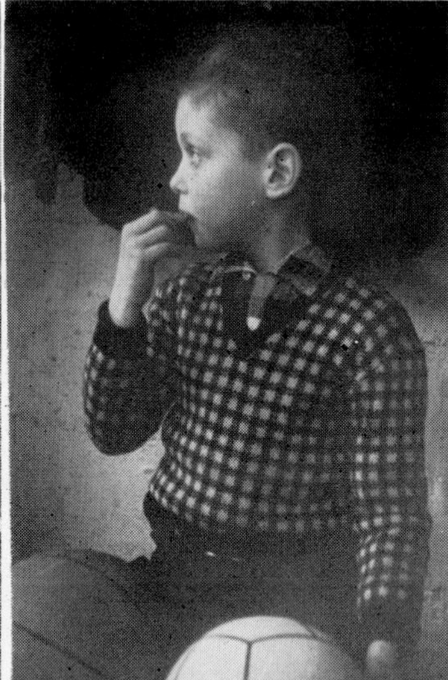

1.3, 4, 5 HARVEY SHAMAN *Nikon S, 50mm f/1.4 Nikkor*
Play school *Available light; Tri-X, 1/20, f/2.8*

exact framing which make a photograph as truly interpretive as any other form of visual art.

Even more than any other hand-held camera, the 35mm has added a new element to visual communication: the isolation of a significant instant caught from the flow of life. This may be apprehended and exposed so rapidly that a full logical understanding of the human meaning and formal relationships within the picture frame follows rather than precedes the opening of the shutter. This is a completely different way of perceiving and thinking than the way of the view camera with its studied and calculated effects of subject matter and design. The contact proof-sheets of a 35mm photographer of honesty and experience reveal the stages of growth in his understanding of the living, changing dynamics of the event, personality or even a locale until it matures into a visual expression which will communicate to others.

In this act, the man is much more important than his instrument. The 35mm camera, however, has extended his means of recording and interpreting for a continually growing audience. The ability to photograph not only accurately but under conditions of poor lighting, spontaneous action and difficult locales, emphasizes the necessity of a precision tool to capture what his eye perceives.

The Nikon and the line of Nikkor lenses were recognized as just such precision tools when experienced American photojournalists encountered them, almost by accident. A few Nikon outfits were in use in the United States in 1949. They attracted no attention and, in fact, the Japanese products were not then considered as serious competition to German optical goods despite the acknowledged high standards of military and naval equipment captured in the Pacific theater during World War II.

In mid-1950, Horace Bristol, a former *Life* photographer resident in Tokyo, saw and tested the 85mm f/2 Nikkor. Impressed, he and David Douglas Duncan of the *Life* staff visited Nippon Kogaku K.K. (Japan Optical, Ltd.), the firm from which the lens came and which had been chief supplier of precision optical goods for the Japanese armed forces. At Nippon Kogaku, they made arrangements to test a selection of lenses and cameras chosen at random from the production line. The original individual 85mm Nikkor proved to be no "freak"; all the Nikkors tested gave remarkable results, consistent from lens to lens.

When Duncan went to Korea a short time later to cover the conflict there, the stirring photographs he sent back to recreate the war for the American public were made with his set of Nikkor lenses. When Carl Mydans, Hank Walker and, later, John Dominis of *Life* came through Tokyo on their way to cover the Korean front each of them, too, picked up Nikkors and used them almost exclusively. When the Nikons and Nikkor lens outfits reached New York, *Life* sent them out for rigorous mechanical and optical tests. The results of these, confirming the field experience, led to a pooled order for over 20 complete outfits for photojournalists working with *Look* as well as *Life*, together with extra Nikkors to fit other 35mm cameras. The active professional grape-vine carried the word of the excellence of the Japanese products and Jacob Deschin in his camera column of December 10, 1950 in the Sunday *New York Times* announced the discovery to a wider public.

Popular Photography magazine, always alert to professional trends of general interest, published fuller accounts of Nikkor performance in their issues of February and March, 1951. The first carried an item on the lenses [Tools and Techniques, page 28] by Norman Lipton, telling the story of their "discovery" and use in Korea; the second, a feature story on the work of David Douglas Duncan by Bruce Downes, which commented on his use of Nikkor lenses and noted that his negatives "according to Frank Scherschel, [then] *Life's* assistant picture editor . . . turned out to be the sharpest 35mm negatives the lab ever processed."

For the June, 1951 issue of *Modern Photography*, John Wolbarst wrote a sober evaluation of the camera and lenses, concluded that the Nikon line offered a direct challenge to the cameras which were then better-known in this country. The success of that "challenge" is demonstrated by the increasing numbers of Nikons and Nikkor lenses used in the United States. The demand for them has kept steady pace with supply, even though this has been greatly multiplied as Nippon Kogaku K.K. has increased production while holding to its own standards of perfection which are even more exacting than the rigid official quality requirements for all photographic export goods enforced by the Japanese Camera Inspection Institute.

Probably the most sincere compliment the Nikon line receives is the common assumption that Nikons have been around "forever." In only a few years, they have been so extensively tested and proven that they are a standard of recognized quality against which the performance of equipment of other manufacturers must be judged.

The company, Nippon Kogaku K.K., from which the Nikon and Nikkors come, is not a new name in the field of precision optics. Japan, like the United States and many other countries, was largely dependent before the first World War on German optical glass as well as finished lenses and instruments. With the Allied blockade of Germany, the rest of the world turned to building domestic optical production and the Japanese found themselves literally sitting on

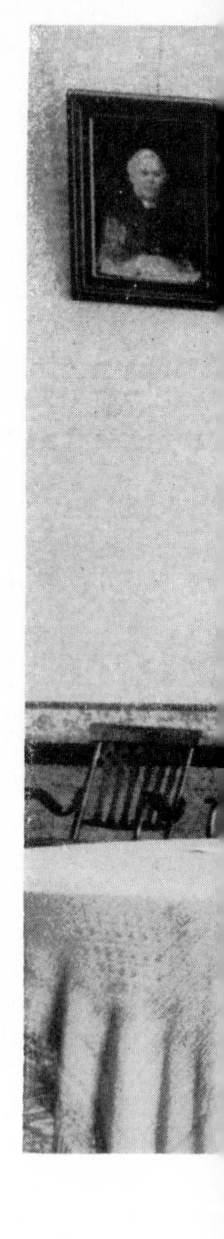

1.6 JACQUES LOWE
Bishop's residence, Haiti

Nikon S2, 25mm f/4 Nikkor
Tri-X, 1/30, f/5.6

volcanic earths with superior qualities as ingredients for the special glass formulas from which lenses are made. In July, 1917, Nippon Kogaku K.K. was founded and began production and active research. In 1923 it began compounding and melting its own glass, developing data and experience which now covers over 100 types with distinctive characteristics. Even as it grew to be a large company, it did not become well known, even in Japan. Like some optical goods manufacturers everywhere, its production went largely to the government rather than to the consumer market.

When World War II ended, Nippon Kogaku K.K. converted entirely to civilian production: binoculars, telescopes, microscopes, optical instruments for science and industry, and (in 1948) the first model of the Nikon camera. Precision made from the first, the study of Nikon performance for its users has continued and produced the improvements and innovations of the Model S2 and the new Model SP, each an original and important step ahead of the field in 35mm design.

The line of Nikkor lenses has kept in advance of other recent remarkable advances in 35mm objectives, too. New speed and wide-angle coverage have been achieved together with the unsurpassed acutance of image which impressed

the American photojournalists who first used them. The line of accessories is also growing to extend the Nikon precision to many applications of photography.

Some of these other fields of 35mm usefulness to industry and science receive little public notice compared to photojournalism and the vast film consumption of the amateur market. Yet this kind of photography is a more important part of the foundation of our technical civilization than is usually realized. It has become essential for research and for the vital communication of results among engineers. The Nikon and the Nikkor lenses are being "discovered" for use in these fields, with apparently the same pleased astonishment that was evoked from professionals and amateurs some years ago.

In the next chapter (and elsewhere in this *Manual*), Nikon equipment is described. The remaining chapters cover the essentials of 35mm technique and useful amateur and professional practices. A book such as this can only serve as the beginning, as an introduction to the possibilities which open before the man standing with a Nikon in his hand. When he looks through the Nikon view-finder, his photography is not limited by the instrument he holds, but extends to the horizons of his own creative perception.

2.1 *The 35mm camera is an intricately made precision instrument. Above is a cut-away view of the Nikon S2, with the 105mm f/2.5 Nikkor and Variframe Finder.*

NIKON EQUIPMENT

2

Getting Acquainted with the Nikon

ESSENTIALLY, ANY CAMERA IS A LIGHT-TIGHT BOX with an arrangement for holding film flat along one side and advancing (or changing) it regularly from exposure to exposure. Opposite the film, there is a lens to collect and focus the light from the subject, with an arrangement to open a shutter to admit this light for controlled intervals. Each of these features has only a few basically different designs, yet the variations between camera brands and models is a bewildering one. The photographer must choose between them on the basis of their record of dependability and performance, and on their convenience for him in use.

It is this latter which is first quickly evident when handling the Nikon. Some cameras, even those of the compact and convenient 35mm size, seem to have been designed by someone ignorant of the precise shape of the human hand and of the way fingers are attached. The position and movements of the controls on such cameras require learning a special digital dexterity before concentrating on photography itself. When the Nikon, however, is picked up and held to the eye, the focusing wheel, shutter release and film advance lever (on the currently produced SP and S2 models) fall naturally under the fingers of the right hand. They are all "where they belong" and the slight awkwardness in handling any new camera passes away before the examination and appreciation of the Nikon's other features is concluded.

Some of these Nikon features are visible to immediate examination and others are not. The single-stroke rapid advance lever of the current models, for example, is built-in to perform the same function which other brands provide as a separate "professional accessory" to match the Nikon sequence-shooting speed. Other design niceties remain invisible. The prisms of the range-finder system, for instance, are front-surfaced in gold. Silver is ordinarily used for this purpose and is somewhat brighter when first applied, but oxidation soon brings down its reflectivity to a point lower than that of the stable gold film. The unseen shutter mechanism is so engineered that it is thermally compensated, its actual delivered speeds much less affected by extremes of cold than are many others. The Nikon has given professional service in the far Arctic and on the recent Antarctic expeditions. Few owners will actually put their Nikons to such tests, yet features such as this are evidence of the skill and honesty of its construction.

The description and operating instructions of the Nikon models S, S2 and SP are on the next pages, with brief descriptions of camera accessories and notes on the proper care of the Nikon following. Some readers in the United States and elsewhere may encounter an earlier Nikon which does not seem to fit these descriptions exactly. The first Nikon (Model 1) was produced during 1948-49, contemporary with the first four Nikkor lenses for 35mm photography. This camera resembles the Model S, has speeds from 1 to 1/500 second, bulb and time settings, but no flash synchronization. Its most distinctive characteristic is an automatic exposure counter numbered past 40, for it exposes a 24x32mm area on the film and gives extra exposures on each cartridge film length.

From 1949 to 1952, the Model M was produced. Some improvements were introduced during this period, but typically the M has the same shutter speeds as the Model 1 and the majority of them are also without internal flash synchronization. The automatic exposure counter, however, is numbered only to 36 and the frame area is expanded to 24x34mm with slightly greater separation (2mm) between the negatives along the strip than is usual. This model served the photojournalists who originally used it in Korea. In 1952, the Nikon left behind this first period of testing and of evaluating professional and amateur suggestions from a market grown world-wide. The appearance of the Model S, introduced a Nikon capable of comparison with the best then current in this sharply-competitive field. The definitely improved S2 followed in 1955, and the further considerably redesigned SP is reaching photographers as this *Manual* is printed. The battle of the drawing-boards (and of the optical glass melting pots) accelerates new design thinking which we, as camera-users, can enjoy and utilize.

A camera is only as important as the photographs it makes possible. Nikon redesign has not been chrome stripping nor "fish-tail" body lines with fake jet-exhausts. It is instrumentation for more closely blending the act of perception with the act of instantaneous and more precise recording.

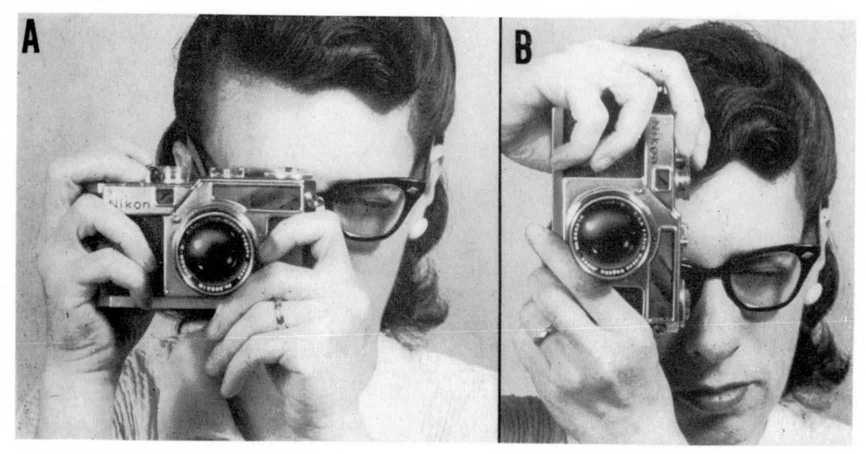

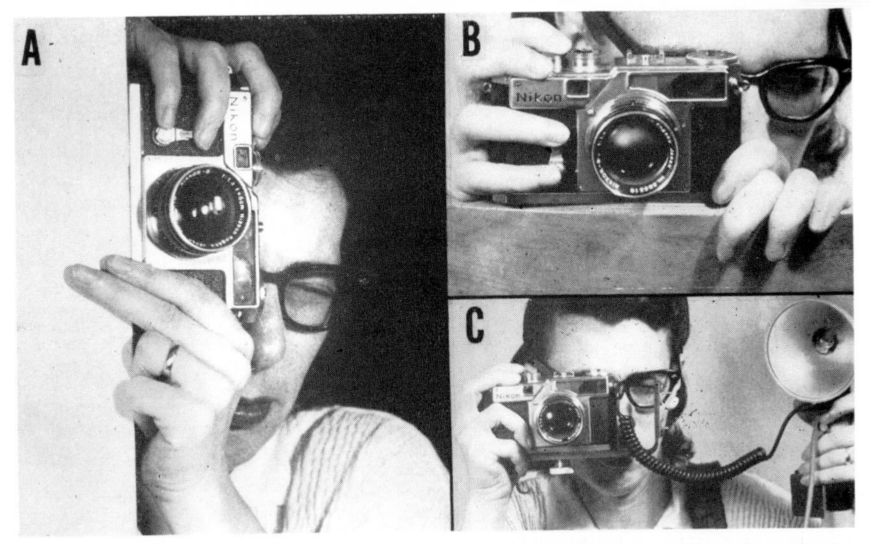

2.2 *(Opposite) the usual ways of handling the Nikon horizontally and vertically, with the fingers correctly held for three-finger operation.* **2.3** *(Above) The Nikon may be steadied against a wall, doorway or other vertical surface (A), or against a horizontal surface (B), for firmness. The Nikon may also be held in one hand when using a flashgun off the camera (C).*

How to Take Care of Your Nikon

Wiping the outside of the Nikon body with a soft cloth should be sufficient to keep it clean. Waxes, leather polishes and metal cleaners are unnecessary and may harm the mechanism if they seep inside.

Clean the inside of the Nikon frequently to remove dust which will create tiny, clear spots on negatives difficult to remove after printing, and any tiny film chips which could damage the shutter curtain or scratch the film. A hand-blower or, better, a vacuum cleaner with *mild* suction followed by a wiping with a soft, lintless cloth is an excellent periodic routine.

See Chapter 4 for lens cleaning instructions.

When the Nikon is in the eveready case, be sure the locking nut holds it firmly so it will not drop out.

Do not allow the Nikon to remain in over-heated spots (such as the glove compartment of a car) or in the direct sun when not in use. If it is left lying uncapped in the sun, the Nikkor may act as a burning glass, concentrating the sunlight on the focal plane shutter which will scorch and weaken or actually char.

When not in use, move the focusing wheel back to the infinity position so the lock catches.

The lens-cap is an excellent investment to protect against accidental damage and finger-prints. However, it has been demonstrated millions of times (often by those who should know better) that it functions very poorly as a "filter" if it is left on when shooting. Acquire the habit of slipping it on when the Nikon is not in use *and* automatically removing it when anticipating picture opportunities.

SP

Introduced 1957

Image: 24x36mm (0.945x1.417-in.) Shutter traverse 13 milliseconds

Body weight 20 ounces

The Model SP Nikon has been re-designed to incorporate a number of distinct improvements over previous models. Here are the names and locations of the parts:

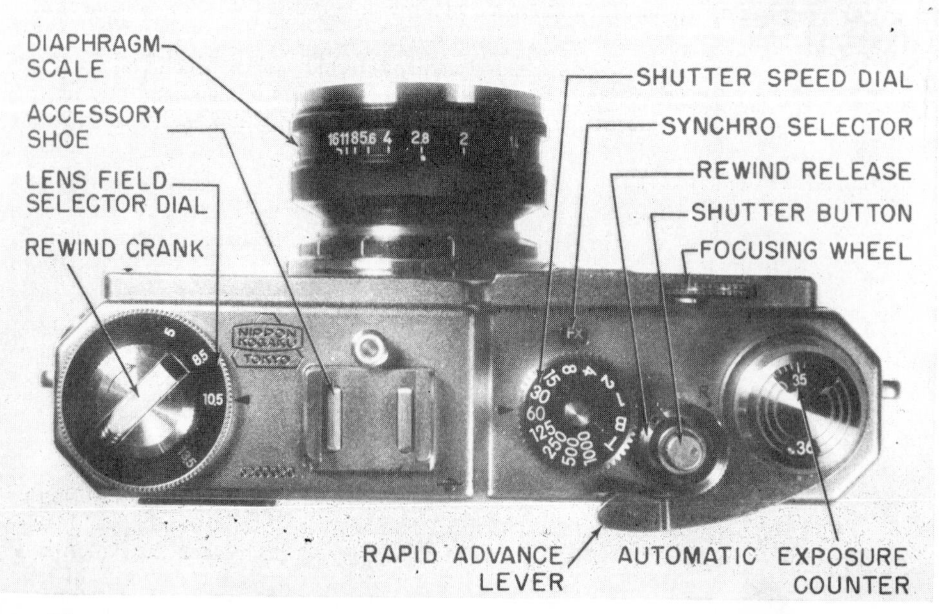

SP Universal Viewfinder System

The unique feature of the Model SP Nikon is the viewfinder which gives the front of the camera its distinctive appearance The rear eyepiece [right, above] is divided into two windows, and the right-hand one serves as viewfinder for the 50mm, 85mm, 105mm and 135mm focal-length Nikkor lenses as well as for the rangefinder (the light-tinted rectangle in the center) with which they all couple. The left window, which a very slight movement of the eye will bring into use, outlines the areas which the 35mm and 28mm Nikkors will cover [left, bottom].

The lens field selector dial [center, above] controls the projected frame lines which appear in the right window. As it is turned, a series of these rectangles appear, one at a time, to outline the life-size image covered by each focal length [left]. The proper choice of lens will be instantly visible as the scene is viewed. Notice that the viewfinder field is slightly larger than the frame lines for the 50mm Nikkor: this is an aid in determining exactly what should be included in the picture without cutting off important details. (It is a help, too, to those of us who wear glasses and find some of the area invisible on other rangefinder-viewfinder systems.) Shown left: 50, 85, 105, 135mm frames.

Focusing is done with the small wheel which is directly under the middle finger when the Nikon is properly held [see later]. Notice, as the wheel is turned, how the frame lines automatically shift to correct for parallax (the separation between the view through the viewfinder and the actual view through the lens). This small difference becomes quite important at close camera distances and parallax correction will prevent cutting off areas unintentionally.

The left window presents the areas included by the commonly used wide-angle Nikkors which also couple to the rangefinder. The solid black line defines the 35mm field, and the dotted lines the parallax correction at 3 to 7 feet. The full window indicates the 28mm field which is so wide that parallax is rarely, if ever, any problem in framing.

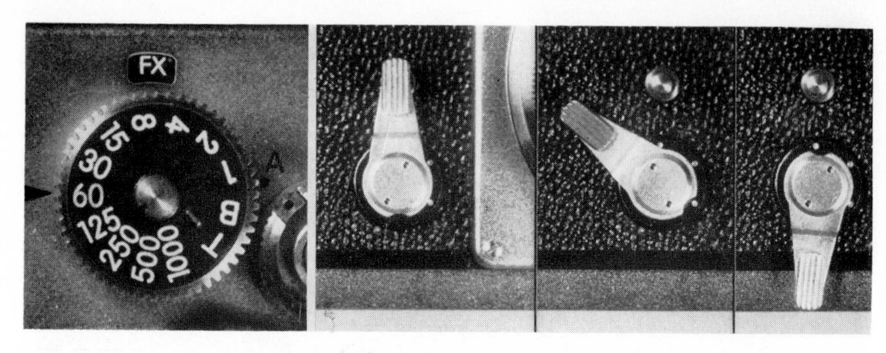

Setting the shutter speed

On the Nikon SP all the shutter speed settings are on a single click-stop dial which rotates freely a full 360° in either direction and which may be set (without lifting) for the required speed either before or after the shutter is wound (by a single stroke of the Rapid-advance Lever). The speeds are arranged in a linear scale, that is, each is approximately half that of the preceding setting: 1 second, 1/2, 1/4, 1/8, 1/15, 1/30, 1/60, 1/125, 1/250, 1/500, 1/1000, Time and Bulb. The "1," the numerator of each fraction, is omitted on the dial for clarity. The speed numbers are color coded to correspond with the proper flash synchronization settings [see later].

The figure for the chosen speed should be set opposite the small arrow to the left of the dial (when the camera is held in operating position). Set at *B,* the shutter will remain open as long as pressure is maintained on the release button. Set at *T,* the shutter will remain open until a slight movement of the speed dial permits it to close. For these latter two settings, the Nikon should be on a tripod or other firm support, and no exposure should be made at speeds slower than 1/30 without firmly bracing the Nikon in some manner, particularly with Nikkors of focal lengths longer than 50mm.

The self timer

The self-timer lever on the front of the camera permits a delay of approximately 3, 5 or 10 seconds between the time the release is pressed and the actual tripping of the shutter. Notice the small notch at the bottom of the timer lever [upper right] and the three white dots it successively reveals as it is rotated in a counter-clockwise direction. These mark the measured intervals of delay, although the lever may also be set for any intermediate position. The tiny release button revealed by moving the lever activates the self-timer and this, in turn, releases the shutter when the lever returns nearly to its original position. The shutter, of course, must be wound and set for the proper speed, just as if the normal release button were to be used. If it is decided not to use the delay after the self-timer has been wound, proceed as usual to make a normal exposure with the shutter release button on the top of the Nikon and after the exposure but *before* winding the next film frame, press the self-timer release and let the spring tension run off.

The amateur thinks most frequently of using this delay when the Nikon is on a tripod and he wishes to get into the picture scene himself. The professional, however, also uses it to trip the shutter when he is using a long, hand-held exposure and he wants to use both hands (and all ten fingers) to hold the Nikon rock-steady.

16 11 8 5.6 4 2.8 2 1.4

SP

1/1000	1/500	1/250	1/125	1/60	1/30	1/15	1/8
f/1.4	f/2	f/2.8	f/4	f/5.6	f/8	f/11	f/16

Aperture (f/stop) settings

The aperture on all Nikkor lenses is set by placing the required f/number opposite the dot or line on the lens barrel (inside the front ring on wide-angle Nikkors). Like the shutter speeds, these are in a linear scale, with each larger number (except for the first interval in some cases) representing an opening which admits half the light of the preceding one [see Chapter 3]. The scale immediately above, indicates this relationship: if the correct exposure setting is 1/1000 at f/1.4, all of the other combinations shown will admit an equivalent amount of light and may be chosen instead.

Depth of field, or zone of acceptable sharpness, may be read directly from the double f/stop scale around the lens bayonet of the Nikon, next to the distance scale on the 50mm Nikkor (and on the barrel of Nikkors of other focal lengths which hide this scale on the Nikon body). When the Nikkor is focused for a given distance, say 15 feet, the depth of field for the f/stop employed may be read from the distances opposite the f/stop marking on either side; in this case (for f/8) from about 10 to 30 feet [left, above].

Hyperfocal distance [see chapters 3 and 4] is found opposite each f/stop marking to the right on this scale when the camera is focused at infinity [right, above]. The greatest possible depth of field is secured for any f/stop when the camera is focused at the corresponding hyperfocal distance; the zone of sharpness will extend from infinity to half the hyperfocal distance.

Infrared focus [right below] differs somewhat from visible focus. After the Nikon is focused by rangefinder, shift the distance scale slightly clockwise (as indicated in the illustration) so the focused distance is opposite the f/2.8 (red R) mark for the 50mm f/2 Nikkor, opposite the f/4 mark for the 50mm f/1.4 Nikkor, or opposite the f/5.6 mark for the 50mm f/1.1 Nikkor. A red mark on the barrel of other Nikkors indicates the point of correct infrared focus for these lenses. (The red R at the f/2.8 position indicates this point of correct infrared focus for the 50mm f/2 Nikkor only.)

SP

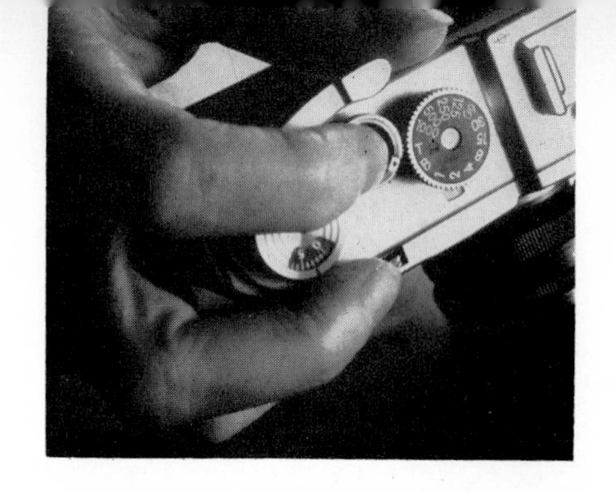

Operating sequence

The Nikon Model SP and S2 are characterized by their rapid, three-finger operation. Form the habit of placing the forefinger on the shutter-release, the middle finger on the focusing wheel and using the thumb to operate the rapid-advance lever. The left hand should be used to steady the Nikon, but when you need one hand for your own balance or when holding a flash reflector above and to the side, the Nikon may be operated for one or even a series of exposures entirely in one hand.

Look through the viewfinder at the light, inner rangefinder rectangle. When the camera is not in focus, a double image will be seen. Rotate the focusing wheel until the two images exactly coincide. If in doubt, run the wheel *slightly* beyond the point where they seem to coincide, then back. The rangefinder is very easy to use when there are definite vertical lines at the point of important focus or where there is a distinct, bright highlight or pattern. If the image is less definite or has prominent horizontal lines, turn the Nikon 90° or to an intermediate position while using the rangefinder. With a little practice, it will become easy to follow focus on moving subjects while awaiting the instant to expose.

Press the shutter release gently so the camera is not jarred. Notice how the button may be depressed before it actually trips the shutter. When anticipating action, take up this slack so a tiny "hair-trigger" movement will set off the shutter, with the least delay and possibility of camera motion.

When shooting a series or anticipating action, advance film immediately after each exposure so the Nikon is set up for the next release of the shutter.

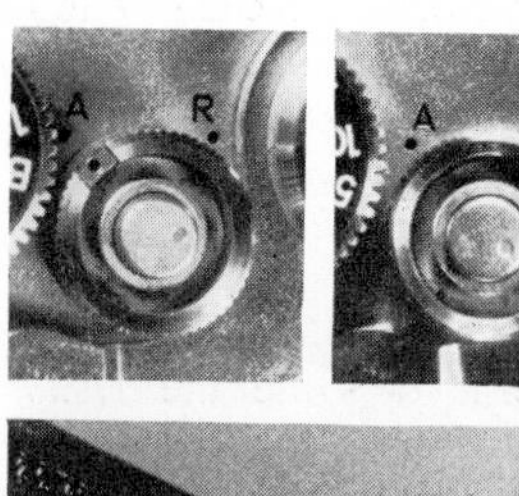

Rewinding and reloading

When the automatic exposure counter [see next page] indicates that film in the cartridge or cassette is exhausted (or when the rapid advance lever suddenly binds in mid-stroke if you have forgotten to watch the count!), replace the lens cap to prevent fingerprints and turn the collar around the shutter release button from the *A* to *R* position [lower left, opposite page]. Raise the rewind crank and rotate in the direction indicated by the engraved arrow. It is best to leave part of the film leader extending from the cartridge to prevent light leaks through the felt light-trap. Notice the off-center red dot on the shutter button: this will revolve as long as the film is threaded on the sprocket wheels [lower right, this page]. The instant this ceases to move, halt the crank and return to its normal depressed position. Hold the Nikon in the palm of the hand, lens down and the barrel between middle and forefinger, or in an equally secure manner, and raise and turn the lock in the left end of the camera base.

Slide the back off and place it in a clean, secure spot. Slip out the used cartridge (toward the base) and slide in a new one so the prongs on the rewind axle slip into the core of the cartridge and engage the little plastic bar. Continue holding the camera with one hand and loading with the other: At first, this may be clumsy but the design of the Nikon makes it perfectly feasible and you will find it a habit of great value when you must load quickly or in semi-darkness or in a moving vehicle.

Hold the new cartridge in place with your thumb [see pictures below] and draw the film leader across, insert the tongue end in the take-up spool slot and give this a *reverse* (counter-clockwise) half-turn [see pictures below]. This little tooth in the slot should have engaged a film sprocket-hole and the rotation taken up the slack in the film leader so it now fits down over the two sprocket-wheels on the axle next to the take-up spool with the teeth through a sprocket-hole at either side. This can be performed more rapidly than it can be described, thanks to the fact that the take-up spool is fixed in place in the Nikon and the back opens for perfect visibility and access.

If there is any slack left in the film leader, draw it tight by a further partial turn on the take-up spool (without drawing any unexposed film out of the cartridge, of course). Replace the back and turn the lock on the base to secure it in place. Turn the collar around the shutter button back to *A* and use the rapid advance lever (it may require an additional short stroke the first time) and make two "blank" exposures to draw unexposed film into position for use. Notice as you do this: the red dot on the top of the shutter button should turn at each use of the advance lever, indicating that the new film is advancing properly. The rewind crank will also turn as soon as all slack within the cartridge has been taken up.

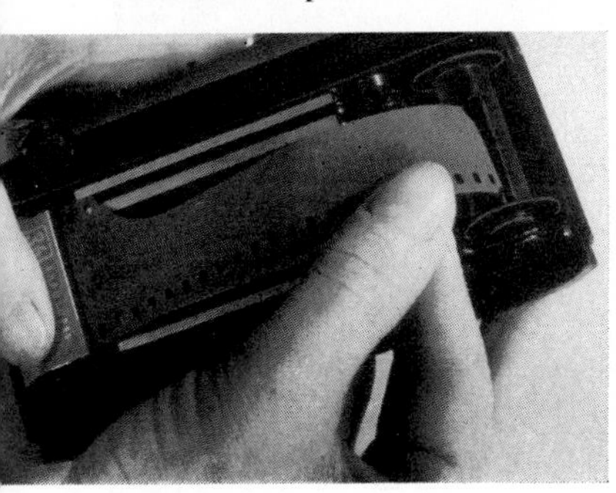

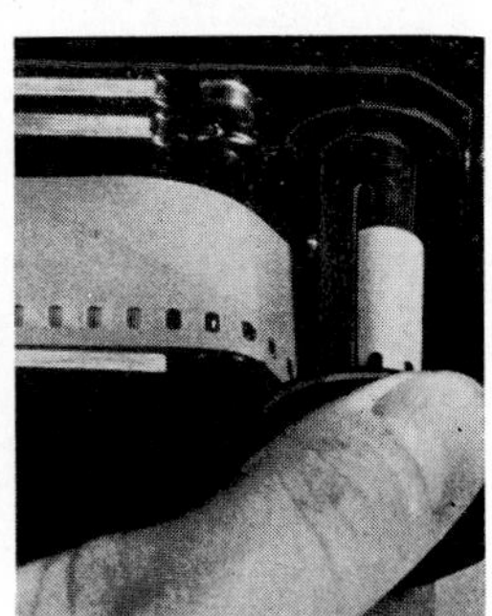

SP

The *automatic exposure counter* [right] on the SP returns to zero when the back is removed and will not register the first two shutter movements which dispose of the exposed leader. When the advance lever is operated for the third time, the counter will register "1" and advance automatically with each exposure to 36.

The *film load reminder* beneath the exposure register indicates whether a 20- or 36-exposure cartridge has been loaded and can be shifted with the fingernail against the little pin between the figures.

On the base-plate of the camera is a *film-type reminder dial* which may be set for the (color or black-and-white) Exposure Index of the film loaded in the camera, or on E for "empty."

Changing lenses

The 50mm Nikkors fit into the *inside bayonet* of the Nikon body. To remove, first turn the lens back to infinity, so the focusing wheel locks in position. Then depress the end of the locking spring found just to the left of the "infinity" mark on the distance scale as you look down on the lens with the top of the camera toward you. Turn the lens clockwise until the red dot on the lens barrel (on the small projecting flange) is opposite the red dot on the Nikon body, then lift out. Replace in the same way: match the dots, insert and twist counter-clockwise until the spring clicks into place. Nikkors of other focal-lengths (up to 135mm) attach to the outside bayonet. Be sure both lens and camera are turned back to infinity, then match the red dots and slip the lens straight in, and turn counter-clockwise until the springlock clicks. A thumb-catch on these other Nikkors opens the retaining spring. Test the focusing wheel which should move freely (turn the lens barrel on Nikkors longer than 50mm to test). If there is a click or two inside the barrel as you do this, you've been careless and the mount is finding the correct alignment with the focusing mechanism. Doing it correctly will save wear and tear. Use front and back lens caps when the Nikkor is removed and placed in its case. A body cap is available to cover the opening if the Nikon body is left for a while without a Nikkor inserted.

Flash synchronization

The connecting cord from the Nikon BC III Flash Unit (or other guns) is inserted in the *synchro-socket* [above right] at the upper left side of the SP. For positive synchronization use the Nikon snap-lock cord, although the socket will accept other cords in an emergency. The Nikon BC IV Flash Unit slides into the accessory shoe and makes contact with the flash terminal in the front, so no external connections are necessary. Exact synchronization is easily set for the recommended FP and F bulbs or for electronic flash (see tables, *Data and Formulas,* pp. 274, 5) by matching the color of the shutter speed number and the color of the proper symbol in the selector aperture [right lower]. Raise the knurled ring of the shutter speed dial and rotate it so one of the four symbols appears in the little window. With a small FP (focal plane) flashbulb, match the color of the dot in this window to the chosen shutter speed. With F-type flashbulbs, match the color of the F in the window. (There is no green F, so speeds of 1/125 and faster are not suitable for this class of flashbulbs.) Electronic flash is synched at the X position of the selector and at 1/60 or slower speeds, except units with built-in delay circuits which require 1/30 or slower. (See Chapter 9 for a full treatment of flash photography.)

NOTES

The *eveready case* is useful to protect the Nikon from dirt and accidental damage. The locking screw at the bottom fastens to the tripod socket in the bottom of the Nikon body, and is itself threaded to screw directly on a tripod. Remove the front of the eveready case by prying up the snap at either end rather than trying to wrench it off with a direct pull.

Many professionals when actively at work prefer a *neck strap* which clips to the eyelets at either end of the Nikon body. The Nikon may be quickly reloaded without the delay of removing it from the case. However, professionals are prepared to accept greater wear on their cameras, and the neck strap is not a substitute for a case when the Nikon is temporarily stored or carried in a car.

The Model SP and S2 Nikons are available in the regular body, (like that in the S2 illustrations), finished in leather and chrome-plated brass, with black dials (like the SP illustrated) for slightly better visibility in dim lighting. A professional all-black model is also available on special order with the external portions black nickel-plated and then lacquered to eliminate all reflections and make the camera as inconspicuous as possible in use.

See also descriptions of the Nikon Exposure Meter (which links directly with the SP shutter speed dial), Nikon filters and lens hoods, and other equipment on the following pages.

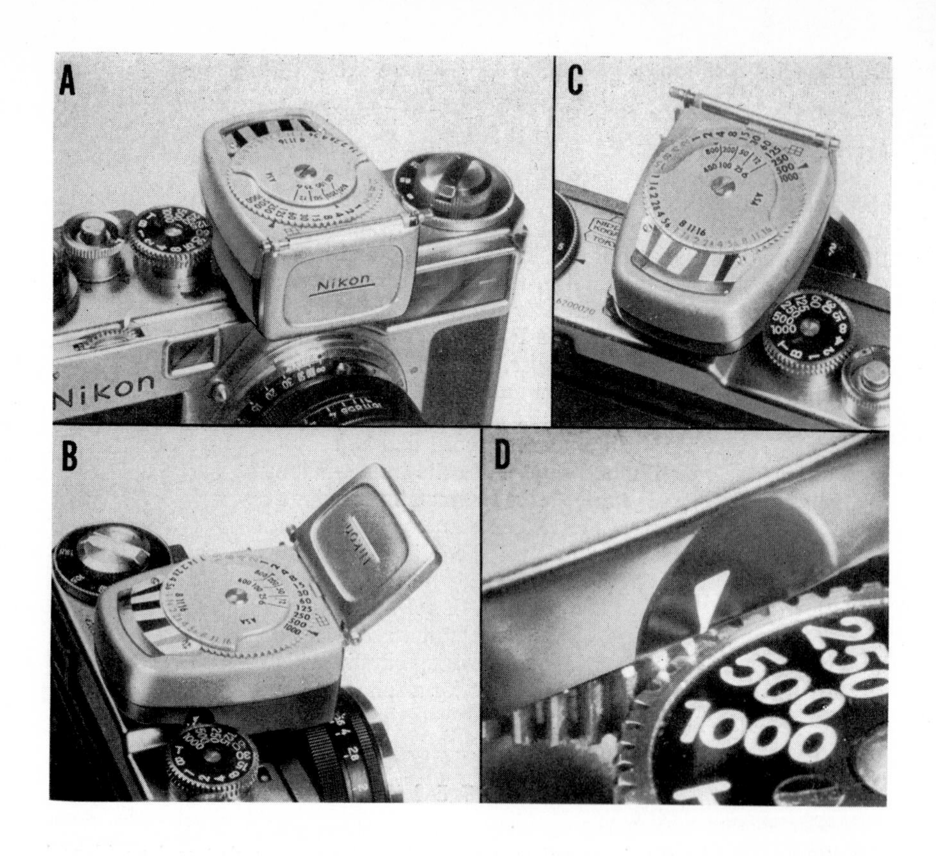

NIKON EXPOSURE METER

The Nikon Exposure Meter is inserted into the accessory shoe from the front. Slide it in as far as it will go, then push it slightly to the left to disengage it from the gear around the Nikon speed selector dial. Set both dial and meter at a 1/1000 speed and allow meter and speed selector dial to engage (see D in illustration). Now set film speed correctly on the dial at the top of the meter.

Suggestions for making meter readings accurately are found in Chapter 3. To calculate exposures, revolve the Nikon shutter speed selector to set f/stop for which the Nikkor lens is set against the position of the indicator needle. When the cover is closed for bright light, use the black f/stop scale; when the cover is raised in dimmer light, use the red f/stop scale. If the Nikon is already set for the desired shutter speed, re-set the Nikkor diaphragm instead to the f/stop indicated by the needle reading. With either method, the Nikon SP will be set for the proper exposure.

The amplifier plate for very dim light is inserted in the side clip of the meter itself. When this is in place, use the red f/ numbers, but read the shutter speed opposite the square mark at the top of the meter rather than at the usual arrow. Then reset this speed by moving the shutter speed dial so that the indicated speed is opposite the arrow.

NIKON ELECTRIC MOTOR DRIVE

An electric motor drive is available for the Nikon SP for manual or semi-automatic operation for quick sequence exposures. Film may be shot in bursts of two or more exposures at a rate of approximately three frames per second or as single, manually controlled shots.

A three-position ring on the rear of the special back may be set at lock, for manual operation or for continuous operation. The connecting cord may be plugged into the battery case in either of two sockets, one of which is for remote control at the battery case position.

The film counter on the motor back may be set for any number of exposures from 1—36 and the electric drive will automatically cut off when the desired number of exposures has been reached. When the end of the roll is reached, the clutch will automatically slip to prevent tearing the film if the drive has been set for exposures beyond this length.

The Electric Motor Drive for the SP may also be used for rapid single exposures (at all speeds except "T") using the normal shutter release on the top of the camera. The motor will wind the shutter and advance the film more quickly than is possible with the rapid advance lever. (At shutter speeds of 1/30 or slower, it is necessary to hold down the shutter release button until the full shutter cycle is completed.)

For remote control, the connecting cord is inserted into the "R" socket of the battery case and the ring on the rear of the Motor Drive is turned to "K". Action is then controlled by the button on the battery case.

The battery case requires 6 1-1/2 volt batteries. These will drive the motor for about 30 (36-exposure) cartridges of film. Nikon Film Cassettes (see Chapter 5) are recommended for use with the Nikon Electric Motor Drive because their construction results in less film friction than with standard cartridges.

S2

Introduced 1955

Image: 24x36mm (0.945x1.417-in.) Shutter traverse 17 milliseconds

Body weight 18 ounces

The Model S2 has by no means been rendered "obsolete" by the introduction of the Model SP. It is a sturdy, dependable camera with many design features of the SP, including its rapid, three-finger operation and makes a desirable second body for professional use.

Rangefinder-viewfinder (with life-size image)

The viewfinder window also includes the centered light-colored rectangle of the rangefinder. This shows a double image until it has been brought into focus by rotating the focusing wheel on the Nikon body. With the camera held in a horizontal position, the rangefinder is simple to use when vertical lines, a bright highlight or strong pattern lies at the point of intended focus. The correct setting may sometimes be found more easily by turning the Nikon to a vertical position or to an intermediate angle. With a little practice, it is not difficult to follow focus on a moving subject while waiting for the best moment to expose the negative.

Shutter speed dials

There are two shutter speed dials on the S2. The speeds are linear, that is, each represents approximately half the shutter-open time of the preceding setting: 1 second, 1/2, 1/4, 1/8, 1/15, 1/30, 1/60, 1/125, 1/250, 1/500, 1/1000. (The "1," the numerator of the fraction, is omitted on the dials.) The *X* setting is approximately 1/50 second, the most rapid speed at which the focal plane shutter curtain is fully open during exposure and is used for electronic flash synchronization. (See below and Chapter 9.)

Fast Speeds are set by moving the lower dial to the 30 mark and setting the upper dial to the selected speed [below, left]. The upper dial may be turned freely in either direction when lifted slightly. Align the proper speed number with the inner arrow (before or after winding shutter with the rapid advance lever) and drop the dial back into place. *Note* that the dial will remain slightly raised at the "1000" setting. At the *B* setting, the shutter will remain open as long as the shutter release button is held depressed.

Slow speeds are set by moving the upper dial to the 30-1 setting and rotating the lower dial to align the chosen mark with the arrow on the top of the Nikon body. The *T* setting will open the shutter when the release button is depressed and the focal-plane curtain will *remain open* until it is released by moving the lower dial to the 1 position. (There will be about a second's delay and a buzz as the spring tension runs off.)

Double exposures may be made by turning the upper dial (without raising it) counter-clockwise to rewind the shutter without using the rapid advance lever. The dial will catch after about a full turn and the Nikon is ready for another exposure on the same film frame. A different shutter dial setting may be chosen for this second exposure.

1/1000	1/500	1/250	1/125	1/60	1/30	1/15	1/8
f/1.4	f/2	f/2.8	f/4	f/5.6	f/8	f/11	f/16

Aperture (f/stop) settings

The aperture on all Nikkor lenses is set by placing the required f/number opposite the dot or line on the lens barrel (inside the front ring on wide-angle Nikkors). Like the shutter speeds, these are in a linear scale, with each larger number (except for the first interval in some cases) representing an opening which admits half the light of the preceding one [see Chapter 3]. The scale immediately above, indicates this relationship: if the correct exposure setting is 1/1000 at f/1.4, all of the other combinations shown will admit an equivalent amount of light and may be chosen instead.

Depth of field, or zone of acceptable sharpness, may be read directly from the double f/stop scale around the lens bayonet of the Nikon, next to the distance scale on the 50mm Nikkor (and on the barrel of Nikkors of other focal lengths which hide this scale on the Nikon body). When the Nikkor is focused for a given distance, say 15 feet, the depth of field for the f/stop employed may be read from the distances opposite the f/stop marking on either side; in this case (for f/8) from about 10 to 30 feet [left, above].

Hyperfocal distance [see chapters 3 and 4] is found opposite each f/stop marking to the right on this scale when the camera is focused at infinity [right, above]. The greatest possible depth of field is secured for any f/stop when the camera is focused at the corresponding hyperfocal distance; the zone of sharpness will extend from infinity to half the hyperfocal distance.

Infrared focus [right below] differs somewhat from visible focus. After the Nikon is focused by rangefinder, shift the distance scale slightly clockwise (as indicated in the illustration) so the focused distance is opposite the f/2.8 (red R) mark for the 50mm f/2 Nikkor, opposite the f/4 mark for the 50mm f/1.4 Nikkor, or opposite the f/5.6 mark for the 50mm f/1.1 Nikkor. A red mark on the barrel of other Nikkors indicates the point of correct infrared focus for these lenses. (The red R at the f/2.8 position indicates this point of correct infrared focus for the 50mm f/2 Nikkor only.)

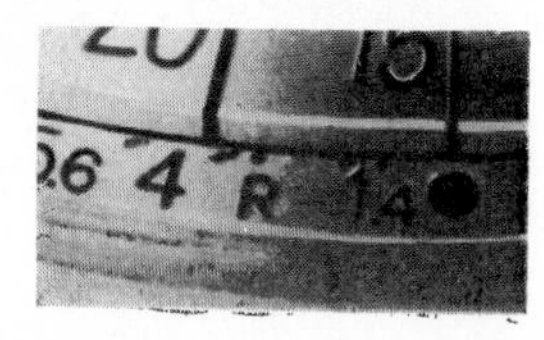

Operating sequence

The Nikon Model SP and S2 are characterized by their rapid, three-finger operation. Form the habit of placing the forefinger on the shutter-release, the middle finger on the focusing wheel and using the thumb to operate the rapid-advance lever. The left hand should be used to steady the Nikon, but when you need one hand for your own balance or when holding a flash reflector above and to the side, the Nikon may be operated for one or even a series of exposures entirely in one hand.

Look through the viewfinder at the light, inner rangefinder rectangle. When the camera is not in focus, a double image will be seen. Rotate the focusing wheel until the two images exactly coincide. If in doubt, run the wheel *slightly* beyond the point where they seem to coincide, then back. The rangefinder is very easy to use when there are definite vertical lines at the point of important less definite or has prominent horizontal lines, turn the Nikon 90° or to an focus or where there is a distinct, bright highlight or pattern. If the image is less definite or has prominent horizontal lines, turn the Nikor 90° or to an intermediate position while using the rangefinder. With a little practice, it will become easy to follow focus on moving subjects while awaiting the instant to expose.

Press the shutter release gently so the camera is not jarred. Notice how the button may be depressed before it actually trips the shutter. When anticipating action, take up this slack so a tiny "hair-trigger" movement will set off the shutter, with the least delay and possibility of camera motion.

When shooting a series or anticipating action, advance film immediately after each exposure so the Nikon is set up for the next release of the shutter.

Rewinding and reloading

When the automatic exposure counter [see page 36] indicates that film in the cartridge or cassette is exhausted (or when the rapid advance lever suddenly binds in mid-stroke if you have forgotten to watch the count!), replace the lens cap to prevent fingerprints and turn the collar around the shutter release button from the *A* to *R* position [upper left, bottom of page]. Raise the rewind crank and rotate in the direction indicated by the engraved arrow. It is best to leave part of the film leader extending from the cartridge to prevent light leaks through the felt light-trap. Notice the off-center red dot on the shutter button: this will revolve as long as the film is threaded on the sprocket wheels [lower right, page 35]. The instant this ceases to move, halt the crank and return to its normal depressed position. Hold the Nikon in the palm of the hand, lens down and the barrel between middle and forefinger, or in an equally secure manner, and raise and turn the lock in the left end of the camera base.

Slide the back off and place it in a clean, secure spot. Slip out the used cartridge (toward the base) and slide in a new one so the prongs on the rewind axle slip into the core of the cartridge and engage the little plastic bar. Continue holding the camera with one hand and loading with the other: At first, this may be clumsy but the design of the Nikon makes it perfectly feasible and you will find it a habit of great value when you must load quickly or in semi-darkness or in a moving vehicle.

Hold the new cartridge in place with your thumb [see pictures below] and draw the film leader across, insert the tongue end in the take-up spool slot and give this a *reverse* (counter-clockwise) half-turn [see opposite page]. The little tooth in the slot should have engaged a film sprocket-hole and the rotation taken up the slack in the film leader so it now fits down over the two sprocket-wheels on the axle next to the take-up spool with the teeth through a sprocket-hole at either side. This can be performed more rapidly than it can be described, thanks to the fact that the take-up spool is fixed in place in the Nikon and the back opens for perfect visibility and access.

If there is any slack left in the film leader, draw it tight by a further partial turn on the take-up spool (without drawing any unexposed film out of the cartridge, of course). Replace the back and turn the lock on the base to secure it in place. Turn the collar around the shutter button back to *A* and use the rapid advance lever (it may require an additional short stroke the first time) and make two "blank" exposures to draw unexposed film into position for use. Notice as you do this: the red dot on the top of the shutter button should turn at each use of the advance lever, indicating that the new film is advancing properly. The rewind crank will also turn as soon as all slack within the cartridge has been taken up.

On the base-plate of the camera is a *film-type reminder dial* which may be set for the (color or black-and-white) Exposure Index of the film loaded in the camera, or on E for "empty."

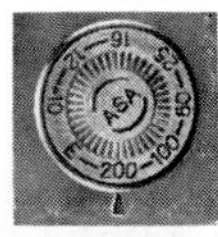

Changing lenses

The 50mm Nikkors fit into the *inside bayonet* of the Nikon body. To remove, first turn the lens back to infinity, so the focusing wheel locks in position. Then depress the end of the locking spring found just to the left of the "infinity" mark on the distance scale as you look down on the lens with the top of the camera toward you. Turn the lens clockwise until the red dot on the lens barrel (on the small projecting flange) is opposite the red dot on the Nikon body, then lift out. Replace in the same way: match the dots, insert and twist counter-clockwise until the spring clicks into place. Nikkors of other focal-lengths (up to 135mm) attach to the outside bayonet. Be sure both lens and camera are turned back to infinity, then match the red dots and slip the lens straight in, and turn counter-clockwise until the springlock clicks. A thumb-catch on these other Nikkors opens the retaining spring. Test the focusing wheel which should move freely (turn the lens barrel on Nikkors longer than 50mm to test). If there is a click or two inside the barrel as you do this, you've been careless and the mount is finding the correct alignment with the focusing mechanism. Doing it correctly will save wear and tear. Use front and back lens caps when the Nikkor is removed and placed in its case. A body cap is available to cover the opening if the Nikon body is left for a while without a Nikkor inserted.

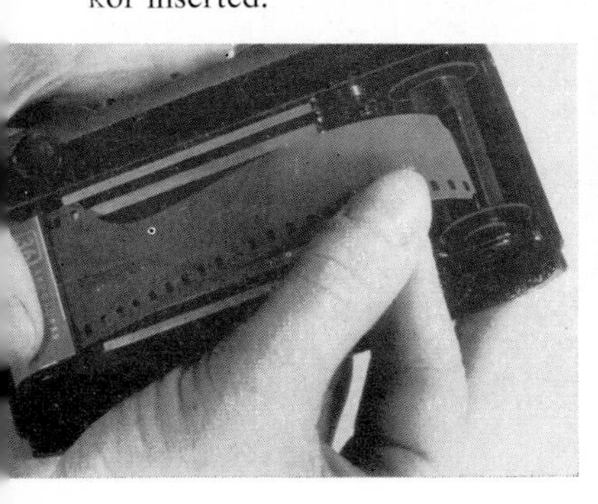

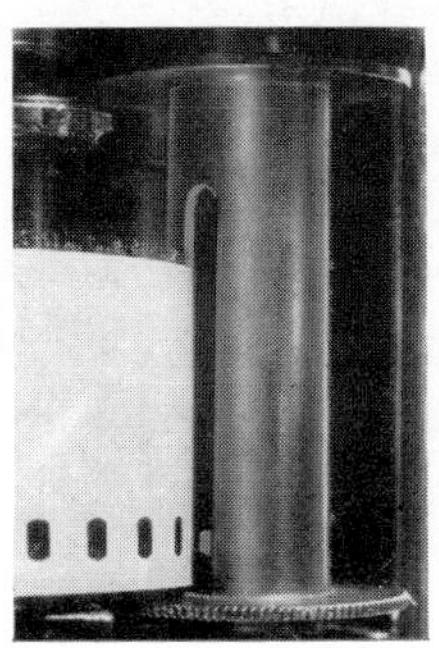

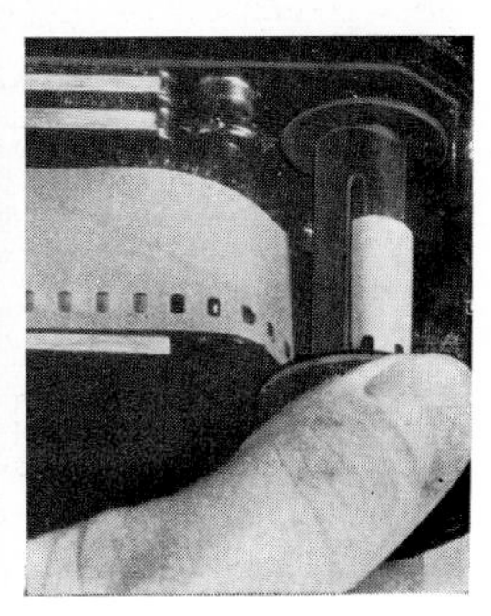

Automatic exposure counter

After two "blank" exposures have been made and the first frame of usable unexposed film has been advanced to a position behind the shutter, turn the automatic exposure counter [left] to "O", using the fingernail against the two small lugs on its face. The counter will move one notch every time the film is advanced.

Flash synchronization

The model S2 Nikon provides internal synchronization for most flashbulb types generally available as well as for electronic flash. The "synchro-selector" [above, right] provides the proper (millisecond) interval between the instant of shutter release and the ignition of the bulb so light is at its maximum when the shutter is open. Set the proper delay interval on the selector dial to correspond with the chosen shutter time and bulb type. A table is provided in *Data and Formulas,* page 274, classifying suitable American flashbulbs in current supply, and there is a chart on page 275 which indicates proper shutter speeds and selector dial settings for these flashbulbs.

For electronic flash, set selector dial and shutter speed dial both to *X*. If the unit has a built-in delay, use 1/30 or slower speed.

Flash cords are connected in the socket [below, right]. The Nikon BC IV Flash Unit, connects through the accessory shoe and the contact pin at the front.

Note: The S2 shutter release button (on earlier models) will close the internal circuit and fire the flash even when the shutter is not wound. This may be put to advantage when repetitive flash (with the shutter remaining open) is required, see Chapter 9. Late in 1957, however, a safety interlock, like that on the SP, was added to prevent accidental closing of the flash circuit.

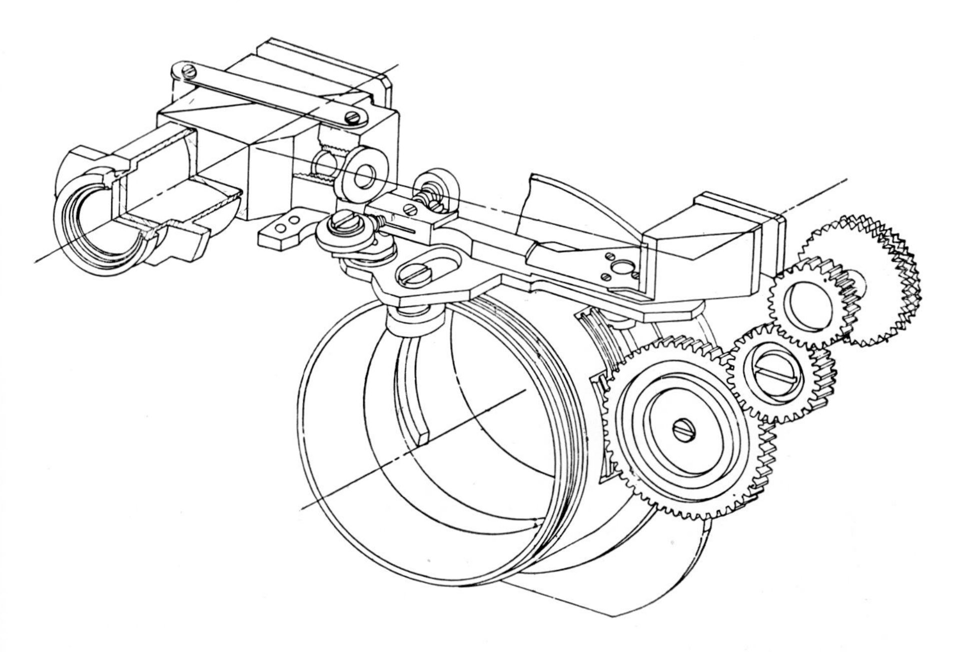

2.4 *The coincident-image Nikon rangefinder requires the precision mechanism diagrammed above (for the S2). This shows the rear view and indicates how the focusing wheel (upper right) is linked to a moving prism and to the lens mount.*

NOTES

The *eveready case* is useful to protect the Nikon from dirt and accidental damage. The locking screw at the bottom fastens to the tripod socket in the bottom of the Nikon body, and is itself threaded to screw directly on a tripod. Remove the front of the eveready case by prying up the snap at either end rather than trying to wrench it off with a direct pull.

Many professionals when actively at work prefer a *neck strap* which clips to the eyelets at either end of the Nikon body. The Nikon may be quickly reloaded without the delay of removing it from the case. However, professionals are prepared to accept greater wear on their cameras, and the neck strap is not a substitute for a case when the Nikon is temporarily stored or carried in a car.

The Model SP and S2 Nikons are available in the regular body, (like that in the S2 illustrations), finished in leather and chrome-plated brass, with black dials (like the SP illustrated) for slightly better visibility in dim lighting. A professional all-black model is also available on special order with the external chrome portions black nickel-plated and then lacquered to eliminate all reflections and make the camera as inconspicuous as possible in use.

S

Introduced 1952 Discontinued 1954
Image: 24x34mm (0.945x1.339-in.) Shutter traverse 24 milliseconds
Body weight 23 ounces

Although the Model S Nikon is now out of production, there are many of them still in active use and appearing on the re-sale market. It is well-built and by no means "obsolete" for even advanced amateur use.

Rangefinder-viewfinder

The viewfinder window also includes the centered light-colored rectangle of the arngefinder. This shows a double image until it has been brought into focus by rotating the focusing wheel on the Nikon body. With the camera held in a horizontal position, the rangefinder is simple to use when vertical lines, a bright highlight or strong pattern lies at the point of intended focus. The correct setting may sometimes be found more easily by turning the Nikon to a vertical position or to an intermediate angle. With a little practice, it is not difficult to follow focus on a moving subject while wating for the best moment to expose the negative.

Shutter speed dials

There are two shutter speed dials on the S. The speeds are 1 second, 1/2, 1/4, 1/8, and 1/20 on the lower dial, and 1/20, 1/30, 1/40, 1/60, 1/100, 1/200 and 1/500 on the upper one. (The "1," the numerator of the fraction, is omitted on the dials.)

Fast speeds are set by moving the lower dial to the 20 (red) mark and setting the upper dial to the selected speed [below, left]. Always set this *after* the shutter has been wound for correct timing. Lift this top dial slightly and bring the proper number opposite the arrow on the top of the Nikon body. Be sure that the dial is seated down into place before shooting. The dial rotates as the shutter is released and the time for which it is set may be noted opposite the rear lug which arrests the movement of the lever on the lower dial. At the *B* setting, the shutter will remain open as long as the shutter release button is held depressed.

Slow speeds are set by raising and turning the upper dial to the 20-1 setting and moving the lower dial to the proper mark. The *T* setting will open the shutter when the release is pressed and the focal-plane curtain will remain open until it is released by moving the lower dial just past the 1 position. There will be a second's delay and a buzz as the spring runs off.

Double exposures may be made by rewinding the upper speed selector knob (without raising it) counter-clockwise until it catches. (Do not wind the film advance knob, of course.) The Nikon is now ready for another exposure on the same frame. A different shutter speed setting may be used for this second exposure.

S

Aperture (f/stop) settings

The aperture on all Nikkor lenses is set by placing the required f/number opposite the dot or line on the lens barrel (inside the front ring on wide-angle Nikkors). These f/numbers are in linear scale, with each larger number (except for the first interval in some cases) representing an opening which admits half the light of the preceding one [see Chapter 3].

Depth of field, or zone of acceptable sharpness, may be read directly from the double f/stop scale around the lens bayonet of the Nikon, next to the distance scale on the 50mm Nikkor (and on the barrel of Nikkors of other focal lengths which hide this scale on the Nikon body). When the Nikkor is focused for a given distance, say 15 feet, the depth of field for the f/stop employed may be read from the distances opposite the f/stop marking on either side; in this case (for f/8) from about 10 to 30 feet [left, above].

Hyperfocal distance [see chapters 3 and 4] is found opposite each f/stop marking to the right on this scale when the camera is focused at infinity [right, above]. The greatest possible depth of field is secured for any f/stop when the camera is focused at the corresponding hyperfocal distance; the zone of sharpness will extend from infinity to half the hyperfocal distance.

Infrared focus [right below] differs somewhat from visible focus. After the Nikon is focused by rangefinder, shift the distance scale slightly clockwise (as indicated in the illustration) so the focused distance is opposite the f/2.8 (red R) mark for the 50mm f/2 Nikkor, opposite the f/4 mark for the 50mm f/1.4 Nikkor, or opposite the f/5.6 mark for the 50mm f/1.1 Nikkor. A red mark on the barrel of other Nikkors indicates the point of correct infrared focus for these lenses. (The red R at the f/2.8 position indicates this point of correct infrared focus for the 50mm f/2 Nikkor only.)

Operating sequence

The Nikon S may be operated quite rapidly when its controls become familiar. Form the habit of placing the forefinger on the shutter release button and use the middle finger to operate the focusing wheel. When holding the flash reflector off the camera or photographing from an unsteady position, the Nikon may be operated with one hand to focus and expose. When following continuing action, the Nikon may be wound with the film advance knob without removing the eye from the viewfinder window.

Look through the viewfinder at the light, inner rangefinder rectangle. When the camera is not in focus, a double image will be seen. Rotate the focusing wheel until the two images exactly coincide. If in doubt, run the wheel *slightly* beyond the point where they seem to coincide, then back. The rangefinder is very easy to use when there are definite vertical lines at the point of important focus or where there is a distinct, bright highlight or pattern. If the image is less definite or has prominent horizontal lines, turn the Nikon 90° or to an intermediate position while using the rangefinder. With a little practice, it will become easy to follow focus on moving subjects while awaiting the instant to expose.

Press the shutter release gently so the camera is not jarred. Notice how the button may be depressed before it actually trips the shutter. When anticipating action, take up this slack so a tiny "hair-trigger" movement will set off the shutter, with the least delay and possibility of camera motion.

When shooting a series or anticipating action, advance film immediately after each exposure so the Nikon is set up for the next release of the shutter.

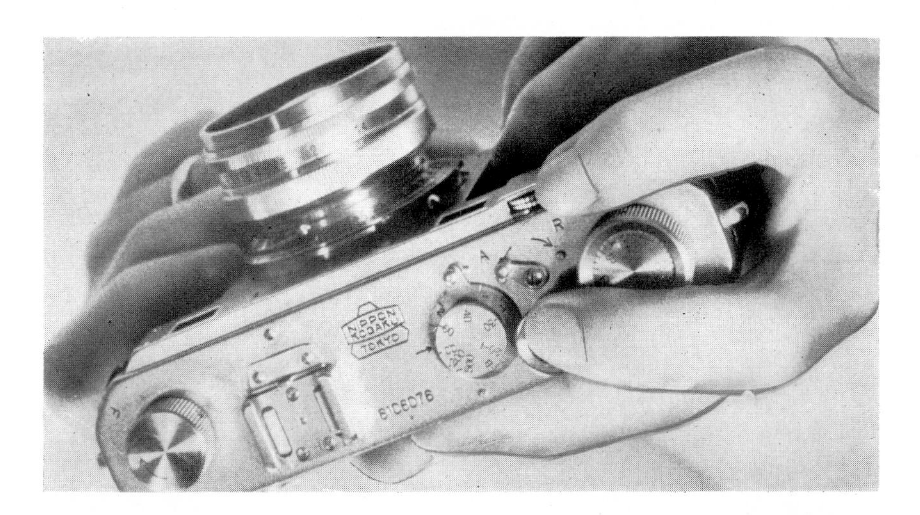

Automatic exposure counter

After two "blank" exposures have been made and the first frame of usable unexposed film has been advanced to a position behind the shutter, turn the automatic exposure counter [right] to "0", using the fingernail against the two small lugs on its face. The counter will move one notch every time the film is advanced.

Rewinding and reloading

When the automatic exposure counter [previous page] indicates that film in the cartridge or cassette is exhausted, replace the lens cap to prevent fingerprints and turn the lever in front of the shutter release button [upper left, below] to the *R* position. Rotate the rewind knob [upper left, below] in the direction indicated by the engraved arrow. It is best to leave part of the film leader extending from the film cartridge to prevent light leaks through the felt light-trap. Notice the off-center dot on the shutter button: this will revolve as long as the film is threaded on the sprocket wheels [see bottom right]. The instant this ceases to move, stop rewinding. Hold the Nikon in the palm of the hand, lens down and barrel between middle and forefinger or in an equally secure position and raise and turn the locks at either end of the base.

Slide the back off and place it in a clean, secure spot. Slip out the used cartridge (toward the base) and slide in a new one so the prongs on the rewind axle slip into the core of the cartridge and engage the little plastic bar. Continue holding the camera with one hand and loading with the other: At first, this may be clumsy but the design of the Nikon makes it perfectly feasible and you will find it a habit of great value when you must load quickly or in semi-darkness or in a moving vehicle.

Hold the new cartridge in place with your thumb [see pictures below] and draw the film leader across, insert the tongue end in the take-up spool slot

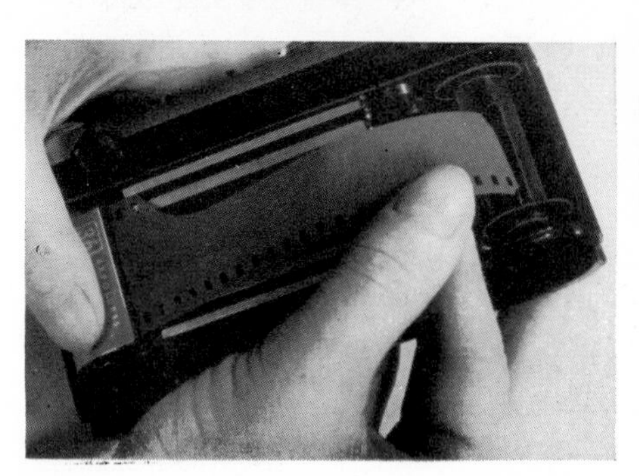

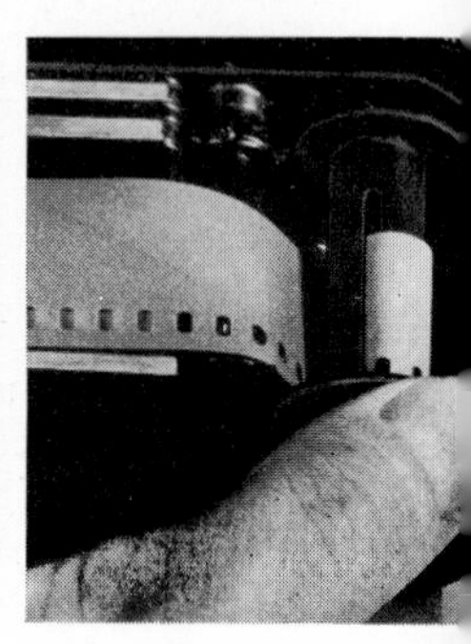

and give this a *reverse* (counter-clockwise) half-turn [opposite, lower]. This little tooth in the slot should have engaged a film sprocket-hole and the rotation taken up the slack in the film leader so it now fits down over the two sprocket-wheels on the axle next to the take-up spool with the teeth through a sprocket-hole at either side. This can be performed more rapidly than it can be described, thanks to the fact that the take-up spool is fixed in place in the Nikon and the back opens for perfect visibility and access.

If there is any slack left in the film leader, draw it tight by a further partial turn on the take-up spool (without drawing any unexposed film out of the cartridge, of course). Replace the back and close the two locks on the base to secure it in place. Turn the advance-rewind lever to *A* and make two blank exposures to draw unexposed film into place for use. Notice as you do this: the top of the shutter release button will revolve as the film is advanced, indicating proper loading. The rewind knob will also turn simultaneously as soon as any slack within the cartridge has been taken up.

Changing lenses

The 50mm Nikkors fit into the *inside bayonet* of the Nikon body. To remove, first turn the lens back to infinity, so the focusing wheel locks in position. Then depress the end of the locking spring found just to the left of the "infinity" mark on the distance scale as you look down on the lens with the top of the camera toward you. Turn the lens clockwise until the red dot on the lens barrel (on the small projecting flange) is opposite the red dot on the Nikon body, then lift out. Replace in the same way: match the dots, insert and twist counter-clockwise until the spring clicks into place. Nikkors of other focal-lengths (up to 135mm) attach to the outside bayonet. Be sure both lens and camera are turned back to infinity, then match the red dots and slip the lens straight in, and turn counter-clockwise until the springlock clicks. A thumb-catch on these other Nikkors opens the retaining spring. Test the focusing wheel which should move freely (turn the lens barrel on Nikkors longer than 50mm to test). If there is a click or two inside the barrel as you do this, you've been careless and the mount is finding the correct alignment with the focusing mechanism. Doing it correctly will save wear and tear. Use front and back lens caps when the Nikkor is removed and placed in its case. A body cap is available to cover the opening if the Nikon body is left for a while without a Nikkor inserted.

S

Flash synchronization

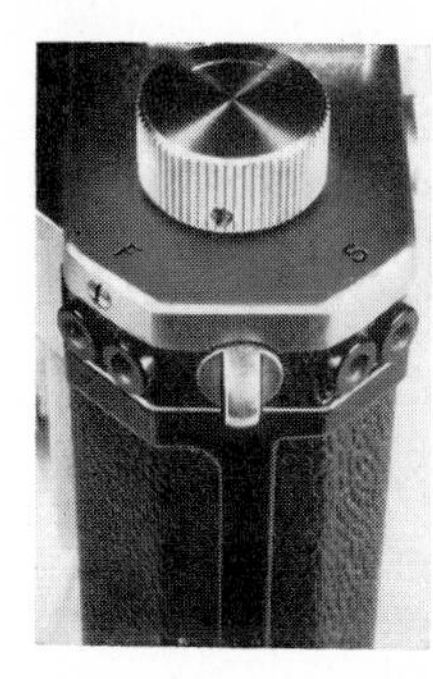

The Model S provides internal synchronization for several types of flashbulbs and for electronic flash. Two flash sockets are provided [left]. Use the front set for shutter speeds of 1/30 to 1/500, the other for slower speeds. See flashbulb list and synchronization chart in *Data and Formulas,* pp. 274, 5.

Note: The shutter release button will close the internal circuit and fire the flash even when the shutter is not wound. This may be put to advantage when repetitive flash (with the shutter remaining open on *T*) is required, see Chapter 9. *Note*: If the rewind lever is not pushed fully to the *A* position, the internal circuit may remain closed and bulbs will fire when they are inserted and burn fingers!

Connect flash plugs before inserting bulb. For a 1/500 exposure or when more than two flashbulbs are simultaneously fired, use the Nikon BC III Flash Unit or one with not less than 4.5 volts output.

NOTES

The *eveready case* is useful to protect the Nikon from dirt and accidental damage. The locking screw at the bottom fastens to the tripod socket in the bottom of the Nikon body, and is itself threaded to screw directly on a tripod. Remove the front of the eveready case by prying up the snap at either end rather than trying to wrench it off with a direct pull.

Many professionals when actively at work prefer a *neck strap* which clips to the eyelets at either end of the Nikon body. The Nikon may be quickly reloaded without the delay of removing it from the case. However, professionals are prepared to accept greater wear on their cameras, and the neck strap is not a substitute for a case when the Nikon is temporarily stored or carried in a car.

2.5 Ray Shorr
Siobhan McKenna rehearsing "St. Joan"
(courtesy "Mademoiselle")

Nikon S2, 35mm f/2.5 Nikkor
Plus-X, 1/60, f/8

2.6 Eric Meacher
Ibn Saud and President Eisenhower
(Photo: INP)

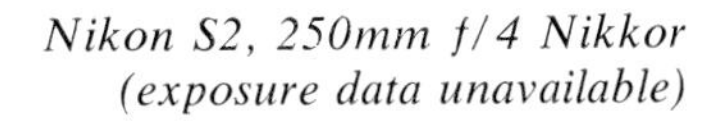
Nikon S2, 250mm f/4 Nikkor
(exposure data unavailable)

NIKON SNAP-ON LENS HOODS

These lenshoods are quickly attached by depressing the buttons on either side and slipping the hoods onto the front of the lens. Lens caps with a similar attachment are also available. The hoods may be placed on the lens in a reversed position and will fit into the Nikon leather case when it is closed. Snap-on hoods are available also for Leica-mount lenses, but cases for these cameras usually may not be closed with the hood mounted in reverse position.

When snap-on lens hoods are used with screw-in Nikon filters, these are attached first before the hood which then snaps onto the filter ring. (On the 35mm f/1.8 Nikkor, the hood attaches to the lens barrel directly even when a filter is used.

NOTE: Screw-in lens hoods (which accept Series-size filters) are available for most Nikkors through 135mm focal length.

The table below indicates the proper snap-in hood and cap sizes for Nikkor lenses.

Nikkor Lenses	in NIKON mounts	in LEICA mounts
34.5mm	50mm 1:3.5 (Micro Nikkor)	28mm 1:3.5 35mm 1:2.5 35mm 1:3.5 50mm 1:3.5
40.5mm	50mm 1:2	50mm 1:2
43mm	50mm 1:1.4 28mm 1:3.5 35mm 1:2.5 35mm 1:3.5 135mm 1:3.5	50mm 1:1.4 35mm 1:1.8 135mm 1:3.5
48mm	85mm 1:2 35mm 1:1.8	85mm 1:2
52mm	105mm 1:2.5	105mm 1:2.5
62mm	50mm 1:1.1	50mm 1:1.1

NIKON UNDERWATER HOUSING

The all metal Nikon underwater housing can be used at depths up to 165 feet. It has a frame finder attached at the top, with provision for parallax correction. A handle is used to advance the film and wind the shutter. Either a 50mm standard lens or a 35mm wide angle lens can be used with this housing. Among the other features located on the outside of the unit are: focusing and diaphragm setting; automatic exposure counter; use of a yellow or orange filter, both of which are built into the unit.

A special flash gun is available, supplied with a 23 foot extension cord. The housing has a specific gravity of 1.0, contributing to its ease of handling.

The Nikon Underwater Housing is supplied in a fitted wooden case with provision for holding camera, lenses and accessories.

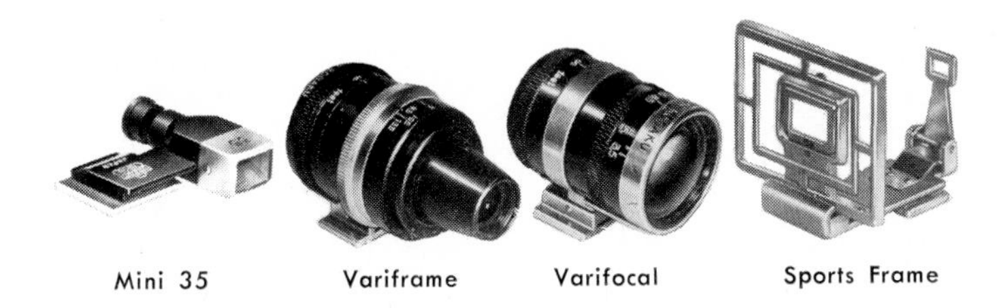

Mini 35 Variframe Varifocal Sports Frame

NIKON VIEWFINDERS

Viewfinders to slip into the accessory shoe of the Nikon are illustrated above. Types available include: *Individual finders* for each lens from 25mm through 135mm. Except for the 35mm finder these give a life-size image, and all have full parallax adjustment. The new, compact *Mini 35* finder for 35mm Nikkors used on the S2 Nikon. *Variframe finder* which varies the frame-size to conform to the field of view of Nikkors from 35mm to 135mm. *Varifocal finder* which changes the size of the image to correspond with that of any Nikkor from 35mm to 135mm. The latter two also have full parallax adjustment and adaptors for the 28mm field of view are available. *Sports Frame finder* which has four fixed frames corresponding to the field of view of the 35mm, 50mm, 85mm and 135mm Nikkor lenses. All finders are supplied with leather carrying case except Mini 35 and 25mm Individual finder.

3.1 GENE COOK
Actress Brigitte Bardot

Nikon S, 135mm f/3.5 Nikkor
Plus-X, 1/100, f/8

3

Basic Shooting with 35mm

THERE ARE PROBABLY MORE PICTURES—certainly amateur ones—made outdoors than indoors under artificial or available light conditions. Out-of-doors under adequate sunshine is the best place to learn how to utilize fully the versatility and control which the Nikon affords. The familiarity with the camera itself and with the response of films (both black-and-white and color) gained here, will make the more complex situations later encountered comparatively easy to understand and master. [See film data, Chapter 5 and *Data and Formulas*.]

It is especially important for the new camera-user to begin his picture-making career under circumstances where no great technical ingenuity is required. It is his eye, which isolates pictures from the flow of life around him, which is his most important "instrument." The Nikon he holds in his hand is a wonderfully sensitive and flexible tool, but it is the servant of the eye. Its real value lies in its simplicity and convenience for recording what the user sees.

In the beginning, the Nikon itself may occupy much attention. With use, however, as operation becomes more and more automatic, adjustments will be made almost unconsciously to fit the changing circumstances encountered. When this moment arrives, the Nikon will become, almost literally, an extension of the eye. If the user sets about acquiring this facility systematically, such complete control over the instrument will arrive more quickly than he expects.

The Three Basic Camera Controls

ON ANY camera, including the Nikon, there are *only three basic controls*: the aperture (diaphragm or "lens opening") setting, the shutter speed, and the focus (distance setting). The inter-relationship between the first two govern correct exposure, and the intelligent use of all three controls will distinguish a good photograph from a mere snapshot. For the amateur, the best way to learn the effective use of these three basic settings is outdoors in daylight.

Aperture

Modern camera lenses are equipped with *iris diaphragms,* an arrangement of extremely thin metal leaves, linked to a ring on the outside of the Nikkor lens barrel (or to a small lever on some other equipment). As the ring is turned, the leaves open or close, changing the size of a nearly circular hole around the optical axis of the lens through which light passes to form the image on the film. [See diagrams, Chapter 4.] One effect of this change of size is obvious: as the opening is made smaller, less light will pass through during any given interval of time, and vice versa. Consequently, when the size of the opening is altered (as from f/2.8 to f/4), cutting the entering light by one half, the shutter speed must be correspondingly doubled (as 1/60 to 1/30 second) under constant light conditions, if the exposure is to remain correct. The converse is equally true. (Other, less self-evident optical effects are explained below.)

f/numbers

The series of numbers, engraved on the lens barrel, which indicates the relative sizes of the aperture settings on any lens, may seem at first arbitrary and confusing. In the past, there have been several systems of indicating these diaphragm openings. The modern system (with which Nikkor lenses are marked) is the one which has been found to be the most convenient in practice and is the one approved by the American Standards Association. It is a measure of *aperture ratio.* In simple terms, this means that when a lens is focused at infinity and the diameter of a certain diaphragm aperture is found to be say, ¼ the distance between lens and film, this ratio is expressed as f/4. (More precise optical information will be found in Chapter 4.) Each engraved number (with "f/" omitted) on the aperture scale is thus the denominator of a fraction. Hence, the larger this number, the smaller the relative size of the opening.

The marked stops on Nikkor lenses are an orderly series of fractions (powers of $\sqrt{2}$, for the mathematically minded), each representing an opening which admits ½ the light of the preceding one, thus: f/1, f/1.4, f/2, f/2.8, f/4, f/5.6, f/8, f/11, f/16, f/22, f/32, etc. Note that the relationship between the light-admitting power of each marked stop is the same as the relationship between the shutter-speed settings of the Nikon S2 and SP models, each of which is (for all practical purposes) ½ the time of the preceding one. The speed settings of the model S are sufficiently close to this (linear) relationship for all but the most critical exposure determination. For constant exposure, a change of one place in either series can be matched by a compensating change of the other setting, as will be explained below.

Lens speed

The "speed" of a lens is expressed as the maximum diaphram opening permitted by its particular design. This maximum aperture is marked on the ring around the front glass surface on Nikkor lenses (and on most other lenses as well) in the form of a ratio, as "1:1.4." (The focal length is also found here, as "f-50mm," for example, as well as the serial number for that particular lens. Letters on the ring [S, P, etc.] designate lens construction, see Chapter 4.)

This maximum opening, however, is not a complete measure of the light-gathering power of a lens. This depends, as well, upon the characteristics of the various glasses employed and on the presence of anti-reflectant surface coating on the elements, indicated by the "C" on the front ring. In the last few years, the use of optical glass incorporating certain rare-earth elements has enabled Nippon Kogaku K.K. and other advanced manufacturers to produce exceptionally rapid lenses without sacrificing either resolution or precise color correction. (This is the ability of the lens to focus colors of the spectrum simultaneously to the same plane, and is important for image resolution on panchromatic film as well as for color film.)

The presence of anti-reflectance coating on the surfaces of the elements tends to prevent internal reflections which block the transmission of an appreciable percentage of the light and which cause halations which degrade the image.

Aperture and depth of field

When a camera is focused on any plane, objects both closer and further away tend to blur, to become "soft." Since the fall-off of definition is gradual, there is a band on either side of this plane in which objects are still reasonably sharp for all practical purposes, a band which is usually called "depth of field." In large part, the limits of this field of acceptable sharpness are a function of the size of the aperture used. The smaller the stop, the deeper the zone of useful sharpness. We should note here, in passing, that certain other physical and psychological factors are involved, such as the contrast of the subject, the resolving power (acutance) of both film and paper, and the viewing distance of the final print.

The depth of field varies also with the distance from the camera to the object on which the lens is sharply and accurately focused. The zone of useful sharpness becomes rapidly shallower as this point approaches the camera. At a distance of 12 inches, for example, a 50mm Nikkor lens set at f/8 will have a depth of field of about ½ inch. The same lens set at the same aperture but focused at 33 feet, will give an acceptably sharp image of objects from about 16 feet, 6 inches, to infinity.

The depth of field is different for lenses of various focal lengths: the "shorter" the lens, the greater the zone of acceptable sharpness under similar conditions. A 35mm Nikkor lens, for example, when focused at a point about 16½ feet from the camera, will produce a sharp image of objects from about 8 feet to 3 inches to infinity at f/8. A 50mm Nikkor lens, focused at the same distance, must be stopped down to f/16 to give the same depth of field.

Shutter speed

Let us turn to the less-complicated subject of shutter speeds, the second of the three basic controls of any camera. The principal factor in the choice of shutter setting is the rate and direction of movement of the subject. It is obvious that when the camera is focused on a moving object, the image of that object will also move across the surface of the film during the time that the shutter is open. The extent of this *image displacement* depends, in turn, upon three factors.

The first of these is the rate of movement or speed of the object; the second is the direction of this movement. An object directly approaching the camera (with its image slowly enlarging on the film) will show less displacement than one moving at an angle to the lens axis (all other factors being equal). The greatest movement, of course, will be that of a subject crossing the lens axis at right angles (parallel to the film plane). The third factor is the distance of the moving object from the camera itself. The farther away the object is, the smaller the movement of its image on the film. (A fourth factor may also be noted here: the longer the focal length of the lens, the larger is the image of any given object and the greater its relative movement across the film plane. Long-focus and telephoto lenses are more apt to show image movement on the negative than are short-focus or wide-angle lenses.)

Almost every outdoor subject includes some objects in motion. This may be so slight as to be completely disregarded, for example the movement of distant foliage in a landscape, or as extreme as a racing car passing the photographer at a right angle. However, for complete control of the ultimate result on the print—and this is the purpose of every exposure—this subject motion must be considered in choosing a shutter setting. [An approximate guide will be found in the table of *Shutter speeds for moving subjects* in *Data and Formulas*.]

The choice of aperture and shutter settings should now be seen as a compromise. The total amount of light admitted to the film must be sufficient for a proper exposure (see below). A wide choice of aperture-speed combinations will admit the necessary amount of light under most circumstances, but the exact combination of settings chosen will depend on the necessary zone of sharp focus needed to include all of the important subject area, and on the speed necessary to "stop" whatever action there may be in the picture. On very many occasions there will be no great conflict between these two, and a range of settings may be used. In other situations, either depth or stopping power may have to be sacrificed. Photographers have learned to turn these "limitations" of material and equipment to pictorial use, however, as we shall see (later in this chapter) after a brief exposition of the last basic camera control and an explanation of determining correct exposure.

Focus

The Nikon is focused by rotating the focusing wheel on the camera body or the barrel of Nikkors 85mm or longer [see Chapter 2] to increase or decrease the distance between the lens itself and the film plane. As this distance increases, the camera is in focus for closer and closer objects. Precise focus is always important. The principal subject should be as sharp as possible. The Nikon range-finder assures this accuracy and, since it is the distance between camera and subject which is critical, the range-finder assures correct focus no matter which of the interchangeable Nikkor lenses (up to 135mm) is used on the camera. (The Nikkor 180mm, 250mm and 500mm telephoto lenses require the Nikon Reflex Housing incorporating a ground glass on which the depth of field may be seen directly.)

As was noted above, when the camera is focused on any point, there is a zone of acceptable focus extending on either side of that point along the lens axis. This zone expands as the distance from the camera to point-of-focus increases and also expands as the lens is stopped down. [See diagrams, Chapter 4.] A part of the pictorial effectiveness of any photograph depends on the depth of this zone and on its location in the scene.

Zone focusing

The depth and distance from the camera of this zone of acceptable focus may be read on the scale on the body of the Nikon for the 50mm Nikkor lenses or on the lens barrel of Nikkors of other focal lengths. On each Nikkor lens (except the 50mm focal lengths) an engraved line moves along the distance scale to indicate the point of sharpest focus (distance to which the lens is focused). On either side

3.2 Jacques Lowe
Nikon S2, 50mm, f/1.4

Circus horse
Super-XX, 1/60, f/11

of this line the series of possible f/stops for that lens are also repeated. At any distance setting, the f/stop markings for the aperture setting in use will indicate the near and far limits of the zone of focus. For instance, when the 105mm Nikkor is focused at 22 feet, the scale shows that at f/16 there will be a depth of field of (roughly) 17 to 30 feet. Under the same conditions, the 35mm Nikkor (wide angle) lens would produce a depth of field from about 6 feet, 3 inches to infinity.

In the case of the latter lens, such a setting does not make use of the full capacities of the lens for extreme depth of field. This setting places the f/16 mark on one side of the scale far beyond the infinity-distance marking. If such an extremely small (for a wide-angle lens) aperture is required, the f/16 mark may be brought back to the infinity mark, which will place the distance setting between 8 and 9 feet and the near limit of acceptable sharpness (read under the other f/16 mark) at approximately 4 feet, 4 inches.

It is thus possible, especially with the shorter-focus lenses, to achieve what amounts to *universal focus* under conditions of bright sunlight which allow small apertures. The distance setting (focus) of the lens is adjusted so that the line corresponding to the f/stop in use falls on the infinity mark and all objects at a reasonable distance from the camera will be in focus without further adjustment. When the far background is not important, or when it might be distracting, the focus may be adjusted so the proper f/stop falls at 50 or even 30 feet and the zone of sharpness will cover action at medium and closer distances.

Under conditions of weaker light or when the need for a rapid shutter speed make a large working aperture necessary, this placement of the zone of focus at a medium or close distance will still insure sharp pictures without constant attention to the exact point-of-focus. However, the range-finder should not be neglected even under these circumstances. Distances are deceptive and sometimes difficult to estimate even for the experienced. When employing this technique of *zone focus,* the range-finder should be used to establish the near and far limits of sharp focus required by the picture situation (actual or anticipated). Focus on these limits successively and read the distances off the scale. Then set the camera lens so that the markings for the f/stop in use overlap these limits.

Film Characteristics

BLACK-AND-WHITE FILM is essentially a light-sensitive silver halide, plus certain dyes, suspended in gelatin and coated on a flexible, transparent base. There are many different types of film available in 35mm width and the amateur may be caught up in some confusion over which kind to choose for best results. Three characteristics which differentiate various films are important in choosing one for ordinary use. These are *speed* (degree of sensitivity to light), *latitude* (margin for exposure error), and *grain* (the microscopic nature of the negative image which controls the possible size of enlargement.)

Note: The film recommendations in this chapter assume that film is correctly developed [see Chapter 5] by the photographer himself, or by a processing studio experienced in the careful handling of 35mm materials. Correct development is not difficult, but results will be unpredictable and generally unsatisfactory with commercial, "drug-store" processing and printing.

3.3 TED RUSSELL *Nikon S2, 50mm f/1.4 Nikkor*
Plus-X, 1/250, f/4

Color films consist essentially of *three* layers of sensitive emulsion, each of which responds to one band of the spectrum [see Chapter 7]. To gain proper color response, many compromises are necessary which lead to lower speed and a generally narrower latitude. In addition, another factor must be considered: *color balance*. There are great differences in the actual color of the illumination present under either artificial or natural lighting. The human eye adjusts for such variations over an exceedingly wide range, but color films must be especially designed for each type of illumination. For practical reasons, 35mm color films currently available are balanced for three common lighting conditions: average middle of the day sunlight; clear-glass, wire-filled flashbulbs; and photoflood illumination. There is reason to expect that new negative-positive color materials will in the near future substantially broaden the range of lighting conditions under which acceptable color photographs can be made.

Speed

Films differ in the amount of light required to produce a satisfactory negative image. There are many systems of rating this speed for black-and-white films, but since 1946 there has been a general tendency to settle on the method recommended by the American Standards Association. Many meters currently manufactured are scaled to correspond with this system, and most published exposure information is based on speed ratings expressed in this scale, which doubles the index number (e.g., 50 to 100) as response to light is doubled. Manufacturers' ratings of their own films are (for good reason) somewhat conservative and it is also possible to classify the same film under different index numbers, depending on the way the exposure is calculated (see the next section of this chapter) and on the way it is developed.

Since the American Standards Association itself does not rate films and since film ratings may be arbitrarily altered (under controlled conditions), terms such as "ASA 50" or "ASA (equivalent speed) 800" are avoided in this manual in favor of the neutral term "Exposure Index" ("E.I.") or "speed index." Such Exposure Indexes may be used with any meter calibrated to the ASA scale. [For older meters or other calculations, see *Table of Comparative Film Ratings*, in *Data and Formulas*.]

While there are no official "ASA ratings" for color films (a standard for such ratings is due in 1957) for practical purposes it is possible to rate them along this same scale on the basis of comparative exposure tests. The Exposure Indexes suggested for color may consequently be used with any exposure meter calibrated in the ASA scale of ratings.

Film manufacturers enclose a printed leaflet with each 35mm cartridge. These instruction sheets should be read with more care than they seem to receive ordinarily. They contain recommended Exposure Indexes for the film under daylight and other lighting as well as development recommendations for quality negatives. These instructions are derived from a consideration of the film characteristics as the manufacturer knows them and from experience with ordinary—and frequently careless—handling of film in amateur cameras.

Consequently, there are many *safety factors* included in these black-and-white recommendations. (If all your exposure calculations are accurate and development follows the manufacturer's recommendations, these safety factors will result in at least 1 1/3 stops over-exposure. Such a negative will be slightly dense and more grainy than is desirable.) As the photographer's own experience increases, he can modify these instructions to get more flexibility than even the manufacturer suggests from any one of these films. The next section of this chapter, *Light and Exposure,* outlines the specific conditions under which the limits of speed may be safely extended.

Latitude

Since black-and-white Exposure Indexes suggested by the manufacturers are a safe "middle of the road" recommendation, it is possible to make a considerable error in judging exposure conditions and still arrive at a printable negative. As film is "pushed" to higher speeds or to cover more extreme conditions of lighting contrast, much of this margin for error necessarily disappears and more accurate calculation of exposures is required. Even the most expert photographer will be aided under these circumstances by a photo-electric exposure meter such as the Nikon Exposure Meter *and a knowledge of how to interpret its reading.* The purpose of much of the rest of this chapter will be to provide a basis for such knowledge. In the case of color film, as was noted, there is comparatively little latitude although some films may be "pushed" to a somewhat higher speed when they are to be appropriately developed. This technique will be covered in the chapter on color.

Grain

The image in the developed black-and-white negative consists of extremely tiny clumps of metallic silver grains produced by the action of the developer on those silver halide crystals which were affected by light during the exposure (or accidentally exposed to light by careless handling of the film). The size of these clumps of silver and the pattern of their distribution, particularly over solid areas of the middle tones of the picture, determine the magnification of the final print which can be secured without unpleasant, "sandy" tones, a loss of smooth gradation and a general breaking down of the image definition.

Negative grain depends partly on the characteristics of the original film and partly on the developing formula and other processing conditions. However, almost any film, except under the most extreme exposure conditions, may be processed to produce a *reasonably* fine-grain result: a 35mm negative from which an 11x14-inch print may be made without a break-down of the image. The practical means of achieving the finest grain with any film are covered in more detail in Chapter 5.

With color film, normally exposed and processed, there is no effective control of grain other than the original choice of material. All current 35mm color films are sufficiently fine-grained for amateur use as projected transparencies or as an intermediate step for color prints. For professional use, however, particularly when 35mm transparencies are to serve as the basis for engravings for publication, relative graininess becomes a factor. As currently supplied, Ektachrome gives the greatest apparent grain and Kodachrome the least, with Anscochrome occupying an intermediate position (when it is normally processed).

Film types

In very general terms, black-and-white films group into three major types (excluding special-purpose emulsions): the slow, very fine-grain (thin emulsion) films with little latitude; the very rapid, somewhat coarser-grained films which may be "pushed" to cover great extremes of light conditions; and a third, middle group of films intermediate in its characteristics.

3.4 GENE COOK *Villager, Ceri, Italy* — *Nikon S, 50mm f/1.4 Nikkor Plus-X, 1/100, f/8*

This medium speed group of films is the most suitable choice for all ordinary outdoor shooting. (You will discover, too, as have many professionals who are not bemused by the inherent speed of the rapid emulsions, that these films are also excellent for indoor work at moderate light levels, see Chapters 5, 8 and 9.) Used outdoors, the medium speed films will permit a considerable enlargement when properly developed, and have enough latitude to give the amateur confidence that moderate exposure errors will not ruin his negatives. It should always be remembered, however, that the more accurate the exposure for the given conditions the more satisfactory the negative and the subsequent print will be. Latitude is not the excuse for carelessness.

In *Data and Formulas* there is a list of the black-and-white films with recommended Exposure Indexes, and information on many of the available developers. These films differ in many of their characteristics, but the Nikon user who standardizes on any one of the medium speed group until he learns to exploit its image-recording capabilities to the full will obtain technically excellent negatives. Experimentation and comparison of materials is of great value, but only when it is done under controlled conditions and the results properly evaluated. Constantly changing from one film to another or, even more fatally, from one developer to another, will delay rather than accelerate an understanding of the photographic process. Elsewhere in this Manual, other films of the fine-grain and the extra-rapid types will be noted in connection with specific situations. This should not mislead the beginner into abandoning the sound practice of standardizing on one film and one developer until he can add flexibility to his methods without confusion—one film or one developer at a time.

Light and Exposure

IT IS NOT NECESSARY for the photographer to become expert in the physical theories of the nature of light. However, many of its characteristics are important to understand, particularly for color photography, and these will be introduced as they are necessary to explain the photographic process. For black-and-white films it is sufficient here to consider light as it illuminates an object against a background in terms of three factors: intensity, contrast and direction. (We assume, for the next pages, that the illumination is correct for either daylight-balanced color film or for Type F color film with an 85C conversion filter or for Type A color film with the 85 conversion filter.)

Estimating light intensity

The latitude of the medium speed black-and-white films is so great that it is possible to make a rough division of daytime lighting conditions into four categories, to memorize the proper settings and then expose accordingly.

A base speed of 1/125 second is rapid enough to eliminate the danger of camera movement or slight subject movement. When using film with a manufacturer's rating of 80 in daylight (such as Kodak Plus-X), the aperture diaphragm or f/stop can be set as follows:

Bright sunshine with large areas of blue sky visible, f/16.

Hazy sky, sun visible through clouds, shadows present but indistinct, f/11.

Cloudy bright, sun invisible, no shadows, f/8.

Open shade, under trees or other shadow on a bright day, f/5.6. (This exposure is for the darker areas and small patches of highlight may receive enough exposure on the negative to remain almost pure white on a print.)

From this basic exposure, variations are easily possible. Exposures will remain identical for all practical purposes if the speed dial on the Nikon is advanced one notch (say from 1/125 to 1/250) and the aperture is simultaneously opened one stop (say from f/8 to f/5.6) and so on in successive steps. To stop action in bright sunlight, for example, it would be desirable to use a 1/500 second speed at f/8 or 1/1000 at f/5.6, either of which are equivalent to the recommended 1/125 at f/16.

Similarly, if a faster or slower film is used, the base speed may be varied or the series of stops shifted along the scale on the barrel of the Nikkor lens employed. As (ASA-scale) Exposure Indexes are doubled (or halved) a shift of one f/stop is required to compensate.

This basic exposure is calculated for subjects of average reflectance and contrast. Nearby landscapes, houses or people generally fall into this category.

When the principal subject is quite dark in color or when a person, for example, is standing against the sun with no near-by surface reflecting light back into the shadow side, the exposure should be increased (opened up) by one f/stop or by using the next slower shutter-speed setting. Similarly, if the subject is very light or if the highlight detail and texture are more important than the shadow areas, the exposure may be decreased by one f/stop or by using the next faster shutter-speed setting.

The photo-electric exposure meter

The Nikon Exposure Meter [see Chapter 2] is a clip-on meter which slides into the accessory shoe of the Nikon. It links directly with the shutter speed dial of the SP model for semi-automatic operation, or may be used on the other Nikon models (or hand-held) for accurate and convenient exposure calculation.

In a photo-electric meter light is directed onto a selenium cell, activating it to produce a minute electric current. This current flows through the coil of an extremely sensitive ammeter, swinging a needle across a dial. The amount of current produced (and registered by the needle) is proportionate to the amount of light which reaches the selenium photocell. For additional accuracy in photographic work, the light is admitted to the Nikon Exposure Meter through a set of moulded lenses which admit light from one direction only. These are so designed that this angle of acceptance is approximately the same as the angle of view of the Nikkor 50mm lens. The front plate of the Nikon Exposure Meter may be easily snapped open to multiply the sensitivity of the meter to suit the general level of illumination. An accessory selenium cell may be quickly attached to the meter to raise the response to dimmer light. To measure incident light, a translucent opal plate is inserted in the front to collect light from a wider angle for this type of reading.

The needle-reading of the Nikon Exposure Meter may be converted into exposure data (or used for semi-automatic operation on the Nikon SP). The Exposure Index of the film in use is set on the calculator dial, which is then adjusted to correspond to the needle-reading. This aligns a range of possible shutter-speed—f/stop combinations which will produce correct exposure with the Nikon, or any other camera.

Using the Nikon Meter for reflectance readings

The meter (on or off the Nikon) may be used to measure either the over-all light reaching the camera lens from the picture scene, or to measure the light reflected by the principal subject or by the most important area of that subject.

If landscapes and other general scenes contain no extremes of illumination or of subject reflectance which are important, they may be measured by an over-all reading. The Nikon Exposure Meter is used on the camera and aimed directly at the scene. Care should be taken to point the meter somewhat downward to avoid including too much of the sky in the area being read, otherwise the meter reading will be deceptively high.

For many subjects, the results will be more satisfactory if a close-up reading is taken of the principal subject. This is particularly true if the background is conspicuously lighter or darker than the main subject, as in the case of a portrait made against the sky or against a background of dark trees. In these cases, the meter will average the over-all values of the scene and the main subject may be under- or over-exposed. The meter should be brought close to the subject, or the most important area of the subject (as the skin-tone of an outdoor portrait), keeping the meter in line with the position from which the photograph will be made. Care should be taken that the meter and Nikon do not cast a shadow which will influence a close-up reading.

For subjects of greater contrast, the most accurate exposure readings are derived from measurements of the lightest and darkest areas. If these are within the range of the film, the meter may be set half way between them for calculating exposure. If the contrast range is too great, it will be necessary to sacrifice either highlight or shadow values.

When it is impractical to approach the subject so closely, a *substitution reading* may be made from a nearby object of the same approximate reflectivity and receiving the same illumination as the main subject. In the case of portraits or any subject of average tones, this may be the photographer's hand, held in such a manner that the light strikes it at the same angle from which the most important subject area is illuminated.

Using the Nikon Meter for incident-light readings

An over-all reading for scenes of average contrast may be taken with the opal glass slide inserted and the meter either close to the principal subject or close to the shooting position, if the lighting conditions are the same at either location. In either case, the translucent light-collecting slide of the meter should point back along a line from subject to camera position for an accurate reading.

When reading the incident light, the meter will not be influenced by large areas of exceptionally light or dark tones which may falsify a reflectance reading. On the other hand, since it measures the light which *strikes* the subject, it will not compensate for the contrast of tones within the subject area. With either reflectance or incident-light readings, therefore, some interpretation of the result is frequently necessary.

Selecting proper exposure

This leads to the question: what is a "correct" exposure? The meter reading is only one step (although frequently an essential one) in determining the answer to this question. In the first place, the meter will permit a choice of f/stops or shutter speeds (even when it is linked to the SP for semi-automatic operation), from which the photographer must choose a combination which will give him sufficient depth of field and a speed which will stop subject motion in the picture (see above). This may be sufficiently accurate for all practical purposes with an over-all reading correctly made. However, it is frequently necessary to make a further correction for the best results. The photographic process contains so many variables, from exposure through the final printing process, that any photographer may find a certain consistent error in his readings. On the basis of such experience, it is necessary to determine an individual correction factor. With this in mind, he can modify the film speed setting on his meter to compensate for individual idiosyncracies in handling the meter or camera, or in processing and printing the film.

Beyond this, the meter reading must be interpreted in many picture-situations. With either black-and-white or color film, more than one exposure may be "correct" in terms of film response, but give entirely different results in the pictorial interpretation of the scene before the camera. Some instances of this will be considered later in this chapter.

Exposure-development ratio

It should be obvious that no meter is "intelligent" enough to substitute for the photographer's judgment. This is particularly true in cases where the contrast of a given scene is particularly extreme (in terms of the response of either black-and-white or color film). In these situations, it will be necessary either to measure only the important area (the principal subject) and to expose for that, or (with black-and-white film) to compress or expand the response of the film to the gradations encountered within the limits to which this is under the control of the photographer. This latter expedient may be used whenever the important subject is particularly contrasty or, conversely, has so little differentiation of tones that they must be exaggerated for clarity of image or for more desirable pictorial results.

The most effective tool for this is manipulation of the exposure-development ratio. In general terms [see also Chapter 5] it is the exposure which determines the *density* of a negative, and the development which controls its *contrast*. From a practical standpoint, this means that by increasing or decreasing development times, we may add or subtract image contrast in any (except the most extreme) situation. However, to keep the over-all density of the negative within proper limits, we must slightly modify exposure times correspondingly. The actual procedure is less formidable than this rather abstract rule.

On a bright summer day, for example, we may have exceedingly bright highlights from surfaces in direct sunshine, yet the shadows may be very dark and reflect little light back into the lens. The result on film will be usually more contrast than is visible to the eye which adjusts rapidly to see detail in both extremes. The photographer may either exploit this contrast pictorially or modify the film response for an image sufficiently reduced in contrast to record both highlight and shadow details. He will accomplish the latter by basing his exposure time on a correct reading for the shadows, and reducing the development time so the highlights will not over-develop and "block up" before the shadow areas on the negative have reached proper density.

It is impossible to give an exact numerical formula for this modification of the exposure-development ratio. Any rule sufficiently accurate to apply to a particular film and developer under a range of reflected light readings would be too clumsy to employ in actual practice. It is rather a matter of judgment, a "feeling" which will come readily and easily with little experience. In most high contrast situations encountered, the modifications will be within a range of 1/3 to ½ stop "over-exposure" from an over-all reading of both shadows and highlights (when a close-up reading is impractical, as it frequently is) and within a range of 25 to 50 percent less development time than ordinarily employed for that particular film and developer formula.

In the opposite case of a dull, gray day and a subject of little inherent contrast, or of a portrait subject under deep shade, a converse rule may be applied: the exposure may be more or less "normal" (to assure sufficient final density of the negative) or slightly less (up to ½ f/stop) than an over-all meter reading would indicate, and the development time may be increased (by 50 percent or even more) to build additional contrast into the negative image.

In the case of color film, the only effective way to control excessive contrast is actually to change the illumination reaching the subject by the use of a reflector or by synchro-sunlight flash. [The description of this latter technique will be found in Chapter 9.] Flash may also be used to increase the relative brightness of a subject against the background, but in most instances we must depend on color contrast to make interesting photographs under conditions of low contrast such as diffuse illumination. However, excessive brilliance is not always desirable in color photography and "flat" lighting is more useful in color work than in black-and-white.

Light, Form and Texture

FOR PICTURE-MAKING, there are other characteristics of light which are as important as its actual intensity. Illumination, for example, may be divided broadly into two types: direct and diffused. The bright sunshine at the beach or in the country on a clear day is an obvious example of direct illumination; while the light under the shade of a tree in full leaf, or anywhere out-of-doors on a cloudy or overcast day, is a case of diffused illumination.

There are many intermediate situations, as when a light haze partially obscures the sun, but nearly every outdoor situation falls into one of these two categories. Pictorially, direct light and diffused light will produce somewhat different results, particularly in terms of the rendering of form and texture, while

3.5 BURT OWEN *50mm f/1.4 Nikkor Plus-X, 1/50, f/11*

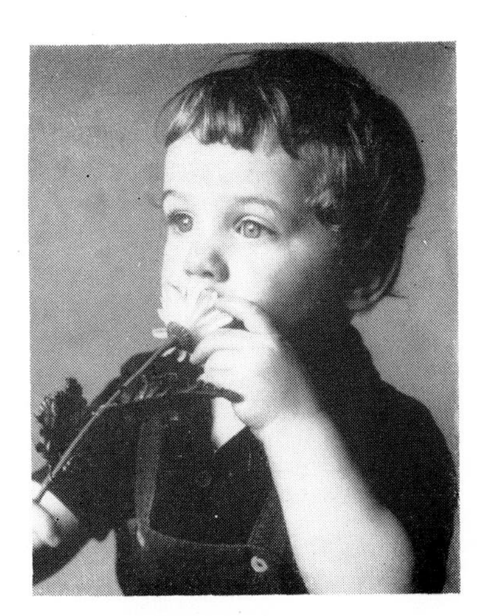

3.6 Jacques Lowe
Nikon S2, 105mm f/2.5 Nikkor
window light, Tri-X, 1/30, f/4

control measures can swing the results one way or the other in lighting situations which are intermediate between the two extremes.

Form

The rendering of three-dimensional form, i.e., the shape of an object, on two-dimensional photographic paper is an illusion which depends on a number of factors, the most important of which are *contour gradations* and the position and intensity of *cast shadows*. These, in turn, depend on the type of illumination, whether diffused or direct, and in the latter case upon the direction or source of the main light. When light is modulated around any object, the planes or curves reflect more or less light back toward the eye or the camera lens depending on how much of the illumination actually strikes the object and the acuteness of the angle from which it is reflected. These contour gradations may be abrupt on an object with distinct planes or smooth and gradual on a rounded object. In fact, it is the character of this gradation, abrupt or smooth, which is our visual clue to the shape of every object which we encounter.

A third factor in the identification of objects and their characteristics both in real life and in photographs is the presence of *local color*. Objects, as well as areas within most objects, differ in actual hue and in reflectivity (the difference, for example, between the color of lips and cheeks or between the face and the garment in the case of a portrait).

Both contour gradation and differences of local color are always present, although they may be masked to some extent by the strong highlights and deep shadows under bright, directional light, or reduced sometimes to very subtle values under extremely diffuse "directionless" light. In the majority of cases, all three factors (cast shadows, contour gradation and local color) are present to the eye and their recording is to some extent under the control of the photographer in his pictorial version of the scene. He may choose to subdue contrast and reduce shadow strength and even contour gradation, and select or control his subject to minimize differences of local color to arrive at a "flat" rendering of reality, or choose to emphasize cast shadows and to work for the greatest illusion of roundness and depth. His choice depends on the mood and effect he wishes his picture to produce.

The depiction of surface *texture* is linked with the illusion of form. The appearance of surface textural qualities depends upon the same effects of contour gradation and cast shadows. Diffuse light which minimizes these factors tends to subdue texture, while direct sunlight (or direct light from any source) tends to emphasize it. This result depends on both the intensity and the length of the cast shadows. Consequently, textural effects (as well as the rendering of form) depend in large measure on the direction of the light, the angle from which the light from the main source strikes the object and is reflected back to the eye and to the camera lens.

Classifying lighting

If we move a direct light source around an object, there is an infinite number of positions from which the light will strike the object. However, there are six basic positions which are easily distinguished by even the untrained eye and each of which has certain distinct pictorial characteristics. Terminology for identifying these positions varies somewhat, but current practice seems to have settled on: *front lighting, top front lighting, top lighting, angle lighting, side lighting* and *back lighting.* Some of these lighting situations are more useful than others in particular situations—if the photographer has any choice in the matter.

Outdoors, the photographer has small chance of moving the sun, but he may wait until lighting conditions are more favorable (in the case of an immovable object), or he may either move the subject or move himself around the subject for better lighting in many instances. Where the circumstances are such that he cannot postpone his exposure nor interfere without losing or falsifying his picture, then he must do what thousands of photographers have done before him: make the best of the lighting as he finds it.

Front lighting: When the light source is directly behind the photographer, the illumination tends to flatten out most subjects. Depending on how "pure" this position is, the cast shadows are either non-existent or very short, and modeling and texture depend upon contour gradation alone. Picture contrast depends in large part on differences in local color and reflectivity of objects.

Out-of-doors, this straight-on lighting occurs only when the sun is very low in the sky or when a subject is illuminated by reflected light from some surface such as the wall of a building. With color film, either of these light sources is apt to be a different "color temperature" than that for which the film is balanced and an appropriate color balancing filter must be employed (see *The ABC's of Filters,* below) or the over-all hue will be distorted from "normal" color. Excellent results, however, have been obtained when photographers have deliberately used this color distortion for a planned effect.

Top front light: When the sun (or other source of illumination) is behind the photographer, but somewhat higher than the pure front light position, cast shadows are longer (depending in part on how high or how far to the side the light source is located) giving an appearance of rounder form and more emphasis to texture. This is a more generally useful lighting angle than the pure frontal lighting for either color or black-and-white.

This is the typical lighting for many snapshot portraits which follow (or rather, slightly misinterpret) the old injunction to have the sun over the photographer's shoulder. This rule had some purpose when it was first formulated fifty years ago. Films were relatively slow and it was necessary to illuminate faces strongly for proper negative exposure. Today, it is more apt to result in over-exposure of skin areas in relation to the surroundings unless the film development is compensated to reduce the natural contrast of such lighting. It is a difficult light for a portrait subject, also, because the victim must look almost directly toward the sun, leading often to squinting eyes and a strained expression. The pattern of cast shadows on the face (under the nose and in the eye-sockets) is not apt to be a flattering one, unless there are natural reflectors present at the scene.

Top lighting: When the sun is almost directly overhead, values and gradations on the film may be considerably exaggerated. Horizontal surfaces are flatly illuminated, losing form and texture while vertical surfaces are either in shadow or illuminated with such sharp cross-light that texture is considerably exaggerated. All cast shadows are apt to be almost opaque unless there are natural reflectors on the scene. Sand, water or snow serve as such reflectors and top (noon) lighting is sometimes effective when they are present. For full shadow detail on black-and-white film, increase exposures by 1/2 to 1 full stop more than indicated by an over-all meter reading of the scene, or make a direct close-up shadow reading. (Decrease developing time to correspond.)

In some narrow city streets, this top lighting is the only direct illumination which penetrates, but it is apt to create excessive contrast. Films are fast enough today so such direct light is not necessary, even to stop action or gain adequate depth of field. Except when special effects are desired or when some action requires coverage at this hour, many photographers (unlike mad dogs and Englishmen) rarely go out in the noonday sun.

Angle lighting: When the light source is farther around to the side than in top front lighting and not yet so high as "pure" top lighting, there are a wide range of plastic lightings which may all be classified together. The intermediate position when the sun is half-way around and half-way up the sky (sometimes called the "double 45°" position) is one which is generally accepted as the most useful and least troublesome photographic lighting. With the light source at approximately this angle, cast shadows and contour gradation are brought out for effective rendering of both form and texture.

Control over contrast is important with this angle lighting. The photographer may, of course, take his contrast as he finds it, particularly when natural reflectors "open up" the shadows so surface detail is visible within them. He may soften contrast, giving a rather full exposure and cutting back on developing time, to preserve form yet reveal full shadow detail, or even use the opposite technique to exaggerate the depth of his shadows and to emphasize the impression of bright sunlight in some pictures. It is generally the best practice, however, to cut down contrast slightly so the negative registers detail in both shadow and highlight areas. With such a negative, greater contrast may be restored in printing if the "full sunlight" feeling is wanted. Control is thus shifted to a point when further reflection and judgment may be exercised and different effects may be actually printed and compared.

With color film, excessive contrast must be avoided. Rendering detail in both shadow and highlight areas is often beyond the effective latitude of the film and there may be color distortion in either or both illumination levels. It is better with color film for the photographer to move around whenever possible so the light more closely approximates a top front position, or to make use of natural reflectors to open up the shadows and raise their illumination level. Where this is impossible, it is best to expose for the most important highlight area. In other situations, a fill-in flash may be useful [see Chapter 9].

Side lighting: When the sun is all the way around to one side, contrast is usually exaggerated, form is brought out very fully and textures (on surfaces facing the camera lens) are usually strongly rendered. This emphasis on form and texture is frequently so harsh that this side lighting is a cruel one for portraiture.

3.7 K. Tateishi — *Nikon S2, 50mm f/1.4 Nikkor Super-XX, 1/60, f/8*

There is usually too great a contrast for any color film to record properly and even black-and-white film should have an increase in exposure of from 1/2 to 1 full stop with a correspondingly shorter development time for lowered contrast to produce negatives which will print without further exaggeration of the extremes of illumination present at the scene.

Back lighting: When the picture subject is between the photographer and the sun, a useful and interesting variety of light effects is possible. These range from the pure silhouette to a print which presents the subject flatly illuminated against a very light background. The key to these *contre-jour* effects is the accurate selection of exposure.

If an over-all reading is made of the scene, the results will approach the silhouette, an almost black figure against a correctly exposed background. If an accurate reading is made of, say, the face of a person standing with his back to the sun and illuminated only by reflected light, detail in the face will be recorded but the background will be over-exposed. With the Nikon Exposure Meter used for a reflectance reading, close-up, be careful that the direct rays of the sun do not strike into the sensitive cell of the light-meter, or make a reading from the palm of the hand, held so it is against the sun in the same manner as the subject. An incident light reading with the opal plate inserted may be made either close-up at subject position or with the meter shielded from the direct rays of the sun by the palm of the hand and facing back toward the photographer.

In working in these against the light situations, the sun ordinarily should not be included in the picture area. It may be shielded from the camera lens by the subject itself or by some object, such as a tree branch. A Nikon lens-shade, always a useful accessory, is especially valuable here to keep direct sunlight out of the lens. However, with the internally-coated Nikkor lenses, the Nikon may be pointed very closely toward the sun without too much danger of internal flare and halation which will fog the film or at least cut down considerably the acuity of the image. The internal coating also permits the inclusion of less intense sources of illumination such as sunlight reflections on the surface of a body of water without the danger of excessive halation.

"Seeing" light

It is useful, in the beginning, to identify these "base points" of illumination and to study the effects of light even when the Nikon is not being carried or used. A consciousness of light and its pictorial effects should be stimulated until it reaches the point where, like the mechanical operation of the Nikon, it becomes an automatic part of a total picture-reaction.

The six lighting positions which we have identified here rarely exist in "pure" form, and they tend always to blend into one another. However, as base points, they will serve to aid the photographer in sharpening his awareness of light and its effects.

The A B C's of Filters

Before concluding this general introduction to photography with the examination of specific picture-making situations, we must take one more look at light itself. In sunlight, out-of-doors, we are bathed with light which the eye accepts as "white"—which is almost a way of saying *neutral* or non-colored illumination. Yet we know that when this white light is passed through a prism, it will break up into a band of colored rays, ranging from violet through blue, green, yellow, orange and red. We can collect these colored rays in a simple optical system and merge them together to produce a result which is again "white." Nature itself sometimes supplies the "prisms," for example, the fine mist particles which create a rainbow.

Exactly how this rainbow mixture of colored rays produces the subjective impression of white is not yet well understood by physiologists or psychologists. There is a long-standing theory, open to question and by no means "proven," that there are three separate receptors in the eye, each one sensitive to certain wave lengths of light, that is, to certain sections of the rainbow (spectrum) and that their combined stimulation produces the sensation we call white. Certainly, it is possible experimentally to combine three very narrow bands of monochromatic (single-color) light from the blue, green and red areas of the spectrum and to have the eye fail to distinguish this from the full spectrum we receive from the sun. (Ordinary fluorescent lighting is an example of discontinuous spectral bands which seem to result in white light.) But, somewhat disconcertingly for the three receptor theory, it is possible to achieve a subjective impression of "white" from only *two* monochromatic bands, if these are correctly chosen.

Local color

While the light from the sun itself (usually combined with reflected light from the sky) is accepted as white, each object which we see as we look around the world seems to have its own color. This is a phenomenon of *selective absorption*: in other words, each object absorbs a portion of the spectral "rainbow" and reflects the rest. Foliage absorbs much of the blue and red ends of the spectrum and reflects a great deal of the middle, green, portion, while an apple (if it is ripe)

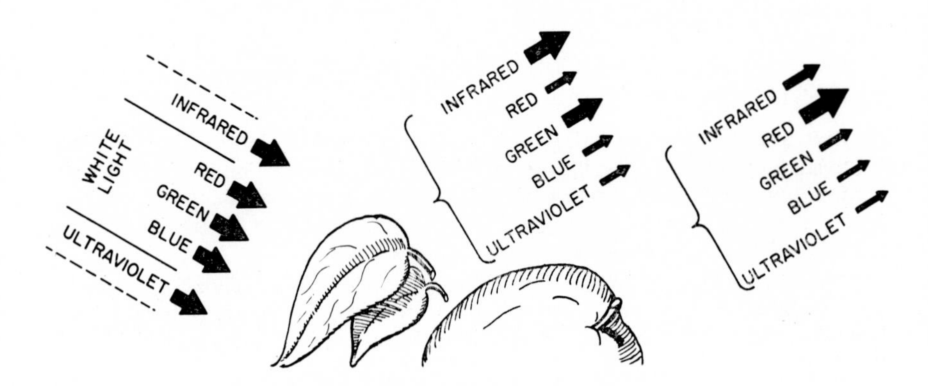

3.8 *White light is partially absorbed and partially reflected from objects in nature. This gives them their distinctive color.*

absorbs much of the blue and green and reflects a large proportion of the red rays. Transparent objects also exhibit this selective absorption. Each piece of stained glass in a church window absorbs a portion of the spectrum and transmits the rest.

When we understand that white light is a "bundle" of colored rays, that objects reflect only certain portions of the white light which strikes them, and that a colored glass will transmit only a certain portion of "the bundle," we have the basis for understanding how filters function in photography.

How filters work

The earliest term for photographic filters was *ray screens*, and they are still sometimes called "screens" in British photographic literature. It is an equally appropriate term for they screen off or filter out a more-or-less extensive portion of the spectrum and prevent some of the rays which make up white light from entering the lens of the camera. Since most objects reflect only a portion of the white-light spectrum back toward the camera lens, and since it is possible to choose a filter which will either pass or screen off the reflected rays from this particular object [see diagram, Figure 3.9], it is possible to exercise a large measure of control over how light or dark this object will register on the film and on the print which is made from it. (We will look first at filters for black-and-white photography. Filters for color films will be considered in the second part of this section.) We must remember, of course, that few objects absorb all of

3.9 *Filters absorb part of the light and transmit the rest. Proper filter choice gives great control over film recording of the colors of nature.*

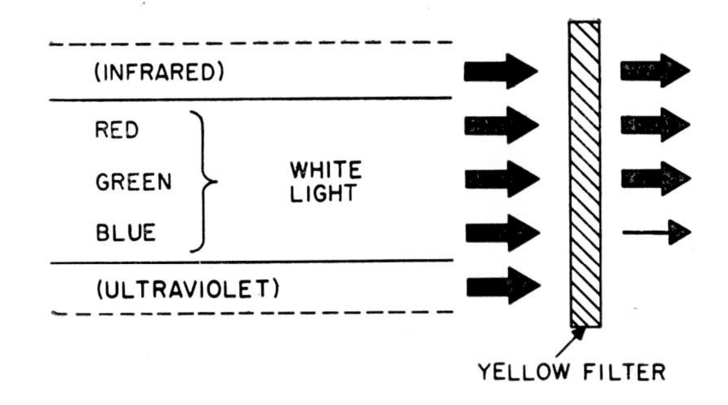

the rays in any portion of the spectrum and that filters have not yet reached a theoretical "perfection." Within these limits, a great degree of practical control is easily and simply possible.

The construction of filters

Technicians have attempted to solve the problems of manufacturing uniform and stable photographic filters from two directions. One is the introduction of various materials into a batch of optical glass to affect its color, and then casting this glass into a thin slab which may be cut into the proper sizes. This method, for reasons which are immaterial here, has certain limitations particularly in the range of appropriate colors (more accurately, wave length transmission characteristics) which can be obtained. However, such solid glass filters are stable in color and more rugged than those constructed by other methods. These are supplied as Nikon filters bound in a metal rim. They are available as screw-in filters to fit most of the Nikkor lenses or in "series" sizes. [See table in *Data and Formulas*.]

The more common method is to mix dyes (usually organic) into a batch of gelatin which is then spread in a thin coating of uniform depth on a specially prepared glass surface and allowed to harden. This is then stripped off, tested and prepared for use. These gelatin filters are available for 35mm photography in two forms: as small squares or disks of gelatin film, lacquered on both sides for protection; or as cemented between two thin pieces of glass which are very carefully ground exactly plane-parallel so they will not distort the image as formed by a good lens.
when the photographer has need for some unusual or specialized filter, or one for use in the darkroom [see Chapters 6 and 7], but they are delicate and easily damaged. Filters which are to be used frequently should be of the solid glass or glass-sandwich type which are relatively rugged in normal use.

Filters for Nikkor lenses are also classified by *size*. Since the diameter of the front ring of camera lenses differs between various makes and focal lengths, manufacturers classify their filters by *series sizes*. One minor, but very useful, advantage of Nikkor lenses is the fact that most of the Nikkors from 35mm to 135mm focal lengths take *Series VII* filters, so a filter purchased for one of these Nikkors will fit any of the others which are owned or acquired. (The exceptions are the 50mm f/2 Nikkor which accepts a Series VI size, the 50mm f/1.1 which requires a 62mm filter, and the 85mm f/1.5 which takes a Series VIII.) The

180mm and 250mm telephoto Nikkors are necessarily larger in construction and require a Series IX size, while the longest Nikkor, the 500mm, requires filters which are 110mm in diameter.

Filters are used at the front end of Nikkor lenses and are secured there either by threads on the filter itself, by a retaining ring which is supplied with the lens or by a ring which is part of the Nikkon lens shade for that lens. Since a lens shade is an invaluable accessory under any shooting conditions, it is excellent practice to use the filter in conjunction with the Nikkon lens shade.

The care of glass-sandwich filters

In use, a filter is part of the optical system of the camera and should be treated with as much respect as the Nikkor lens itself. A filter which is dirty, scratched or discolored will degrade the film image. Filters are adversely affected by both dampness and heat and should always be stored in a dry place and, if possible, never subjected to temperatures above 120F. Properly handled, they should rarely require more cleaning than wiping with a soft, dry, lintless cloth. If they become finger-marked, wipe them with lens tissue or clean cloth moistened slightly with Kodak Lens Cleaner or a similar preparation. Do not use water. Moisture which enters the glass sandwich may cloud the gelatin film or may expand the gelatin to strain the filter and alter its optical characteristics.

Do not leave filters in direct sunlight or other extremely bright light for long periods of time. Heat, intense light, moisture and the passage of time will all alter filter characteristics. However, despite these warnings, a glass-sandwich filter handled with ordinary care will give satisfactory service for at least several years.

The kinds of filters

There are well over 100 different kinds of filters available, without counting duplications by several manufacturers. Each of these has a useful purpose, but only five need concern the amateur who shoots black-and-white, and he may even get along quite comfortably with three filters for a large measure of control in every ordinary shooting situation. [Filters for color photography will be explained further on in this section and in material on color later in the book; a full listing of the most useful filters for black-and-white photography will be found in *Data and Formulas*.]

Filters for black-and-white photography may be divided by function into three general categories: *corrective, contrast,* and *selective and special purpose.* (Some filters fit into more than one group depending on their use and the shooting conditions.) Here, we will be concerned only with the first two of these categories.

Corrective filters are employed to alter the response of film to make it correspond more closely to the color response of the human eye. If the actual light reflectance from a number of differently-colored surfaces is made equal, those which are in the yellow-green region will seem brighter to our eyes than those which are in either the blue or the red region. Most 35mm films presently available respond approximately the same way, but introducing certain filters into the optical system will further correct their response. The amateur (and the professional in normal practice) uses black-and-white films which are termed *Type B panchromatic*. In direct sunlight, a medium yellow Nikon Y (or K2) filter is used for full color correction. Tungsten light (household bulbs, and some photofloods and wire-filled flashbulbs) is generally poorer in blue and richer in red than is sunlight, even though the human eye rapidly adjusts to it and accepts it as "white." A light green (Nikon X1) filter is used for correcting Type B panchromatic film under tungsten light. (Artificial light will be considered in detail in Chapter 9.)

Contrast filters are used to deliberately exaggerate the color response of black-and-white film for a more interesting pictorial result. A medium red Nikon R (or A) filter, for example, will render a blue sky very dramatically dark. The light green Nikon X1 filter becomes a contrast filter under daylight, rendering yellow-green subjects slightly lighter and red subjects slightly darker than they are perceived by the eye. This filter will also somewhat darken blue subjects (such as a clear sky). This "rule" is the key to the effect of any filter (used with panchromatic film) on color rendition in the photographic print: it will lighten its own color and darken the other portions of the spectrum. [See filter table in *Data and Formulas*.]

Controlling aerial haze

Distant landscapes are always covered with a bluish haze which becomes a deep violet in the far distance. This (like the blue color of the sky itself) is caused by the scatter of light by air molecules and by suspended dust and water droplets. This scattering effect is strongest in the blue end of the visible spectrum and extends into the invisible ultraviolet to which all sensitive materials respond very strongly. The obscuring effect of haze in distant landscapes, in aerial shots and in photographs made in high altitudes is thus greater in the negative and print than it is to the eye. Most filters, however, tend to block the passage of ultraviolet. Distant detail will be better in filtered pictures. In order of their increasing effect in blocking ultraviolet, any of these filters may be used: ultraviolet Nikon L (or UV) medium yellow Nikon Y (or K2), orange Nikon O, Wratten G, and red Nikon R (or A).

Exposure factors

Since, as we noticed above, a filter functions by absorbing part of the light and passing the rest, less total light reaches the film during any given time when a filter is employed. Consequently, exposures must be increased by a specific multiple for each different filter. These are expressed as *filter factors*. The leaflet enclosed with each package of film gives the manufacturer's recommendations for filter factors for the commonly employed filters. These have been reasonably constant for some years, but this leaflet should be checked with each batch of film purchased, particularly if the photographer shifts from one kind of film to another.

Exposures with filters should be accurate. No filter is absolutely perfect and all will "leak" through a certain amount of the colors they are intended to screen. Over-exposure will partially nullify the effect of any filter as well as tend to excessive negative density and film grain. Under-exposure will also lead to color distortions and to a negative which is difficult to print.

The filter factors [*Data and Formulas*] are expressed as "2X", "1.5X", "4X", etc. These figures indicate that exposures through these filters must be multiplied by these factors. There are several convenient ways to do this. The very commonly used medium yellow (Nikon Y) corrective filter, for example, has a 1.7X filter factor, indicating that exposures through this filter must be nearly doubled. On the matched linear shutter-speed—diaphragm-opening scales of the S2 and SP Nikon models, an exposure may be easily doubled by moving the speed dial one notch to a slower speed or by opening up the diaphragm by one setting. Or the compensation may be made by changing the Exposure Index of the film on the photo-electric meter. For a 2X factor, any of the Exposure Indexes listed in this book may be halved and the meter calculator changed to this new setting. For a 1.5X factor, reduce the Exposure Index by 66 percent or open the diaphragm about 2/3 stop, as nearly as this can be estimated.

Neutral density filters

There is also a set of "gray" filters which admits all the colors of the spectrum fairly evenly but which cuts down the total amount of light which passes through. These have achieved a new usefulness with the advent of extremely fast emulsions. In bright sunlight, with the Nikon loaded with such sensitive films as Kodak Tri-X or Ilford HPS, even though the Nikkor lens is stopped down to the smallest opening it may still be necessary to use a shutter speed of 1/500 or 1/1000. This is a needless limitation and hampers full control over selective focus and other factors. The neutral density filters are supplied by Nikon in screw-in and "series" sizes such as VI and VII which fit the most commonly used Nikkor lenses. Of the wide range of possible densities, Nikon has selected as the most useful those with 4X and 8X filter factors.

A neutral density and a corrective or contrast filter may be combined in front of the lens for more complete control of color rendition. However, there is some inevitable *loss in acuity* of image. Two filters interpose *four* air-glass surfaces, each of which contributes a slight degradation of image. A single filter, even an 8X neutral density, rarely interferes seriously with the sharpness of the Nikkor image in a print of moderate enlargement, but as additional filters are included in the optical system the image will begin to suffer a slight "softness."

Note: When any two (or more) filters are used together their filter factors must be multiplied to arrive at a corrected exposure. Thus, a 4X neutral density filter and a 2X medium yellow Nikon Y (or K2) corrective filter, used together, will have an 8X filter factor, and require either 3 stops greater exposure or a shutter speed three places down on the speed dial.

Polarizing filters

There is a completely different kind of "gray" filter which is useful in subduing certain kinds of reflections, particularly those from nonmetallic surfaces, and for darkening blue skies without affecting the other colors in the scene. This is the polarizing filter, marketed by several manufacturers under various trade names (Polaroid, Pola Screen, etc.). These filters control another variable of light. In completely nonscientific language, we may consider each ray of light from the sun or other source, whether received directly or reflected from any surface, as if it were a piece of cord stretched to the camera lens. Ordinarily these imaginary cords may be considered to "vibrate" in all directions around their axis. Under some special circumstances they will be *polarized,* that is, they will vibrate only in one direction at right angles to their axis [see diagram, Figure 3.10]. The polarizing filter always acts as a screen, accepting only light which is "vibrating" in one direction (in relation to the axis of the ray). It will thus admit *part* of ordinary light rays (which accounts for its brownish gray visual appear-

3.10 *Polarizing filters pass only light rays vibrating in one plane at right angles to the lens axis.*

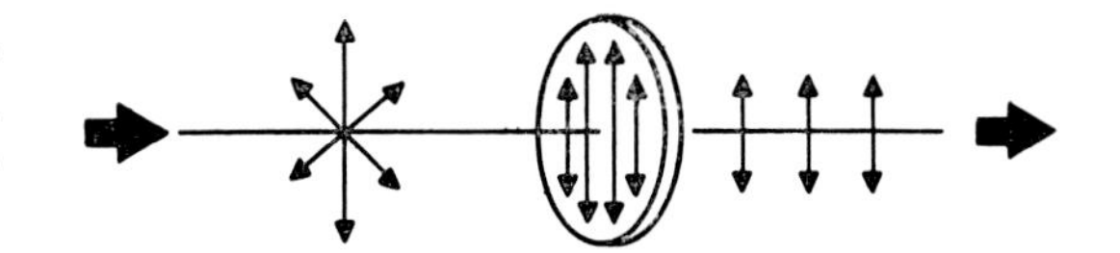

ance), consisting of almost *all* of the light which is "vibrating" in the correct direction in relation to the filter, and almost *none* of the light which is vibrating at right angles to the direction of complete acceptance. A reference to the diagram [Figure 3.10] again, may make this somewhat clearer.

There are two sources of strongly polarized light in out-of-door situations: light reflected from nonmetallic surfaces (such as wood, paint, glass, water, etc.) at about 35°; and light reflected from a clear blue sky at right angles to the position of the sun. The polarizing filter may be rotated to block this polarized light almost completely, allowing the lens to "see" the non-polarized light from details masked by bright, specular reflections; or to allow the sky to print more deeply in the final picture.

In use, nonmetallic reflections may be examined visually through the filter to determine the precise angle which reduces them most effectively, an angle which must be maintained when the filter is placed over the lens. (It is important to note that it is not always possible to subdue reflections.) Some polarizing filters have a small viewing filter on an arm extending from the rim of the camera filter, which simplifies handling in use. When this arm is pointed directly toward the sun, the filter will function most effectively (for that particular situation) when a darkening of the sky is desired. Polarizing filters are also useful in work with color film [see below] and in copying and close-up work [see Chapter 11].

Because of the extreme variation in the proportion of light which is polarized (and may thus be screened out) in any situation, it is very difficult to establish a uniform filter factor for the polarizing filter. When the filter is used to subdue reflections, with other black-and-white or color film, exposure should be increased by a 3X filter factor (1 2/3 stops). With the side or top lighting which produces polarized sky illumination a further increase of 1/2 to 1 full stop is recommended. These factors apply to both panchromatic and color films.

Filters in color photography

None of the filters mentioned previously (except the polarizing) is useful in color photography. Filters for color alter the light passing through them somewhat less drastically than do filters for black-and-white. (This observation does not apply to three-color separation filters and the other special purpose filters. These will be considered in later chapters.) Color filters fall into four general classifications: *color conversion, light balancing, color compensating,* and *special purpose.* Here, we will consider the commonly used filters in these classifications.

Color conversion and light balancing filters

Color films now available in 35mm size fall into types according to the illumination sources for which they are balanced. The light from a clear-glass flashbulb, for example, contains red, green and blue light in somewhat different proportions than does average daylight. Film is manufactured for use with either of these two light sources, but may be exposed under other conditions if a proper filter is employed which will change the characteristics of the light admitted to the film to approximate that for which the film is designed. (A third kind, Professional Kodachrome, formerly called "Type A," is balanced for 3400K tungsten (or photoflood) bulbs. This is used largely by professionals and is not so widely stocked in camera stores as are the other types.) These filters entail a loss in speed which ranges from slight to considerable.

[See *Data and Formulas* for table listing currently available 35mm color films and filter recommendations for their use under other lighting conditions.]

Note: "Universal" (color negative) film, such as Kodacolor, may be exposed with either daylight or clear flash and proper filtering supplied during printing. As this book went to press, negative color films were not yet available in 35mm cartridges loaded by U. S. manufacturers.

Color compensating filters

It is often desirable to shift color characteristics only slightly, either to correct response more fully or deliberately to distort film response for a rendition which is "warmer" or "cooler." These shifts are accomplished by the "CC" series of filters. (Their other uses will be covered in later chapters.) These CC filters are available in several degrees of density in each of six colors: red, green and blue, and their complementaries, cyan (green-blue), magenta (blue-red) and yellow (red-green). A table listing all of them and other relevant data will be found in *Data and Formulas*.

UV and skylight filters

As we noted in the material above on filters for black-and-white work, many outdoor scenes contain an excess of ultraviolet radiation. While this is invisible to the normal eye, color film, like all other photographic sensitive materials, responds strongly to these wavelengths. This unwanted radiation will obscure detail in distant landscapes, as well as in pictures made from the air or in very high

3.11 MORRIS JAFFE

Nikon S2
35mm f/2.5 Nikkor
Plus-X, 1/500, f/11

altitudes. Most experienced color photographers employ an ultraviolet-absorbing filter such as the Nikon L over the camera lens when they photograph such scenes. These filters may also be useful in color pictures made in outdoor shade (illuminated by scatter light from the blue sky, a source rich in ultraviolet).

The *UV filters* (ultraviolet screening) have a tendency in certain situations, particularly with color photographs made under open shade, to impart a slightly yellowish cast to the transparency. The *skylight filter* blocks off not only the ultraviolet but also small amounts of visible blue and green light, and has a slight pinkish appearance. This filter consequently will serve both purposes: cutting distant haze and minimizing the slight bluish cast of scenes illuminated only by sky light. Many photographers use the skylight filter for most color work out-of-doors. No increase in exposure is necessary for either the Nikon L (or UV) or the skylight filter.

Subjects Frequently Encountered

THE FOLLOWING SECTIONS include brief notes on the subject matter most frequently encountered, particularly by the amateur. There are a few words of general advice which apply to almost every situation.

Whenever it is possible or convenient, the important subject matter, including all necessary and useful background, should be so composed that it fills as much as possible of the whole film frame. The ideal of many photographers is a picture so accurately "seen" at the time of exposure that the film may be printed, corner to corner, on the final print. It is not always possible to accomplish this, but a fully utilized negative or color transparency is a sign of photographic competence. Even from a technical standpoint, using the full negative tends to minimize grain in the final picture. If several lenses of different focal-lengths are available, this ideal composition is more easily achieved.

Variety in working angles and distances for recording scenes should be sought, particularly with close and middle-distance subjects. It is always useful to work around any subject, exploring for new angles which are more interesting pictorially or which tell a story more effectively. Changing the working distance or shifting from one focal-length Nikkor to another also adds versatility to subject coverage. Moving in very closely or using a telephoto Nikkor to isolate an especially interesting detail will sometimes produce photographs of more than ordinary interest.

This leads to the question of how many photographs are necessary for any subject or situation. The box-camera beginner often has the approach of "one subject, one exposure." On the other hand, with a 36-exposure cartridge in the Nikon, an amateur may be tempted to shoot many pictures which are virtual duplicates. The optimum number lies somewhere between these extremes. With a comparatively static landscape or distant scene, one or two exposures may be all that are necessary. When the effectiveness of a photograph depends upon catching peak action, or upon the shades of expression in a portrait, or upon picturing the relationships between several persons, then many more exposures may be useful. Film is relatively cheap. The photographer should expose as many shots as seem necessary in a specific situation, provided that each exposure is potentially different and useful.

In many instances, the number of exposures may decrease with a growth in confidence. The rapid, "three-finger" control of the Nikon is a valuable aid to

3.12 GERRY LOW

Nikon S2
50mm f/1.4 Nikkor
Plus-X, 1/500, f/4

recording the optimum relationship of elements in the picture as quickly as they are perceived. With practice in seeing and practice in the instantaneous shooting which the Nikon design permits, he will be more and more likely to seize what has been called "the decisive moment" accurately as it occurs.

Landscapes

Distant views are often improved by including an interesting foreground object or a human figure to emphasize the depth of the scene. A wide-angle Nikkor will increase the feeling of panorama and distance, while a longer than normal focal length will increase the apparent size of distant mountains, etc., at the expense of inclusiveness of the view. [See material on perspective and print viewing distance, Chapter 4.] The medium-speed films such as Plus-X are excellent, but the slower, fine-grain films (Panatomic X, Adox KB14, Ilford Pan F, Perutz Pergrano 14, or Agfa Isopan FF) are recommended when very large prints are anticipated. The medium yellow Nikon Y (or K2) filter is recommended for the best rendition of a blue sky; the light green Nikon X1 will help bring out good foliage detail; while the orange Nikon O (or G) or red Nikon R (or A) filters will exaggerate the depth of the sky tones on a clear day. The polarizing filter is a good choice if the camera is pointed approximately at a right angle to the sun.

Color adds interest to almost any landscape. The relatively slow Kodachrome (E. I. 10) is an excellent choice, although any of the color films may be used. The Nikon L or a skylight filter will improve the rendition of distant detail on a clear, bright day. Do not overlook the dramatic possibilities of color photography on a gray or rainy day, however. Color need not be vivid to be interesting.

Scenes which are almost monochromatic (yellow-red in late afternoon sunlight, for example) may be even more interesting than those taken in "normal" lighting.

Sunsets

Sunsets are dramatic even on black-and-white film, although color is the more usual choice. In either case, an interesting horizon line, silhouetted against the color display, makes for a more effective picture. Slight under-exposures with color film often lead to more intense and saturated colors. To establish exposure, one useful method is to take a reading with the Nikon Meter pointed straight up to the zenith, then take a second reading with the meter pointed toward the sunset. A camera-setting half-way between the two readings will often yield excellent color rendition. When the sun is still relatively high and too bright to view directly with the eye, it should be shielded from the camera lens by a distant tree or building.

Groups

Groups of people who are lined up or formally posed outdoors rarely make interesting picture subjects. Try, instead, to catch moments of more natural action, waiting for characteristic or interesting groupings which will tell a story or form a desirable pictorial pattern. With either black-and-white or color film, the diffused light of a slightly hazy day or open shade is often better than harsh lighting for studies of groups in action. Under open shade always use a skylight filter with daylight color film.

Individual portraits

Head-and-shoulder portraits are best made at a moderate working distance (at least six feet) to avoid distortion. The 85mm, 105mm and 135mm Nikkors are excellent choices to preserve a proper working distance yet fill the full frame with the principal subject. If it is necessary to work at a relatively close distance, there will be less danger of any possible distortion in the features of the subject if he is turned so his face is either three-quarters or full profile to the camera lens. For full-figure portraits, particularly with action, the 50mm or a wide-angle lens (such as one of the 35mm Nikkors) may be effectively used, especially when it is desirable to relate the figure to its background. In most outdoor situations, the medium-speed films are rapid enough to stop action and still provide a useful depth of field. On very dull days or under deep shade, the fast films such as Tri-X or HPS may be necessary. When blue sky is used as a background, the medium yellow Nikon Y (or K2) filter will usually darken it enough for good separation. The red Nikon R (or A) filter will give better separation, but will often give unsatisfactory flesh tones. A ruddy appearance of the skin will be recorded in more satisfactory tones by the light green Nikon X1 filter. Under proper lighting conditions (see above) the polarizing filters are effective with both black-and-white and color. A skylight filter is almost a necessity for close-ups or medium shots of individuals under open shade with daylight color film.

Children

Often, the most interesting photographs of children are the informal, unposed action shots, made while they play. Such pictures usually require a fast shutter speed. The photographer must be alert to keep children in focus as they move around, or employ zone focusing when circumstances make this possible. If children are occupied with a game or a toy, activity may be confined within a a reasonable area. Strong light and harsh shadows are not the best lighting pattern for children. A softer contrast, open shade or even back-light often result in more satisfactory pictures. In most indoor circumstances, medium speed black-and-white film or the color films rated at an Exposure Index of 32 are generally fast enough to record even active children but the new Super Anscochrome [E.I. 100] will provide a greater freedom.

Action

Arresting action on film depends on shutter speed in relation to how close the movement is to the camera and on its direction in relation to the camera. [See speed table *Data and Formulas.*] However, the photographer has a choice between "freezing" the action, with every detail sharp, or stopping the movement of the principal part of the subject while allowing details to blur, or of deliberately permitting a great deal of subject blur. His choice will depend entirely on his pictorial purpose. When it is impossible to shoot rapidly enough to freeze movement (as with a racing car passing in front of the photographer at a near distance) he may "pan" with the action, that is follow the moving object in the finder, swinging the camera to follow the movement, as he exposes. This will produce a relatively sharp image of the principal subject against a completely blurred background, often an extremely effective pictorial device.

When light conditions permit, setting the Nikon for zone focus is the most generally satisfactory solution for recording action which cannot be precisely anticipated. This is especially effective with either the 50mm or a wide-angle Nikkor. With the latter, on a sunny day, almost "universal focus" is usually possible. With the longer-focus Nikkors, depth of field is somewhat more shallow, but is often completely adequate at distances of thirty feet or more from the camera. For the greatest possible field set the infinity mark on the distance scale opposite the f/marking corresponding to the diaphragm setting in use. From a spectator's position, Nikkors of 135mm or longer are an excellent choice for "close-ups" of sports action. On dull days, or when it is desirable to stop down for greater depth of field, it is preferable to change to a faster film such as Kodak Tri-X or Ilford HPS. Some color films, Anscochrome and Super Anscochrome in particular, may be exposed and developed for a much higher Exposure Index when it is necessary to record fast action. [See Chapter 7 on color.]

City Streets

The active and often unpredictable human activity on city streets has served as the "school" for many contemporary photojournalists and as photographic subject matter for countless amateurs. Some of the most interesting travel records, also, are pictures of the sometimes exotic "public life" of foreign cities. Success depends, in large part, on learning to shoot rapidly and on remaining unobtrusive. The compact Nikon controls are an aid to both, for it may be set, properly zone-focused, and carried under a coat until the actual instant of exposure, or focusing and shooting may be done very rapidly while the camera is at eye-level. Telephoto lenses, from the 85mm to the 135mm Nikkors are useful, also, for hand-held use at a distance from the action photographed. Some professionals prefer the all-black Nikon body which has no chrome trim to catch attention.

3.13 MORRIS JAFFE *Nikon S2, 35mm f/2.5 Nikkor Plus-X, 1/250, f/8*

In other situations, the wide-angle Nikkors (such as the 35mm, 28mm and 25mm) are useful because of the greater area included in each picture and the considerable depth of field they provide. On sunny days, even in narrow, shaded streets, the medium-speed panchromatic films or color films will be found adequate in speed for most situations. Where exceptionally fast shutter speeds are required or when a greater depth of field is necessary, the faster Tri-X or HPS should be used. With either film, exposures should be calculated for any large shadow areas which have important detail and development held back to prevent the highlight areas from overdeveloping and blocking up on the negative. When rapid action is encountered, Anscochrome or Ektachrome may be exposed at an Exposure Index of 64 or Super Anschrome at 200 without significant loss of color fidelity. (Special development is required for this extra speed.)

Architecture

Dramatic photographs of buildings, monuments, etc., may be made on bright days, particularly with filters such as the red Nikon R (or A), or orange Nikon O, or Wratten G to allow blue sky to print almost black. For pictures, however, in which detail is especially important, a hazy or slightly overcast day is a better choice. There is lowered contrast between highlight and shadow, and the film will register full detail in both. Contrast (in black-and-white) may be restored, without losing this detail, by a slightly prolonged developing time and by printing on a more contrasty grade of paper. [See Chapters 5 and 6.] Color film, too, will give improved results when the lighting is less contrasty. On the other hand, side lighting and strong shadows will bring out form and texture much more boldly, if that is the purpose of the photograph.

Building lines will tend to converge sharply if the camera is close-up, particularly if a wide-angle lens is necessary to encompass the whole scene. [See notes on perspective in Chapter 4.] This effect will be further exaggerated if the camera is tilted upward to include the whole of a tall structure. Horizontal lines which converge in this fashion will not be as obtrusive (and possibly annoying) to the eye in the final picture as will vertical lines. Part of this "distortion" (which is, in reality, a reproduction of what the eye actually sees—and ignores) can be corrected by working from a greater distance, if this is possible, and by choosing a focal-length Nikkor which fills the full frame of the film from that standpoint.

The medium-speed panchromatic films will ordinarily produce a completely satisfactory picture, but the fine-grain films such as Kodak Panatomic-X, Adox KB14, Ilford Pan X and others, will give the ultimate in detail and a negative which may be enlarged many more diameters without the interference of grain.

Beach scenes

Sand (like snow) forms a highly reflective surface. While normal contrast between highlight and shadow areas in open landscapes may measure about 6:1, readings at the beach with *front* or *angle lighting* [see above], with sunlight reflecting off the sand into shadow areas, may show a contrast reduced to 4:1 or less. However, with *side lighting* or with *back lighting*, there may be less reflection into the shadow areas and the contrast may climb to an extreme of 8:1 or more. When a human subject moves a few feet away to a grass or other surface with less reflectivity, the contrast may also become quite extreme. The best practice is to take both shadow and highlight readings with a reflectance meter used either close to the subject or against the palm of the hand, held so it is first in the direct light of the sun, then angled to correspond to the shadow lighting. Exposure should be calculated to give good shadow detail. Black-and-white development should be curtailed to prevent highlight blocking. With color film, the extremes of illumination may be too great for the film to register, leading to loss of detail in either, or both, ends of the scale. Front lighting or less extreme angle lighting will usually compress the contrast ratio to within the capacity of color film.

A medium yellow Nikon Y (or K2) filter is excellent for separation of tones and is the best choice for panchromatic film when there are people included in beach scenes. A red Nikon R (or A) filter gives more dramatic effects but will bleach out skin tones. A green Nikon X1 filter will slightly exaggerate the effect of suntanning or ruddy skin.

Snow scenes

When snow is on the ground, conditions will be much like those outlined under *Beach scenes* (above). When the snow is actually falling, conditions are similar to those mentioned under *Rain and fog* [below]. On a clear day, with snow on the ground, use the Nikon exposure meter for an accurate camera setting.

3.14 Philip O. Stearns

Nikon S, 50mm f/1.4

Guardsman, London

Plus-X, 1/60, f/2

The shadows on snow are surprisingly blue, particularly with back-lighted and side-lighted scenes and this will be particularly evident with color film. A Nikon L (or UV) or a skylight filter will reduce this excessive blue somewhat to make the transparency more acceptable in color rendition. A medium yellow Nikon Y (or K2) filter with black-and-white film will darken these shadows just as it darkens blue sky, while a medium red Nikon R (or A) filter will exaggerate their contrast. Filtering with either of these will bring out snow texture very strongly when cross-lighting exists. The slower, fine-grain films are usually fast enough for many brightly lit situations. To restore normal control over speed and depth of field, it may be necessary to use either the 4X or 8X density filter with the ultra-fast panchromatic films.

The construction of the Nikon shutter mechanism is such that it is not appreciably affected by extreme cold. Nikons have been used for months in the Arctic without mechanical difficulties, and have even been taken into rooms designed to break down equipment with intense cold and used there to record the effect of such tests. However, there are certain precautions which will ensure successful pictures in extremely cold weather. Whenever possible, carry the Nikon under the outer layers of clothing to keep it moderately warmed for best shutter operation. It should not be kept so warm, however, that moisture condenses on the lens surfaces. Rapid change of temperature from outdoors to indoors should always be avoided, for moisture will condense on cold lens surfaces and cloud them. It is better to leave the camera in a relatively cold place if the photographer is going indoors only temporarily. When the camera is brought indoors for any period, the lens should be removed and carefully wiped with lens tissue, or a very clean, lintless handkerchief, or with facial tissue to remove all trace of condensation. The Nikon body should be left open until it is thoroughly warmed to allow condensation an opportunity to evaporate. Professionals working under Arctic conditions use two sets of Nikon bodies and Nikkor lenses for indoor and outdoor use.

Film will become very brittle with extreme cold and the danger of small discharges of static electricity as film is advanced or rewound increases. (These static discharges show as jagged "lightning" streaks across the film where they have exposed the silver halide. They are impossible to remove from negatives.) Film should be advanced and rewound slowly to lessen any danger of static discharges or of breaking the now brittle film base.

These cold-weather practices are advisable in northern-latitude winters or in any weather when the temperature drops close to or below freezing. A few precautions will ensure the technical success of photographs made, for example, on a skiing week-end.

Rain and fog

Strong sunshine is not necessary for excellent pictures; in fact, many beautiful ones have been made in rain and fog. Low subject contrast is the usual problem here and black-and-white film may require extra development to compensate. Often, it is useful to load the Nikon with the fastest available film so it

3.15 TED RUSSELL *Nikon S2, 50mm f/1.4 Nikkor*
Tri-X, 1/4, f/2 (forced development)

3.16 TED RUSSELL *Nikon S2, 50mm f/1.4 Nikkor*
Tri-X, 1 sec., f/2 (forced development)

may be stopped down for depth of field without too great a sacrifice of shutter speed in the dimmer light. Filters are of little use with black-and-white, but a skylight filter may "warm up" color film slightly for better results. Do not be afraid, however, of almost monochromatic bluish color results which may have a beauty of their own.

Protect the Nikon from moisture as much as practicable. Keep it under a coat when not in use and use the lens shade whenever shooting to keep off some of the rain. If possible, stand in a doorway or under some other protected spot when actually shooting or have a companion hold an umbrella over you and the camera. Wipe the front surface of the Nikkor gently before each shot with either lens tissue, a soft, well-laundered handkerchief or with facial tissue. Rub off moisture gently, do not scrub! Occasional moisture or dampness will probably not harm the sturdy Nikon, but prolonged exposure or a real drenching is dangerous. In professional work, pictures are important, whatever the weather. But if the Nikon is subjected to a jet of water or to prolonged exposure in very wet weather, it should be returned to your Nikon dealer or to Nikon, Inc., 251 Fourth Ave., New York City, for examination and a thorough cleaning.

Night scenes

Night-time exteriors—city streets, theatre marquees, flood-lighted buildings, neon signs—provide interesting subject matter for the Nikon. It is difficult to

3.17 DAVID LINTON
Aerial view, Japan

Nikon S2, 85mm f/2 Nikkor
Plus-X, K2 filter, 1/500, f/4

establish an exposure guide, for conditions vary widely. In many instances it will be found that an exposure meter will give no reading under these dim lighting conditions. It is best to bracket exposures, making the first at a speed established by experience (or by pure guess) and another at two stops each way. In scenes with a moderate amount of light, with fast films such as Tri-X or HPS, the basic exposure might be 1/15 to 1/30 at f/2.8. Color film under the same circumstances might require from 1/5 to 2 seconds (on tripod) at the same aperture. The inclusion of bright light sources as the principal subject may shorten correct exposure by one or two stops. Effects will vary considerably with exposure and one which is "incorrect" may produce a very interesting result.

This is particularly true with color film. The types balanced for clear flash bulbs or for tungsten illumination will generally give more natural results at night than will the daylight type, but night color sources range over such extremes of color that no transparency will record exactly the colors which the eyes see. Anscochrome may be exposed at an Exposure Index as high as 125 or Super-Anscochrome up to 200 or more (with appropriate development). There will be some color distortion, but it will be unimportant under these circumstances.

Rainy nights, which add reflections, often produce excellent night pictures. Another useful effect is obtained by placing the Nikon on a firm tripod before sunset and making a fairly long exposure (1/2 to 2/3 of the meter reading) in the fading light to register some detail in the scene. Leave the Nikon on the tripod (without winding the film) and wait until the lights have come on in the scene and then *double-expose* to register them on the film. Extreme care must be taken not to move the camera, particularly when re-winding for the intentional double-exposure. [See Chapter 2.]

Aerial

When photographs are made from the air, as from the window of an air liner, the Nikon should be left locked at infinity focus. The panoramic effect which is generally desired may be obtained with either the normal 50mm or with a wide-angle Nikkor. With black-and-white film, a light yellow Nikon Y (or K2) filter will usually give better rendition of detail on a sunny day. With color film the Nikon L (or UV) filter or a skylight filter is essential for there is generally more bluish haze evident, even on a clear day, than in shots from ground level. When haze is not excessive, exposures made when the ground is side-lighted are generally more interesting than front-lighted shots. Back-lit scenes, even on the same day, are usually more obscured by haze.

Exposures should be as short as possible to minimize the effects of plane vibration, and no part of the arm or upper body should rest on the plane itself. Brightness range, on the film itself, varies considerably with altitude. On a sunny day, this may shift from about 100:1 at very low altitudes to 8:1 at 10,000 feet and above. While exposures, as a general over-all rule, are the same for aerial shots as for the landscapes taken from the ground under the same conditions, contrast correction may be made in exposing and developing black-and-white film, but can be controlled only during the exposure of color film. Correctly-exposed color film taken from the air generally appears somewhat darker than a similar landscape taken from the ground, but will be found to contain full details in the shadow portions as well as the highlights when it is projected. Increasing exposures will tend to obliterate proper gradation in the highlights. Because of the compression of the brightness range with increased altitude, the actual latitude of film is considerably increased. However, exposures should be determined as accurately as possible and then slightly compensated for altitude: between 1000 and 2000 feet, open the diaphragm about 1/3 stop; up to 4000 feet, about 1/2 stop; and above that altitude, about 1 full stop.

4

Image Formation and Nikkor Lenses

LENSES AND THEIR RELATIVE MERITS are a popular subject of discussion. There is a considerable body of "folk-lore" on the subject, largely rooted in misconceptions about the process of image formation. Some professionals, as well as the more affluent amateurs, are veteran lens-shoppers, pursuing the "ideal" lens which will solve all problems of definition, perspective, depth of field and light-gathering speed in an automatic and fool-proof manner.

In this chapter, the essential facts about image formation are outlined, as well as the ways in which focal length and lens apertures influence performance. This outline may indicate why no one lens is—or ever will be—"ideal" for every picture-making situation. A well-designed and carefully made lens, like those included in the Nikkor line, is a tool, an instrument with definite characteristics which should be understood and fully exploited, but supplemented by other Nikkors of different characteristics more suitable for other occasions the photographer may be expected to encounter. The latter part of the chapter lists the full line of Nikkor lenses for use in 35mm photography with the important specifications of each.

Image Formation

A PHOTOGRAPH can be made without even employing a lens. A light-tight box with a film along one side opposite a pin-hole and with a piece of tape for shutter is a functioning camera. As Figure 4.1 indicates, when light strikes any point on an object and is scattered off by reflection, the pin-hole accepts a tiny pencil of rays from each point. These cross at the hole and form an image on a flat surface behind, an inverted image and one reversed from left to right. All image formation follows this essential pattern: light reflected (or emitted by) each tiny object-point is gathered by the system and formed into an image-point on a surface within the camera.

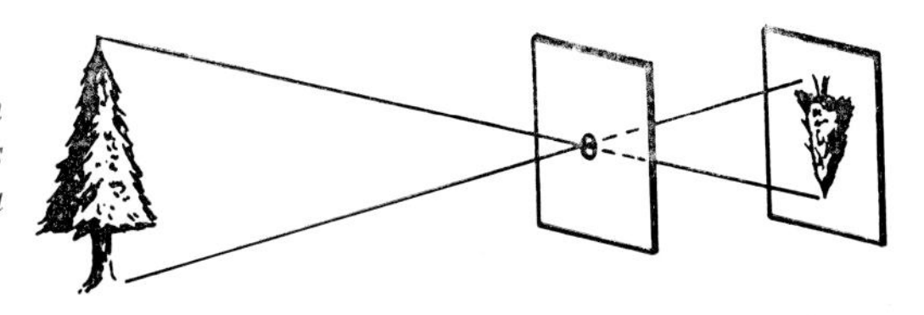

4.1 *Light rays from each point on an object pass through a pinhole to form a reversed, inverted image.*

A pin-hole is more effective for demonstration than for use. The image is a very dim one. It is brightened if we enlarge the hole, but this enlarges the image-points which overlap and rapidly destroy the "definition" of smaller pin-holes. It can be calculated that the best size of this hole for a sharp image is equivalent to f/217 for a 50mm "focal length" or f/490 for approximately the 105mm separation between pin-hole and image surface.

The image-forming characteristic of a pinhole was noticed in quite ancient times, and long before the invention of photography glass lenses were devised to admit greater relative amounts of light without losing sharp, clearly defined image points.

The simple lens

To understand how a lens functions, one characteristic of light must be defined. Light travels through a vacuum somewhat faster than 186,000 miles per second. When it enters a denser, transparent medium such as air, water or glass, it is slowed down. If it enters at an angle, rather than "head-on," it is also bent away from its original straight-line path. (See diagrams, Figure 4.3). Similarly, when light emerges from the opposite surface into another transparent medium, it is again bent away from a straight-line path. This effect is called *refraction*. Two factors influence the path of the light ray: the density of the transparent medium, such as optical glass, (called its *index of refraction*), and the angle at which the light ray reaches the surface between two materials.

These are the first variables with which the lens designer works. He chooses optical glass of a particular index of refraction from the constantly-growing list

4.2 GENE COOK *Nikon S2, 135mm f/3.5 Nikkor*
New York skyline *Tri-X, 1 sec., f/6.3*

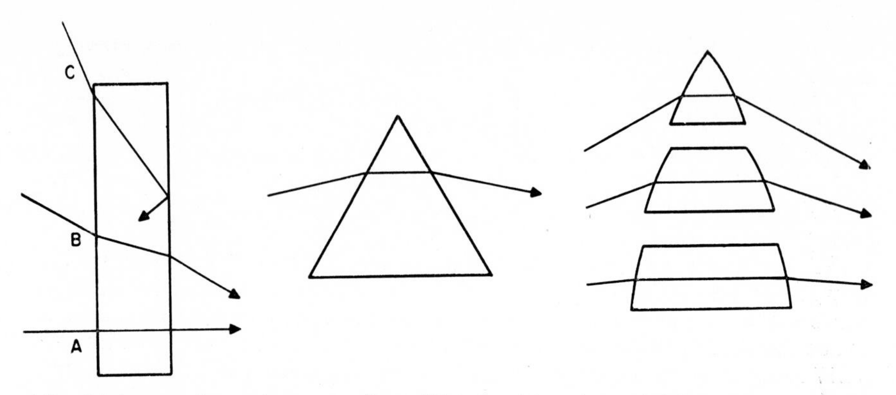

4.3 *Light entering a denser medium (like glass) is refracted, left; a prism, center, bends rays away from original path; lens is shaped to bring rays to a point-focus, right.*

of those available, and he specifies the surface curvatures of the two faces. The six basic shapes of simple lenses which either bend light rays together (positive or convergent lenses) or bend them apart (negative or divergent lenses) are shown in Figure 4.4.

Errors of simple lenses

Life would be quite easy for the lens designer if a simple lens bent the light from each object-point to an exact tiny image-point along a flat surface behind the lens. His glass, however, is subject to many annoying perversities. Lens surfaces (as they depart from the flat plane) are spherical, as if they were thin outside slices from balls of various diameters. Such a spherical surface brings the rays emerging from the outer edges of the lens to focus at a slightly different distance than the rays which pass through the center. (See Figure 4.5). This is called *spherical aberration.* It is accompanied by another phenomenon, familiar to anyone who has seen a prism. When white light is bent as it passes through glass, the beam is broken into a tiny rainbow. Red light is refracted least, blue-violet refracted to the greatest extent. This is diagrammed in the first part of Figure 4.5 as the *chromatic aberration* of a simple lens. This spreading of the light into a rain-

4.4 *Simple lens shapes either concentrate the rays of light reaching them (positive), or tend to spread them out from the lens axis (negative).*

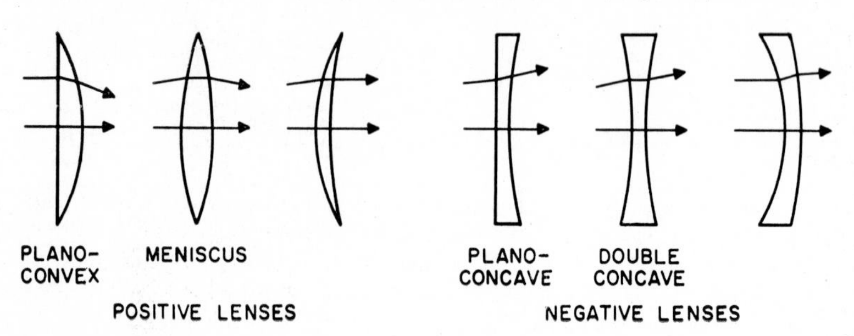

bow is also called *dispersion* and optical glasses differ, also, in their index of dispersion.

The lens designer conquers these aberrations by combining simple lenses (elements) cut from optical glasses of different indexes of refraction and dispersion so the errors cancel each other out. The simplest (two-element) lens form for adequate correction is illustrated in the third part of Figure 4.5. A principal virtue of the newer optical glasses is their stronger powers of refraction without a corresponding increase of dispersion, simplifying the designer's problems in finding combinations which will cancel out errors without introducing other limitations of speed and construction.

These aberrations may serve as a simplified example of the errors of simple lenses, although there are other aberrations which distort the formation of sharp, small image-points in true focus on a flat plane behind the lens. Despite their importance, we can ignore them here, although it will be necessary to introduce one of them later when we come to aperture setting and the greatest possible sharpness of images.

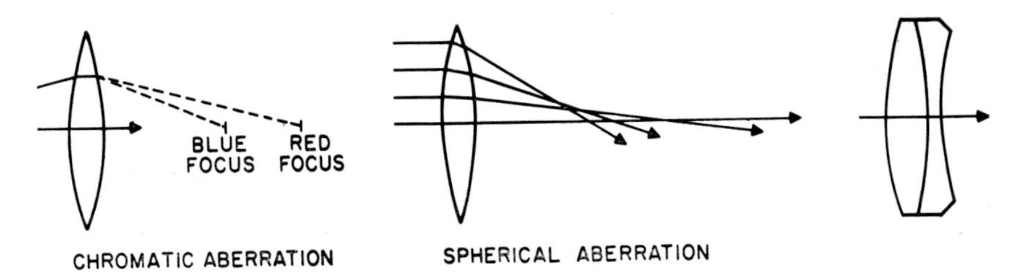

4.5 *Two of the many errors or aberrations of simple lenses. Glasses with different characteristics are combined by the lens designer to cancel errors (right).*

Depth of Field

PERHAPS THE EASIEST way to explain the relationship between focus, aperture and depth of fields is by means of the diagrams drawn to exaggerated scale, of Figures 4.6-7. The first of these shows a lens focused on the plane at the left. Points along this object-plane are brought into focus as tiny points (we can assume here) on the focal plane at the right. Other points either nearer or farther from the lens than the object-plane are not brought to such exact focus, but form somewhat larger circles on the focal plane. These are termed *circles of confusion.* Obviously, the farther from the object-plane any point before the lens lies, the larger will be its circle of confusion.

When these circles are very small they will be indistinguishable from the "points" of accurate focus. As the negative is enlarged, the circles of confusion will be correspondingly enlarged and the apparent depth of field will decrease. In 35mm work the permissible size of the circle of confusion on the negative is ordinarily considered as 1/30mm.

The next diagram of Figure 4.7 illustrates, to exaggerated scale, how the depth of field is increased without exceeding this permissible size of the circles of confusion when the object-plane on which the lens is focused is at a greater distance, and how the depth of field at any distance is increased when the aperture size is reduced (lower diagram, Figure 4.6).

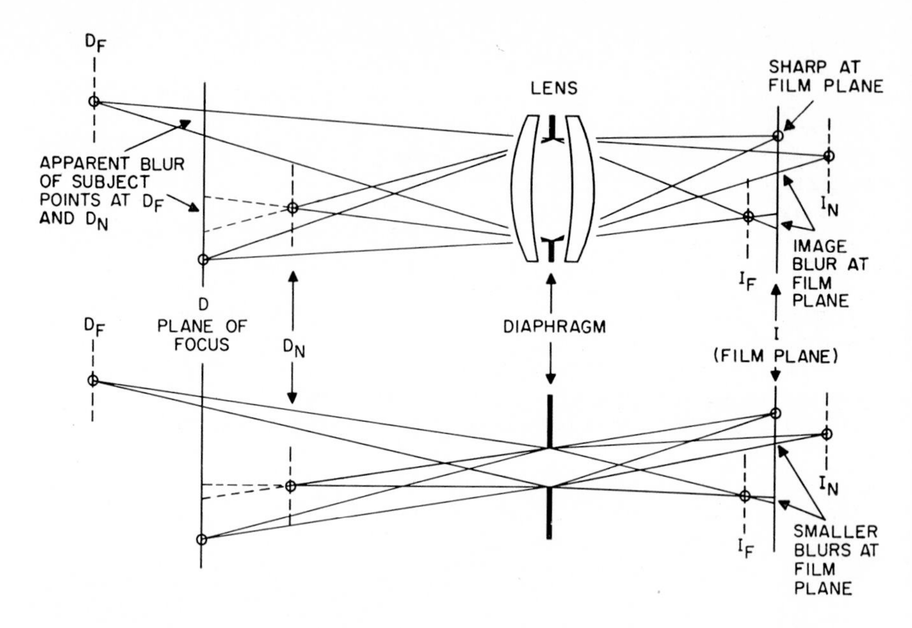

4.6 *Light rays from the plane of focus (D) form an approximate point image on the film (I), shown to exaggerated scale, top; while rays from other distances (Df, Dn) form larger spots. Below, stopping down the aperture reduces size (and brightness) of these out-of-focus spots.*

As depth of field tables indicate, the distance at which objects are in acceptably sharp focus is greater beyond the object-plane than nearer the camera. These tables are quite accurate but may apparently fail in practice. Since distant objects appear relatively smaller than near-by objects, we detect the out-of-focus blur of distant objects more readily in some photographs. This reduces the useful depth of field beyond the plane of sharp focus.

It should be noted that a highly corrected lens with great resolution has a depth of field which is quite sharply defined. In the informal language of working photography, it "pops" in and out of focus. Lenses of lesser acutance which have large residual errors of spherical aberration and other ills which optical glass is heir to, have much less sharply defined fields. Points in the object-plane are not imaged so nearly to true "points" on the focal plane; there is no internal standard of comparison. Lenses which are claimed to have greater depths of field (at comparable apertures and distances) than Nikkors of the same focal length must have greater residual aberrations left uncorrected.

Focal length and depth of field

Two "rules" for depth of field have been mentioned: the total depth increases at greater distances from the lens, and increases with smaller apertures. These are true for lenses of any focal length. However, the focal length influences depth of field in other ways.

At the same subject to lens distance, the depth of field with any given aperture will be shallower as focal lengths increase. The longer lenses require more

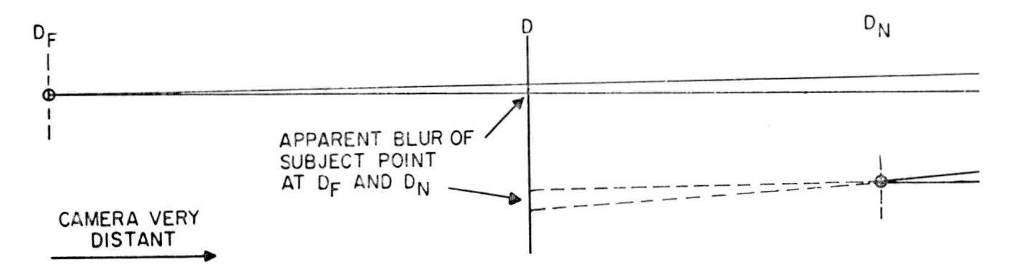

4.7 *Light rays from very distant objects form a narrow angle through the lens diaphragm, consequently, give much greater depth of field than when the lens is focused on near distances.*

accurate focusing, particularly for near-by subjects, than do shorter lenses. (This greater depth of field of shorter lenses, incidentally, is the reason for the usually greater depth of acceptably sharp focus of Nikon negatives compared with those made with larger cameras.)

However, if an object is imaged to exactly the same size *on the film* by lenses of various focal lengths, they will all have the *same* depth of field at the *same* aperture. The longer focal length lenses will be further away from the object than the lenses of shorter focus. The lens-to-object distance "rule" increases the depth of field of the longer lenses to match the depth of field of the shorter lenses working at closer distances. This is important to remember in close-up applications, particularly, where lenses may be set up for particular subject magnifications.

There is a fifth "rule" which may be added for completeness and occasional usefulness. As you look into the front of a Nikkor, you will see the iris diaphragm somewhat magnified by the front portion of the lens. The diameter of this opening as seen magnified is the *entrance pupil* of the lens and marks the outer limits of the bundle of light rays admitted to the lens at the particular f/number (relative aperture) for which the lens is set. (It is not the same actual diameter as the iris diaphragm, but somewhat larger depending on the construction of the particular Nikkor.) Any two Nikkors will have exactly the same depth of field at the same working distance when their entrance pupils are adjusted to the same diameter. This, too, is a "rule" with occasional useful application, particularly in critical close-up work when there may be an advantage in changing focal lengths.

The Hyperfocal Distance

When the Nikon with its Nikkor lens is set at the infinity mark, the depth of field of acceptably sharp focus will extend back toward the camera a considerable distance. In fact, the near limit, will approach the Nikon to a point approximately equal to 1000 times the actual diameter of the lens aperture used. The smaller the aperture, the closer will this near limit, or *hyperfocal distance,* fall.

If the Nikkor is then re-focused to this hyperfocal distance, the depth of field will extend from infinity back to a point *half* the hyperfocal distance from

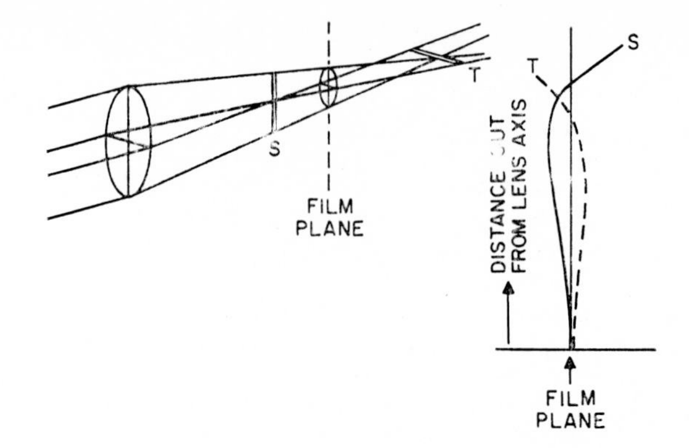

4.8 *Light rays entering lens from an angle tend to form tiny line-images in front of and behind film plane. This astigmatism (shown to very exaggerated scale) increases with distance from lens axis as charted, left.*

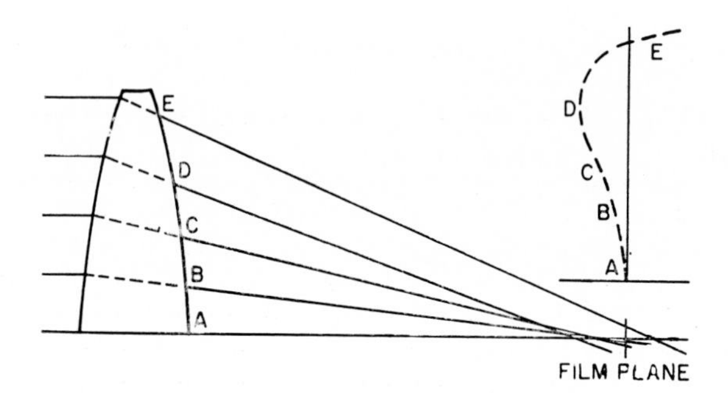

4.9 *Spherical aberration also increases with distance out from lens axis as shown to very exaggerated scale in both diagram and chart.*

the Nikon. This setting obviously will give the greatest possible depth of field for any focal length and aperture.

It is not necessary to establish this hyperfocal distance by calculation. The depth of field scale on the barrel of every Nikkor, when the lens is set at the infinity mark, places the proper hyperfocal distance opposite each f/stop marking on that scale. When the Nikkor is refocused to this hyperfocal distance the infinity mark will fall next to the chosen f/stop on the opposite side of the scale. In practice, immediately setting the infinity mark opposite the chosen f/stop on this depth of field scale will automatically focus the Nikkor for extreme depth.

The use of this scale for zone focusing has already been mentioned in Chapter 3. The distance limits between the same f/stop marks on either side indicate the field in acceptable focus at that f/stop, and the camera may be pre-set for rapid use.

Aperture and Critical Sharpness

IN THE PRECEDING discussion, the depth of field was considered in terms of "acceptable sharpness" and the means of extending this depth were examined.

It is a common misconception to conclude from this that a lens "becomes sharper" at ever smaller apertures. This is quite incorrect, but the explanation requires some technical detail. In brief, the correction of the last vestiges of residual aberrations is always a trifle less complete near the outer edges of even lenses as beautifully designed as the Nikkors which are probably as highly corrected as any lenses available for 35mm work. Stopping down two or three stops blocks off the edges of the lens so image formation is accomplished only by the central areas. Stopping down further, however, increases light-scatter around the aperture and counteracts any further gain in sharpness.

However, except in the most critical applications, any Nikkor may be used at any aperture with no differences in the acutance of its image which will be noticeable at any ordinary degree of enlargement. Setting any Nikkor for its full extreme degree of exceptional sharpness has no point unless all of the subsequent steps in the photographic process are so precisely controlled that this sharpness may be preserved. This requires a "laboratory" rather than a "darkroom."

Astigmatism

To explain why the point of maximum critical sharpness of a Nikkor and other well-corrected lenses lies at an aperture smaller than maximum, we must examine another of the many aberrations which affect simple and compound lenses. We assumed above that a point on an object was imaged as a point on the focal plane. This is, of course, an over-simplification; it is rather a formless blob of light under high magnification. Two principal factors which distort it, particularly in the regions at a distance from the central axis, are the spherical aberration previously encountered and *astigmatism.* This latter results in a rather peculiar distortion as encountered in the simple lens, which is diagrammed to exaggerated scale in Figure 4.8. A point-image (if no other factors disturbed it) formed by rays at a distance from the lens axis will actually come to sharp focus a little ahead of the film plane as a distinct short *line* pointed toward the lens axis. At the focal plane, the ray is a tiny unfocused blur and, if it were allowed to continue, would again come to focus as a short, distinct line now at right angles to the first. The diagram presents this odd behavior in perspective.

With Figures 4.8-9 are two scales. The first shows how the small remaining astigmatism is usually charted for a well-corrected lens. The changing positions of the first (radial or sagittal) and the second (tangental) lines are indicated by their distance out from the lens axis and by their shift in percentage of focal length. The lower scale shows how traces of residual spherical aberration are similarly charted. These are typical for a lens of pre-World War II quality for purposes of exaggeration.) These scales make it obvious that closing down the aperture admits light through a relatively better-corrected portion of the lens.

However, we soon encounter a characteristic of the wave-nature of light: as a beam of light passes an opaque edge, it is slightly bent in the direction of that edge. Passing through the circular aperture, a beam is expanded. The effect of this diffraction is slight but enough to increase the size of each image spot.

Stopping down increases diffraction and decreases aberrations. The point of best maximum critical sharpness varies somewhat with focal length but may be assumed to be about three stops down from maximum aperture for Nikkors of 50mm or shorter focal lengths and one or two stops more for those of longer focal length.

(Text continued on page 96.)

25mm f/4 (W.C) NIKKOR

introduced 1954 4 elements
click stops to f/22
focus to 3 feet
couples to Nikon range-finder
diagonal angle of view: 80.5°
(50°x70°)

Nikon bayonet 4 ¼ ounces
lens accessory size (Series VII)
screw mount (Leica thread)
3 3/16 ounces
lens accessory size (Series VI)
34.5mm snap-on; screw-in

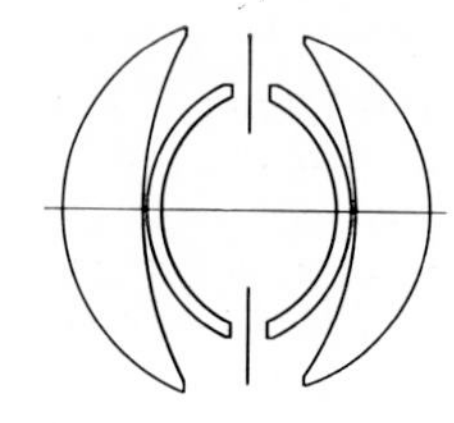

An unusually wide angle of view, with excellent flatness of field due to the symetrical design, and with vignetting reduced to a minimum. Rare earth glass enables the aberrations to be controlled for this extreme angle yet obtain a reasonable aperture.

Lens Descriptions

ALL OF THE CURRENTLY-PRODUCED NIKKOR LENSES are illustrated and described on the following pages. Specifications include the year of introduction, diagonal angle of view (followed by the vertical and horizontal angles), the proper sizes of lens attachments and availability in threaded mounts for Leica, Canon, Nicca and other cameras requiring this construction.

The weight given is for the currently-produced models. The first Nikkors were brass-mounted; later models partly brass and partly aluminum. Current Nikkors have barrels which are largely aluminum except for the bearing surfaces which are still brass to maintain the careful factory accuracy of the construction. An all-aluminum mount would have slight weight advantages but at the cost of perfect performance over the years.

The mounts of all Nikkors are carefully and individually adjusted so the variation between two new lenses of the same design from a dealer's shelf never exceeds a maximum of 0.5 percent. This is negligible in practice and Nikkors do not have to be "fitted" to Nikon bodies as is the common practice with many cameras of "professional quality." However, a Nikkor purchased second-hand may require checking and correction if it has been previously used on cameras other than the Nikon. The Nikkor mount may have been altered to compensate

28mm f/3.5 (W.C) NIKKOR

introduced 1953 — 6 elements
click stops to f/22
focus to 3 feet
couples to Nikon range-finder
diagonal angle of view: 74°
(45°x64°)

Nikon bayonet — 3 ½ ounces
lens accessory size — (Series VII)
43mm snap-on; screw-in
screw mount (Leica thread) — 3 ⅞ ounces
lens accessory size — (Series VI)
34.5mm snap-on; screw-in

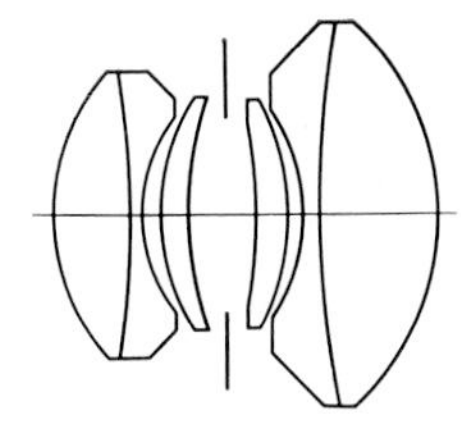

Professionals who take the 35mm Nikkor as "standard" use the 28mm for their wide-angle. This design utilizes older optical glasses, but is a new formula, especially computed for high acutance across the field and control of vignetting, including use of a very large rear element.

---

for depth variations permitted by many other manufacturers in their camera bodies.

Although lenses are produced in relatively large volume, they cannot be "mass-production" items if quality is to be maintained. Lens performance deteriorates drastically, for example, if there is imprecision in the centering of the two tiny glass bits which may be cemented together to form an element. The extreme care and repeated inspections which the Nikkors receive at Nippon Kogaku K.K. account for the unusual uniformity between Nikkors of the same design. It accounts in part, too, for the performance of those Nikkors which are by no means radically different in design from established types, yet seem to have a greater correction all across the field. (Treatment of the glass itself during the melt, contributes considerably to this final effect, of course.)

All current Nikkors are internally surface coated with magnesium fluoride, the thickness controlled to produce a coating 0.1μ (micron), or 0.0001mm, in thickness. This treatment is indicated by the C on the front rim of each Nikkor. All glass-air surfaces in the Nikkors are hard-coated (not merely the front and rear surfaces). If it is ever necessary for a qualified lens repair man to dismantle a Nikkor for any reason, it will not be necessary to re-coat all of the interior surfaces.

The other letter on the rim indicates the number of elements in that Nikkor: Q = 4, P = 5, H = 6, S = 7 and N = 9. (Wide-angle Nikkors are all marked W. The number of elements in each is given in the specifications here.)

35mm f/1.8 (W.C) NIKKOR

introduced 1956 — 7 elements
click stops to f/22
focus to 3 feet
couples to Nikon range-finder
diagonal angle of view: 63°
(37°x53°)

Nikon bayonet — 5 ½ ounces
lens accessory sizes (Series VII)
48mm snap-on; 43mm screw-in
screw mount (Leica thread)
6 ⅜ ounces
lens accessory size (Series VII)
43mm snap-on; screw-in

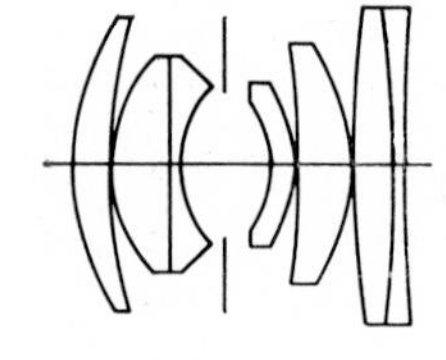

An extremely rapid wide-angle lens, collecting 2X the light of the f/2.5. Rare earth (lanthanum) glass enabled designers to achieve a flat field and excellent corrections at previously impossible speeds. A Gauss type, but utilizes seven elements in five groups, with unusually large front and rear elements (the front diameter would cover f/1.4) in order to decrease vignetting so illumination at the corners of the image is considerably improved over that of other wide-angle formulas.

The A B C's of Perspective

THE OFTEN-MADE COMPARISON between the camera and the human eye is really a misleading one. True, they both serve as light-collecting systems bringing an image into focus, but as soon as we begin to compare them in detail their differences become more important than their similarities.

The (single) human eye takes in a field of moderate sharpness of about 45°, closely identical with the 46° angle of acceptance of the 50mm "normal" focal length Nikkor lens. (A much more vague perception extends the field of the eye to as much as 150° horizontally and 120° vertically.) But in vision only a narrow angle of about 6° within this wider field is actually sharply in focus, and the depth of sharp field is a comparatively shallow one. In life, our eyes are in almost continuous motion, scanning the scene before us, shifting focus rapidly to accommodate for the actual distance of the objects we perceive. We build up our impressions from a very rapid, unconscious *summation* of "exposures" each about 1/10 second in duration.

The old-fashioned approach to photography—a style which may still be seen in some conventional studio portraiture—led to prints which "duplicated" a single glimpse of the human eye. A portrait, for example, would be sharply focused on the nearer eye-socket of the subject and the ear and back of the head (and sometimes even the tip of the nose) would slide foggily out of focus.

35mm f/2.5 (W.C) NIKKOR

introduced 1952 — 6 elements
click-stops to f/22
focus to 3 feet
couples to Nikon range-finder
diagonal angle of view: 63° (37°x53°)

Nikon bayonet — 3 ⅞ ounces
lens accessory size (Series VII)
43mm snap-on; screw-in
screw mount (Leica thread) — 4 7/16 ounces
lens accessory size (Series VI)
34.5mm snap-on; screw-in

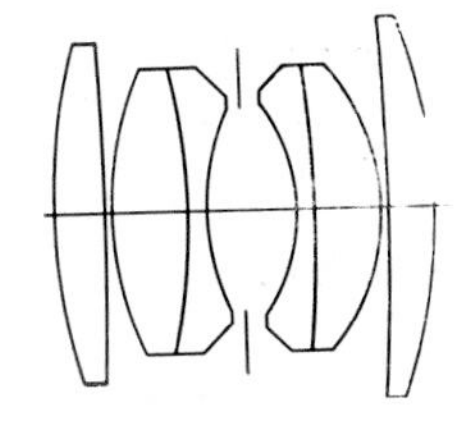

A rapid wide-angle lens for professional use. It is a new lens design, rather than a re-working of older approaches to wide-angle, and is beyond former limits of speed at acceptable minimums of residual aberration.

35mm f/3.5 (W.C) NIKKOR

introduced 1948 — 4 elements
click stops to f/22
focus to 3 feet
couples to Nikon range-finder
diagonal angle of view: 63° (37°x53°)

Nikon bayonet — 3 ½ ounces
lens accessory size (Series VII)
43mm snap-on; screw-in
screw mount (Leica thread) — 4 ¼ ounces
lens accessory size (Series VI)
34.5mm snap-on; screw-in

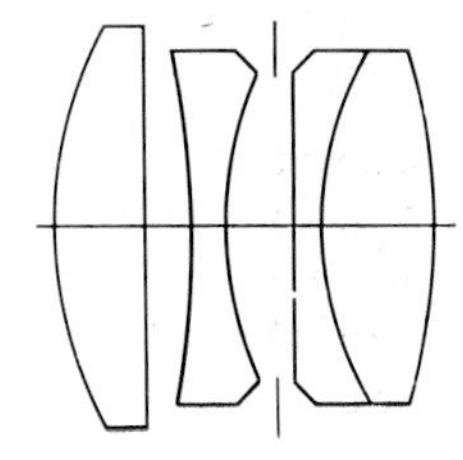

A standard wide-angle lens with sufficient speed for all general photography. This is a proven design, recomputed for maximum corrections, with a maximum aperture probably near the upper limit for this wide-angle formula.

50mm f/1.1 (N.C) NIKKOR

introduced 1956 — 9 elements
click-stops to f/22
focus to 3 feet
couples to Nikon range-finder
diagonal angle of view: 46°
(26°x39°)

Nikon bayonet — 12 3/16 ounces
lens accessory size — (Series IX)
62mm snap-on; screw-in
screw mount (Leica thread) — 15 ounces
(same accessory size)

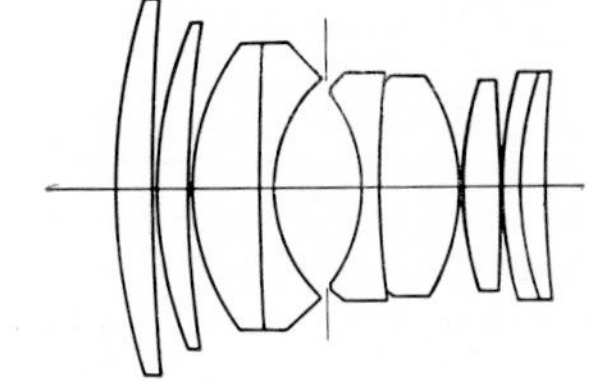

Greater light-gathering power than any other lens with comparable acutance and freedom from aberrations. Introduced 1956, after surface coating and glass technology made radical redesign with split elements and air-spacing possible.

50mm f/1.5 NIKKOR

Introduced 1950
Discontinued 1950

50mm f/1.4 (S.C) NIKKOR

introduced 1950 — 7 elements
click-stops to f/16
focus to 3 feet
couples to Nikon range-finder
diagonal angle of view: 46°
(26°x39°)

Nikon bayonet — 5 ⅜ ounces
lens accessory size — (Series VII)
43mm snap-on; screw-in
screw mount (Leica thread) — 8 ⅛ ounces
(same accessory size)

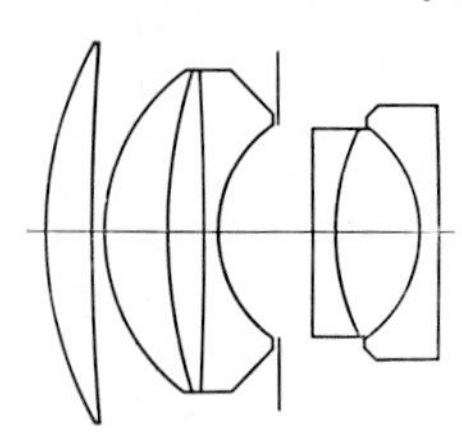

First lens faster than f/1.5 for 35mm cameras, with appreciable gains over previous design. Glass is processed for higher refractive index, enabling recomputation for better corrections as well as greater speed.

50mm f/2 (H.C) NIKKOR

introduced 1948 — 6 elements
(originally with collapsible mount)
click-stops to f/16
focus to 3 feet
couples to Nikon range-finder
diagonal angle of view: 46°
(26°x39°)

Nikon bayonet — 4¾ ounces
lens accessory size (Series VI)
40.5mm snap-on; screw-in
screw mount (Leica thread) — 7 9/16 ounces
(same accessory size)

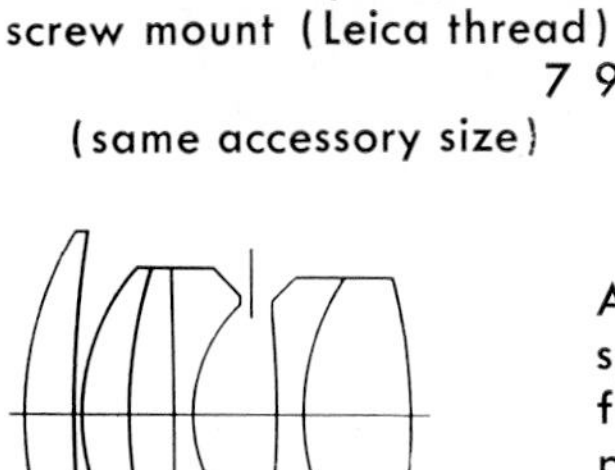

A standard focal-length for 35mm, with sufficient speed for all general work. Excellent acutance at full aperture. This f/2 is a recomputation of a proven design, for greater correction of aberrations and a minimum of vignetting (fall-off of illumination at the corners of image).

The argument that this represented a truthful statement of what our eyes perceive neglected our rapid and unconscious summation of impressions as we look at a face or any other subject. It was, in fact, a rationalization of the inadequacies of old, slow lenses which had to be used at wide apertures, particularly in portraiture, to get a sufficient exposure in a reasonable length of time on the slow plates and films of the era.

Today's approach to pictures is considerably different and the largest single factors in the change are the deep, crisp depth of field possible with 35mm cameras and their range of interchangeable lenses and the fast films which have been developed for 35mm photography. As has been true throughout the history of photography, the availability of better and more versatile equipment and sensitive materials has led to changes in the style of the photographs which are made and published. The introduction of the Nikkor line of lenses, for example, which are widely acknowledged among professional photographers as the standard of sharpness and reliability, has given photography another nudge toward crisp definition, from corner to corner and front to back of the imaged scene.

There are occasions, as we shall see immediately below, when this universal definition is not pictorially desirable, but a photograph which shows the whole scene in relatively perfect focus does not violate the facts of human vision. For we use our eyes in a normal manner when we examine any print, focusing on each area and scanning the photograph just as we scan an actual scene. In a sharp print there are no areas which the eye cannot bring into focus, just as there are no areas in the original scene which the normal human eye may not bring into focus and study at leisure.

50 mm f/3.5 (P.C.) MICRO-NIKKOR

introduced 1956 5 elements
collapsible mount
click stops to f/22
focus to 3 feet (mount extended)
to 1.5 feet (mount collapsed)
auxilliary aperture control device
(for collapsed position) available
couples to Nikon range-finder
diagonal angle of view: 46°
(26°x39°)

Nikon bayonet
lens accessory size (Series VI)
34.5mm snap-on; screw-in
screw mount (Leica thread)
(same accessory size)

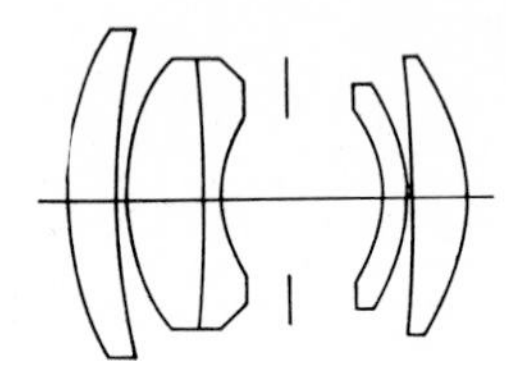

Greater fine-line resolution than any other lens available for the camera. It is a development of the Petzval symmetrical formula, especially computed for extremely high acutance at comparatively short object-to-lens distances, reaching maximum at image reductions of 1:12. It is especially suited for microfilming, but the corrections at greater distances make it useful for many other applications. At very close distances, the lens mount is collapsed and a device is inserted to make aperture settings convenient. The Micro-Nikkor may also be used with the Nikon Repro Copy Outfits, Models S and P, at reductions down to 1:1.

The human eye has sharp vision only over an angle of about 6° within a much wider, but out-of-focus field of perception. The 500mm Nikkor telephoto lens has an angle of acceptance of 5° while the so-called "normal" lens, supplied with the Nikon, is the 50mm which takes in an angle of 46°. Why, then, is the 50mm, rather than the 500mm, accepted as the normal? And why, if it is "normal," is there any necessity for using other focal lengths for satisfactory pictures? To answer these two questions, we must review some optical facts.

Perspective, in the sense in which we use it here, means the relationship between the size of objects as they recede with distance. Paradoxically at is may seem at first acquaintance with the rule, from any one camera position two objects in the picture at given distances will be imaged to the *same proportion* by lenses of *any focal length.*

Their *absolute sizes* on the film will of course be different with each focal length. The longer the focal length, the larger will be the two objects on the film. Their *proportional sizes,* however, will remain the same. The more distant object will be the same *fractional size* of the closer object, even though the actual sizes on the film are different.

The *angle of view,* however, differs with each focal length in any series of lenses, such as the Nikkors. The lens specifications included in this chapter lists them for all of the Nikkors, from the 80°30′ acceptance angle of the 25mm

(Enlarging Lens)

EL-NIKKOR

50mm f/2.8

6 elements
marked click-stops: 2.8, 4, 5.6, 8, 11, 16
diagonal angle of view: 46°
(26°x39°)

surfaces amber-coated
furnished with Leica thread
adapter ring available for enlargers requiring long lens barrel
plastic case supplied

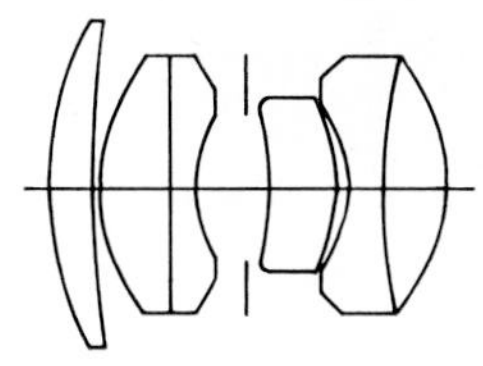

Six elements arranged in four groups for speed, with special corrections of lens aberrations at the near-image distances of projection printing. This correction extends into the near ultraviolet, to which black-and-white printing papers are sensitive, to eliminate all difference between visual and actinic focus. Amber surface coating of magnesium fluoride 0.08μ (0.00008mm) in thickness and specially-selected optical glass to pass the shorter wave lengths freely. The front and rear elements are especially large for maximum illumination to corners. At full opening, resolution is higher than that of any taking lens, and there is no shift of focus as El-Nikkor is stopped down. Aperture settings in white figures at nearly equal intervals.

---

f/4 Nikkor, the 63° acceptance angle of the 35mm Nikkors, through all of the others up to the 10° angle of the 250mm f/4 and the previously mentioned 5° acceptance angle of the longest Nikkor, the 500mm f/5. Consequently, all of the objects included in the spreading field of the short, wide-angled lenses will be imaged in a smaller size than the same objects from the same viewpoint which are included in the field of the longer focus lenses.

Print viewing distance and the size of enlargement are the keys to reconciling the optical rules above with the actual impression of altered perspective in prints made from negatives taken with different focal length lenses.

If we were to make contact (same size) prints of 35mm negatives and view each picture from a distance equal to the focal length of the lens with which its negative was made, we would have the illusion of normal (human vision) perspective with any one of them. No matter what the focal length of the taking lens, if the contact print were viewed (by one eye) at the correct distance, we would observe no difference in perspective between prints of the same subject made with lenses of various focal lengths, or between these prints and the view over the camera at the moment of exposure. Viewing prints in this way is obviously impractical—and in most cases would be acutely uncomfortable. We normally examine only enlargements of 35mm negatives.

Even in enlarging, however, we can maintain identical perspective if we follow this rule exactly: print viewing distance should equal focal length multiplied by the degree of enlargement. In practice, this means that when a (full frame) negative is enlarged to fill the horizontal dimension of an 8x10-inch sheet of printing paper, for example, the viewing distance should be this degree

85mm f/1.5 (S.C) NIKKOR

introduced 1953 — 7 elements
click-stops to f/32
focus to 3.5 feet
couples to Nikon range-finder
magnification 1.7X
diagonal angle of view: 28.5°
(16°x24°)

Nikon bayonet — 19 ¼ ounces
lens accessory size (Series VIII)
60mm screw-in
lens hood supplied
screw mount (Leica thread)
18 11/16 ounces
lens accessory size
58mm screw-in

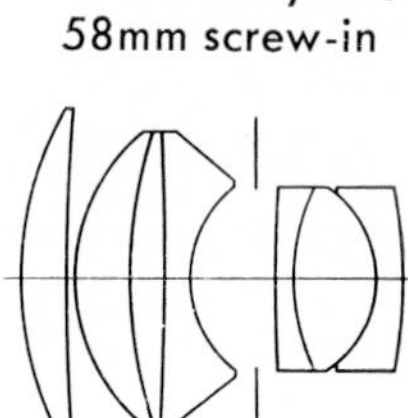

The patient recomputations and the advances in glass technology which made possible the 50mm f/1.4 were used for this rapid long-focus version of that formula, not quite as fast, but with all of its excellent corrections and acutance.

85mm f/2 (P.C) NIKKOR

introduced 1949 — 5 elements
click-stops to f/32
focus to 3.5 feet
couples to Nikon range-finder
magnification 1.7X
diagonal angle of view: 28.5°
(16°x24°)

Nikon bayonet — 11 ⅝ ounces
lens accessory size (Series VII)
48mm snap-on; screw-in
lens hood supplied
screw mount (Leica thread)
12 ⅞ ounces
(same accessory size)

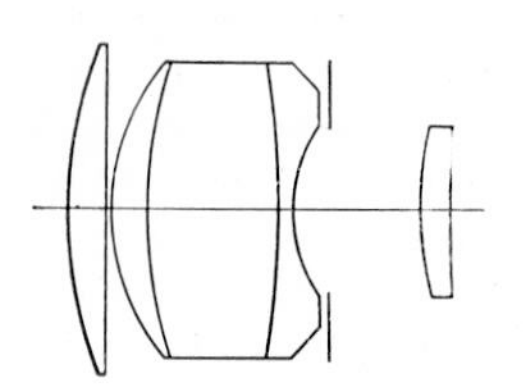

A fast, medium telephoto, designed on the same principles as the 105mm Nikkor. The speed is a measure of the success with which this formula has been made to produce full useful correction so far out from the axis with older types of optical glass skillfully computed and treated by modern technology.

105mm f/2.5 (P.C) NIKKOR

introduced 1954 5 elements
click-stops to f/32
focus to 4 feet
couples to Nikon range-finder
magnification 2.1X
diagonal angle of view: 23.5°
(13°x19.5°)

Nikon bayonet 18 11/16 ounces
lens accessory size (Series VII)
52mm snap-on, screw-in
lens hood supplied
screw mount (Leica thread)
18 7/8 ounces
(same accessory size)

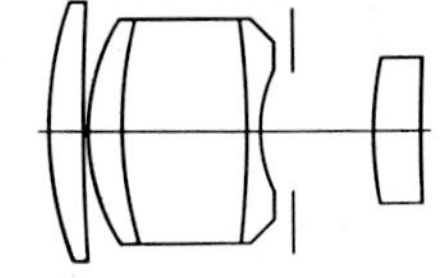

A general purpose, medium telephoto, similar in formula to the 85mm f/2. The perspective of the 105mm is useful, particularly when accompanied by the especially good acutance and light-gathering power developed in this design.

---

of enlargement (about 6.5X, allowing for margins on the paper) times the focal length of the taking lens. If this is a 50mm lens, we arrive at a proper viewing distance of approximately 325mm. This distance is very close to 12 inches. If the negative were cropped slightly, with a consequent slight increase in the factor of enlargement, the correct viewing distance would become almost 14 inches, which is accepted as a comfortable viewing distance for a print held in the hand.

The 50mm Nikkor, then, is "normal" in the sense that *it produces natural perspective in the ordinary print held at ordinary viewing* distance. (We almost automatically hold an 11x14-inch print further away from our eyes in order to take in the whole print at a glance and thus restore in part the proper viewing distance.)

But what of other focal lengths? If we enlarge the full frame to the same 8x10-inch size, our viewing distance will have to change in order to restore the "normal" perspective. In the case of the 500mm Nikkor, we would have to view an 8x10-inch print from approximately 10 feet away! In the case of the print made from a negative taken with the 25mm Nikkor, we should view it at 5 inches!

On any particular occasion, our viewing distance remains constant for photographs we see as prints or as reproductions in books and magazines, whatever the focal length of the taking lens. Consequently, the impression of perspective "distortion" occurs *as we view the print,* rather than when the image is formed by lenses of various focal lengths. In almost all cases, prints made with wide-angle lenses are viewed from "too great" a distance and prints made with long-focus or telephoto lenses are viewed from "too short" a distance, and perspective is exaggerated *at this point* in the photographic process. A similar exaggeration will be obtained by unusual enlargements from a negative (or from

135mm f/4 **NIKKOR**

Introduced 1948
Discontinued 1951

135mm f/3.5 (Q.C) **NIKKOR**

introduced 1951 4 elements
click-stops to f/32
focus to 5 feet
couples to Nikon range-finder
magnification 2.7X
diagonal angle of view: 18°
(10°x15°)

Nikon bayonet 13 ¾ ounces
lens accessory size (Series VII)
43mm snap-on; screw-in
lens hood supplied
screw mount (Leica thread)
16 ¾ ounces
(same accessory size)

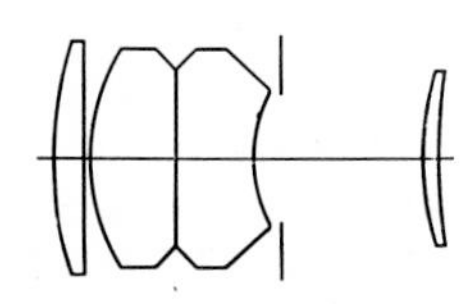

An advanced development of the triplet (see also the 250mm), this incorporates an additional negative rear element which makes it a true telephoto. This focal length is about the upper limit for linkage with camera range-finder mechanisms, because of the inevitable weight and the strong leverage they exert on the range-finder gear train and linkage system.

135mm **NIKKOR**

short mount focus ∞ to 1:1
for use with Bellows Focusing Attachment
(in preparation)

---

a section of one) made with a 50mm, normal lens. An unusually great enlargement, viewed at too close a distance, or a smaller one viewed from far away, would introduce the same factors of distortion.

Up to this point, we have considered only the image formed by normal, wide-angle and long-focus lenses used with a constant distance between camera and subject. When the camera itself is moved so the image of the principal subject is kept constant as the focal length of the taking lens is changed, a somewhat different "distortion" of perspective and space occurs, one which professionals who use 35mm extensively have learned in recent years to exploit for more effective pictures. In brief, when a wide-angle lens is employed and the camera is moved in close to the principal subject, space "expands" and there seems to be a greater separation between objects at different distances from the camera. Conversely, when a long-focus lens is moved back so the image of the principal subject is the same size on the film it would have been with a normal focus lens, space "contracts" and distance objects seem closer and larger.

180mm f/2.5 (H.C) NIKKOR

introduced 1955 — 6 elements
stops to f/32 — pre-set diaphragm
focus to 7 feet
requires Prism Reflex Housing
magnification 3.6X
diagonal angle of view: 13.5° (7.5°x11.5°)

Nikon bayonet — 59 15/16 ounces
lens accessory size (Series IX)
82mm screw-in
lens hood supplied
screw mount for Leica Reflex Housing — 59 15/16 ounces
(same accessory size)

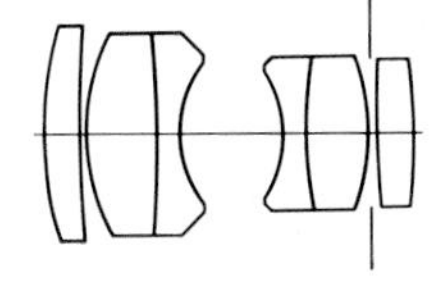

A high-speed telephoto of unusual aperture. The correction of residual aberrations this far out from the axis in a lens of this focal length is an achievement in optical design.

It must be emphasized that these shifts in drawing (image perspective) are not, of themselves, either good or bad, except as they are used intelligently to make more effective photographs. And, as we will note in the following pages and elsewhere in this book, there are other, equally practical, reasons for employing a range of focal lengths to improve one's photography.

Lens speed

The size of the largest aperture setting in relation to the focal length is an indication of the possible brightness of the image formed by the lens under given lighting conditions. Lens designers have recently broken through old limitations to produce designs of remarkable speed. The difficulty has been to gain this speed without significant losses in correction of the aberrations previously mentioned, which grow progressively more difficult to handle at greater distances from the lens axis. The combination of speed and full-aperture acuity of the f/1.1 50mm Nikkor is a revolutionary achievement as yet unmatched.

Fast lenses are invaluable—in their proper sphere. They have extended the possibilities of photography under difficult conditions and photojournalists, in particular, find the f/1.1 Nikkor enables them to work under conditions previously impossible. For others, particularly amateurs, this speed may be a rarely needed luxury, much less valuable to him than an f/2 50mm Nikkor, *plus* a Nikkor of a different focal length. Particularly for non-professional use, it seems more sensible to stretch a budget to its limits to own a minimum of three Nikkors of different focal-lengths than to exhaust it on Nikkors of two focal-lengths and the highest speeds. The professional, of course, should regard lenses which give him the greatest flexibility under all circumstances a necessary investment.

250mm f/4 (Q.C) NIKKOR

introduced 1955 — 4 elements
stops to f/32
focus to 10 feet
requires Prism Reflex Housing
magnification 5X
diagonal angle of view: 10° (6°x8°)

Nikon bayonet — 36 11/16 ounces
lens accessory size (Series IX)
68mm screw-in
lenh hood supplied
screw mount for Leica Reflex Housing
36 11/16 ounces
(same accessory size)

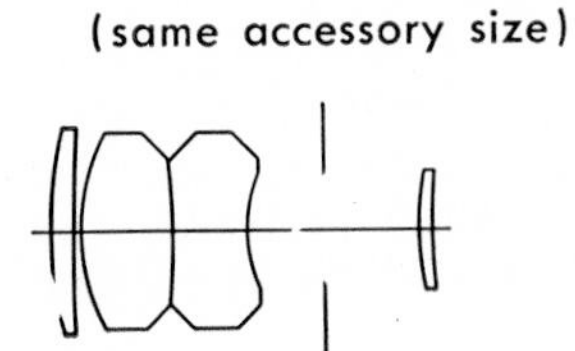

A telephoto lens, standard for the Prism Reflex Housing and the length most often used. The design follows the principles of the 135mm f/3.5 retaining its high acutance with excellent speed for a lens of this focal length.

Lens Design

PLOTTING THE CONSTRUCTION of a new lens is a strategy of devising combinations of positive and negative simple lenses to make up the several components of the design. Each optical glass (and there are hundreds of formulas) has its own individual index of dispersion and refraction, further influenced by the thickness of the element and by the radius of its surface curves. The aberrations of each single element must be computed and employed to cancel out the aberrations of the other elements so corrections "come out even" within the limits of any useful application of the lens, even when an individual Nikkor is selected for the most rigorously critical recording. The complex process of lens computation involves the simultaneous solution of all the inherent distortions to which a ray of light is subject on its way through the elements. In addition, these problems must be solved within rigid limits of practical manufacturing techniques and solved to produce lenses of required speed (large apertures and minimum light loss in transmission through the lens), great sharpness, an angle of acceptance and a focal length needed to serve a function within the Nikkor series, a reasonable total weight of glass, and with a (back focus) distance between the last element and the focal plane within the narrow tolerance which allows complete interchangeability on the Nikon body.

The lead in optical design which is being maintained by Nippon Kogaku K.K. is a product of intensive research into the problems of the formulation and exact manufacturing processes of new kinds of glass with indexes of dispersion and refraction more useful for cancelling aberrations. The most important advances have been made with the so-called "rare earth" glasses which permit greater corrective control than with older materials. A second factor has been the perfection of surface coating techniques, the addition of thin films of transparent substances such as magnesium fluoride with regulated thicknesses to

500mm f/5 (T.C) NIKKOR

introduced 1955 3 elements
stops to f/45 pre-set diaphragm
focus to 25 feet
requires Prism Reflex Housing
magnification 10X
diagonal angle of view: 5°
(2.5°x4°)

Nikon bayonet 298 ⅜ ounces
110mm filter
lens hood supplied
screw mount for Leica Reflex Housing
298 ⅜ ounces
(same filter size)

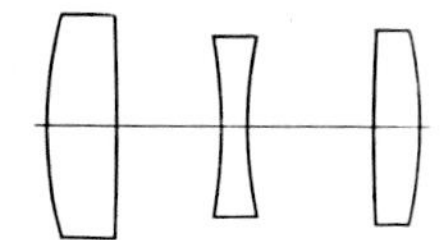

A long focus lens, longest available Nikkor for 35mm photography. Corrections are excellent with this comparatively simple formula since image-forming rays lie close to the central axis.

---

fractional light wave-length tolerances and with definite refractive indexes. It had been observed for many years that some lenses which tarnished actually gained in their transmission of light as this natural coating reduced internal reflection. A distinct gain in image contrast, with less light scattered into the shadow areas of the image by multiple internal reflections, was also observed. It was not until the 1930's, however, that the theoretical and practical body of knowledge reached the point where surface coating could be efficiently employed.

Surface coating immediately gave the lens designer a new degree of freedom. Previously, the number of air spaces between elements (which, of course, serve as additional useful elements) was limited because of the transmission loss and contrast-destroying internal reflections set up at glass-air surfaces. Components were constructed of cemented elements, glass surface to glass, as far as possible. Now, the lens designer may work more freely with the air-space, treated as an element in the total construction. Or he may split an element into two separate glasses for more effective speed or sharpness.

Using these new glasses and the greater freedom to employ air-spacing, some of the most spectacular gains have been made by the brilliant recomputation of certain older designs. There is one arrangement of seven elements into three members, for example, which is described as "best avoided entirely" for satisfactory image formation at apertures greater than f/4.5, in an authoritative book not quite ten years old. Yet the properties of the new optical glasses poured by Nippon Kogaku K.K. gave its lens designers the materials to recompute this seven-element triplet arrangement to produce not only the f/1.5 85mm Nikkor, but also to modify it into the f/1.4 50mm Nikkor, a lens which has been described as unequalled in critical sharpness and useful light-gathering power, a lens with a performance which converted many professionals to the use of Nikkors and, in turn, to the Nikon.

Some of the other Nikkors are equally outstanding recomputations of older designs, although the fact is not obvious to the user who is only aware that each

Nikon Prism Reflex Housing

The Nikon Prism Reflex Housing is designed for use with the Nikon and the 180mm, 250mm and 500mm Nikkor lenses. The Reflex Housing is also required with the Nikon Bellows Focusing Attachment. It may be added between the top stage of the Nikon Repro Copy Outfit, Model S, and the Nikon body to add 74mm of extension for a larger direct image on the film with the Repro Copy Outfit, and a direct view of the image during focusing. The front and back bayonet mounts are used in the standard way: red index dots are matched and the added attachment turned counter-clockwise to lock in place or in the reverse direction to separate.

After the Housing is attached, adjust the eye-piece of the 4.3X magnifier above the image-erecting prism until the small circle on the groundglass is sharp. This prism magnifier may be removed from the housing, if desired, by a short counter-clockwise rotation of the magnifier in its bayonet mount.

Two types of cable releases are provided: one for releasing the Housing mirror immediately before film exposure, the other to transfer the action to

---

produces an image free of aberrations at previously impossible maximum apertures. Other Nikkor designs have been so altered from previous solutions of the optical problems by the splitting and re-combination of elements and the use of air-spacing that family resemblances have disappeared and new design has grown from the characteristics of the glasses now available.

There is a final additional factor which has given the Nikkor line a superiority of performance equalled by few, if any, other lenses. There are manufacturing variations with any product, especially one requiring the extreme precision of a compound lens. The highest standard of uniform quality can be maintained only by methods of inspection and rejection which are exacting and ruthless. The tolerance of deviation from ideal specifications is held to such small limits that any Nikkor of any focal length may be taken from a dealer's shelf and fitted to any Nikon body which has not actually suffered damage from mistreatment and the two will fit together with smaller deviations from an ideal alignment (by fractional thousandths of an inch) than will the lenses and bodies from other manufacturers with established reputations for precision equipment. Similarly, any two lenses ever sold may be given elaborate optical tests and their slight, inevitable residual spherical aberration and their residual radial and tangental astigmatism measured, even though these are far below the level which will affect the film image. However, the differences to be found between any two Nikkors of the same design and their deviation from the standard are so slight that the common practice of "trying out" new lenses to find the best available example of a type has become meaningless with Nikkors. Each lens shipped from the factory will deliver the same perfection of image as any other of the same design.

the Nikon shutter release. First attach the end of the connecting cable with the black band to the adjustable release socket of the Housing, and the other end around the shutter release button on the Nikon. Then attach the cable release to the mirror release socket on the Housing. Wind the Nikon film advance after each exposure and release shutter with the cable release to the housing.

To change film-frame orientation from horizontal to vertical, depress button at left side of housing and turn camera 90°. The format masks inside the Housing back and top will automatically rotate correspondingly.

For series photographs, the connecting cable may be removed and the mirror held in a raised position. Turn lock ring on cable release counter-clockwise until red dots on ring and base meet. Then depress releasing cable. For normal cable release action, keep lock ring in its closed position.

Synchronizing shutter and mirror action If the shutter of the Nikon releases before the mirror is raised, or lags behind the mirror action, adjust synchronization by first loosening the locking knob just below the connecting cable socket on the housing, then rotating the knurled socket by small degrees until synchronization is reached. Tighten locking knob firmly.

This adjustment may be so accurately made that the Nikon Prism Reflex Housing may be used for fast action coverage, in contrast with other housings which have a built-in ½- to 2-second "safety factor" between the mirror action and shutter tripping. Gravity action returns the mirror immediately to viewing position so there is no appreciable "blind period" while following subject action.

Lens Care

To clean the surface of the Nikkor, dust lightly (preferably with a blower) to remove any possible grit, then wipe very gently with lens tissue or a very soft, lintless cloth which has been through the laundry several times. *Never use the silicone-treated tissues sold for cleaning eye-glasses.* These will damage the surface coating of the lens. Alcohol is not advisable unless the cloth is only slightly dampened for it will loosen the cement between elements if any quantity works its way into the mount.

Do not screw in a lens hood or other attachment so firmly that it may loosen the front portion of the Nikkor mount when it is removed. Do not try to disassemble a Nikkor for any reason. In case of accident or damage, return it to the manufacturer through your dealer or through an authorized repair service.

Note that optical glass may sometimes contain small bubbles (although glass from Nippon Kogaku melts is remarkably free from these). There will be no effect on image quality if these are present. You may also notice small "slicks" on the coating which show up when light is reflected from the surface of the front or rear element as you handle a Nikkor. These, too, will not affect the transmitted light through the lens nor the image quality and may be easily removed if desired.

Always keep the lens capped when not in use and in a dust-tight case when it is not on the Nikon.

5

35mm Film and Development

PHOTOGRAPHERS TEND TO TAKE FILMS FOR GRANTED. We expect complete uniformity from cartridge to cartridge. Sometimes, we even seem to expect film to anticipate our requirements and to respond adequately no matter how severe the test. To a remarkable extent, modern film does all of these things. Despite the complex and difficult nature of the manufacturing process, film bought under any of the leading trade names behaves identically, within practical limits, with other packages of the same emulsion type. Modern speed indexes and latitude characteristics are sufficient to permit a gross error of many stops in exposing medium speed and rapid black-and-white films under many conditions before the resulting negative becomes useless.

Film for the Nikon is supplied in two forms, the most common of which is the light-tight metal *cartridge* which is loaded into the camera and which contains sufficient film for either 20 or 36 exposures. For reasons of economy or in order to employ certain specialized types of film not available in factory-loaded cartridges, 35mm film may be purchased in bulk and loaded by hand into either old cartridges or into the Nikon metal cassette. [See picture-series, page 124.] Both conventionally used and special purpose 35mm films are often supplied in bulk lengths of 27 1/2 (sometimes 30) feet, as well as 50 and 100 feet. Some emulsions are supplied with notches at 36-exposure lengths. The film data at the end of the book includes information on types available in bulk lengths only.

Film structure

Black-and-white 35mm film is conventionally a three-layer material. There is first a flexible support or *base* on which is coated an *emulsion* of gelatin containing light-sensitive silver halides and certain additives which impart greater sensitivity. Above this is a clear gelatin overcoating for protection. The precise thickness of each of these three layers varies, depending upon manufacturing requirements and the speed and purpose of the emulsion.

The structure of the emulsion will be considered in the next section, *The latent image*. In appearance, the emulsion is a tannish, translucent layer which does not become transparent until the undeveloped silver halides are converted in the fixing bath.

The early motion picture film used in 35mm still cameras employed a cellulose nitrate base. This was not only dangerously inflammable but subject to spontaneous decomposition in storage. Many early 35mm negatives (as well as movie classics) have perished with their nitrate base. In recent years, most films for the Nikon and other 35mm still cameras are coated on "safety base": a transparent, flexible and relatively stable cellulose acetate (most commonly the "high acetyl" or triacetate form). This is made from a cellulose ester plus a plasticizer, and sometimes retains traces of the volatile solvents used in manufacture. The slow evaporation of these solvent traces and of the plasticizer itself eventually lead to brittleness and shrinkage of the base. However, it will literally last a lifetime, will not spontaneously decompose, and is classified in insurance terminology as "slow burning," with the comparatively negligible storage hazard of an equivalent amount of strips cut from newsprint.

Research has continued to produce candidate materials to replace cellulose triacetate as a film base, substances which would have the dimensional stability required for very critical work and which would not need the somewhat excessive thickness of the acetate for reasonable strength. Vinyl and polystyrene resins are in use for some sheet films and DuPont *Cronar* is used as a base for both sheet and movie films. These still have many disadvantages, notably their cost. Much more promising for Nikon users are the new polycarbonates (like General Electric's *Lexan*) with excellent base characteristics and the promise of future economical production. In any event, a greatly improved film base seems nearly at hand.

Film base for black-and-white 35mm films designed for still camera use normally contain a gray dye to prevent halation. Light which is intense enough to penetrate the emulsion completely during exposure must traverse this gray "filter" incorporated in the base. The small percentage of this stray light which is then reflected back by the rear surface of the base and the black pressure plate behind the focal plane of the Nikon must again traverse the thickness of the dyed base before re-entering the light sensitive emulsion to produce an unwanted secondary image. The dye thus has a double effect. It remains in the base after processing but will have no practical effect on the printing characteristics of the negative.

The top surface of the emulsion is generally covered with a layer of clear gelatin which has been hardened to serve as an anti-abrasion coating as the film is advanced in the camera, re-wound into the cartridge, processed, and during subsequent storage. The actual light-sensitive emulsion itself is thus protected in a "sandwich" of base and overcoating.

Handling and storage

Film materials are remarkably tough and stable, considering their structure, but they are susceptible to mechanical and other damage. They require reasonable, but not excessive care. Cartridges should be kept in the factory packing until loaded into the Nikon especially when the weather approaches hot, wet tropical conditions.

Scratches may occur as the film travels through the camera, if fine grit is allowed to accumulate in the Nikon. Clean the inside of the camera regularly as suggested in Chapter 2. Dirt on the felt light-trap of 35mm cartridges, particularly those which have been re-loaded from bulk film by the photographer, will cause fine, lengthwise gouges which will appear as lines on the final print. Following development, film should be cut into lengths of four to six frames and filed in envelopes to eliminate scratching or the accumulation of dust or grit.

Heat is destructive to film, before and after development. Temperatures above 120F will accelerate the evaporation of the plasticizer in the base as well as produce an over-all silver deposit (fog) in the unexposed emulsion. If film is to be retained for long periods of time, particularly during the summer months, it is best to seal it in a moisture-proof container and keep it in the bottom of a refrigerator. This is more essential with color films than with black-and-white films which will withstand conditions which are far from optimum.

Humidity, above or below the limits of human comfort, is also an enemy of film stability. Dehydrated safety base may crack during handling, while excessive moisture may encourage complex chemical changes and breakdown of the gelatin layers and provide favorable conditions for the growth of air-borne fungus and micro-organisms which proliferate in the organic gelatin. Under tropical conditions, film should be dehumidified with silica gel and sealed in moisture-proof containers.

Chemical vapors as well as actual contact with reactive materials may lead to deterioration. Even after processing, sulfur complexes and other atmospheric contamination normally present in urban areas will produce a slow change of the gelatin and of the silver image itself.

These notes are intended to encourage a reasonable precaution in handling film and irreplaceable negatives. In practice, film materials will not be damaged by anything except gross carelessness—and the slow decay of time.

The Latent Image

THE LIGHT-SENSITIVE layer of the film is actually a colloid, a dispersion of silver halide crystals in gelatin, although the technically incorrect term, *emulsion,* is now firmly established even in the scientific literature of photography. This suspension of halides in a gelatin carrier originated in a series of rule-of-thumb experiments (plus fortunate accidents) but its superiority to other light-sensitive systems in everyday work has been conclusively demonstrated since its introduction, originally as a coating for printing papers, in 1873.

Silver halides

Light-sensitive crystals are formed by combining silver nitrate with one or more of three halides: bromine, chlorine and iodine. In film preparation, this is accomplished by adding silver nitrate and potassium bromide simultaneously at a controlled rate to a warm, aqueous solution of gelatin which holds the crystals in suspension as they are formed. Up to about 7 percent of potassium iodide is usually included. This leads to the formation of mixed crystals with slight irregularities of structure which increase their sensitivity to the action of light.

These silver halide crystals produced in emulsion making are sensitive primarily to radiation in the ultraviolet and in the visible blue. H. W. Vogel, however, discovered (also in 1873) that certain dyes added to the emulsion would sensitize the crystals to colors of longer wave length. There has been much

5.1 JACQUES LOWE

Actress Susan Harrison

Nikon S2
50mm f/1.4 Nikkor
(window light)
Plus-X, 1/30, f/5.6

research in this field and it is now possible to sensitize the emulsions selectively to all of the visible spectrum and into the far infrared. The color response of the human eye may be matched with films for ordinary use, or the photochemical response exaggerated in certain bands in emulsions for special purposes.

Some hundreds of dye compounds have been used. The most frequently employed are from a group known as cyanines. These sensitizers are adsorbed to the surface of the halide crystals and absorb wavelengths of radiation to which the crystal itself is insensitive. This absorbed energy causes, in turn, crystalline changes which render the silver halide developable. Other admixtures to the emulsion, such as traces of gold salts, have multiplied the over-all sensitivity of films in the last few years. The exact nature of these compounds are usually protected as commercial secrets.

Gelatin

The choice of gelatin as the basis for the emulsion was a fortunate one, even though it is in some ways a difficult material. It is an organic substance, a by-product of hide-clippings and bones from meat-packing. It is difficult to maintain uniformity from batch to batch as it is supplied to the manufacturers for purifying and processing, and it is sensitive to storage conditions as noted above. Attempts have been made to replace gelatin by manufactured materials such as the water-permeable cellulose esters, but satisfactory techniques are not yet developed.

Gelatin has the useful property of changing from a *sol* (liquid) condition to a *gel* (semi-solid) or vice versa, depending on the temperature and the amount of water present. It may be chemically treated to become reasonably stable in a gel state under the full range of conditions encountered in photographic practice. It will remain permeable, however, permitting processing solutions to penetrate and interact with the silver halide crystals or with the developed silver image.

The original choice of gelatin as a carrier for the halide crystals was also fortunate for it was subsequently discovered that certain "impurities" normally present, notably silver sulfide, acted as sensitizers, enormously increasing the response of the silver halides to light even when present as 1:1,000,000 traces. Completely purified gelatin produces an extremely slow emulsion unless the silver sulfide is restored or another sensitizer substituted.

Photochemical reactions

When light strikes the silver halide crystals (or a dye substance adsorbed to its surface), a structural change within the crystal occurs so that when it is subsequently brought into contact with a suitable reducing agent (developer) the crystal will be converted to metallic silver. This change may be induced by visible light and by radiation of other wave-lengths, by x-rays, α-particles and other sub-atomic particles.

Since the beginnings of photography there have been a succession of theories to account for this photochemical process. As in all science, newer hypotheses are regularly published to serve as the basis for further experiment and eventual replacement. Current theories involve quantum mechanics and sub-atomic physics and are stated in a difficult mathematical language. Fortunately, it is not necessary for the photographer to understand these theories in order to make satisfactory and creative pictures.

However, these investigations have revealed the essential gross mechanics of the process from which much useful information may be drawn. It is evident that the silver halide crystals contain minute impurities which act as *sensitivity centers.* The energy absorbed from light apparently results in the clustering of atoms of metallic silver at these points which act, in turn, as *development centers* to convert the whole crystal to metallic silver in the presence of a reducing agent. Other behavior patterns of the crystals are apparent from both theory and observation. A slight percentage of them will always develop to metallic silver even though they have not been affected by light. On any negative there is a light over-all veiling of general fog which has no appreciable effect on image quality. Many chemical vapors will render crystals developable, as will sharp pressure (as in a tightly-creased film). If development is considerably prolonged, the percentage of unexposed crystals which are converted to silver will rise until the whole film area ultimately reaches maximum density.

Examined under extremely high magnification (at least 2500X) the granular structure of the undeveloped emulsion becomes evident. The largest of the crystals are about 1/25,000-inch in size. The range of size distribution is a factor in establishing the speed and contrast of the emulsion. In general, the larger crystals are more sensitive, but factors of shape, structural deformities, adsorbed impurities (including sensitizers), and the depth of the crystal in the thickness of the emulsion influence their threshold of response, that is, the amount of energy they must absorb from the radiation which strikes them before they become readily developable. However, each crystal operates on an all-or-nothing basis: it is either sensitized or remains inert during development under ordinary conditions of time and temperature (except those which make up the slight "fog" mentioned previously).

This variation in individual sensitivity makes possible the negative image. If all crystals had identical thresholds of response, in many circumstances the film would receive a minimum exposure which would make all of the crystals develop simultaneously to full over-all uniform density. Only subjects of the

5.2 MORRIS JAFFE
Nikon S2
50mm f/1.4 Nikkor
Plus-X, 1/30, f/4

highest contrast would register as an image in tones of pure black and white with no intermediate gradations. The proportions of crystals with various levels of sensitivity may be controlled in manufacture to considerable precision, making it possible to construct emulsions of homologous nature for a uniform (high threshold) response characteristic of very high contrast, extremely short gradation films such as Kodak Microfile. Emulsions of mixed sizes and sensitivities produce the longer, even gradation of response in materials suitable for ordinary photography.

Following exposure, the latent image formed by the selective exposure of the silver halide crystals in the emulsion remains relatively stable. Development may be postponed for days or even weeks without obtaining perceptibly different results from those of immediate development. A fully-exposed latent image will hold up better than one weakly exposed; shadow detail is lost first. Subsequent exposure to radiation, heat or certain chemical vapors between exposure and development, however, may either destroy or tend to strengthen the latent image. If development is postponed for a year or more, many factors may influence the stability of the latent image. Some evidence indicates there may be a slight growth in the intensity of the image for a period of approximately a year, followed by a gradual decay, but this is difficult to predict with accuracy. Films exposed by the Andrée Expedition (1897) before its members perished in the Arctic were found preserved in the perpetual cold and developed into printable negatives after holding their latent images for thirty-three years.

Image granularity

Following development, a considerably lower level of magnification exhibits the grain character of the photographic image. In fact, there are occasions when a 35mm negative enlarged to 8x10 inches may reveal a dismaying non-homogeneity of image if, for example, development has been prolonged to gain the ultimate possible speed response from the film. This nonuniformity of image may be objectively measured in the laboratory and, as such, it is termed *granularity*. The perception of this image structure in negative or print is properly termed *graininess*. While all photographic images are necessarily granular in nature, in practice efforts are usually made to keep this granularity below the visible level. [See "Development and grain" following.]

The halide crystals which are developed to metallic silver lose their crystalline shape and under the microscope resemble tangles of black thread. These individual grains are larger than their parent crystals but are far below the resolution of the human eye. Visible graininess is a product of several factors. One of the most important of these is the tendency of the developing grains to clump together to form larger masses of silver. This tendency is more apparent in closely-packed, non-homogeneous, rapid emulsions than in slower, more evenly dispersed ones.

There is also a tendency for crystals which are closely adjacent to exposed ones to develop spontaneously by "contagion." The fast emulsions are richer in crystals than are slower ones and the greater variation in crystal sizes in rapid materials permits a closer packing of the silver halide crystals. Under these circumstances, development is more likely to spread to adjacent crystals. There is some practical advantage in this tendency; a weak exposure which may set up development centers in only a few crystals in one (tiny) given area may result in a (relatively) massive deposit of silver, heavy enough to form part of a printable image. This spreading of the image in development contributes to the effective speed of some rapid emulsions, but it does so at the cost of increasing granularity, sometimes to the point of visible graininess at moderate enlargements.

Uniformity of crystal dispersion in the emulsion, irrespective of their size is an important factor in granularity, but one not under the control of the photographer. Considerable advances have been made in improving this uniformity in recent years and both slow and rapid films have been improved in this respect.

Still another factor influences graininess. A thick emulsion of identical granularity characteristics as a thin emulsion will exhibit more tendency to graininess. As light penetrates the developed thicker emulsion during the printing process, it will encounter grains which overlap at different levels and blend together in the projected image. The thin-emulsion films [see list, *Data and Formulas*] which are intended for fine-structured images and great enlarging potential have much thinner emulsions than films with faster speed indexes.

In the thicker emulsions, crystals closer to the top surface tend to build development centers slightly more rapidly than crystals lower in the layer which are partly shielded by the upper crystals and the turbidity of the gelatin carrier. If exposures in the Nikon are always kept to the *minimum correct* level for adequate detail and contrast, the granularity of the faster films will be minimized. Normal recommended development times and formulas which contain relatively large amounts of a silver halide solvent such as sodium sulfite will also control grain in the faster films.

Minimum correct exposure will also reduce *irradiation*, the internal reflection of light from grain to grain within the emulsion. This scatter of light not only produces additional graininess but also reduces the acutance or edge-sharpness of image detail.

5.3 *In many situations the important tone values cover only part of the gradation represented between clear film base and maximum silver deposit. In 35mm photography, it is usually best to give a "minimum correct" exposure and place these tones toward the "toe" of the curve, as shown here.*

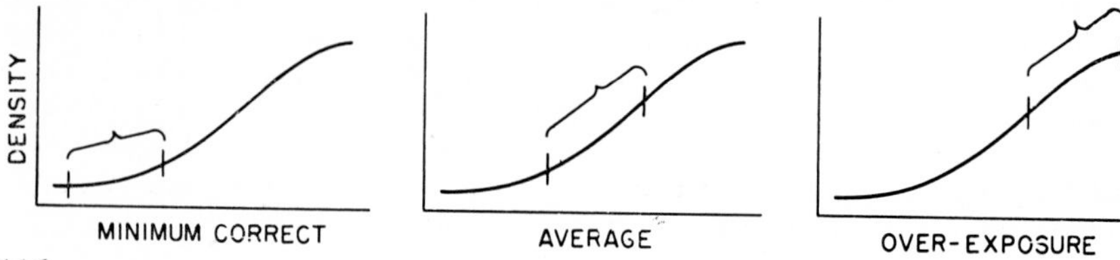

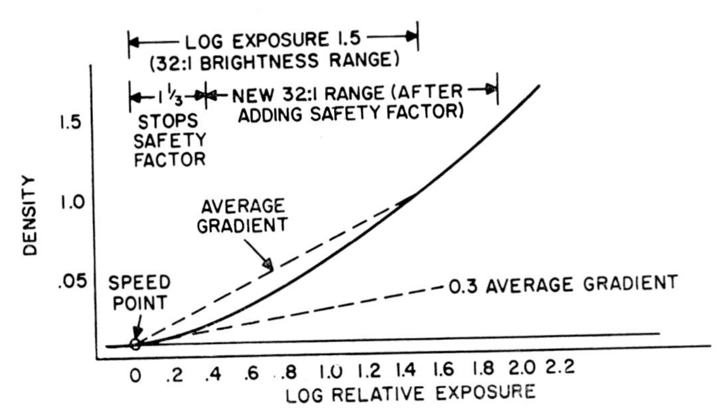

5.4 *This diagram shows the "fractional gradient" method of the ASA method of rating film speeds. A test film is very accurately exposed and developed in the sensitometric laboratory (not in any actual situation). The speed number is based on the point where the graduated test exposure has produced a gradient equal to 0.3 of the average gradient over a 32:1 brightness range. This point is then arbitrarily moved 1 1/3 stops to introduce a "safety factor."*

Film speeds

The subject of film speeds (Exposure Indexes) is sometimes confusing because the available information does not often distinguish between the "speed" of the material by the standards of the sensitometrist, and the useful response of particular films in practice. The most useful rating system so far devised is that of the American Standards Association [see diagram above]. This includes a 1 1/3 stop safety factor as well as the usual assumption that the important values of the scene are distributed along the whole slope of the curve from the shadows on the left to the brightest highlights on the extreme right.

If these ASA ratings were to be used with film on the Nikon, the resulting negatives would almost always be too dense, grainy, and of poor quality. It is necessary at least to double this ASA rating (i.e., to halve the exposure time or close down one stop) with most films. The speed should be further increased to secure proper *minimum correct* exposures and often increased again when the subject is low in contrast.

Film rating recommendations throughout this *Manual* are given with these speed advances taken into consideration and are based, also, on the specific developers and development times given in the text [see also *Data and Formulas*]. Most of these recommended E.I.'s for various situations assume that the film will be given "normal" or very slightly increased development times. Consequently, it is possible to use different E.I.'s (providing exposures are accurately calculated) on the same cartridge of film with subjects and illumination of various types, indoors and out, and to produce acceptable densities and contrasts in each with the recommended development.

The thin-emulsion films are by no means as "elastic" in rating as are the medium speed or rapid emulsions. The foreign ones usually produce best results with a 1/2 stop increase over manufacturer's ratings; Kodak Panatomic-X with a one stop increase. Film speed with faster emulsions may be considerably increased at the expense of graininess and acutance, as noted previously. Note carefully the specific recommendations in Chapters 3, 8, 9 and 11, as well as the chart of films and developers in *Data and Formulas*.

Developer Formulas

IN DEVELOPMENT, the latent image in the film is converted to metallic silver by the action of one or more suitable reducing agents in the developer formula. In general photography, the developer should be chosen to bring out all possible detail and full gradation without losing any significant emulsion speed and without building a grain structure which limits the useful size of enlargements. To achieve this end, there have been hundreds of formulas and packaged products offered on the photographic market. Many of these have real merit. Others, however, enjoy only a limited and faddist popularity for they actually produce no better results than may be obtained with such standard and well-established developers as D-76 and D-23 [see *Data and Formulas*].

Some of the early developers for 35mm film had as many as 17 or 18 ingredients; at least one excellent formula (D-23) contains only two, plus the necessary water for compounding it. However, the "standard" formula contains four ingredients in addition to the water which acts as solvent:

1. The *developing agent:* There are many substances which reduce silver halides to metallic silver. It is essential that the formula be built around one (or more) of these compounds which acts *selectively,* i.e., which reduces those silver halides which have been affected by light and thus form the latent image, without reducing any appreciable amount of the other silver halide crystals present in the emulsion during the normal duration of development. There is a long list of such developing agents and we will describe only the ones in common use (below).

2. The *preservative:* Many developing substances have an affinity for oxygen which combines with them and reduces their effectiveness. Formulas frequently include a sulfite, bisulfite or metabisulfite which serves to protect the developing agent.

3. The *accelerator:* The common developing agents operate best (or exclusively) in an alkaline solution, so formulas generally contain a compound such as sodium carbonate, sodium or potassium hydroxide, or borax, depending upon the level of alkalinity desired. Normally, the components of developers constitute a *buffer system* which maintains the alkalinity level (pH) throughout the useful life of the solution.

4. The *restrainer:* This is usually potassium bromide (sometimes benzotriazole) which acts to protect the unexposed silver halides and inhibits development fog.

The developer penetrates the gelatin emulsion and acts on the silver halide crystals which have been affected by light. The exact process which enables it to act selectively has not been satisfactorily covered by chemical or physical theory. We know, however, that some agents tend to restrain the newly-formed silver grains from tending to clump while the gelatin is saturated, and that some developer components, notably sodium sulfite, tend to prevent this increase in granularity. Strong alkalies swell the gelatin and tend to obliterate fine detail, hence 35mm film is generally developed in solutions containing minimum amounts of weaker compounds such as borax (sodium tetraborate).

Developing agents

While the list of substances which act selectively to reduce the exposed silver halides is a long one, there are only a few in common use. (The identity of the reducer in some proprietary preparations has not been published.)

Before World War II, many formulas for 35mm film development were built around *paraphenylenediamine* and this is probably the only true "fine grain" developing substance ever discovered, at least for ordinary developing procedures. No other agent gives as fine a dispersion of the silver particles forming the image. Its unfortunate disadvantage is a considerable loss in emulsion speed (at least 1 1/2 stops) as well as a very long developing time. It is also quite toxic and may lead to dermatitis.

Metol (also known under other trade names: Elon, Pictol, Rhodol, Genol, etc.) is paramethylaminophenol sulfate. It begins to work very quickly, building up detail even in very slightly exposed areas but builds density slowly. Used alone, it usually gives extremely soft results and a slight general fog. Some Metol contains traces of a highly poisonous impurity which results in dermatitis for some users.

Metol is frequently combined with *hydroquinone* (paradihydroxybenzene). Used alone, hydroquinone produces an image of strong contrast, shadow detail appearing relatively late in the course of development. In combination with Metol, the two agents act to supplement each other's action. Hydroquinone is strongly susceptible to changes of temperature, its action slowing down rapidly below 60F and ceasing entirely below 40F.

Phenidone is the trade name for a product (1-phenyl-3-pyrazolidone) first prepared in 1890 but only discovered to be a developing agent by the Ilford laboratories in 1940. Large-scale manufacturing processes were devised after World War II and the excellent characteristics of Phenidone have given it a considerable popularity, particularly in 35mm work. It is not particularly toxic, has a long life in solution and is relatively inexpensive since it may substitute for five to fifteen times its weight of Metol in formulas. Its rate of exhaustion is also less than that of Metol. As a reducing agent, it produces a silver image very rapidly but the action slows down and, used alone, produces low density even with prolonged development. In combination with hydroquinone, it forms a "compensating" developer, building excellent shadow detail without blocking up highlights even with moderately prolonged developing times to "force" speed with brief film exposures.

Replenishers

As developing solutions are used, some of it is carried away in the film, the developing agent (or agents) is exhausted, and complex by-products of the reducing action tend to accumulate. Increasing the time of development will partly compensate for these changes, but it is best to add small quantities of replenisher solution regularly. These are formulas similar to that of the original developer but so balanced as to replace the developing agent and to compensate for the restraining effect of the accumulating reaction products. Generally, adding an amount of replenisher sufficient to replace the volume lost as developer is carried away, is sufficient.

The fixing bath

Following development, it is necessary to remove the undeveloped silver halide crystals in order for the negative image to remain stable. This is accomplished by converting the halides to a form soluble in water so that they may be washed out of the emulsion. Since the early days of photography, this has been accomplished by bathing the emulsion in *hypo,* an abbreviation for "sodium hyposulfite" which is now more correctly known as sodium thiosulfate. A plain

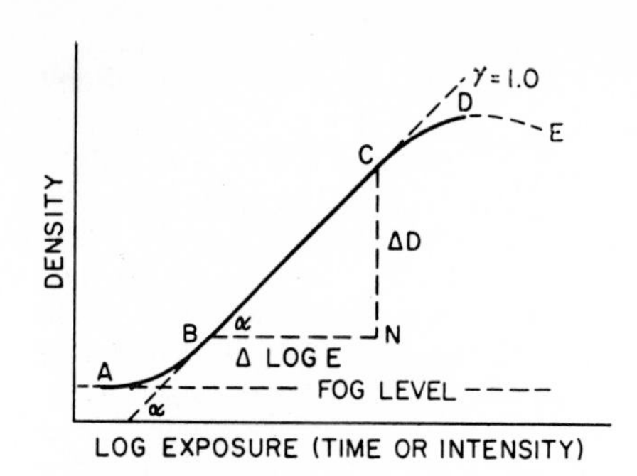

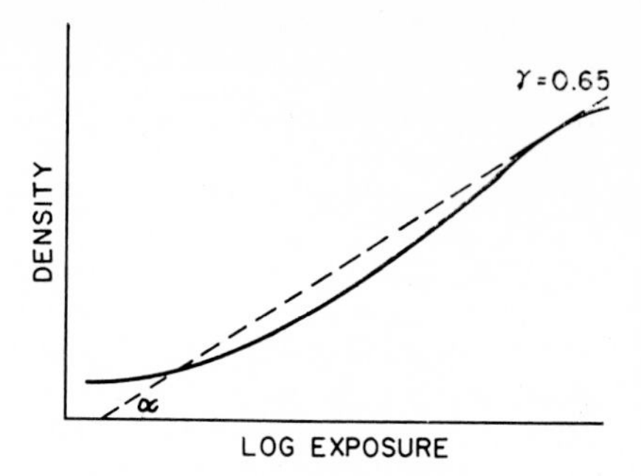

5.5 *Left, above, is the "typical" H&D curve, graphing the response to light of the film emulsion. Its structure is explained in the text. At right is a curve which more nearly represents the actual shape of the plotted response of modern films (see also 5.7).*

solution of sodium thiosulfate and water will accomplish this end, but such a bath has an extremely short life. Formulas for the hypo or fixing bath generally contain, in addition, acetic acid to neutralize the alkalies carried over from the developer, sodium sulfite to check the decomposition of the sodium thiosulfate, boric acid to prevent the formation of sludge, and alum as a hardener for the emulsion.

Ammonium thiosulfate has also been employed as a fixing agent since useful formulas were devised in 1942. It is more rapid in its action and serves as a base for several prepared fixing products. [See *Data and Formulas*.]

The Development Process

BEFORE OUTLINING development procedure, step by step, some general remarks about the behavior of the exposed silver halides during development will be useful.

Developer and gradient

The terms *contrast, gamma,* and *gradient* are often used interchangeably, although there is actually a very useful distinction between them. The diagram of Figure 5.5 is a simplified characteristic (or H&D) curve of film response, identifying the names applied to the various portions of this schematic way of charting film response. The steepness of the angle which the center "straight-line" portion makes with the base is a direct measure of the *comparative* contrast of the original scene and the developed negative. In this simplified drawing, it makes a 45° angle. The tangent of this angle, (α) as the dotted lines show, gives the numerical value of this angle:

$$\tan \alpha = \gamma \text{ (gamma)}$$

$$\textit{or } \Delta D / \Delta \log E = \gamma$$

Conveniently enough, when scene and negative contrasts are equal, $\gamma = 1$. Higher values represent a negative with contrast greater than the original scene; lower values a lesser negative contrast. (Nikon negatives are generally developed to "gammas" of 0.6—0.8.)

Actual films do not chart so neatly as this, as Figure 5.5B will make clear. This is a rapid film, with its characteristically extended "toe" region and a re-

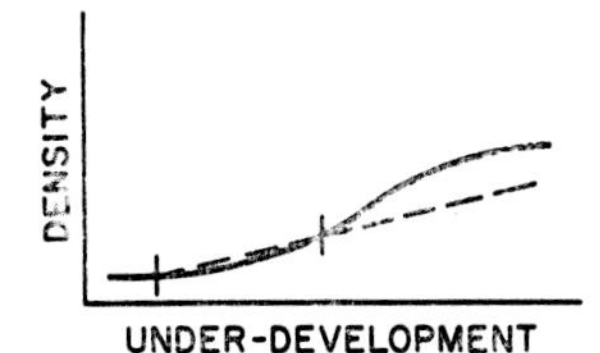

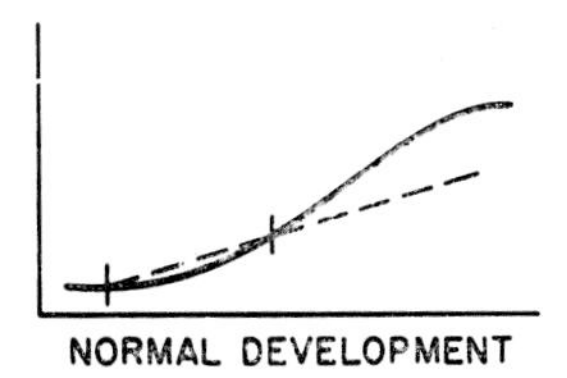

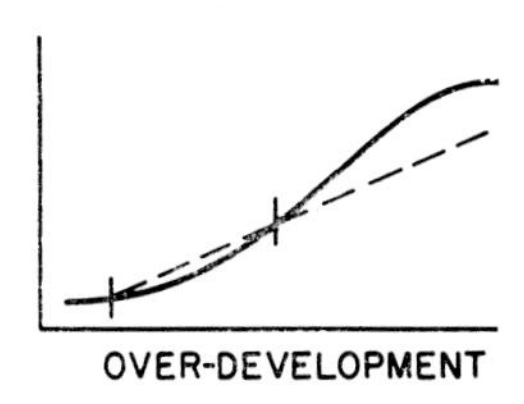

stricted "straight line" portion. In many cases, all of the important portions of the scene are represented by negative densities on this toe section which has a continuously changing "gamma." Consequently, the *average* over the important part of the slope must be used, and this is termed *gradient*.

The family of curves (5.7) indicates graphically what occurs with a normally-exposed film as development is prolonged. The lower curve depicts the results after six minutes of development: shadow details (at the toe of the curve) have some separation of tones, while middle and high-light details have begun to assume a long even gradation. The gradient or average gamma (γ) is 0.51, about half the contrast of the original scene. As development is prolonged to 10 minutes, there is greater separation of tones at the lower portion of the curve as well as throughout its entire length. The gradient at this point is 0.72 which is approximately the contrast considered desirable for 35mm negatives. As the time is further increased to 15 and then to 25 minutes, the high-light values increase proportionately more than do the shadow values, until the film reaches a gradient of 1.04 or slightly greater contrast than that of the original scene.

A fully-exposed negative developed to this extent would be difficult to print and would probably have excessive grain and a lack of acutance [see below]. However, one which is given minimum exposure, so that all of the important values lie toward the left on the curve, would be more normal in appearance.

There are limits to the useful employment of increased development to gain contrast (steeper gradients). As contrast increases, the right end of the curve rises also, bringing highlight values closer to maximum silver density in the

5.6 *(Top of page) shows the increasing contrast (dotted line) as films are given various development times. (Compare with 5.3.)* **5.7** *(below) shows the response of a film similar to Kodak Tri-X as contrast is increased by prolonged development. The "time-gamma" curves indicate how contrast rises as development times are prolonged in three different developers.*

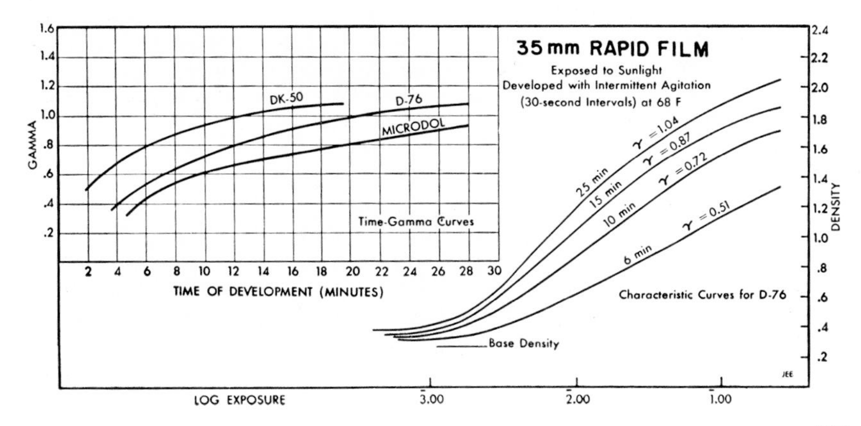

negative. The highest values tend to compact and this small area *decreases* in gradient. Beyond a certain critical point for any particular film-developer combination, additional development time begins to bring more and more tones at the right on the curve up to maximum undifferentiated density. Simultaneously, the fog level increases rapidly, forcing up the foot of the curve. All gradation is lost at either end and the gradient of the curve as a whole begins to decrease; the negative becomes very dense and of poor contrast. The limiting point of maximum possible gradient is called by the old name, *gamma infinity*.

The gradient of all films in common use can be altered by changes in development. The effects are not identical with all types of film, however. The ultra-rapid films which have a relatively enlongated "toe" on their characteristic curves, [see Figure 5.7] may be considerably "pushed" when the exposure has placed most of the important values in this region. Medium speed films may be considerably increased in contrast, also. The slow, thin-emulsion films accept prolonged development only within narrow limits before losing their granularity and long gradation superiorities.

It is important to note that the curves of Figure 5.7 are for development at 68F and with specified agitation during development. If developer is warmer than this, it will act more rapidly, and vice versa. More rapid or violent agitation will also cause a proportionally greater increase of gradient.

These curves furnish the information for constructing the center trace of the graph inset in 5.7 which compares the effects of three different developers in terms of the gradient produced for various development times (at 68F). This is a *time—gamma* chart. It will be seen that DK-50 builds contrast much more rapidly with this film than does D-76. If a straight-edge is laid across the chart at the level of the desired gradient (usually between 0.6 and 0.8) the proper development times (at 68F with specified agitation) for each of the three developers may be read off directly. Time-gamma charts are published by Kodak and several other manufacturers and photographers should be aware of the information which may be easily read from such curves.

Development and emulsion speed

It was noted in the previous section that the important tone-values in the original scene will be shifted toward the straight-line portion of the H&D curve with full exposure or toward the toe of the curve with a shorter exposure in the Nikon. With subjects of low or moderate contrast range, if the film is accurately exposed for the important shadow detail, that is, given minimum correct exposure, the tone values will lie toward the left, or toe, of the curve. Extended development will increase the gradient of this portion of the curve (Figure 5.6) to give it a reasonable density and contrast. Effectively, this increases the speed of the film, frequently from one to two stops or even more.

This is most effective with high speed emulsions such as Tri-X and HPS (which show curves with elongated toe portions). These films have a considerable development latitude. The possibility of exposing these rapid films over a very wide range of Exposure Indexes, however, has apparently obscured the superiorities of the medium speed films (Kodak Plus-X, Perutz Peromnia 21 and Agfa Isopan ISS) within a considerable section of this range. In very many situations which require up to an Exposure Index of 400, these latter films will produce superior grain and tone rendition as well as perfectly adequate speed. It is not ordinarily desirable to develop medium speed materials for gradients

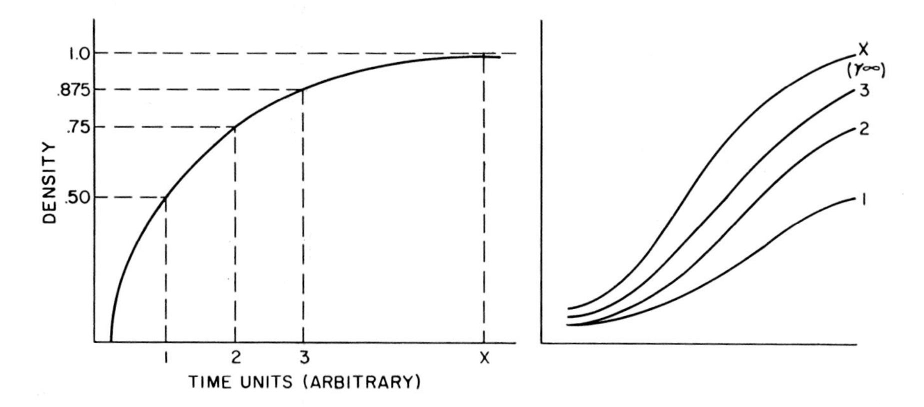

5.8 *(Left) indicates the pattern of increased density in the exposed areas of a negative as the development is prolonged.* **5.9** *(right) shows schematically the H&D curves these development times would produce.*

much beyond 0.8 in the effort to gain speed for there will be a concurrent increase in graininess and in the level of over-all fog. The thin emulsion, fine-grain films do not respond well to this forced development and lose much of their excellent acuity and grain characteristics.

More energetic development will tend to increase effective emulsion speed, also. The time-gamma chart illustrated indicates that D-76 will produce a much higher gradient with a typical fast film than will Microdol, and that DK-50 will build a gradient equal to that of D-76 in a much briefer time. D-76, D-23 and Ethol UFG are favorites of most professionals for preferred Exposure Indexes [see *Data and Formulas*], and Microphen is often used for pushing the rapid films to extreme speeds when negative quality must be sacrificed to obtain useful density.

It might be added here that the Exposure Index chosen for various situations must be appropriate for either the "normal" or "pushing" development times used. For example, a cartridge of medium speed (manufacturer's E.I. 80) film which contains exposures made outdoors at an E.I. of 160 as well as other exposures made indoors at up to E.I. 320 may often give good negatives of both at "normal" development times. The 160 "doubled Exposure Index" is correct for average outdoor light and the minimum correct exposure indoors is approximately 250 for contrasty lighting or up to 320 for more evenly illuminated scenes. At worst, with these elevated indexes, E.I. 250 will give good rendition of middle tones and highlights and E.I. 320 will give excellent highlight detail, even though shadow detail may occasionally be lost. [See text elsewhere on the relation between contrast and Exposure Index, especially Chapters 3 and 8.] This applies, of course, to the exposures on a cartridge of any film of whatever speed.

Development and grain

Often, it may be important to avoid purchasing any speed increase at the expense of grain. The high energy developers and prolonged development times tend to increase grain clumping and graininess. Full film speed and good grain

5.10 *Loading the Nikon cassette. Left, bulk film is trimmed so tab fits through slit in spool. Center, parts of the cassette. Right, film is removed from spool for development by cutting off the tab which will not pull out after being inserted.*

are not incompatible, however, and the complicated paraphenylenediamine and glycin-metol formulas of ten years ago are not necessary with modern films. Kodak D-23 and Ethol UFG will produce excellent granularity at all reasonable Exposure Indexes, and D-76 gives nearly as good results in this respect.

Negative grain will also result from irradiation [see above] which no developing formula will prevent. Incipient reticulation, described more fully below, will also produce a granular effect no matter what developer is being used.

Development and acutance

The resolution of fine detail is partly a matter of the size and the disposition of the developed silver grains. Negative quality in this respect is best preserved by developers which have relatively low alkalinity. Developers with stronger alkalies (or large amounts of the weaker ones) tend to swell the emulsion and promote clumping of the developed silver into larger grains. Developers with an excess of silver halide solvent such as sodium sulfite or sodium thiosulfate give lower graininess only at the cost of this acutance. Although there is an apparently large amount of sulfite in D-76, this functions primarily as a preservative and this developer is still one of the best choices for maximum acutance. Ethol UFG also produces excellent image sharpness.

Choosing a Developer

THE SOUNDEST ADVICE about developers has been often repeated and too often ignored: find a satisfactory developer and standardize on it, despite the claims for the merits of other products. After you understand this formula thoroughly, how it performs with the films you use and with your own shooting habits with the Nikon, then (and only then) can you begin to test other developers intelligently. Probably no photographer who changes from developer to developer following the winds of fashion can exhibit a consistent run of technically excellent negatives.

The *Data and Formulas* section lists a number of well-accepted general purpose developers. If only one formula were to be used for all films, the choice of a great many photographers would be D-76. This is almost universally accepted as a standard against which to test the results of other developers. The amateur will discover that he can get excellent negatives with all films, medium speed to ultra-fast, and completely satisfactory results with the thin-emulsion films of high resolution and fine grain. The formula is easily compounded and it is also available in packaged form as a Kodak product. (In other parts of the world, the same formula is available as Ilford I.D.11 in prepared packages. Additional developer energy for forcing film speed may be obtained by increasing the amount of borax in the solution and maximum activity by substituting Kodalk for the borax. [See directions *Data and Formulas.*] D-76 gives excellent acutance and moderate grain as well as full emulsion speed, but is not the best choice for pushing film to especially high Exposure Indexes. Many professionals as well as the custom finishers who deal with professionals often use D-23 instead for their regular formula. This is very simple to prepare, soft-working, and will not block highlights readily when development is extended beyond the normal times. It will not give quite the excellent acutance of D-76 but is another very satisfactory choice as a standard developer.

The rapid-acting but essentially fine-grain Ethol UFG (a proprietary packaged formula) has been widely adopted by press associations, newspaper photographers and other professionals. It will produce excellent negatives with Panatomic-X and Adox KB-17 at E.I. 50-64 and 3 to 4 minute development, or speeds of 80-100 with 4 to 6 minute times. The medium-speed films may be shot at E.I. 160-200 and developed for 4 to 6 minutes, or at 320-400 and developed 6 to 9 minutes. The rapid emulsions will produce E.I. 400-500 in 4 to 5 minutes and E.I. 800-1000 in 6 to 8 minutes. With maximum development times of 12 minutes, medium speed films may be exposed up to E.I. 800 and rapid films to 2000, and still produce negatives from which very good quality prints for publication may be made.

5.11 *Reloading film cartridges: (A) bulk film in daylight loader, end taped to spool; (B) cartridge is re-assembled and (C) placed into loader; (D) film is wound into cartridge with crank; (E) loader is opened and film is cut off, and then (F) trimmed to fit into Nikon take-up spool.*

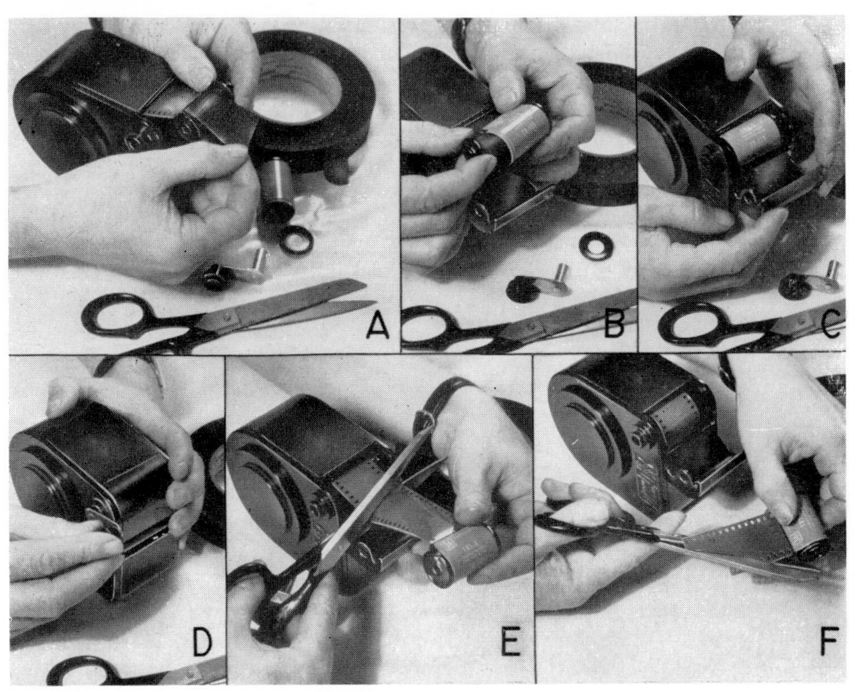

Many Phenidone developers have gained a wide acceptance, particularly because of their "compensating" action, their ability to develop full shadow detail without blocking highlights, which makes them particularly useful for the contrasty subject matter often encountered in available light work. The utmost in quality may also be obtained from the thin-emulsion films with developers which are especially compounded for them, such as Neofin Blue, X-22 and Minicol. The older fine-grain developers such as DK-20 and Microdol do not seem to work as well with contemporary films as they did with those of a few years ago, particularly with the new high-resolution, thin-emulsion films.

A rough but effective test of developer claims may be made under any photographer's own working conditions by selecting a subject which contains a full range of tones with important detail in both shadow and highlight areas. Two lengths of film should be exposed successively in the Nikon, each containing a wide range of shutter settings above and below that indicated by a careful meter reading of the scene. One of these identically exposed strips should be developed in D-76 and the other in the developer under comparison, following exact processing instructions in each case. When the films are dry, they may be compared under a magnifying glass. Detail in both high-light and shadow should be compared critically as well as any apparent gain or loss in speed between frames identically exposed. Grain and actuance are best compared by selecting a small middle tone area and making the largest possible enlargements on glossy paper. It will often be discovered that new, "miracle" developers have little, if any, discernable advantage over D-76.

Development by Time and Temperature

THE "SECRETS" of good processing for Nikon negatives are care, consistency and cleanliness. It is not difficult, even in a kitchen or bath room, to produce perfectly developed 35mm negatives with a minimum of equipment and preparation. Each step should be performed with care, however, and without deviation from film to film. Cleanliness is essential, for dirt, scratches or other defects will show up strongly at the magnifications necessary in printing the negative.

There are two basic proceedures for developing. One is the standard method of developing film for a precise time (see time-gamma chart, 5.7) at exactly the correct temperature. The other method is development by inspection, that is, checking the progress of development by quick glimpses of the film under the proper safe illumination. This latter method will be reviewed following the description of time-temperature processing.

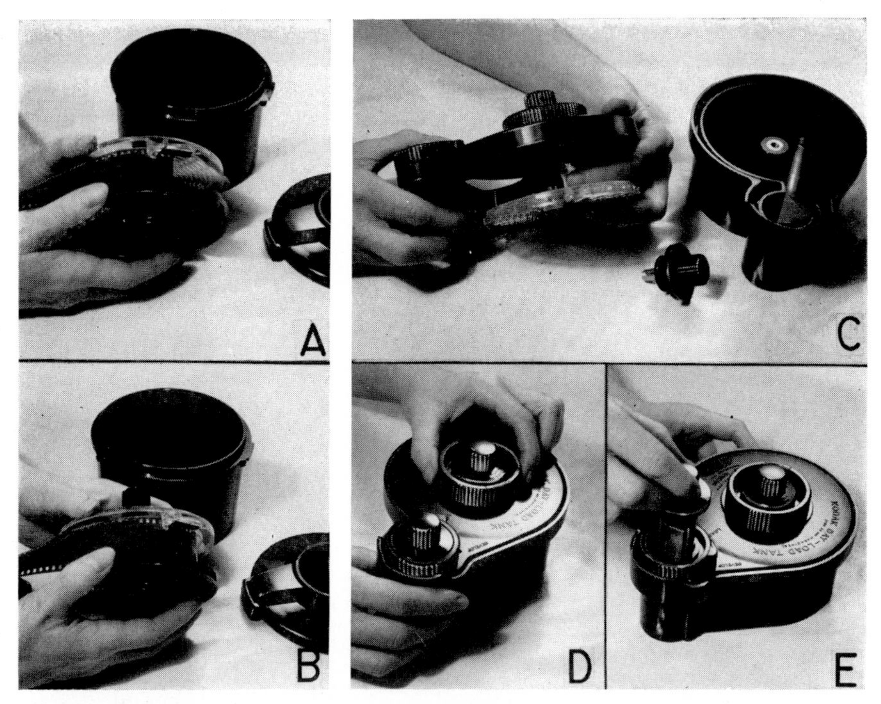

5.12 *(Opposite). For development, cartridges are (A) snapped open, (B) the end placed in the center of a spiral-wire reel, and (C) film curved slightly as it is fed into the reel.* **5.13** *(above) Ansco tank (A, B) has spring-grip reel fed from outside edge. Kodak Day-Load Tank (C-E) has center slot and roller, loads from unopened cartridge when tank is closed.*

Equipment for film processing

The minimum desirable equipment for negative processing includes: brown glass or polyethylene bottles to hold the solutions; a reliable thermometer, accurate to within one half degree (F); a clear glass graduate; a light-tight tank; and several film clips. Other useful items will be noted later.

If the photographer mixes his own processing solutions from bulk chemicals, a reliable scale for weighing amounts from a few grains to several ounces (or their metric equivalents) will be necessary. It is also useful to have a heavier scale to weigh the several pounds of hypo which go into a gallon of fixer. (Directions for mixing formulas will be found in *Data and Formulas.*)

Loading the film tank

There are several types of film developing tanks especially designed for 35mm work, including the spiral plastic reel, wire spiral reel and apron types. Two of these illustrated in Figures 5.12—5.16, are *daylight developing* models: they must be loaded in total darkness, but all subsequent operations may be continued in normal illumination, the processing solutions being poured in and removed through a light-tight trap. There are also *daylight loading* tanks [see Figure 5.13] which will accept the cartridge of exposed film and enable the entire

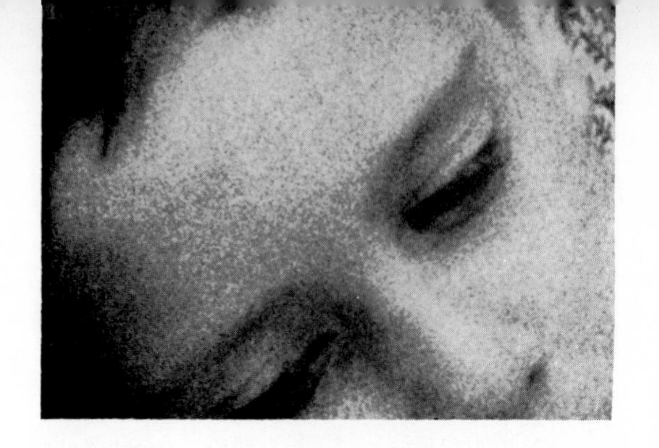

5.14 *This mottling is often mistaken for film graininess; it is actually incipient reticulation caused by too-great a difference in temperature between solutions or between hypo and wash-water.*

operation to be conducted under normal lighting. Some tanks will accept several spiral reels of film, but those accepting more than two reels do not have the light-tight trap for liquids, consequently, the light in the processing room must be extinguished when developer, short stop and hypo are poured into and out of the tank.

The only developing step difficult for the beginner is loading the 35mm film on the spiral reel. The steps in this process are illustrated in Figures 5.12 and 5.13. It is best to practice this several times in normal illumination, using a length of practice film, and then to repeat it once or twice with the practice film in total darkness. The necessary dexterity will be acquired rapidly. The Nikon film should be handled only by the edges, as illustrated. The natural skin oils will act to restrain development if the emulsion side of the film is touched. The tank itself and the reel should be clean and dry before loading.

Before beginning development, all the processing solutions should be at the correct temperature, usually 68F. Most developers will give good results between 65 and 70F, but the developing time must be adjusted if the solutions are not exactly at 68F (or the exact degree indicated in the directions with the particular product or formula). The proper compensation for developing at slightly cooler or warmer temperatures may be found by consulting *Time-Temperature Charts* published by Kodak and some other manufacturers. This 68F temperature provides good developer action without softening the emulsion unduly. At temperatures below 65F, many formulas particularly those with hydroquinone, do not develop properly. Processing may be successfully performed at elevated temperatures when this is unavoidable [see *Tropical and hot weather processing, below*].

Whenever possible, bring the solutions to 68F, however, and be certain that developer, short-stop (or rinse water) and fixer are all at exactly the same temperature. Working either at home or in the laboratory, the bottles containing the solutions may be immersed in a waterbath (tank, sink or bathtub) until they are uniformly warmed or cooled to the correct point. Apply only gentle heat to solutions to avoid chemical decomposition. In the summer, the bottles may be placed in the refrigerator or in an ice-bath if the water from the faucet runs above 68F [see *Film washing* below]. The contents of a larger tank may be cooled by placing ice cubes in a plastic bag or in a rubber glove which is tied tightly and placed in the tank. (Ice should never be added directly, as it will obviously dilute the solution and change its characteristic action.) It is important that the thermometer used be accurate and that it is left in each solution long enough to reach an exact reading. Keep the bulb from direct contact with the sides or bottom of the tank for correct readings.

Using a daylight developing tank, observe the time carefully on a watch or clock, or set the timer, and pour in the developer as quickly as possible. As

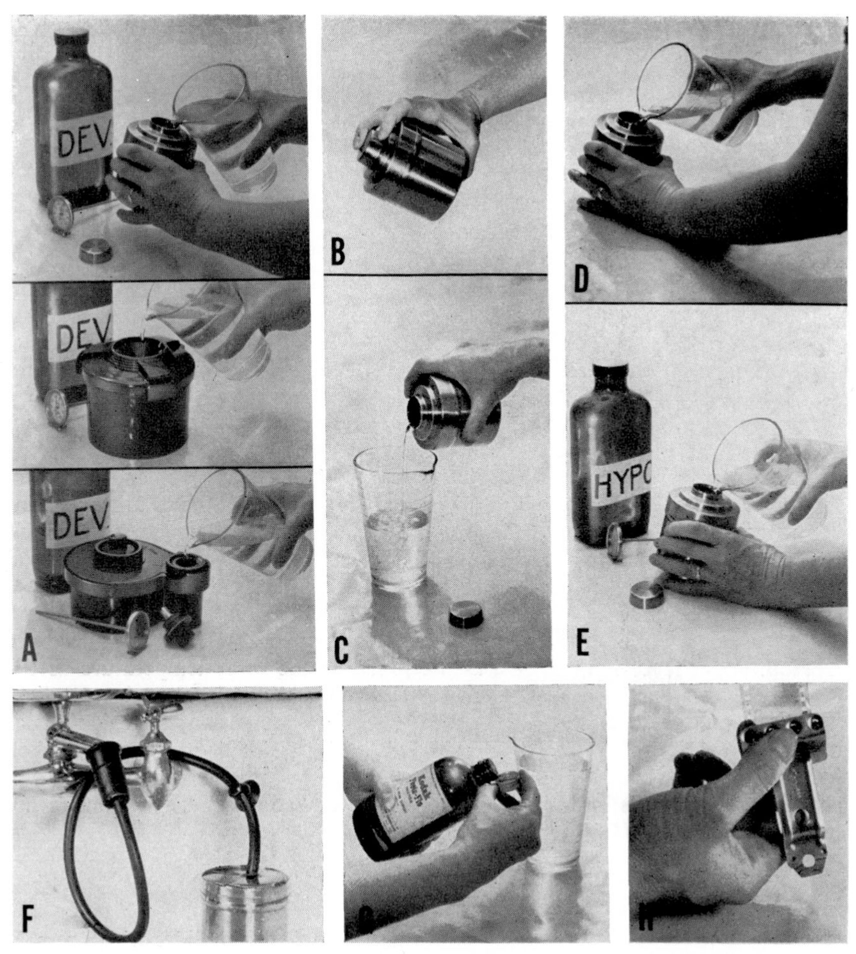

5.15 *Steps in film developing. A shows developer being poured into three types of tanks. B shows method of agitation of common type of wire-reel tank. Other types shown are agitated by revolving reel in tank. C shows solution being rapidly dumped from tank. (Timing should extend from time solution enters until next one goes into tank.) D shows short-stop or intermediate water bath, and E, hypo being poured into tank. All solutions must be kept at the same temperature. Film is then (F) washed, bathed in wetting agent (G) and hung on clip to dry.*

soon as this action is completed, the tank should be agitated to dislodge any potential air-bells clinging to the film and preventing the developer from beginning to penetrate [Figure 5.15]. Thereafter, a regular pattern of agitation should be employed. This is usually a five-second period every 30 seconds unless the developer directions indicate differently. It is very important that this be *intermittent* and *standardized.* A lack of agitation will cause local exhaustion of developer on portions of the film with a strong latent image, leading to loss of contrast, and may also allow the heavier by-products of the reducing action to flow down the film, producing less-developed streaks from the restraining action of these complex by-products.

5.16 *Brown-Forman "Lazy Susan" processor incorporates tanks in light-tight vessel for either black-and-white or color development in full daylight.*

Short-stop

Immediately upon completion of the proper development time, pour the developer out of the tank and re-fill it with either plain water or with short-stop. There is some division of opinion among working photographers as to the desirability of using a short-stop solution, a mildly acidic wash intended to stop the action of the developer quickly and to neutralize the alkaline solution remaining in the film before it enters the (acid) fixer. Short-stop does prolong the life of the fixing bath, which is in any case relatively cheap. However, in some cases, there does seem to be some slight possibility of tiny film blisters from the chemical action of the short-stop. These are important defects on the Nikon negative, and if they occur, a plain water-bath should be used after development and before fixation. Whichever is used, it must be *precisely* the same temperature as the developer. The emulsion is softened by immersion in developer and even slight temperature changes may cause *incipient reticulation:* the faintest beginnings of a wrinkling of the gelatin carrying the developed image. This produces a marked increase in grain clumping which will show up strongly in enlargement. The film should remain in this intermediate bath for about two minutes (the time is not critical) and receive fairly vigorous agitation.

Fixation

The developed Nikon negative still contains the silver halides which remain undeveloped and these must be removed to ensure the permanence of the image. The intermediate bath (short-stop or water) is poured briskly from the tank and discarded, and replaced by the fixer. Again, it is very important that the exact temperature be maintained to prevent the possibility of reticulation, incipient or actually visible. The tank should be frequently agitated during the first two or three minutes and intermittently thereafter. After about 3-5 minutes, the lid of the tank may be opened.

The film as it leaves the short-stop has a creamy, opalescent appearance which rapidly disappears in fresh fixer. The usual duration of proper fixation is twice the time necessary for this creamy appearance to completely disappear. This will vary somewhat depending on the formula employed and upon its age and the amount of previous use. In a usefully fresh sodium thiosulfate fixer, the total immersion time should not exceed about ten minutes. Rapid (ammonium thiosulfate) baths require less time. As the bath approaches the point where it requires nearly twice the original time to clear the film to the point of complete transparency, the bath should be discarded. It is false economy to overwork a fixing solution, and negatives may stain after a few years because of such improper fixation. In laboratories with a steady flow of negatives, some economy and assured complete fixation may be obtained by using two fixing baths. The film is left in the first until it clears and is then transferred to the second to complete the action. When the first bath begins to appreciably slow down in its clearing action, it is discarded and replaced by the second bath and a new second bath provided.

It is important, with the Nikon negative, not to allow it to remain in fixer for a period too much beyond twice the clearing time. The fixer has a slight reducing action and may begin to attack the thin (shadow) areas and remove the metallic silver which forms the image. This is especially true of the rapid-acting ammonium thiosulfate fixing solutions. About 50 percent beyond the twice-clearing time is the maximum limit for leaving films in fixer before this silver reduction begins.

Hypo removal

Films may be immediately transferred from fixer to wash water, but complete removal of the thiosulfate and its fixation by-products is accelerated by an intermediate bath in a hypo eliminator after a brief preliminary wash. A number of such preparations are on the market or a 2 percent solution of Kodalk (2 ounces, 245 grains per gallon of water) may be used for 3 minutes.

The final washing of the developed film removes all but residual traces of the thiosulfate and the fixation by-products. The temperature of the wash water at the start should be as close to 68F as possible, although it may gradually change to a few degrees colder or warmer without harm to the emulsion which has been hardened by the fixing solution. However, the washing rapidly loses efficiency as it approaches 60F and removal of the absorbed chemicals is extremely slow below that temperature. If the water in the washing tank is completely replaced every five minutes, the film should be completely washed in from 20 to 30 minutes.

In the case of severe water shortage, almost complete hypo removal may be obtained by using one of the hypo eliminators followed by soaking the film in at least six changes of water for five minutes each. The volume of water for each of these soakings should be as large as possible under the circumstances. It is also practical to wash films in sea water which is free of foreign matter or organic scum in cases of fresh water shortage. The sea water will dissolve out the processing chemicals remaining in the film emulsion. However, there should be a final washing in fresh water for at least five minutes to remove the salts left by the sea water.

Drying negatives

This is the final stage at which a sharp change in temperature may lead to incipient reticulation and a consequent increase of graininess. Cold air effects the film more than does warm air under these circumstances. The ideal temperature seems to be in the range of 68-85F for preservation of grain and for the least amount of warping of the film base. It is best when the film is removed from wash water to immerse it for about 30 seconds in a dilute wetting agent, a detergent which will prevent the water adhering to the film from forming droplets and the consequent danger of watermarks from uneven drying. The film should be hung from a clip with another at the free end to keep the roll straight. Films should be hung far enough apart so they will not come in contact with each other if they curl or are blown by a breeze. Many photographers give the film a final wipe with a viscose sponge or with their fingers to remove drops but care must be taken that no gritty particles are present which will leave fine scratches on the film. With an efficient wetting agent and a drying temperature in the 70-80F range, films may be lifted from the wetting agent, drained for a moment and hung to dry without further attention.

It is important that the film be hung in a dust-free location. Depending on the temperature and the circulation of the surrounding air, it will be completely dry in from 20 minutes to an hour. Do not touch the film during this period under any circumstances, except the unexposed or fogged leader at the bottom of the strip as it hangs. When this portion is completely dry, the film may be taken down and cut into short sections for filing [see Chapter 6]. If film is left to dry too long beyond this point, it may lose so much moisture that an excessive curl will develop.

Development by Inspection

WHILE DEVELOPMENT by time and temperature is the standard method, some advanced amateurs and many professionals prefer to process by a method which permits an occasional quick observation of the developing silver image. Processing services catering to professionals also find this necessary because of the extreme variations of exposure and subject lighting conditions in the films they handle. If lighting conditions are not particularly abnormal and if films are carefully exposed within normal speed indexes for the particular emulsion, time-temperature methods are ordinarily completely adequate for Nikon negatives. However, when working under available light conditions [see Chapter 8] or when pushing film beyond its normal speed limits it is extremely useful to be able to check the progress of development visually. Since the technique is not difficult to learn by experiment with several practice rolls, many photographers incorporate it into their everyday methods.

Equipment and procedure

It is most convenient to have at least three tanks (either small daylight development tanks used without covers or larger tanks which will accommodate several reels of Nikon film) for developer, rinse water and hypo. In addition, there should be a safelight equipped with a Series 3 Wratten filter or equivalent and a 7 1/2-watt bulb. The best arrangement is to control this light by means of a foot-switch. This eliminates fumbling with a switch with wet fingers and ensures that the light may be promptly extinguished before any danger of fogging.

The general proceedure is identical with that of development by time-temperature in that all solution temperatures should be carefully checked and maintained. The film reel is immersed in developer and properly agitated for from half to three-quarters of the normal recommended development time for that particular film emulsion. At this point, the developer action will have considerably reduced the sensitivity of the emulsion to light (without completely destroying the natural sensitivity of the undeveloped halide crystals). It is now possible to turn on the dim green safe-light for a few seconds in order to examine the film. It is then immediately returned to the developer solution and agitation is continued. A series of such brief glimpses is possible at short intervals until optimum silver deposit in the image is reached. The subsequent processing is identical with that outlined above.

This visual control is an extremely useful technique. The best way to learn how the film should appear at various stages of development is to expose several rolls of film under normal conditions and to use them for practice. It will be possible to work under somewhat stronger illumination (a Wratten 7 safe-light filter) or to take more frequent observations with these trial rolls, if the film is first bathed in a *desensitizing solution* which partially inhibits the response of the halide crystals in the emulsion. This may be either Kodak Desensitizer (Pre-Bath Type) or Ansco Pinakryptol Green. The latter will slow development action somewhat and necessitate about a 50 percent increase over the normal time. The Kodak product does not seem to have a pronounced restraining effect with ordinary film-developer combinations. The film is first soaked in this desensitizer (following directions with the package) and then transferred to developer.

After development has reached the normal half-way point (plus 50 percent with Pinakryptol Green) the safelight may be turned on for periods of no longer than ten seconds at one-minute intervals. Remove the film reel from the developer tank, unroll just enough of it to free the first two or three exposed frames, and turn on the safelight—a foot-switch is shock proof and convenient for this. Hold the film about two feet from the safelight. Do not try to look *through* the film. Instead, look at both emulsion and base sides. At this point, there will probably be a perceptible darkening of the emulsion side, while the base side will show no change. Extinguish the light promptly and continue development. Allow development to proceed the full normal time (plus 50 percent with Pinakryptol Green) for these trial films, inspecting the film at intervals. With these first practice rolls, do not shorten or lengthen the development time no matter what the film seems to look like. This is important, for you will be learning the changing appearance of a film during the course of development. It may seem to become impossibly dense as you watch and there will be a temptation to curtail development. However, the film will gain its proper transparency when the fixer has removed the creamy appearance and the white light is switched on.

When you have learned to judge the normal appearance of the image, the desensitizing bath may be omitted and the inspection periods curtailed to several very brief glimpses (under a Series 3 safelight) after the normal three-quarter development time has elapsed.

Two- developer methods

Some professional photographers and many technicians processing for the profession have worked out quite elaborate methods for increasing the possible control over the density of the image during development by inspection. Most of these are intended to force out a printable image on film which has been somewhat under-exposed on difficult shooting assignments, or to reduce excessive contrast produced by shooting under existing light. For the most part, these "rescue operations" are achieved at the cost of some negative quality in grain, acutance or gradation.

To force development, a darkroom technician may have in addition to a tank of standard developer (frequently D-23 or D-76), tanks containing one or more stronger developers such as Dektol (or D-72), Promicrol, D-76F, a more concentrated solution of the standard developer, or the replenisher solu-

5.17 PHILIP O. STEARNS

Nikon S
250mm f/4 Nikkor

Queen Elizabeth II
Plus-X, 1/60, f/4

tion of his developer. If he observes that the image is not building properly on the film, he will transfer it to a different and stronger solution and observe its progress there. In the most extreme cases, when it is necessary to attain some kind of printable density at no matter what the cost in quality, he may resort to D-11 [not to be confused with Ilford I.D. 11] or even to SD-19, a developer for producing high contrast in X-ray work.

The water-bath in development

The individual worker will use these stronger developers only when he is aware that his film will need forcing, or he will keep a second developer on hand and at the proper temperature as a general rule if much of his work with the Nikon is done under poor illumination. It is excellent practice for everyone, however, to have a tank of clear water at the proper 68F beside the developing tank. This provides a simple and effective way to build up all possible shadow detail without over-developing highlight areas, particularly with negatives exposed in high contrast illumination. If it is noted that the highlights are building density rapidly before any shadow detail seems evident, the film may be removed to the water-bath and allowed to remain for about a minute *without agitation.* The developer which is absorbed in the emulsion will be quickly exhausted in the highlight areas while the developer present in the shadow areas will continue to reduce silver until it, too, is exhausted. (Agitation in the water-bath would tend to dilute the developer rapidly and prevent its continuing action on the shadow detail.) The procedure may continue: one or two minutes in developer alternated with a minute in water until the highlights reach optimum density.

Many professionals and laboratory technicians have worked out individual "recipes" for this control during development by inspection. In photojournalism, for example, it is possible to obtain extreme speeds from the fast films by processing for two minutes in Ethol UFG, followed by a one minute soak in water, then repeating this before the first inspection by safe-light. If this abnormally "normal" development has not built sufficient density, the development-soak sequence may be repeated once more or the film transferred to Dektol for not over one minute. This method is cited as an example rather than as a model for all Nikon users—shortcomings in the quality of news or photojournalist negatives are masked by the process of engraving for publication. It is always best to begin with a standard developer plus a water-bath and to resort to additional developers or more elaborate procedures only in cases of extreme necessity or if the photographer always or frequently uses his Nikon under unusual conditions.

Tropical and Hot Weather Processing

PROCESSING the Nikon negative in the summer and especially in the hot, humid tropics introduces difficulties. As the temperatures rise there is always some danger from excessive swelling of the emulsion, production of fog, rates of development too rapid for accurate control, and accident while handling the softened emulsion during processing and washing. Developers with moderate alkalinity, suitable for 35mm work, may generally be used at temperatures as high as 75F, if the developing time is shortened appropriately. A hardening rinse should be used (SB-5). Several packaged developers, notably Harvey Panthermic 777 and Ethol UFG, [see *Data and Formulas*], may be used at quite elevated temperatures if directions are followed.

As temperatures rise toward 95F, anhydrous sodium sulfate (not sulfite) added to the developer and hardening rinse restrains the swelling of the emulsion. This acts also as a restrainer, and development times will be approximately the same as at 68-70F. Add sulfate at about 75 grams per quart or liter. Detailed directions for adding sulfate to D-76 for various temperatures ranges will be found with that versatile formula in *Data and Formulas*.

A processing system may be set up for the nearly continuous heat and high humidity of the tropics. A developer of relatively low alkalinity such as D-23 should be used to keep emulsion swelling to a minimum. This may be replenished with D-25R at the rate of 3/4 ounce per roll and the solution discarded after processing 100 rolls per gallon. A short-stop is essential to prevent reticulation and rupture of the emulsion. The best choice seems to be SB-5, a highly sulfated acetic acid bath which is free from scumming or the poor keeping qualities of chrome alum hardening short-stops. This bath should be discarded after about 75 rolls have been run through. F-6 is an excellent fixer for hot weather processing and hardening. It does not discharge as much sulfur dioxide in hot, humid, poorly-ventilated rooms as do most other fixers. Fixation requires about 10 to 15 minutes and should be followed by a 30-minute wash.

At 85F, D-23 will produce a desirable gradient (about 0.8) in 6-7 minutes on many common films in the medium and high speed groups. (Note: Tri-X seems more susceptible to damage in warm solutions than most other films and may not respond well at these temperatures.)

6

Printing 35mm Negatives

THE GOAL OF ALL THE TECHNIQUES outlined in the previous chapters is the photographic print. Ideally, it should convey to others what the photographer saw through the Nikon viewfinder. It may not be merely a straight record but an interpretive one: the visual "facts" isolated within the print borders to display design, human inter-relationships or the universe we live in. Printing the Nikon negative is an integral part of the creative process which links the photographer's eye and mind to those of his audience. Most well-known photographers (with only a few conspicuous exceptions) make their own prints or exercise a close and knowledgeable control over the work of the assistant or the laboratory handling their negatives.

The actual printing process can soon become fairly routine—the technical steps outlined in this chapter are almost "second nature" after a few months of experience. From this point on, the photographer begins to master the intangibles of print quality, the tonal range and brilliance which can make a print a beautiful thing in itself, and to master the nuances which make permanent his individual vision through the Nikon.

Characteristics of Photographic Paper

FIRST, let us look at the printing materials themselves. There is a confusing array of photographic paper on the shelves of a well stocked dealer. This choice of material will become more simple if we examine the structure of the papers and the several variables which distinguish between them. Like film, paper consists of a reasonably stable base and a light-sensitive coating. The paper used is designed to have strength when wet, a fair dimensional stability, and to be as free as possible from any chemical impurities which would destroy the developed image during the long potential life of the paper itself.

Photographic paper has several layers. Next to the base on the upper surface, there is usually a coating of barium sulfate in gelatin, called baryta, which smoothes out the minute surface irregularities natural to paper. In turn, this baryta-coated paper may be passed through calendering or embossing rolls which impart a more or less obvious surface texture, ranging from the almost perfectly smooth *glossy,* through *luster* and *matte* to a variety of rougher patterns like *canvas* or *tweed.* Papers are available with a variety of base thickness and many popular kinds are supplied as either single or double weight. The heavier kind is the usual choice of individual photographers, despite its slightly higher cost, because it is easier to handle during processing and less subject to curling and damage in subsequent handling. Single weight prints are often used by laboratories turning out a large volume of photographs or when prints are made for immediate mounting on a stronger base.

There are many special-purpose papers which differ in some respects from the general scheme just outlined. Kodak Ad-Type, for example, has a tough, thin base with no baryta coating and may be folded without cracking. Other products are emulsions coated on cloth, especially translucent paper, clear or translucent film base, or even on thin aluminum sheets.

Paper emulsions

Whatever the base, it is coated with light-sensitive silver halides suspended in gelatin, usually with a final over-coating of clear gelatin which is comparatively hard and acts as an anti-abrasion protection. The paper emulsions are most frequently mixtures of silver chloride and silver bromide with traces of silver iodide. They are not sensitized, [see *Variable grade papers,* below] as are the usual film emulsions, with substances which induce response to the full spectrum of visible light, nor with those additives which make modern films so extremely fast. There are two very loose groupings: the slower emulsions, primarily composed of silver chloride, used for contact printing, and the relatively much faster emulsions which are made with larger proportions of silver bromide. Within each of these groups, there is a considerable range of speeds and even some overlap between the two types. As in the case of film, light (selectively screened by the negative) produces a latent image in the paper emulsion which is subsequently altered by development to the metallic silver positive picture.

In addition to these *developing-out papers,* there are several *printing-out* papers available, the "studio proof" or "red proof" materials used by many portrait photographers. The emulsion on this material will respond to a strong exposure with a visible image of exceptionally long scale and excellent gradation. It is usually left unfixed and may be briefly examined in subdued light before eventually printing out completely to a uniform full tone. However, it is possible to fix this image or to fix and tone it for permanence, although it has been rarely used in this way for the past fifty years or more.

Paper grades

The contrast or gradient of films may be altered over a wide range by varying the exposure-development ratios. Paper, however, permits a much more limited control over contrast during development. The contrast is a function of the particular emulsion used for coating. Some papers are furnished in only one grade, many others are available in a range of contrasts,

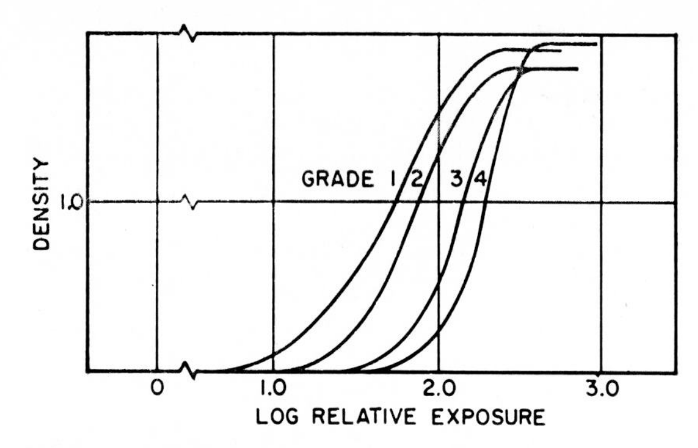

6.1 *Relative contrasts of paper grades (similar to those of Ansco Cykora) are indicated in this chart.*

while a third type combines a high contrast (hard) emulsion with a lower contrast (soft) one to permit a wide range of response.

Graded papers are labeled from 0 (very soft) to 5 (extremely contrasty) with No. 2 representing the "normal" contrast appropriate to recommended negative contrast. Most printing papers are available in three or four grades only, usually in the 1 to 4 range [see Figure 6.1]. Papers marketed by various manufacturers and labeled with the same grade number often differ; two "No. 2" papers may have a "half grade" difference in contrast.

Single grade papers for general photography have a response approximately that of No. 2 in graded papers and have as a general rule slightly more development latitude than do the graded papers. That is, with proper exposure compensation, their development may be extended to produce a somewhat greater contrast without an unpleasant image tone. Their normal contrast may be lowered somewhat also by using a diluted developer for the full normal time. These papers, notably Kodak Opal and Illustrators' Special and Ansco Indiatone, are used by many studios and professionals whose negatives are customarily exposed and developed to a reasonably constant gradient matched to the paper response. Printing papers for special purposes may also be of a single grade, such as those used in document reproduction.

Variable grade papers may be double-coated, with both high and low contrast emulsions, one of which is sensitive to blue-violet light and the second layer dye-sensitized into the green region of the spectrum. Or it may be a mixed single-coated emulsion, with a portion of the silver halides receiving sensitization beyond the blue-violet. The two components of the emulsion may be selectively exposed by the choice of filters. Ilford Multigrade paper, for example, is exposed through one of three filters of deepening shades of yellow which remove progressively larger amounts of the blue-violet light but permit the passage of the green light which affects the harder component of the coating. DuPont Varigram utilizes a series of ten filters, ranging from blue to yellow, with the yellower filters producing a softer gradation. The Kodak Polycontrast paper requires one of a series of seven filters for full contrast control. (Regular CC filters may be used in place of the Polycontrast set: 30Y, 45Y, 25M, 45M, 65M, 85M and No. 34 will produce the range of contrasts from soft to hard.) Multigrade, exposed without a filter, produces an extremely soft result; Varigam and Polycontrast, on the other hand, react to produce an approximately "normal" contrast. These latter two papers are available in two "speeds"—one approximately that of many common enlarging papers, the other about twice as fast and designed for laboratories producing a high volume of printing.

Paper speeds

Printing papers are grouped into two major speed types, those which are fairly slow in response and designed for contact printing, and faster ones intended for projection printing (enlargement). There is a considerable range in the speeds of various projection papers. There is also a speed difference between the several contrast grades of the same kind of paper: the harder (more contrasty) grades become progressively slower. (This speed difference is slightly greater between grades when a bluish fluorescent light source is used than with the yellowish tungsten bulbs.)

Image tone

The metallic silver image of the developed paper may range from a cold bluish black to a warm brownish black. This is primarily a characteristic of the particular paper chosen but the developing formula and the time of development influence the result. The warmer tones result from a finer grain structure in the paper than colder toned images. Kodak Opal and Ansco Indiatone, for example, are warm-toned papers, while Kodabromide and Ansco Jet produce a blue-black image. Polycontrast is also somewhat warmer in tone than Varigam. Softer working developers preserve fine paper grain and warm tones unless the development times are prolonged beyond normal. Somewhat stronger working developers such as the commonly employed Kodak Dektol tend to produce colder tones, particularly when development time exceeds that recommended by the manufacturer for the paper.

Safelights

Printing is ordinarily carried out under filtered illumination bright enough for convenience and for judging the image density and gradation of developed prints but of a color to which the emulsion is not especially sensitive. Ordinary contact and projection papers respond strongly to ultraviolet radiation and to the visible blue-violet (although they have a feeble response to the other colors of visible light). Human vision is excellent in green light, so a yellow-green (OA) safelight filter is usually recommended by U. S. manufacturers. The variable contrast papers, however, are sensitized into this green region of the spectrum so a safelight of an orange-yellow (OC) is necessary. The proper safelight filter for any paper is indicated on the package or on a slip accompanying it and the manufacturer's recommendation should be followed. No stronger bulb than the one for which the particular safelight was designed should be used and undeveloped paper should be protected from all unnecessary exposure even to safelight illumination. (Methods of testing safelight illumination are given later in this chapter under the heading, *Print Quality*.)

Contact Printing

In contact printing, the negative is placed against the paper, film emulsion against paper emulsion, held in firm contact and the exposure made by a light source striking through the base side of the film to reach the paper. Proper contact between film and paper is usually obtained in a contact print box or a print

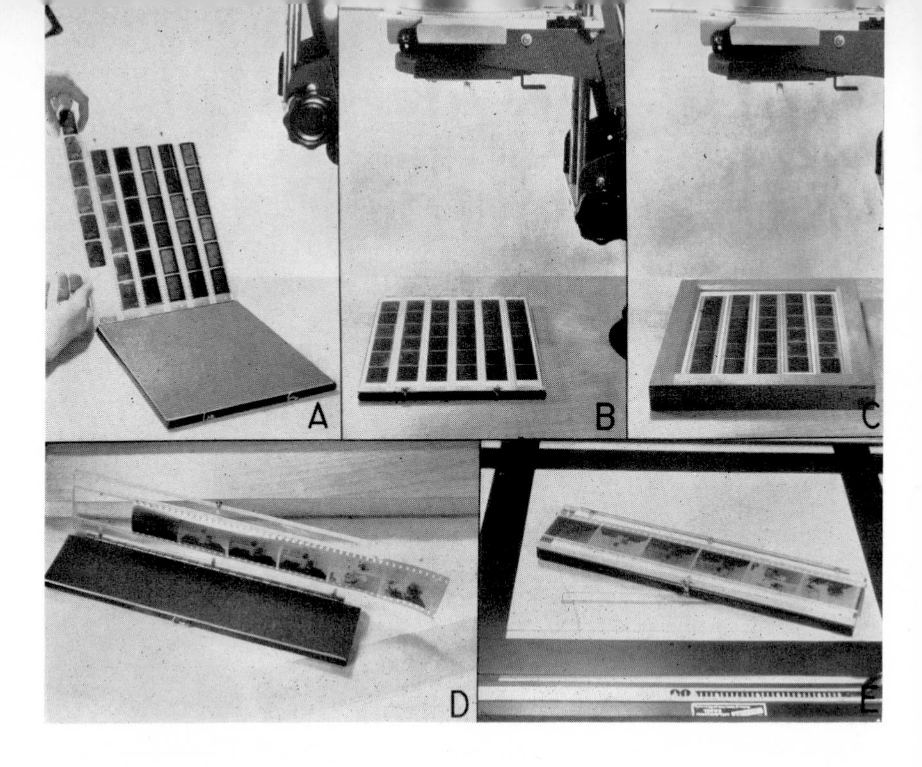

6.2 *Contact proof sheets are conveniently made under the enlarger. A and B show the Multi-Printer with grooves in a plastic plate to accept a full 36-exposure roll. (D and E show the single-strip Multi-Printer). An ordinary 8x10 printing frame, like that in C, may also be used for these contact sheets. (Multi-Printers courtesy M. P. Manufacturing Co.)*

frame. Individual Nikon negatives are rarely contact printed because of their size, but it is common practice to make 8x10-inch *contact proof sheets* of each roll of Nikon negatives.

Usually, the developed film is cut into strips of six frames each. These fit regular negative preservers and may be arranged to cover an 8x10-inch sheet of sensitive paper. Variations of the process are shown in Figures 6. 2, A-D. The slower contact paper may be printed with any available light source, but it is more common to expose these proof sheets in a printing frame placed under the enlarger and to employ the faster projection paper. This also eliminates stocking an extra kind of paper used only for proof. If contact paper is employed, Ad-Type paper is an excellent choice, for it will resist much subsequent handling and reference without cracking. Almost any paper which is on hand may be used, however; papers with a glossy surface will better indicate the precise detail and sharpness of the individual negatives on the proof sheet.

When adequate darkroom facilities are unavailable, printing-out paper (red studio proof) may be used quite satisfactorily. This is exposed under the negative strips in a printing frame, using daylight, a photoflood bulb or some other source rich in ultraviolet. Printing should be allowed to continue for an extra 30-50 percent beyond the time necessary to bring out a well-printed record of the negative. The printed sheet is then immersed for two or three minutes in a solution of sodium thiosulfate (hypo) crystals and water (*not* an acid fixing bath). The strength of this solution is not critical: a heaping tablespoon of these crystals in a quart of water will adequately fix several such proof sheets. This hypo solution will partially bleach the image (hence the necessity for over-printing) to a rather unpleasant brown but give good permanence to the image. The sheet should then be washed for about 30 minutes and dried. The hypo solution will not keep in storage and should be discarded after use.

Frames on the Nikon roll which are thinner or denser than others may be held back or given extra printing time with any of these contact methods with the sheet in a print frame [see section *Dodging* under projection printing, below] or they may be separately printed on smaller slips of paper and stapled in place on the dry proof sheet.

Filing negatives and proofs

Reference numbers, date of exposure and other data may be placed on the edge of the film or on the clear leader at the end of the film if a portion of this latter is included on the proof sheet. India ink applied with a fine point on the emulsion side of the film will work satisfactorily. A red grease (china marking) pencil may be used on the proof sheet before exposure to place a number or date on an area not covered by film. This will block off the printing exposure and the deposited greasy line may be wiped off with the finger during development.

The strips comprising each roll should be carefully filed in negative preservers. These may be of the common glassine type readily available from most dealers. It is wise to avoid using envelopes of paper of unknown quality such as stationery envelopes which may contain sulfur or other compounds which will adversely affect negatives during prolonged storage. Glued seams should be along the edge of any envelopes used, rather than in contact with the surface of the film. Even if no chemical attack occurs from such glued seams, the extra thickness may ultimately cause pressure markings after some years of storage.

Films in their negative preservers may be filed in suitable shallow boxes or file drawers, numbered in such a way that they may be easily found at some later time. All proof sheets should bear corresponding numbers. A search for a particular negative for later printing should be made through these proof sheets, filed by date, by subject-matter, or by some other system appropriate to the needs of the photographer. Those with only an average volume of work will find it satisfactory to keep such proof sheets in loose-leaf binders [See Fig-

6.3 *Contact sheets may be sorted and filed in spring-clamp or loose-leaf binders for convenience in locating the identifying numbers of negatives filed serially.*

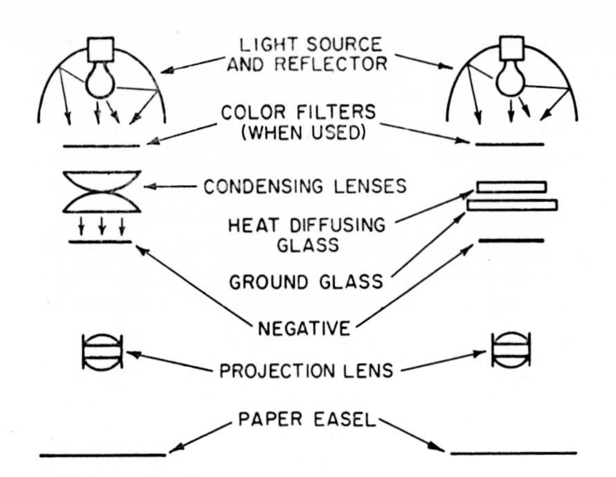

6.4 *The two common types of enlargers are diagrammed here. At left is the condenser type, at right the diffusion type. The latter may also have a fluorescent light source.*

ure 6.3]; a heavy volume of production may call for filing them in folders in standard file cabinets. The easiest method of cross-indexing a large negative collection is duplicate proof sheets.

The amateur may feel that any elaborate filing system is an unnecessary nuisance. However, he will almost certainly find himself very soon with the collection of his Nikon negatives suddenly grown large and unwieldy. From the very first rolls, negatives should be filed by number and corresponding proof sheets held in a file folder or a loose-leaf binder.

Cropping marks and other notations may be made with a china marking pencil directly on these proof sheets (never on the Nikon negative itself) for future reference. These markings may be removed at any time with a solvent such as cigarette lighter fuel and a piece of cleansing tissue.

Projection Printing

THE PRECISION and quality of a correctly exposed and developed Nikon negative demands proper equipment and reasonable care in printing. The superb results the Nikon makes possible should not be destroyed during the production of the final photograph for display or reproduction. The actual steps of projection printing are not at all difficult to learn [see the series Figures 6.5—6.11]. However, the ability to produce the fullest measure of print quality is more slowly acquired through experience and a consistent criticism of one's results.

Enlargers

Enlarger design varies in several important respects. There are two basic types, those with diffusing screen between the light source and the negative and those with a set of plano-convex condensers [see Figure 6.4]. Diffuser enlargers which employ a ground or opal glass produce a picture image of less contrast and slightly less acutance than do condenser enlargers. This has some advantage in obscuring negative grain or scratches and other imperfections on the negative itself, but obtains this advantage at some cost to the great resolution and acutance possible with the Nikon and its Nikkor lenses.

Condenser enlargers preserve the sharpness and quality of image in the Nikon negative, even during extreme enlargement. The difference in picture contrast between the two types may amount to a full paper grade with any given negative. This is a necessary factor to consider when developing the Nikon negative. If negatives, as customarily developed, print correctly on a No. 2 grade of paper under a condenser enlarger, those developed for printing on the same paper grade under a diffusion enlarger will require an additional gamma of about 0.15 which may be obtained by increasing negative development time approximately 50 percent. If the usual run of negatives prints properly on No. 2 paper under a diffusion enlarger, development of those intended for a condenser model should be reduced to approximately 0.15 lower gamma by restraining development by about 25 percent. The slightly shorter development time required by negatives printed in a condenser enlarger tends to hold down grain and preserve full acutance and quality in the Nikon negative.

The condenser enlarger chosen should be one designed specifically for 35mm work or one which has a set of interchangeable condensing lenses matched for use with the 50mm El-Nikkor projection lens.

Light sources incorporated may be either a tungsten bulb or a lamphouse containing some form of fluorescent illumination. Bulbs are more common and furnish a slightly more contrasty source than does tube illumination. Only the bulb for which the enlarger reflector is designed should be used. A bulb which is not in perfect focus in the reflector will lead to uneven illumination across the negative; a bulb which is too strong may lead to excessive heat which will harm the negative. Cold-light (fluorescent) illumination may require somewhat greater negative contrast for proper results and many of these units require an appreciable instant to reach full illumination efficiency, making exact exposure timing slightly more difficult. An important consideration in choosing enlarger illumination is the effective color of the source: if color printing is contemplated it must emit adequate light throughout the visible spectrum.

The enlarger lens should be as sharp and fully corrected as the Nikkor taking lens if negative quality is to be preserved on the print. Lenses specifically designed for the short "throw" to the printing easel will give the best results. Full color correction is necessary if color work is done, and a wide-aperture lens is preferable for an image of full brilliance for accurate focusing.

Other design considerations

The convenience and smoothness of raising and lowering the enlarger head should be noted, as well as its freedom from vibration at all positions. The lamphouse should be adequately ventilated to protect the negative from excessive heat during long exposures, yet there should be no appreciable light leak. The negative carrier should be of the open-frame, glassless type, holding the negative on all four sides without encroaching on the actual image, and permitting the use of strips rather than single frames. The negative carrier should fit firmly without allowing stray light to emerge around it. It is desirable to have some provision for the insertion of a heat-resistant glass and a sandwich of filter foils above the condensers when used for color printing. An enlarger head which swings to a horizontal position or swivels around the baseboard to permit projection onto the floor will allow extreme enlargements to be made. Provision for automatic rather than manual focusing is a convenience, but is expensive and by no means essential.

Other enlarging equipment

A paper easel is necessary to hold the printing paper flat and in the proper position. This may be a simple fixed-size frame, but an adjustable easel with sliding arms to mask off the proper size and proportions of each print is more generally satisfactory. Chemically resistant trays, usually enamelware or hard rubber, to hold processing solutions should be at least an inch larger each way than the paper size used and deep enough so that the sheets may be covered with at least an inch of liquid. Developer and short stop trays 12x15 inches at the bottom are convenient for the usual 8x10 and 11x14 paper sizes. The tray or trays for fixing solution should be somewhat larger and considerably deeper when the processing set-up is permanent or when a reasonably constant volume of work is handled. An accurate thermometer is essential (it may be the same one used for film development) and provision for water-jacket around the processing trays in use is convenient for maintaining correct and uniform temperature. An adequate washing tank and drying facilities may be part of the permanent arrangements or improvised for smaller volumes or occasional work.

Steps in projection printing

The series of pictures, Figures 6.5—6.11, illustrate the sequence of events in printing. The following notes will amplify the picture captions:

A sheet of white paper is placed in the easel (a waste piece the same thickness as the paper to be used), the enlarger is brought into approximate focus and the height of the head adjusted for the required magnification. The image may be projected to fill one of the standard sizes of printing papers (5x7, 8x10, 11x14, etc.) which result in the loss of some negative area; or the whole negative projected within the paper area, with a small "waste" of paper; or a smaller area of the negative may be projected to fill the picture space. It is by no means necessary to confine prints to the exact proportions of standard paper sizes if a more effective picture may be obtained from a rectangle of different dimensions.

After proper cropping is found, the image should be focused as accurately as possible with the projection lens at its widest aperture. A final focusing check should be made on a middle-tone area of fairly uniform tone to assure that the actual grain of the negative is in the sharpest possible focus. This may seem a disadvantage since visible graininess is not a desirable print quality, but it is the only way to assure that the greatest possible image acutance and definition is transferred to the print. This requirement for the most accurate focusing for optimum print quality lies behind the advice given in the previous two chapters (and elsewhere in this Manual) for choosing film, exposure and development for minimal grain patterns. There are several mirror and lens devices to secure perfect focus, but these are not usually necessary with negatives of normal density and an enlarging lens producing a brilliant image like the El-Nikkor f/2.8. The greatest possible acuity is secured with any lens if the aperture is set for an opening larger than 1/100 of the lens-to-paper distance.

6.5 *The first steps in projection printing are to brush dust off (A) or blow it off the negative (B), insert it into the carrier which fits the enuarger (C), and to ad-*

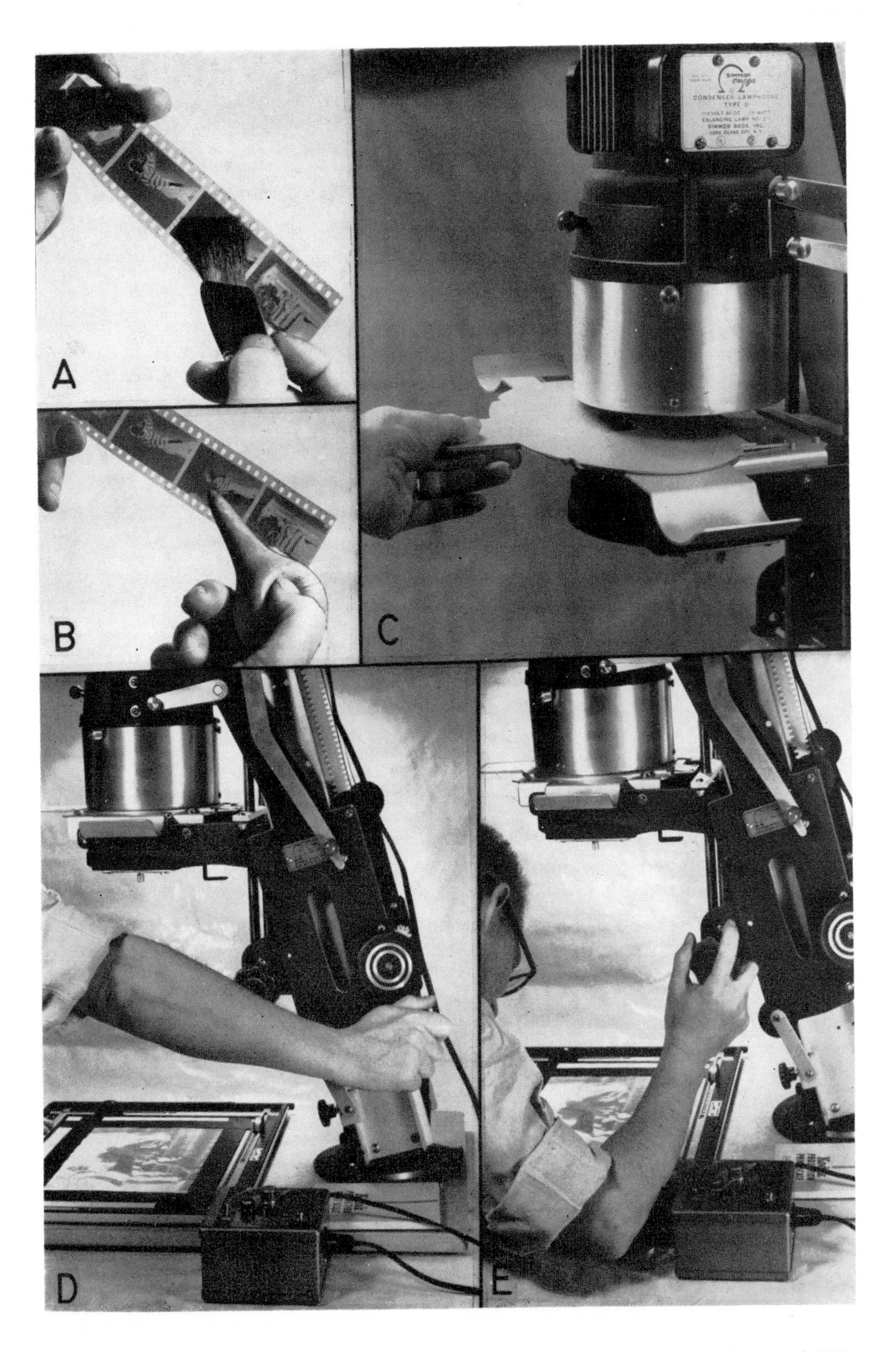

just the height of the enlarger head for the proper size image on the easel (D). Image should be focused very carefully (E). (Simmon Omega D2 enlarger and Saunders easel illustrated).

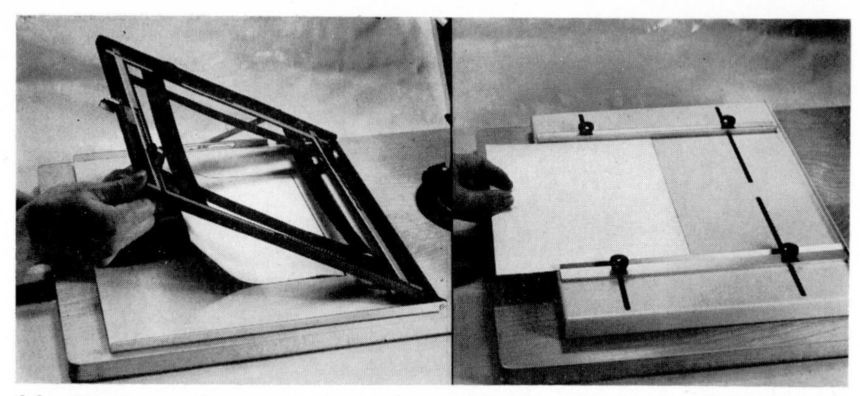

6.6 *Two types of paper easels are those with adjustable borders (left, Saunders "Lifetime") and a newer type, the Saunders adjustable "Bord-r-less" (right), which holds paper without masking off any of the area.*

The test strip

As experience is acquired, it will become possible (with all negatives within a reasonable range of density) to stop down the aperture of the projection lens until the image on the white paper in the easel reaches a level of illumination recognized as proper for a standard printing time, usually from 10-20 seconds.

Before this complete assurance about exposures is acquired, or whenever an unfamiliar paper or developer is employed, or for really critical work, a test-strip will determine proper exposure with minimum waste of time and paper. Cut a strip from the paper to be used, a piece at least two inches wide and eight inches long for 8x10 or 11x14 enlargements; remove the focusing paper from the easel and place the test-strip to include an important area with both highlight and shadow. Cover all but the first inch of the strip with a cardboard and expose for approximately 2 seconds. At 2-second intervals thereafter, uncover successive portions of the strip, giving a final over-all 8-second exposure to the whole strip. Depending on the number of steps, the last portion to be uncovered will have a total exposure of 8 seconds, the previous step, 10 seconds, the next 12 seconds and so on. (With unfamiliar conditions, when exposures cannot be estimated within narrow limits, the steps may be more widely separated, as 4—8—16—32 seconds.)

Paper developer, properly diluted from stock solution, should be ready in the first tray and at the proper temperature. The test-strip is quickly immersed in this developer and the tray tilted from side-to-side and end-to-end "around the clock" for proper agitation. No matter what happens to the test-strip, it must be given precisely the development time recommended for the paper, usually a minimum of 1 1/2–2 minutes. (If it goes completely black or fails to develop a reasonable density, discard it immediately and prepare another at a more appropriate set of times or with the projection lens aperture at a different opening.) At the proper time, immerse the test-strip in short-stop for about 30 seconds with constant agitation, then fix for a minute or two. Rinse in clean water and inspect the strip carefully, preferably under white light. From such a test-strip the proper over-all exposure may be determined as well as whether the proper grade of paper has been chosen. Paper of the proper contrast will show highlight detail without losing shadow detail. If one or the other is lost at all exposures, a softer paper should be used; if all exposures seem too grey and without proper gradation and range a harder paper is indicated. (With variable contrast papers, a change of filters is necessary.) In extreme cases, it may be necessary to manipulate development [see *Processing Prints* below] in order to fit the negative to the paper.

A convenient variation of this test-strip procedure is the use of the Kodak Projection Print Scale [see Figure 6.7] which gives a set of pie-shaped segments of varied density from a single test exposure.

The full-sized print

With a full sheet of paper in the easel, an over-all exposure is given, chosen from one of the steps in the test-strip or an intermediate estimated value. Exposure and development must, of course, be identical with that of the selected step. Accurate timing may be obtained by watching a sweep-second hand, with an electric metronome which clicks off seconds, or with one of the numerous moderately-priced electric timers which may be set for the proper duration and will automatically switch off the enlarger light. These latter will produce the most accurate duplication of timing sequences. Voltage to the enlarger should be as constant as possible: a drop of five volts will require about a 30 percent increase in printing time to compensate. Print development should always remain a constant for best results, so accuracy of exposures is essential.

Until experience builds judgment and confidence, this full print should also be briefly fixed and then examined under white light before being returned to complete fixing. The over-all image density and brilliance should be critically judged. Extreme highlights should have a very slight veil of tone (judged by comparison with the margins which should be completely free of all tone) and there should be some gradation in the deepest important shadow areas. The over-all "depth" (image density) is judged on the basis of the ultimate use of the print. Photographs to be hung under only moderate illumination will require some additional contrast and greater separation of shadow gradations than one intended to be viewed under more intense lighting. At the same time, this first print should be examined for areas which may require more or less local exposure for correct rendition or pictorial effect.

As illustrated in the picture series [Figures 6.8A and B], small areas may be shielded during part of the exposure so less density is built up. Cardboard, cut into a disk or other shape, and mounted on wire is a simple and common tool

6.7 *Test strips to judge proper printing time may be made by uncovering a piece of paper in steps or by using the Kodak Projection Print Scale (right).*

for this. Other areas which require additional exposure for proper density may be printed through a hole in a cardboard or with the rest of the print shielded by the most flexible of all "dodging" tools, the printer's hands. Raising the shielding devices above the easel will result in some edge diffusion to prevent a well-defined and objectionable lighter or darker area from forming—the higher the device the more diffuse the edge. They should also be kept in motion, a constant "tremor" which will blend the edges of the area. The filters may be changed on variable grade paper to give a different contrast to local areas: to bring out highlight or shadow detail, for example.

An area may be *vignetted* by using a cardboard with a hole of an appropriate size over the paper during the complete exposure. This cardboard should be raised about one third of the distance between lens and easel and kept in motion to prevent the formation of a hard edge. Corners or other areas may be *flashed* with a slight fogging exposure by a properly shielded flashlight or by careful exposure of these areas under the enlarger with the negative removed from its carrier. It is easy to over-do this with resulting poor print quality.

Some photographers for some purposes destroy the acuity of the negative image by *diffusion*. There are supplementary lenses which slip over the printing lens to accomplish this. The effect may be obtained in other ways if it is desired, for it is essentially the superimposition of a more or less blurred image over a sharp one. To secure it, leave the enlarger in sharp focus but during part of the exposure interpose a diffusing element such as a crumpled and partly smoothed out piece of Cellophane or a piece of dark nylon stocking material stretched tightly across a ring or a large hole in a sheet of cardboard. Diffusion will degrade print highlights to some extent and reduce over-all contrast.

Processing Prints

ANY OF THE paper developers listed in *Data and Formulas* will give satisfactory results. If in doubt, use the developer recommended by the manufacturer of the paper. While development should always continue for the minimum time suggested by the manufacturer for that particular brand (usually about 1 1/2–3 minutes), some further control over results is possible by manipulation during development. The most common of these is local acceleration of the development action. As the image first appears, decide which areas require additional darkening. Rinse the print quickly in running water and apply a cotton swab saturated with stock (concentrated) developer which has been slightly warmed to about 75F. The most convenient working arrangement for this is a piece of plate glass or an inverted tray set in the sink at an angle. Apply the stock developer for only a few seconds then immediately return the print to the developer tray and resume normal agitation. This process may be repeated two or three times during the development period. Be careful to work quickly to prevent stains from developer oxidation. Maximum effectiveness of this local treatment is obtained if it is begun during the early stages of development; an almost fully developed print will respond very little. (Note: the control methods sometimes observed of rubbing a local area during development or removing the print from the tray to breathe on it, probably relieve the feelings of the printer but have small practical effect on the image. However, a print held for any length of time in the hand may show black spots from developer action accelerated by the warm fingers or palm.)

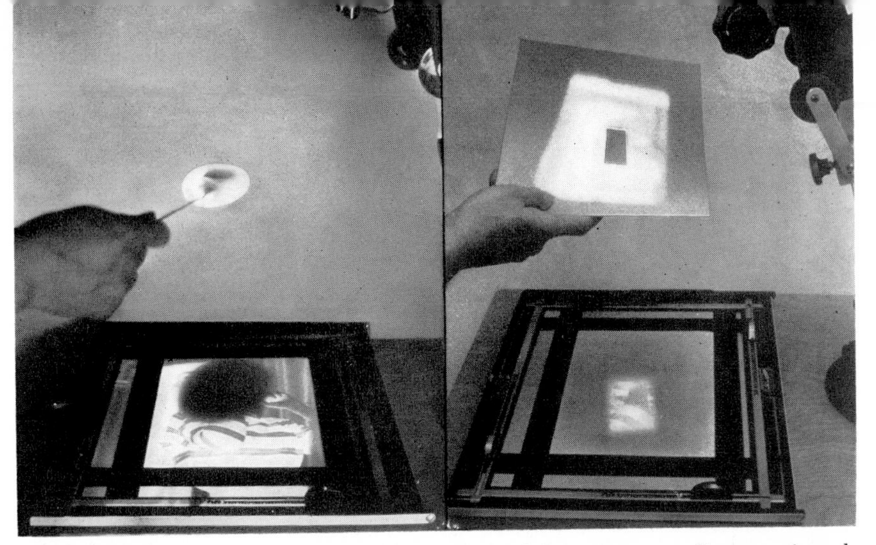

6.8 *Areas of the print may be held back (dodged) by using a small piece of cardboard on a wire or given additional exposure through a hole in a sheet of cardboard. The hands make the most flexible of dodging "tools."*

It is also sometimes possible to develop out fuller detail and slightly longer gradation by using a water bath. Remove the partly developed print from the developer and immerse it in a tray of clear water and allow it to remain there for 30 seconds to a minute without further agitation. If the print has a tendency to float to the surface, immerse it face down but be sure there are no air bubbles trapped beneath it. The print is then returned to developer for the remainder of the normal processing time.

Following development, prints should be placed in short-stop and agitated for about 15 seconds before being transferred to the fixing solution. Prints should not be allowed to soak in short stop or they may develop mottle or other stains.

Prints should be fixed from 5 to 10 minutes in a sodium thiosulfate acid hardening fixing both (or a somewhat shorter time in an ammonium thiosulfate bath) with occasional agitation to bring them into contact with fresh solution and to prevent prints from stacking up and fixing unevenly. In a permanent processing set-up, a two-bath fixer (usually sodium thiosulfate) is desirable. It will prolong the life of fixing baths to fix prints from 3-5 minutes in the first, then a similar time in the second one. After about 200 8x10-inch prints (or equivalent surface area) per gallon have been treated in the two baths, discard the first and substitute the second and mix a replacement. This may be continued until an area equivalent to 1000 8x10-inch prints has been fixed, when both baths should be simultaneously discarded. In any case, the tray life of fixing baths should not substantially exceed a week for best results. (Note: fixer which has been used with film should never be used with paper or stains will result.)

Prints should not remain in fixer for more than 10 minutes when the solution is fresh (as it should properly be). After this period the solution will begin to bleach fine highlight detail; there may be a partial sulfiding of the image, particularly on warm-toned papers; and the paper base will soak up fixer and processing by-products difficult to remove by normal subsequent washing.

Removal of all residual chemicals is important for print preservation. It is comparatively easy to remove most of these from the emulsion but they cling more tenaciously in the base. Washing in running water requires at least one full hour for reasonable print permanence. If the water temperature is below

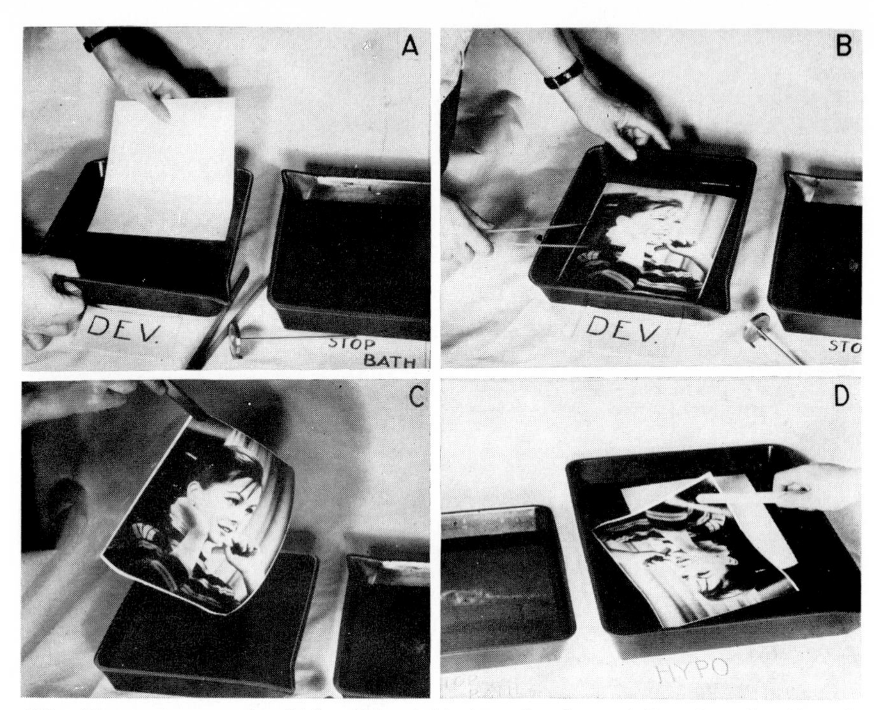

6.9 *Exposed paper should be slid quickly into developer (A), agitated uniformly and constantly (B), and drained for a few seconds (C), before being transferred to short stop and then into hypo (D).*

65F the time must be considerably prolonged; water which is warmer will very slightly accelerate the removal rate but may soften the emulsion dangerously above 70F. The time may be shortened, however, and more importantly the efficiency of removal increased by treatment before and after washing. Following the fixing bath, rinse the print in running water for a minute or two, then place in a tray containing a 2 percent solution (2 oz., 245 grains per gallon of water) of Kodak Balanced Alkali (Kodalk) and agitate continuously for two minutes, then wash for a half hour. This treatment improves image stability and lessens any danger of staining during subsequent toning if this is used. A gallon of this dilute alkali will treat 100 double weight 8x10-inch prints or 150 single weight. There are several proprietary products on the market intended for this neutralization treatment or a one percent solution of sodium carbonate of a two percent solution of tribasic sodium phosphate may also be used.

Ferricyaniding

Many professional photographers and other expert printers employ a dilute solution of Farmer's Reducer (potassium ferricyanide—sodium thiosulfate) for over-all or local print reduction following thorough washing. Mix the A and B solutions of the R-4a formula in the *Data* section for a working solution the light lemon color of a K2 filter. Apply with a cotton swab or small piece of cotton on the end of a toothpick for small areas. (Do not use a brush: the ferricyanide will destroy bristles and react badly with the metal ferrule.) Work under a good light, preferably with the print on a piece of plate glass or an inverted tray placed flat in a sink and convenient to a hose with which to flood the print with water.

Wipe the surface of the print free of standing drops of water and apply the ferricyanide solution to the area to be reduced. Do not use so much that it will flow into surrounding areas. Allow it to work for a few seconds, then arrest the action with an application of solution B and flush the print with water. Be careful that this stream of water does not spread the ferricyanide but washes it away completely. Repeat the action cautiously until enough density has been removed. Wash print thoroughly following this treatment.

Professionals, or those with enough experience, usually use a solution of plain potassium ferricyanide and immerse the print in the fixing bath (not an ammonium thiosulfate formula) to arrest the action. This requires more judgment of the reaction speed so the bleaching action is not carried too far.

This somewhat drastic print retouching method has "saved" many prints from Nikon negatives exposed under dim and contrasty lighting. By printing for correct highlight detail and allowing the shadows to go very dark (while preserving a minimum of gradation to serve as a matrix for the reducing action) a more normal density range and gradation may be "built back" into the print.

Print drying

There are a variety of drying units on the market, many of them employing heat for more rapid results. Lacking these, a satisfactory method for all prints is to wipe them free of surface water and to stack them between the special chemically inert blotters sold for this purpose. After they have been in this stack for a few minutes, transfer them to fresh blotters and hold them under light pressure until completely dry. One of the several print flattening solutions may be used to condition the gelatin so it will resist curling under lowered relative humidity.

Glossy paper will give an agreeable surface if dried between blotters. However, if it is dried under pressure in contact with a polished metal (ferrotype) plate, the surface structure of the gelatin will be altered to produce an extremely smooth surface. For proper results, the gelatin should not be unduly swollen or disrupted at any stage of processing, hardening should be complete and uniform and washing adequate. Despite precautions, perfect ferrotyping may

6.10 *Local reduction of areas which are too dark is accomplished with ferricyanide, applied with small wads of cotton held in the fingers or wrapped around a small stick. (Ready-made "Q-Tips" are shown). See text and also* Data and Formulas *section.*

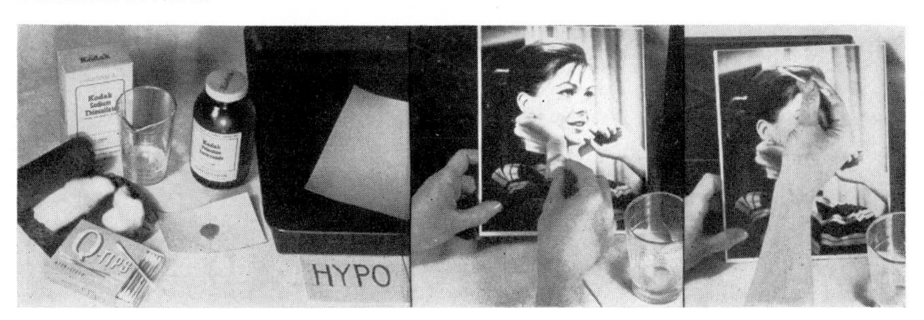

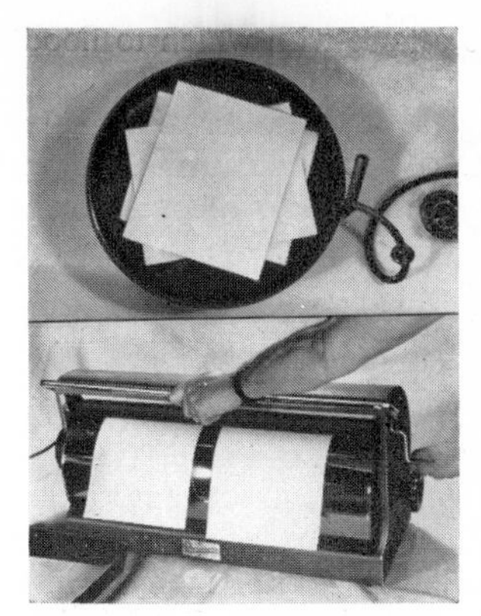
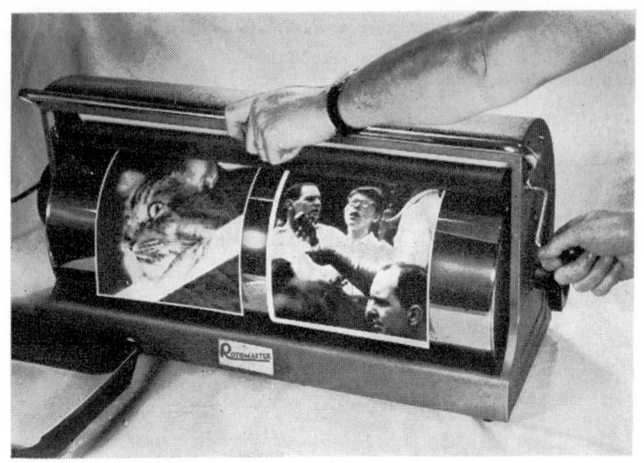

6.11 *Prints should be thoroughly washed (upper left), preferably in a swift-moving current. A small drum-type dryer such as this Lott Rotomaster handles ferrotyping with prints faced toward the chromium drum (left) or matte prints face up toward the canvas belt (right).*

sometimes be difficult for reasons which remain obscure. Prints to be ferrotyped should be fixed between five and 10 minutes in fresh fixing bath, go through the two percent Kodalk solution and be washed for at least an hour. Before ferrotyping, soak them in a conditioning solution (such as six ounces of glycerin and an eighth ounce of wetting agent to a gallon of water) for ten to 15 minutes. Drain prints briefly and place immediately in contact with the ferrotype plate, cover with a blotter and apply a print roller with very heavy pressure. Allow them to sit at room temperature for five to minutes before placing the plate on a dryer. Keep the dryer apron taut until the print is thoroughly dry (the faint crackling noises completely cease).

Print quality

A properly exposed and developed Nikon negative will produce enlargements of beautiful quality. Many amateurs seem to fail to secure this ultimate quality simply because they are not familiar with the appearance of an excellent print: they have not had the opportunity to form an adequate standard against which to judge their own work. Photographs reproduced in magazines or even in well-printed books cannot reveal the full scale and subtle gradations of prints made by an expert (amateur or professional) from a Nikon negative.

The keys to this excellence are the choice of the correct contrast grade of paper and an exposure balanced to a full development time. It is important that all processing solutions be fresh, free of chemical contamination and at the proper temperature. Defective safelighting may be the direct cause of much poor print appearance. Safelight filters will fail with age and from overheating. Paper should be removed from its light-tight container a single sheet at a time; if prints are developed in batches, the undeveloped sheets should be kept in a closed box until processed. The usual test for safelight efficiency is to place a sheet of sensitized paper face up on the bench or paper easel with half of it covered by cardboard. Leave it for about twice the time paper is usually left unprotected during usual handling and then give normal development. There should be no perceptible veil on the half which was exposed to the safelight. A more sensitive test for quality degradation from a safelight is to turn it off completely and extract a single sheet of paper and expose a print from a negative with considerable delicate highlight detail. Then cover half of this sheet of paper with a piece of cardboard and switch on the safelight. Leave it for several minutes, then develop normally. Veiled or degraded highlights in the unprotected half will reveal a fogging effect below exposure threshold but strong enough to affect quality.

Stray light leaks from the enlarger lamphouse or the negative carrier are also suspect. The negative carrier should permit no light to pass around the edges of the negative. If a carrier larger than 35mm is used, all the surplus area must be completely masked off. Dirty lenses are also a cause of poor print quality. The enlarger should be periodically examined and dust and grease gently removed from the upper surface of the lens. The surfaces of the condensers and other interior surfaces must be regularly cleaned.

If possible, all weighing and mixing of chemicals should be done outside the darkroom. Chemical dust settling on paper surfaces will produce a variety of spotting effects.

Even the most efficient housekeeping will fail to eliminate every trace of dust. The proof of this will be several tiny white spots on the finished prints. A few of these are easily dealt with; a print speckled with tiny unexposed spots is better reprinted. Sets of water-colors are sold with which image color may be matched and a tiny fleck of paint applied over each spot. A soft pencil will cover on matte-surfaced papers. However, these pigments rest on the surface of the print and may be accidentally removed or be visible when the print is viewed by glancing light. Much more satisfactory are dyes which actually penetrate into the gelatin coating, such as the Spotone set. Dyes are mixed to match the image color and applied with the very fine point of a 00 sable brush. They are permanent and unfading but may be removed intentionally by re-washing the print after a short soaking in a two percent Kodalk solution. With experience, even white, hairline streaks and fairly large areas can be covered with Spotone quickly and invisibly. Dye sets are available for spotting glossy paper which may then be re-ferrotyped. Small black specks on a print (from tiny negative pinholes) may be removed with the iodine-thiocarbamide bleach listed in *Data and Formulas.*

Print mounting

Prints which are to be handled or displayed are best mounted on stiff cardboard for protection against creasing or surface damage. They may be fastened to a somewhat larger white or cream board such as the familiar 16x20-inch salon mounts, or to some other heavy mounting board and then trimmed down to the actual picture image, a practice known as "flush mounting." Only adhesives specifically sold for photographic use should be employed for this, lest chemical impurities later attack the gelatin or the image. The old flour paste used for wall-paper is satisfactory if it is "flavored" with formaldehyde to resist insect attack. Rubber cement should never be used; over the years it will discolor both mount and print.

The most satisfactory adhesives are the dry-mounting tissues: thin paper impregnated with shellac or other materials which will melt under heat and bond to both paper base and mount. These sheets are readily available in types designed for regular dry-mounting presses or for application with a regular household iron. These tissues also serve to isolate the print base from any future chemical attack from the back.

7

Color Films: Processing and Printing

THE DIRECT RECORDING OF COLOR IN THE CAMERA has been a challenge to ingenious amateurs and to photographic manufacturers ever since the birth of photography. The story of the attempts to solve it and the diversity of methods by which two and three-color records are made possible with a single camera exposure is, unfortunately, too long and heavy with detail even to outline here. The most important single advance in our time, one which multiplied the possibilities of the 35mm camera——and multiplied the number of 35mm users as well——was the introduction of Kodachrome in 1935. This process was based on the work of two amateur photographers, Mannes and Godowsky, who obtained a series of color process patents before and after joining the Eastman Kodak research staff. A little later, the next major forward stride was the appearance of Ansco Color Reversible Film which could be developed with simple equipment and techniques as a positive transparency. Other films with similar characteristics were soon introduced throughout the world. Now, we are awaiting the imminent release of 35mm film cartridges which will produce a *negative* color image with its inherently greater exposure latitude and range of color control during printing.

Structure of Color Films

MOST COLOR films available today for use in the Nikon are *reversal* films: after processing, they become positive transparencies. When viewed or projected by transmitted light, the dye image reproduces a similar color effect in the eye as did the original scene.

Positive transparency films receive three separate coatings of light-sensitive emulsion basically similar in structure and response to that on black-and-white films. These color materials are termed *integral tripacks.* Typically, the top layer which is struck first by the light entering the Nikon is blue-sensitive;

that is, it has not been sensitized to light of other portions of the spectrum [see Chapter 5]. Below this layer is an extremely thin layer of gelatin containing a yellow dye substance which filters out blue light but permits the passage of the green and red components of white light. The two coatings of silver halide emulsion below this filter layer are, like all such emulsions, sensitive to the ultraviolet-blue portion of the spectrum and are treated to respond respectively to green and red light which reaches them. Since the yellow filter layer masks off most of the ultraviolet and blue radiation, the middle layer responds only to the green and the bottom layer only to red. Thus, the image formed in the Nikon of a colored scene is effectively separated into three images representing the relative amounts of blue, green and red light present at each point. There is also typically an anti-halation layer to prevent light from striking through the base of the film and being reflected back to degrade the image, and an extremely thin layer of clear gelatin to separate the green-sensitive and red-sensitive layers. [See Figure 7.1.]

The multiple-layer structure of color film tends to produce more diffusion of the light than there is in single-layer black-and-white films with an accompanying loss of acutance. Techniques of thin-emulsion preparation and coating are used to hold the layers to minimum practicable thickness. The current Ektachrome (Process E-2), for example, is more thinly coated than it was when originally introduced with a consequently much improved acutance; the layers are very rich in silver halides, however, producing better speed and a long, even gradient.

Obviously, the preparation of such an integral tripack is much more complicated than the manufacture of black-and-white negative films. Each of these color recording layers is only about 0.0003-inch thick in the typical transparency films and variations of only 4-5 percent will affect their sensitivity and response to a point which will imbalance their accuracy in forming a color image to an appreciable extent. Consequently, each of these emulsion coatings must be controlled during manufacture to a tolerance of plus or minus *15 millionths* of an inch. This is now accomplished so successfully, however, that almost every package of film purchased, providing it has had proper storage and is reasonably fresh, will give a color response which is accurate enough for amateur photography, although some filter correction may be required for the most critical professional use.

Color Balance

VARIOUS SOURCES of illumination differ considerably in the relative amounts of blue, green and red light which they contain. Within extremely wide limits, the human eye adapts its response to perceive both the yellow light of tungsten bulbs (or even of candle-light) and the relatively much bluer illumination of open shade out-of-doors as neutral or "white." The difference between even such extremes is usually only apparent when the two are simultaneously available for comparison: as, for example, tungsten light within a deep room in contrast to the light visible through a window. Even then we may not notice this difference unless we consciously look for it.

The layers of the color film, however, must be constructed to produce a balanced record with equal contrasts and equal points of minimum and maximum response. The color of the light by which the final transparency is

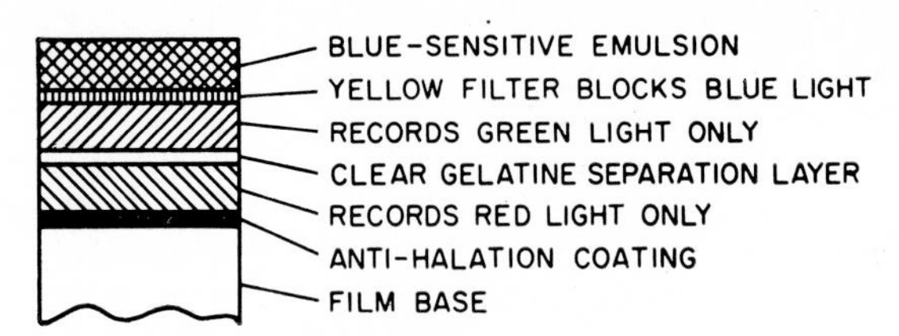

7.1 *The diagram above shows the structure of a typical reversal color film material with its three layers of emulsion, each sensitive to one primary color.*

examined or projected introduces another variable here; a transparency illuminator balanced to 4000K with tungsten or General Electric Photocolor Fluorescent lamps is the accepted standard. The only practical solution for this problem is to select several average and commonly encountered sources of illumination and to construct tripacks balanced to the relative amounts of blue, green and red light produced by these sources.

The color films currently available for use in the Nikon are those balanced for a mixture of direct sunlight and blue reflected skylight such as might occur at noon in the summer within the Temperate Zones *(Daylight Type);* those balanced for the common kinds of clear 3800K flash-bulbs *(Type F);* and film balanced for tungsten illumination at 3400K *(Type A).*

Color temperatures

These film types are often labeled as designed for a particular *color temperature,* such as the 3400K illumination for Professional *(Type A)* Kodachrome. This is a somewhat misleading term, however, and should be avoided whenever possible. It does provide a convenient shorthand for color discussion and is sometimes useful if its limitations are understood. It is derived from the familiar phenomenon that when a bar of iron, for example, is heated it will begin to glow red, then yellow and eventually an intense blue-white as the temperature rises. If a "black body," that is, one which is completely nonreflective, is heated, it will similarly change color as the temperature rises. The color which it emits may be scaled in degrees Kelvin, from the "low temperature" reds through the yellows to the "high temperature" blues. In practice, this becomes a somewhat less than reliable guide: sources of illumination may have similar color temperatures without necessarily having identical distributions of energy in the three blue, green and red areas of the spectrum to which color films respond. Some fluorescent bulbs, to take the most obvious instance, may appear as blue as (6000K) daylight although their spectral distribution is very different and not matched to the response of Daylight Type color films.

Accuracy of color recording

Each of the three sensitive layers of Ektachrome and Anscochrome contains a particular dye coupler. These, upon reversal and redevelopment, produce a positive yellow image in the top, blue-sensitive coating; a positive magenta image in the middle, green-sensitive coating; and a cyan image in the bottom, red-sensitive layer. (Kodachrome does not have the dye couplers incorporated in the layers and must be developed by a more complicated process impossible without elaborate equipment.)

When viewed by transmitted light or projected, the dye images in each of the layers operate as selective filters to block off segments of white light to produce the colored image of the original scene. Because of this filtering action, the yellow, magenta and cyan are termed *subtractive primaries.* [See Figure 7.2.]

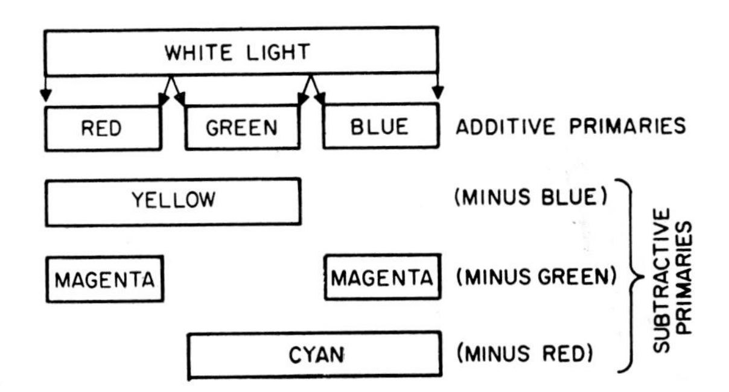

7.2 *The diagram above shows how white light may be divided into the three (additive) primaries, and how the remaining portions of the spectrum, when these primaries are removed, become the subtractive primary colors.*

The colors of nature result from selective absorption of the light which strikes them; part of the spectrum is absorbed and the remainder is reflected to reach the eye. The response within the eye is an extremely complex one and is not yet thoroughly understood as a physiological process. It is obvious, however, that very rapid and minute electro-chemical changes occur in the cells of the retina and produce impulses transmitted by the bundle of optical nerve fibres to the brain. The process is further complicated by the fact that much of the visual discrimination is a function of the brain itself. This seems to account for our automatic "adjustment" to illumination of an extremely wide range of different colors and intensities within which tones and colors are perceived in their correct relative values. In ordinary discussion the somewhat over-simplified assumption is usually made that the visual process responds to three wide bands of primary colors, the relative intensities of which produce the psychological phenomena of color perception.

The superimposed dye images of color transparencies, therefore, can be assumed to filter selectively the transmitted light by which they are viewed and to stimulate correspondingly the tri-color nerve response and the consequent perception of color in the brain. Needless to add, the exact wave-lengths of light as filtered by the transparency are not necessarily identical with those wave lengths reflected to the eye by the original scene. The visual response, however, is comparable whenever there is a reasonably complete (white light) spectrum emitted by the viewing light and the eye is adjusted (accommodated) to this illumination. Color film is in no precise sense ever "accurate," but it may produce a perception which is readily accepted as identical with the perception of the original scene.

This is true, however, only when the film is exposed correctly under illumination of the spectral composition to which the three emulsion layers are balanced and when it has received subsequent correct development. If the scene illumination is different in color balance, the film response may sometimes be held to reasonable correctness by an appropriate filter over the Nikkor lens at the time of exposure.

Color Filters for the Nikon

FILTERS FOR use with black-and-white photography are usually of strong color, many transmitting a substantial percentage of a part of the white light and comparatively little of the rest of the spectrum. Filters for use with color film are, on the contrary, usually pale in color and modify the transmitted light by only the amount necessary to affect the response of one or two of the color layers to any significant degree. These filters may be classified into three general groups, the *color conversion,* the *light balancing* filters and the *color compensating* filters. There are, in addition, a few special purpose filters. All of these are used over the Nikkor lens in the lens shade or filter ring provided or some other suitable holder.

Color conversion and light balancing filters

These are the filters for use when it is necessary to expose color film of one type under illumination of the incorrect color balance. For example, Kodak Ektachrome, Daylight Type, may be exposed by (3400K) photofloods if an 80B filter is employed; Ektachrome Type F would require an 82A with the same photofloods. (*Note:* Wratten filter nomenclature is generally accepted as standard. Other manufacturers employ other identifying terminology to refer to filters of similar transmittance characteristics but frequently add the Wratten designation in parenthesis.) It is generally best to use color films of the correct type under various kinds of illumination whenever this is possible. Often a completely satisfactory conversion is either difficult or the filter strength required cuts seriously into film speed.

Conversion filters for color films are listed in the chart in *Data and Formulas.* These recommendations change from time to time with alterations and improvements in films and the current recommendations should be checked with your dealer or with the manufacturer. The 82 series (bluish) and 81 series (yellowish) light balancing filters may be employed to raise or lower the effective color temperature of light passed by the Nikkor lens to the film. A table of these filters will also be found in *Data and Formulas.*

Color compensating filters

The color compensating (CC) filters are available in six densities in each of six colors: red, green and blue, and yellow, magenta and cyan. They may be used singly or in combination to effect almost any necessary correction and are particularly useful for making the slight but significant changes required to compensate for the small difference in color balance between emulsion batches [see *Critical Standards,* below], for correcting color casts from lamp reflector surfaces and other factors which influence the over-all hue of the result. The amateur will normally find little use for these in shooting, but they are essential for control in direct color printing.

In any application, it is best to use as few of these filters at any one time as are essential to the purpose. Each additional filter tends slightly to increase diffusion and to destroy the exceptional image acuity of Nikkor lenses. A table of the color compensating filters and the required filter factors for each will be found in *Data and Formulas,* together with condensed directions to prevent inefficient filter combinations which introduce needless neutral density.

Special purpose filters

The skylight (1A), ultraviolet and polarizing filters were described in Chapter 3 (page 74). In addition to these, there are "sharp-cutting" filters which are used to isolate a single band of the tri-color response for several processes of color printing [see below].

Critical Standards

AMATEURS, and in fact many professionals, will find that they can obtain satisfactory results with the Nikon by loading it with fresh color film and exposing with reasonable care in accordance with the suggestions provided by the manufacturer of the color film. The Nikon, however, is a precision instrument and suitable for the most exacting professional and scientific employment. The precision worker will find it necessary to compensate more exactly for the many variables of color materials as exposed in the Nikon and as subsequently processed. Frequently, he must work out methods appropriate to his individual working conditions. The very short review which follows indicates a few of the factors which must be considered in critical color work. [See also Chapters 8, 9 and 11.] Even the serious amateur will benefit from becoming aware of these problems of accurate control and may find that his own work with the Nikon will improve with this awareness.

Manufacturing variations

Small variations in the speed of black-and-white films from batch to batch will pass unnoticed in practice. Much smaller deviations in color work become quite apparent to the critical eye: a few millionths of an inch difference in thickness of one or more of the sensitive coatings on reversal color film will appreciably disbalance the color record to trained inspection although the majority of photographers may never notice it. These small changes from one emulsion batch coating to another are masked in average practice by small exposure errors, delays before development, processing variations and similar factors. It is only when these are under extremely accurate control that the differences in speed and color balance between film batches can be isolated and, in turn, controlled. Actually, it is quite astonishing that manufacturing technology is as precise as it is, considering the complex structure of color films and their volume production. Kodak, for example, tests each coating run and only releases for sale Ektachrome which falls within one-half stop of its rated speed and which has a color response which may be restored to its intended balance by the use of the weak (up to .10 density) color correction filters. (These .10 density CC filters require an exposure increase of 1/3 stop.)

It is common practice among professionals and organizations such as magazines with staff photographers to purchase color films in large lots of the same emulsion number and to run several test rolls under actual operating conditions to determine the precise batch speed within a fraction of a stop, as well as the proper CC filtering for accurate balance. While this is not possible for those with limited film consumption, it is an excellent practice even for the amateur to purchase all the color film he requires for a vacation or other trip at one time and of the same emulsion number. Even without accurate correction, this will ensure a matched color balance on all his slides. An audience will accommodate to a reasonable color shift throughout a projected slide show providing it remains constant throughout. Before exposing a batch of any color film, however, a critically examined test roll will provide enough correction data for average shooting. View the slides either on a standard illuminator or by projection. If color shift is apparent or suspected, hold the weak CC filters between eye and slide to determine which improve the over-all appearance and select one for use with that film batch.

Effects of lighting contrast

There is a considerable difference between the color saturation (brilliance) of films exposed under direct illumination, natural and artificial, and those exposed by diffused light. Colors are softer, more pastel, when the Nikon is used in open shade or on an overcast day or when the illumination (flash or flood) is reflected from a suitable white surface before reaching the subject or it is passed through a white spun-glass or other diffuser fastened over the lamp reflector. Subject colors which are already in the pastel range usually give more pleasing results under direct illumination; bright, strong colors usually register well under diffused light.

A very slight difference in color saturation in transparencies is even evident when a dull, matte-surfaced flash reflector is substituted for a bright, highly polished one. Incidentally, as subject contrasts are reduced under diffused illumination, there is a consequent gain in the exposure latitude of films and a wider range of subject tones may be compressed into the useful recording range of the color material.

Surroundings and color casts

An expanse of green lawn, a colored wall indoors or out, and other strong areas of color will exercise an influence on color rendition. The reflected light from these surfaces will be evident in the developed transparency, particularly in the shadows, although the subtle and automatic accommodation of the human eye may suppress perception of this unwanted color as the scene is viewed. Vision must be trained to this awareness.

Even less obvious at the moment of exposure, but quite apparent in the transparency, is the color of the internal surface of lamp reflectors. Daylight Type color films, for example, may exhibit a somewhat warm yellowish cast over-all even when exposed by the bluish light of electronic flash discharge lamps if the reflectors were manufactured by a process which permits them to yellow as they age. This surface change may be difficult to detect by inspection but is a probable culprit if transparencies run consistently too warm in color. Other poorly-made reflectors may create greenish or other undesirable color casts.

Reciprocity-rule failure in color

Like any film depending on the response to light of silver halide crystals, image density in color emulsions tends to fall off under conditions of either prolonged, low-intensity exposures or extremely brief exposures to intensely brilliant light. Since color balance depends upon the nearly equal response of three separate emulsion layers, there may often be some color shifts as well as a loss of film speed under these exceptional exposure conditions. Electronic flash units in common use have a duration of approximately 1/500 to 1/2000 second and higher-powered units produce a flash which may be considerably shorter. Daylight Type color films may require a minor change in guide number with the small, portable units and a somewhat greater change with studio units. This should be determined by practical test under working conditions. At the other end of the time-scale, exposures running into several seconds or even minutes necessitate a speed correction factor which may extend to five or six times the meter reading. Again, practical tests are necessary. Particularly at the lower illumination intensities, color correction filters are usually necessary. Some color films (such as Anscochrome) have a reasonably correct response over a 1/500 to 4 second (2000:1) exposure range, but tests under actual exposure conditions are still desirable.

Increasing film speed indexes

The effective film indexes of Anscochrome, Super Anscochrome and Ektachrome may be somewhat increased with little change in color balance, and even substantially increased whenever speed is more important than the best color rendition. These higher Exposure Indexes require special processing. [See below.] Up-to-date recommendations should be obtained from your dealer or directly from the manufacturer. Color compensating filters will assist in good color rendition at accelerated speeds, although the filter factors tend, of course, partially to negate the higher speed index.

Other critical factors

Precise color control by the use of filters and careful lighting and exposure techniques is meaningless until the end-point is known: the use for which the transparency is intended. While a color slide with rich colors and full detail in every important subject area from shadow to highlight is obviously desirable under any circumstances, slight modifications may improve its utility as an intermediate record. A 35mm slide intended for projection with non-theatrical (home) equipment will benefit from exposure times in the Nikon which are very slightly greater than the meter reading (1/3 to 1/2 stop) to produce a transparency just short of the stage where over-exposure would bleach out important detail in the highlights. A transparency primarily intended for engraving as a book or magazine illustration may transmit highlight and middle tone detail better if it is very slightly under-exposed (1/3 to 1/2 stop) from the meter reading. Shadow detail is more likely to be lost in engraving in any event and excellently delineated high and middle values seem to produce a more agreeable reproduction. It is very important, however, not to decrease exposure beyond the very slight amount necessary for full, rich highlight detail and for a low-contrast subject no such exposure modification will be necessary for full-scale color recording.

An excellent test for a transparency intended for either photomechanical reproduction or printing on color paper or by dye transfer, is to lay the unmounted film on the surface of an illuminated viewer without masking off the remainder of the lighted area and without subduing normal, full room illumination. This light level will prevent the visual mechanism from accommodating to see detail and gradation which may be present in the transparency but which will not reproduce in subsequent printing. It is helpful to include a *grey scale* and a set of *color patches* in subjects such as still-life or wherever practical. [See Figure 11.8.] These will assist in producing a color print of reproduction which matches the original faithfully.

A final factor in critical color work is the intangible of personal taste. Color photography is never an exact reproduction of reality, although it frequently creates the powerful illusion of accuracy. "Reality" is the creation of individual perception, and judgments of color may vary through wide limits of personal appeal. Color rendition of the various films varies, too, through a wide range. Ektachrome is generally "warmer" than Kodachrome, and both produce more color contrast and brighter hues than does Anscochrome. The latter seems to soften reds and yellows slightly more than the greens. Some of these differences are changed when films are exposed at increased speed indexes; a 10M or 20M CC filter may be needed to suppress excess green with Anscochrome used at E. I. 125. Super Anscochrome has slightly paler blues than other films, particularly compared to Kodachrome, but the blue intensity is strengthened when Super Anscochrome is exposed at E. I. 200. Each of these films, however, is used by photographers who stoutly maintain that their choice produces "true" color rendition.

No standard can be established (or, at least, defended) in these matters of taste. Skin tones, for example, may range from pale greens to almost brick reds and seem life-like, depending on the surrounding tones in the transparency or reproduction and upon the mental image of how flesh-tones "really" look. There are scattered psychological studies of the perceptual and personality factors involved: as an example, women tend to prefer the color balance slightly shifted toward the warm yellow-red end of the spectrum and men a somewhat colder, more bluish version of the same subject. The efforts to systemize this material have gained little scientific ground beyond the ancient evasion: *De gustibus non disputandum.*

Handling and Storage of Color Film

HEAT AND MOISTURE are sources of deterioration of color films during their entire life. *Before exposure,* films should be retained in their original packaging until they are loaded into the Nikon. Storage of unexposed films for more than a month at temperatures higher than 70F or at relative humidities much higher than 40-50 percent, may lead to noticeable changes in speed and color balance. Particularly in the summer, films held for future use should be either obtained in vapor-tight packaging or else wrapped in a pliofilm bag or other vapor-resistant container and held in the refrigerator at from 45-55F. If long storage or critical use is intended, they may be kept in a freezer at temperatures down to −10F. Allow films to return to normal temperatures for six to eight hours after removing from the refrigerator, 24 hours with freezer storage, before loading into the Nikon.

Following exposure and before development, film should be removed immediately from the Nikon, sealed in a vapor-resistent container and developed before heat and humidity alter the characteristics of the latent image. If some storage is necessary, keep undeveloped color film in a refrigerator. Processing, however, should always be effected as quickly as possible.

After development color films are relatively stable, but the dye image may also be attacked by heat, moisture and strong light. Store films and slides in a dry, cool place; use only a projector with a heat-absorbent glass shield and adequate forced ventilation; keep them away from direct sunlight. The dyes in color films are still fugitive, although current material seems assured of a much longer life than films produced five or ten years ago. With optimum storage conditions, transparencies will show little fading over many years.

Developing Reversal Color Films

IN ALL the *integral tripack* methods, there are three layers of silver halide emulsion, each sensitized to one of the primary divisions of the spectrum: blue, green and red [see Figure 7.1]. The fi-st step in processing is to develop the latent images in these three layers to black-and-white negative silver images by a process identical in function to ordinary film development. Each layer is then the negative record of the separate color band, red, green or blue, to which it responded. (We will ignore here the very important factor of color overlapping which makes difficult the life of a color technician.) At this stage, each layer still contains, of course, the remaining silver halides which did not receive enough exposure to become part of the latent negative image and which, consequently, were not developed. Instead of fixing these out, as in black-and-white processing, they become the basis of the positive color image.

In Kodachrome, this subsequent color development is a complicated one which only processing stations with automatic machinery and the most precise controls such as constant, pipe-fed chemical replacement of solutions during continuous processing are equipped to perform.

Color reversal processing

Films such as Anscochrome and Ektachrome may be processed even by an amateur without permanent working space. The significant difference between these films and Kodachrome is the addition of a suitable *color coupler* to each layer of emulsion in the user-processed films. These are dispersed throughout each layer and there has been an intense competitive search for ways to prevent one color coupler from "migrating" into another layer.

The exposed color film is first developed in a suitable formula to reduce the latent image in each of the three layers to a black-and-white negative. During this step, the coupler dye-components remain colorless and inert. The film is next given a fogging exposure to white light, sufficient to affect all of the remaining silver halides throughout the three layers. These halides are now developed to metallic silver in their turn, in a different developing solution. The reducing agent used in this second developer creates an oxidation product at the site of each silver halide crystal converted to metallic silver. The oxidation product reacts with the color coupler immediately adjacent and creates a dye. The color of this dye depends on the nature of the coupler dye-component isolated in each layer.

The result of this color development is the formation of a positive color image proportional in density to the silver reduced during the second development. All of the silver is next bleached out, and the transparent positive color image remains.

Color processing procedure

Ektachrome, Anscochrome, Super Anscochrome and other reversal transparency materials (and some color print materials like Printon, Anscochrome Type, see below) all follow approximately the same step-by-step development procedure. *The exact timing and temperature recommendations are changed from time to time by the manufacturer. Read the instructions enclosed with each new kit purchased.* The accompanying charts incorporate the instructions current as this *Nikon Manual* went to press.

Equipment for color processing

Color film may be developed with equipment no different from that used for ordinary negative processing. A stainless steel or plastic daylight-developing tank may be used, providing the film is held in a reel of the spiral-wire type or in a reel at least one end of which is made of clear plastic to permit the free penetration of light during the re-exposure preceding color development. The proper number of bottles for solution storage should be provided; amber glass or colored polyethylene is necessary to inhibit photo-chemical reactions. These bottles should be exactly the capacity of the volume of solution to prevent enclosed air from slowly oxidizing the ingredients. Glass marbles are sometimes added to fill storage bottles to the lip and replace solution lost by absorption in the emulsion during processing. Each bottle should be labeled and not interchanged when new solutions are mixed: glass is actually somewhat absorbent and may alter correct pH (acidity-alkalinity balance) of solutions subsequently stored. Stainless steel tanks should never be used for *storage* of the bleaching solution which is corrosive to these steels, although the brief treatment period in the processing sequence will do no damage.

The thermometer used must be of laboratory accuracy. Color disbalance will occur with deviations from carefully fixed temperatures. (See directions with the latest developing kit purchased.)

Somewhat greater convenience for amateurs or professionals with a comparatively small volume of work is attained with color developing tanks such as those illustrated [Figure 7.3, page 165]. This equipment may be used for black-and-white processing also.

It is important to have a supply of running water which may be maintained at the correct temperature over a reasonable period. A thermostatic mixing valve which can deliver water at a rate of 3 gallons per minute and maintain temperatures within a half degree (F) despite pressure changes is a useful investment in a permanent darkroom. In a less complete set-up, the thermometer should be kept immersed and periodically checked.

It should be unnecessary to note that Ansco and Kodak processing kits cannot be substituted for each other. Only the exact formulas in the outfit specified in the leaflet enclosed with the film will produce satisfactory results.

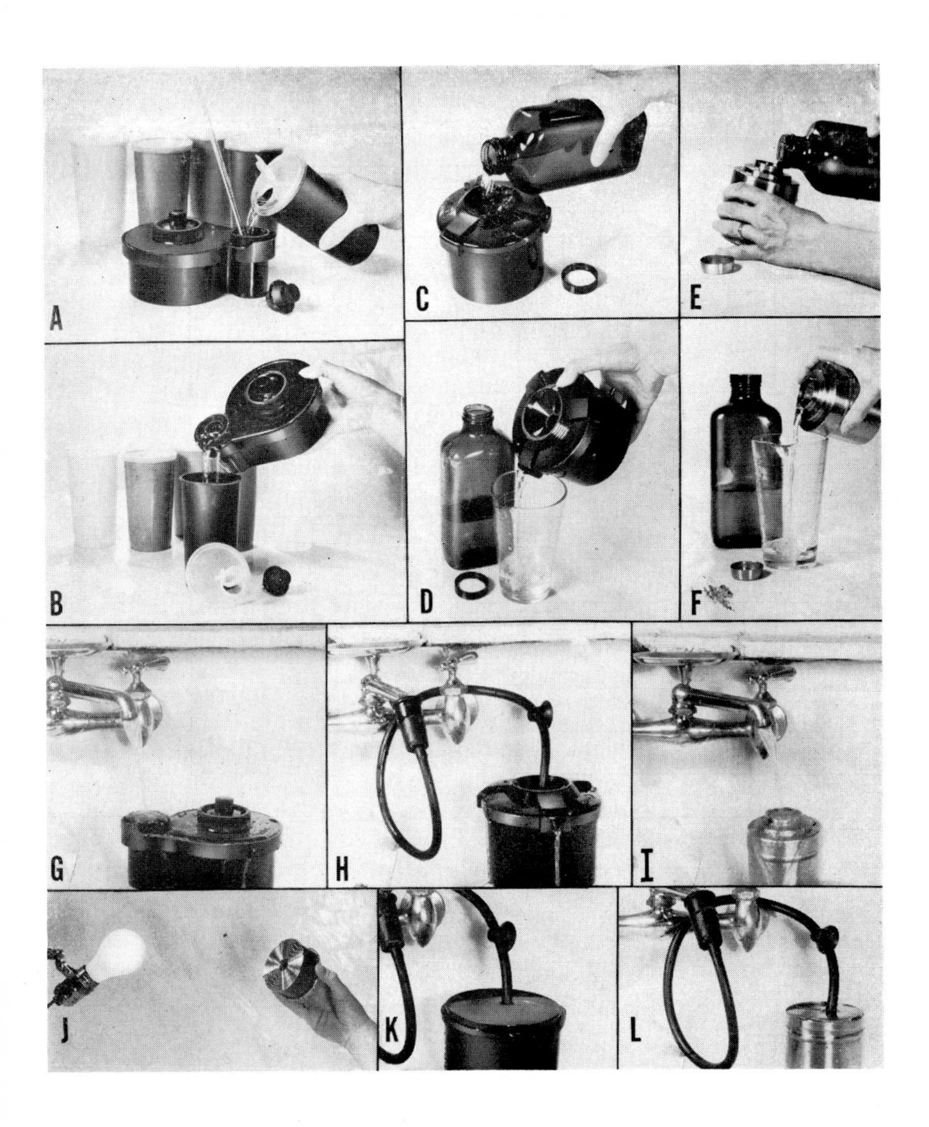

7.3 *Pictures above indicate how color solutions are poured into and emptied from the Kodak Day-Load Tank (A,B), the Ansco adjustable tank (C,D), and the Nikor stainless steel tank (E,F). The method of washing with the lid closed during the first stage of color processing is shown in G, H and I. The method of re-exposing color film during processing is shown in J. Washing with the tank open during later stages of processing is shown in K and L. (The Kodak tank is always used with the lid closed.)*

Time (min)	PROCESSING Anscochrome (E.I. 32) Super Anscochrome (E.I. 100)	°F
16 *	**First developer** * 15 minutes for Super Anscochrome	68 ± ½
2	**Short stop** agitate continuously during first minute	68 ± 2
4	**Hardener** agitate continuously during first minute **Room lights may now be turned on**	68 ± 2
5	**Wash** in running water	60—75
	Reversal exposure expose each end of reel 1 minute at 3 feet from No. 2 photoflood (4 minutes with reels opaque at one end)	
14	**Color developer**	68 ± ½
2	**Short stop** agitate continuously during first minute	68 ± 2
4	**Hardener** agitate continuously during first minute	68 ± 2
5	**Wash** in running water	60—75
5	**Bleach**	68 ± 2
3	**Wash** in running water	60—75
4	**Fix**	68 ± 2
10	**Wash** in running water	60—75

Exact timing and temperature of the first and color development is important. Consider that development begins at the instant the tank is filled with the developing solution and continues until the developer is emptied and the tank is filled with shortstop. Agitate thoroughly when first placed in solution and then agitate for 15 seconds during each minute of the remaining time. See special agitation instructions for shortstop and hardener.

Processing for altered speed ratings

E.I.		First developer	Color developer
64		21 min.	16 min.
100	Anscochrome	25 min.	16 min.
125		30 min.	20 min.
50		12 min.	12 min.
150	Super Anscochrome	19 min	16 min.
200		23 min.	16 min.

Time (min)	PROCESSING Ektachrome (E. I. 32) (Process E-2)	°F
10	**First developer** agitate continuously for first 15 seconds (see directions)	75± ½
1	**Rinse** in running water	73—77
3	**Hardener** agitate continuously for first 15 seconds **Room lights may now be turned on**	73—77
	Reversal exposure Expose open end of reel for 15 seconds 1 foot from No. 2 photoflood (move reel in small circle)	
3	**Wash** in running water	73—77
15	**Color developer**	73—77
5	**Wash** in running water	73—77
5	**Clear**	73—77
1	**Rinse** (not less than 30, nor more than 90 seconds)	73—77
8	**Bleach**	73—77
1	**Rinse** in running water	73—77
3	**Fix**	73—77
8	**Wash** in running water	73—77
1	**Stabilize**	73—77
	Dry: not over 110F	

Agitation (except where specifically mentioned) should be 5 seconds every minute. Begin timing each step after tank has been filled with solution; conclude timing when tank has been emptied and next solution begins to enter tank. Timing on all steps is critical.

For processing Ektachrome exposed at E.I. 64, increase time in first developer to 14 minutes. Add 5 fluid drams per gallon of 10% sodium hydroxide (⅝ fl. dr. per pint) to color developer. Time remains the same. Type F film exposed to gain one stop in speed may require CC-10C or CC-10C+CC-05C over camera lens. Altered color developer may be returned to normal by adding 3½ fluid drams per gallon of 10% (by volume) sulfuric acid (7/16 fl. dr. per pint). Caution: always add acid slowly to water.

Mix all solutions carefully, in accordance with the directions. Some chemicals go into solution with difficulty, particularly color developers, which may require as much as five minutes of constant stirring. Bottle each solution immediately after mixing [see above] and cap tightly. Within a normal temperature range, these solutions will remain stable for a maximum of two weeks. It is better practice to mix them shortly before use rather than put their stability to an unnecessary test. Once used, however, their life is curtailed and used solutions older than two or three days are best discarded. Replenishers are available for developers and bleach but these are useful only to the high-volume processor who can exercise a measure of chemical control. In individual work, it is better to mix up a completely fresh kit of a size matched to the tanks available and to discard it after use. Some compromise can be established between the necessity for developing color films as soon as possible after exposure (to prevent deterioriation of the latent image) and the severely shortened life of solutions after even a single strip of film has been processed. Experience has shown that it is consistently possible to re-use the processing solutions to the limits of the film area for which they are designed (e.g., six 20-exposure cartridges of Ektachrome in the one-pint E-2 Process kit), if they are stored in full, tightly-stoppered bottles and held on the middle shelf of a refrigerator. The two-week maximum storage for unused solutions should never be exceeded with this method of extending useful chemical life. Note that this practice is *not advised* by the manufacturers and that color films of importance or those requiring critical color balance should not be developed with such stored solutions.

When abnormally long delays are necessary between exposure and processing of color films because of such factors as inadequate facilities encountered on an extended trip, if it is not possible to utilize the best alternative of air mailing them to a suitable laboratory, a useful expedient is to give Anscochrome correct first development, short stop and wash, or to develop and wash Ektachrome, harden it for 3 minutes and then bathe it for about 1 minute in 1 percent acetic acid. The films may now be dried in subdued light and carefully re-wound and replaced in their original cartridge or some other container which protects them from mechanical damage and from exposure to strong, direct light. Subsequently, they may be given the usual second exposure and the remainder of the processing steps.

Increasing effective film speeds

Within limits, the speed indexes of reversal color films designed for individual processing may be increased by suitable changes in duration of first and second development (or by increasing developer activity). Beyond certain limits, stronger development to compensate for shorter exposures will not result in matched maximum densities nor equal gradients in each of the three emulsion layers and the color balance of the transparency will be degraded. Anscochrome seems to be the most flexible of the current materials in this respect. Exposed at a doubled E.I. of 64 color rendition is excellent, and when re-doubled to E.I. 125 it usually gives excellent color results with all except the most extremely contrasty subject matter. Super Anscochrome, also, may be exposed at speed indexes of 100, 160 or 200 without significant color distortions. Ektachrome speeds may also be doubled by prolonging first development and by increasing the alkalinity of the color developer. Instructions for this altered processing are noted in the development chart.

The reversal films such as Kodachrome and Gevacolor processed with rigid controls by the manufacturer or his licensees must be carefully exposed at the established speed index. While some very slight development differences seem to occur with Kodachrome, for example, between the several processing stations and with films processed from week to week, these shifts in color balance and effective film speeds are so very small that Kodachrome is always recommended as the most useful film for exposure tests (for example, in establishing proper guide numbers for an electronic flash unit, see Chapter 9) because of this uniformity of processing.

Developing color negatives

In the very near future we may expect color negative films to become available for the Nikon as manufacturing techniques improve and 35mm cartridges are marketed. The basic difference in processing negative color is the omission of the first development to a black-and-white negative image. The latent image formed during the original exposure in the Nikon is immediately reduced to a metallic silver negative image and a dye image of colors, complementary to those of the original scene. In the subsequent steps, both the silver grains formed during this development and the unused silver halides are removed from the emulsion layers. Identical care is required for precise temperature control and freedom from chemical contamination of the processing solutions.

Color Printing Processes

COLOR TRANSPARENCIES are not a completely satisfactory end-product in photography. They must be projected on a screen or trans-illuminated on a viewer. There has always been a desire for a process which would permit a "universal balance" color film to be exposed in the Nikon without corrections over a wide range of lighting conditions, and for simplified processing and for a one-stage printing process, as in black-and-white work. This should result in a properly corrected color print for exhibition, reproduction or record use. It will be a long time before such a color sequence becomes as easy and as flexible as black-and-white photography, but newer materials such as the combination of color negative films and Kodak Color Print Material, Type C, are bringing this ideal process closer to reality.

While color printing is now considerably more complex than making black-and-white enlargements from the Nikon negative, many methods are not beyond the capacity of an advanced amateur with a moderately well-equipped small home darkroom and a willingness to learn from the inevitable errors of his first attempts.

Color recording in photography would offer fewer difficulties if the materials available corresponded with the ideal standards required by color theory. Both the manufacturer and the photographer in his darkroom must "make do" with the actual characteristics of dye substances and of the silver halides, using ingenuity to balance and cancel out the less-than-perfect responses of his materials from stage to stage. This is actually a happy challenge to some printers and there is a definite pride in craftsmanship, a small glint of superiority in the eye of one who has mastered the technique of tri-color

NOTE

The five current methods of color printing are outlined in the next pages. The first two, trichrome carbro and dye transfer, require a semi-technical discussion which may well discourage an amateur or any photographer who, understandably, prefers to use his Nikon creatively rather than discuss the complicated recipes of color print cookery. Turn to page 174, where Printon and Kodak Color Print Material, Type R, enter the outline. These processes can produce excellent prints if the directions supplied by the manufacturer are intelligently followed. Later, some of the more complicated techniques borrowed from older printing methods may seem useful. At that time, the technical underbrush will not seem quite so tangled through pages 170 to 173. Brief notes on Kodak Color Print Material, Type C, are added at the end of this section in anticipation of the date when it will be useful to the Nikon user.

carbro or dye transfer printing as he regards the more simply achieved color print on Ansco Printon material or Kodak Type R color paper.

Trichrome carbro

The color printing standard against which all other methods are still judged is the trichrome carbro process, developed around 1900 from the older carbon printing. The first step is the preparation of three "separation negatives": three black-and-white negatives on a suitable film emulsion exposed in turn through a set of filters, each of which passes only a narrow band of the spectrum. The three films become, like the first stage of integral tripack color transparency films, negative records of the blue, green and red components of a scene. These three black-and-white separation negatives may be exposed in the Nikon, in sequence, with a still-life or other static subject, or they may be made from a 35mm direct-color transparency material. An outline of how these separation negatives are made will be found under dye-transfer methods, below.

Black-and-white enlargements of each of these negatives to the exact size of the final trichrome carbro print desired are next made on a black-and-white printing paper, the emulsion of which is rich in silver bromide, and these prints are developed and fixed in the usual manner but with controls to assure matched contrasts and density ranges. Next, three "pigment papers" are prepared. These are sheets coated with a soft gelatin which contains pigments (originally carbon black when invented, in 1864, and hence still sometimes called "carbon tissues") which today are suitable coloring materials in each of the three subtractive primaries, yellow, magenta and cyan. The pigment papers are soaked in a sensitizing solution containing potassium ferricyanide, potassium bromide and potassium bichromate, and each of the tissues is placed in firm contact with the appropriate bromide print (yellow pigment tissue against the print made from the blue-record negative, etc.). The sensitizing solution diffuses from the tissue into the bromide print and the ferricyanide, working with the potassium bromide, bleaches the silver image on the print and is converted to ferrocyanide. This, in turn, as it is produced in proportional amounts according to the silver in local areas of the print, diffuses back into the pigment tissue. There, the absorbed potassium bichromate of the sensitizing solution oxidyzes the ferrocyanide back to ferricyanide and in the process is itself reduced and locally "tans" (hardens) the gelatin of the pigment tissue.

The positive image of each bromide print is thus transferred to a pigment tissue in the form of a differentially hardened gelatin image. The un-hardened gelatin with its pigment content is removed in a hot water bath; the three images are transferred to sheets of waxed celluloid or other temporary support and the backing of the pigment paper is removed. Finally, the three colored gelatin layers are superimposed in register on a suitable paper base in a final transfer.

Excellent carbro prints have been made in temporarily-requisitioned apartment kitchens, but the process requires the most careful temperature controls and fine adjustments of chemical balances in solutions. Carbro printers all have semi-private "recipes" and individual tricks of manipulation. No finer or more permanent color print can be made than a perfect trichrome carbro, but materials are now in restricted supply and considerable experience is required for success.

Dye-transfer color prints

In dye-transfer work, three gelatin relief images, one for each of the subtractive primaries, are also prepared. They are used, however, as vehicles for suitable colored dyes which are transferred in succession to prepared paper as the final image. The gelatin relief vehicles may be re-dyed and a series of closely identical color prints may be produced. This method, too, is an old one in concept but was difficult to manipulate until the appearance of Eastman Kodak materials (originally called Wash-Off Relief) which have made the process relatively easy and in experienced hands capable of producing color prints nearly indistinguishable in quality from trichrome carbro prints.

Full working details are found in Kodak literature and elsewhere but the sequence may be briefly outlined. Again, three separation negatives are required and these are most often made from color transparencies with suitable filtering and masking procedures [see immediately below]. Each of these negatives is used to print, by contact or projection, a *matrix:* a sheet of heavy film base coated with light-sensitive emulsion suspended in soft gelatin. It is primarily blue-sensitive and may be handled under subdued safe-lighting.

There have been a number of attempts to produce a panchromatic matrix material which could be exposed from positive transparencies and given a *reversal development* to eliminate the need for separation negatives, but none of these has been completely successful. However, Kodak Pan Matrix Film, similar to regular matrix film except for its full color sensitivity, is used for dye-transfer work from color negative materials such as Ektacolor. It is exposed through suitable separation filters and directly developed to a positive record of one of the color layers in the negative. No intermediate black-and-white negatives are required.

The three matrices are each developed to form an image of differentially hardened gelatin, proportional in thickness at each point to the intensity of the printing light penetrating the base of the film during exposure. (The matrix film is exposed with the base uppermost so the image hardening is initiated next to the base.) The unhardened gelatin is then washed off in 120F water. Even after removal of the unhardened gelatin the relief image will continue to cling to the support. In the final steps, each matrix is soaked in a solution containing a dye of one of the subtractive primary colors and is then pressed, in turn, with proper registration into firm contact with a sheet of gelatin-coated paper which absorbs the dyes from the successive matrices to become a full-color print. At each step of the procedure, control measures over contrast and density are somewhat more simple than for trichrome carbro. Problems of registering in succession, the three dye images of the final transfer have been to a large degree eliminated by punching registration holes along the edge of the matrices and positioning them on a registration board with corresponding pins when-they are exposed in succession, or by the use of a special transfer blanket.

Newer printing processes (outlined later in this chapter) are somewhat more straight-forward and simplified than dye-transfer printing. This method is by no means obsolete, however, and may well remain for some time a superior color printing method in all situations where careful and precise color control of the print results and the easy production of matched and inexpensive duplicates are more important than is the expenditure of time and the necessity of acquired skill to make the first print.

Dye-transfer from Nikon-exposed transparencies

Reversal films, such as Kodachrome, Ektachrome, Anscochrome and similar color films manufactured outside the United States may be exposed in the Nikon, developed as positive transparencies and subsequently used as the basis for dye-transfer prints and, of course, for other current color printing methods. A few modifications of technique are required with 35mm, however, during the preparation and subsequent use of the set of three matched color separation negatives from which the matrices are printed. Principally, this is a matter of the most exact control of size and registration when the color image is split into its component primaries. A rigid enlarger is necessary, one which may be locked firmly into position; the negative carrier must be made with precision fit so it may be returned to exactly the same plane between the condensing lenses above it and the projection lens as the matrices are printed from the separation negatives. The enlarger construction must allow no white light leaks, even those too faint to affect black-and-white printing papers, and the carrier should be completely masked off at the borders of the transparency (or negative) image to eliminate stray light from this source. A provision for the insertion of color filters *above* the transparency is very desirable: filters used below the projection lens, especially when a "pack" of several are required, tend to diffuse the projected image.

Almost needless to say, the projection lens itself must be one fully corrected for flatness of field at normal enlargement distances and for projection of all wave-lengths of colored light to precisely the same plane if loss of acutance and the introduction of color fringing are to be avoided.

Color separation negatives

The three black-and-white negatives from which the dye transfer matrices are made may be exposed either by contact printing or by projecting an enlarged image of the transparency. In either case, the black-and-white film used must be capable of being developed to closely matched response curves, with similar gradients throughout the density range, when exposed to narrow-band radiation such as that passed by the Wratten No. 29 (red), No. 61 (green) and 47B (blue) or an equivalent set such as the Ilford 205, 408 and 306. If a suitable enlarger to handle them is available, there are advantages to making enlarged separation negatives; however, with slightly more care to achieve exact registration throughout, contact printing for 35mm size separations is quite feasible.

The transparency may be used to produce a 35mm strip of separations when contact printed in a suitable strip printer on film such as Ilford HP3 or Gevapan 27 Microgran. (Kodak 35mm films do not have response curves so suitably balanced for separation work.) These must be developed as a unit and there is consequently some loss of control over the individual contrasts of the three images (the one exposed through the blue filter tending to be somewhat flat). Contrast correction may need to be partially shifted to the stage of matrix printing. In practice, it seems to be more satisfactory to make the contact separation negatives, as well as projected ones, on sheet film material, trimming them later, if necessary, to 35mm dimensions to fit the enlarger carrier. Sheet films with excellent uniform sensitivity to red, green and blue light include Kodak Super-XX, Ansco Isopan, and Ilford FP3.

These direct separations of the color image into its components as three black-and-white records will produce satisfactory prints from many transparencies exposed in the Nikon. However, before continuing this brief outline, it is necessary to mention an intermediate step required for a more perfect translation of color values from transparency to print.

Color masking

Dye materials in color transparencies and in color printing materials depart somewhat from an ideal response. A perfect cyan dye, for example, would completely absorb all red light and transmit green and blue light without loss. No substance yet produced, however, will absorb large amounts of red without also absorbing some percentage of green and blue. Magenta dyes also absorb some of the blue which they should transmit, while yellow dyes are much closer to a practical perfection. In the transparency as exposed in the Nikon, these deviations are usually unnoticeable except when some scientific accuracy of color recording is sought. When the transparency is reproduced as a print, using dye materials in the second stage which multiply the errors of the first stage may produce a quite apparent color degradation. Flesh tones seem to suffer very little through this re-doubling of inaccuracy, but magentas in the transparency shift toward red, yellows suffer loss of saturation and a shift toward orange, and the blues and greens become noticeably darker and degraded.

A practical solution is to prepare a black-and-white film *mask* which cancels out the unwanted overlap of color response. Two of these are usually made for the most accurate printing results: a negative made with the red filter and developed to a contrast equal to that of the cyan layer in the transparency and then re-registered with the transparency when the separation negative made with the green filter is exposed; and a masking negative made with the green filter and developed to the same contrast as the first mask and similarly bound into register with the transparency when the red filter separation is made.

For even greater tonal accuracy, a highlight mask may be prepared as the very first step even before these other masks are made. This is a very high-contrast film, exposed for developable density only in the very brightest highlight areas of the transparency. Bound into register with the color film and left there for correction when the masks are exposed (but removed for the exposure of the actual separation negatives unless the masking step is omitted) it reduces contrast in the lightest areas to a gradient which dye transfer printing materials can handle. [See *Laminated mask* procedure under Printon directions, below.]

Direct Color Prints

Color printing methods which more closely approximate the direct simplicity of black-and-white projection printing have been a long-term objective of technical research for obvious reasons. Within the last few years, reasonable and even excellent 35mm color results have become possible with positive-to-positive color processes. The printing methods from a positive color transparency are quite easily mastered by any Nikon user who is experienced in the methods of black-and-white printing covered in Chapter 6.

Printon (Anscochrome Type)

Printon is a tripack color emulsion, balanced to a printing light of 3000K and coated on an opaque white base. It is given a reversal development similar to that required by reversal transparency materials such as Anscochrome, although the developing formulas are not identical. The present material replaces Ansco Color Printon, introduced in 1945, the first such user-processed direct color print material with satisfactory characteristics available in the United States.

For best results Printon requires an enlarger with correctly aligned condenser lenses, a heat-absorbing glass and provision for inserting the necessary color correction filters above the transparency. The illumination should be a 150-watt GE 212 or Sylvania E11 bulb or a lamp of similar (3000K) color temperature, with voltage control. (Ten-volt variations in this range may be assumed to equal about 100K color variations which are more than enough to alter color results perceptibly. The projection lens must be one designed for close-distance use and with full achromatism so red, green and blue segments of the spectrum are brought into focus at precisely the same plane.

Standard printing trays may be used for processing Printon: glass, glass-coated steel (enamelware), rubber, ceramic or Type 316 stainless steel. (Bleaching solution will attack the latter on prolonged contact and should remain in stainless steel containers only briefly and during actual use.) Printon may also be developed in sheet film hangers suspended in standard equipment such as the common plastic or ceramic 3 1/2-gallon 8x10-inch or larger film tanks.

The instruction slip with each package of Printon lists the filter or filter combination required to achieve proper color balance with 3000K printing illumination for the particular color emulsion with which the sheets are coated. A UV16P filter to mask off ultraviolet is always necessary. Some changes may be required from this recommendation to compensate for the particular color

PROCESSING PRINTON (Anscochrome Type) and ANSCO COLOR (Type 538) DUPLICATING FILM

Dup'l Film min @ 68F	Printon min @ 68F	Printon min @ 75F	(Printon and Type 538 require **different** processing kits) (temperature tolerance ±2° except where noted)
8	14	9½	**First developer** (± ½° tolerance)
1	2	2	**Short stop** agitate continuously for first 30 seconds
4	—	—	**Hardener** agitate continuously for 1 minute (not required for Printon)
			Room Lights may now be turned on
3	5	5	**Wash** in running water (±5°)
			Re-exposure (Printon) 30 seconds each side 3 feet from No. 2 photo-flood (Dup'l film) 90 seconds each side
7	15	10	**Color developer** (± ½° tolerance)
1	1	1	**Short Stop** agitate continuously for first 30 seconds
4	3	3	**Hardener** (Printon) agitate continuously for first 30 seconds; (Dup'l film) for first minute
5	5	5	**Wash** in running water (±5°)
5	6	5	**Bleach**
3	5	5	**Wash** in running water (±5°)
4	5	4	**Fix**
10	10	10	**Wash** in running water (±5°)
2	2	2	**Rinse** in clean water (±5°)

Agitation, except where mentioned, 5 seconds every minute. Temperatures should be accurate within the tolerances listed. Time each step from the moment solution covers material until it is drained and next solution covers material.

Dry by exposure to air not over 100F and away from strong light.

Ansco Color Duplicating Film (Type 538) may be altered in contrast:

	Lower contrast	Higher contrast
First developer	6 min.	10 min.
Color developer	5 min.	9 min.

Do not alter processing times for Printon (Anscochrome Type).

balance of the transparency to be printed, for the actual printing illumination employed, or for the personal tastes in color rendition of the printer or of the ultimate user of the print.

The simplest way to determine printing time and any necessary changes in the printing filters is to insert them into the enlarger and make a test-strip in the same manner in which one is made in black-and-white printing. [See Chapter 6.] Place a piece of Printon (or a succession of small pieces), cut from a sheet of the same emulsion number as that intended for the final print, on the easel to include an important area of the image with a reasonably full range of colors and densities. Expose successive portions of the strip (or separate pieces placed in the same image area) about 2, 4, 8 and 16 times as long as you normally print black-and-white enlarging paper at the same degree of enlargement and the same lens aperture. Develop this strip or the small pieces of Printon carefully, exactly as the subsequent print will be processed. The density and colors cannot be judged accurately until this test material is completely dry.

Since Printon is a reversal material, test areas which are too dark have received too little exposure and vice versa. One of the steps in the test should be very nearly correct within this range of exposures and a more exact intermediate printing time may be estimated. In the case of doubt or very limited printing experience, a second test strip may be made using a range of exposure times between the two steps which appear most nearly correct. Before printing this second test or proceeding directly to a full-sized print, any needed modification of the filter pack for better color rendition may be estimated by studying the print under white light (ideally, the same illumination as that for which the final print is designed). If color densities seem lacking, hold various color correction filters (yellow, magenta, cyan; red, green, blue) between the test strip and the eye (*never* flat on the print surface). Find the proper color and density of one or of several combined filters which give a proper visual correction with one of the steps of the test (or an estimated intermediate step).

Before proceeding with a second test-strip or a full print, insert this corrective filter or combination into the filter pack used for the test-strip. [*Note:* filter combinations may sometimes be simplified by removing unnecessary duplications: instead of adding a color, an equal density of its complimentary color may be removed. The "rules" for this, applicable for exposing color films in the Nikon as well as for color printing, will be found with the chart of color correction filters in *Data and Formulas.* An approximate indidation of the necessary exposure corrections for various filter densities is also listed there.] Calculate the revised printing time from the test strip and from the alterations in the filter pack and proceed.

A black-and-white negative mask may be made to control the excessive contrasts sometimes found in color transparencies. The most satisfactory method to guarantee the necessary perfect registration required is the laminated-mask procedure.

Laminated masks

Perfect registration of a 35mm contact mask may be assured by exposing and processing the negative without disturbing its original positioning against the transparency. To accomplish this without harm to the transparency requires only a minimum dexterity which can be acquired by brief practice with scrap material. The color original is first centered, base down, on a sheet of thin cover glass such as that used to protect 3 1/4x4-inch lantern slides, and one edge only is taped to the glass. The surface of the glass around the transparency is painted with an adhesive such as Kodak Kodaflat, working up to the edge without actually coming in contact with the color film itself. Allow the adhesive to become tacky. (If this requires more than five minutes, the Kodaflat requires slight dilution with Kodak Print Lacquer Thinner.) Then the edge of the glass plate nearest the taped edge of the transparency is inserted between the rollers of a wringer such as that used for ferrotyping prints. (If the wringer may be brought down so the rolls are horizontal, the operator will not wish he possessed a third hand!) Now, *in the dark,* take a sheet of film (with the black interleaving paper still protecting its emulsion side) and insert one edge into the rollers, align it with the glass plate and with the base of the film toward the transparency. Hold the upper edge of the film away from the glass as the wringer is slowly turned and the glass, transparency and film are passed through the rollers into firm contact, with wringer pressure just short of cracking the cover glass. The sandwich, with the unexposed emulsion of the film now uppermost and with the transparency in a water-tight seal beneath it may then be exposed through the glass base and processed normally.

Dry, the masking negative remains in perfect register and the slight separation of color image and black-and-white image by the thickness of the film base will actually improve the detail rendition of any subsequent step in either black-and-white or color printing. The negative and glass may subsequently be pulled apart and the transparency removed, undamaged.

If this technique appears inconvenient, a mask may be made which is *deliberately unsharp.* Contact print the transparency on a sheet film such as Ansco Isopan or another of the films listed previously under masking for dye transfers. However, place the base side of the transparency toward the emulsion side of the sheet film (i.e., the emulsion side of both transparency and film should face the printing light). Proper diffusion of the black-and-white mask is obtained if there is some additional separation between the two, such as introduced by a .003-inch thick sheet of Kodapak Diffusion Sheet or even a piece of thin cover glass intended for slide binding. Alternately, diffusion may be secured by placing a fixed-out sheet of glossy photographic paper on the easel or in a printing frame behind the sheet film. The halation thus introduced will effectively destroy the sharp image definition on the film emulsion. In either case, there should be firm contact between all the elements during printing, either in a printing frame or under a sheet of plate glass on the easel. The enlarger with the El-Nikkor lens well stopped down or a 10-watt lamp about 10 feet away may be used as a light source.

In this way, a thin negative (with about 50 percent normal development) may be secured to reduce the contrast range of the original transparency. In addition to this contrast reduction, an element of color control may be introduced by exposing the mask through a filter either inserted (alone) into the enlarger or laid over the printing frame. If a transparency, for example, has excessive blue-green values, a mask exposed through a Wratten 67 (cyan) filter will produce densities primarily over those colors, reducing their contrast and brilliance in favor of the reds and oranges present in the transparency and not affected by such a mask.

The transparency and mask (if not made by the laminated-mask procedure) are registered over a light table (a transparency illuminator or a contact printer will serve) in the same relationship: emulsion side of mask against the base of the transparency, so the mask will be above the transparency in the carrier of the enlarger. Use a narrow strip of cellulose tape to bind the two together along one set of sprocket holes and trim away the unused portion of the sheet film if necessary to fit the enlarger. Normal Printon procedure, including the use of corrective filters, may now proceed with either the contrast reducing or the color corrective mask in place.

Local dodging and burning-in may be used as in black-and-white projection printing; however, the effects are *reversed.* Holding back light from an area will darken it, additional exposure will lighten it. Dodging times may be estimated from the test strip steps of correct density for local areas requiring exposures different from the print as a whole.

Kodak Color Print Material, Type R

The production of color prints on Kodak Type R paper is very similar to making Printon as outlined above. The Kodak material is also a tripack emulsion, but is coated on a paper base which some photographers consider gives the final print a more satisfactory appearance than does the Printon base. Type R color paper is printed by enlargement directly from color transparencies exposed in the Nikon. Corrective filter packs are employed and the reversal development (currently Process P-111) follows a similar sequence to that for Printon or for Ektachrome and Anscochrome reversal development. The kit for Type R Color Print Material may not, of course, be interchanged with developing kits for any other of these processes.

The color balance of a test-strip or a full-size print on Kodak Color Print Material, Type R, may be judged before waiting for the emulsion to dry and lose its opalescence, if it is immersed in (undiluted) Kodak Rapid Fixer for one minute following the hardener fixing bath (Step 11 of the usual process; see chart). Inspection of the color balance should be reasonably brief if a full color print is intended for permanence. Thereafter, it is given the usual washing with the time extended to 20 minutes, followed by stabilizing and rinse. Test-strips, of course, may be immediately discarded following inspection. Controls in printing are the same as those mentioned for Printon. *Note:* Type R (and Type C) Color Print Material are sensitive to heat and must be kept under refrigeration (50F or lower) prior to use.

Kodak Color Print Material, Type C

This is a tripack emulsion, with three sensitive layers responding to blue, green and red light, respectively. It is designed for direct printing from color negatives. Prints may be made with suitably filtered white light as with Type R color paper and Printon. However, this color material is primarily designed for *tricolor* exposure: successive printings through Wratten 70 (red), 99 or 61 plus 16 (green), and 98 or 47B plus 2B (blue), or an appropriate modification of these three (or equivalent) narrow-band transmission filters. Prints of a quality often indistinguishable from excellent dye transfer color have been produced on Type C color paper from larger negatives, particularly with the tricolor exposure method. Elaborate control equipment has also been introduced to enable this quality work to be produced in comparatively large volume on a commercial basis. In this respect it is a notable advance over previous color negative-to-positive methods.

PROCESSING KODAK COLOR PRINT MATERIAL (Type R)

Min	Process P-111	F°
3	**Prewet** immerse 5 seconds, drain 10 seconds, reimmerse during first minute. Then drain 2 minutes.	73-77
6	**First developer**	75 ± ½°
8	**First stop bath**	73-77
12	**Wash** in running water with agitation	73-77
	Room lights may now be turned on	
	Re-exposure 15 seconds, emulsion side 1 foot from No. 1 photoflood	
8	**Color developer**	75 ± ½°
8	**Hardener—Stop bath**	73-77
3	**Wash** in running water	73-77
8	**Bleach**	73-77
6	**Wash** in running water	73-77
7	**Hardener**—Fixing bath	73-77
10	**Wash** in running water	73-77

Agitate for first 30 seconds, thereafter lift from solution and drain for 5 seconds every half-minute. Final drain should be 15 seconds. Accurate maintainance of temperatures is essential. Time for each step should extend from moment material is immersed in one solution until the moment it is immersed in the next. Dry at not over 180F.

PROCESSING KODAK COLOR PRINT MATERIAL (Type C)

Min	Process P-122	F°
12	First developer	75 ± ½°
2	Stop bath	73-77
2	First fixing bath	73-77
2	Wash in running water	73-77
	Room lights may now be turned on	
4	Bleach	73-77
2	Wash in running water	73-77
2	Hardener Fixing Bath	73-77
8	Wash in running water	73-77
3	Hardener	73-77
2	Wash in running water	73-77
3	Buffer	73-77

Agitate continuously for first 30 seconds in all solutions. Thereafter, either interleaf prints in tray or use tray-tilt agitation. Drain prints 20 seconds (include this in calculating times).

The advanced amateur and professional may also be able to use it successfully, particularly with the single (filtered) white light exposure which is somewhat easier to control with ordinary printing equipment than is the critically-timed divided (tricolor) exposure method. It is by no means a simple, fool-proof "amateur" printing process even in the sense that Printon and Type R color paper have become.

Test-strips and color balance with Type C

Test-strips on Kodak Color Print Material, Type C, are made in a similar manner to those on other color printing materials, with exposure times and color balance bracketed over their probable range. These tests differ in interpretation from those on Type R (or Printon) in that an area (or step in the test-strip) which is too dark requires *less* exposure just as it does in normal black-and-white printing. Equally, but not quite so obviously, an off-color cast is improved by *increasing* the tricolor printing time of that color or by *adding* filters of the color which is too strong when making white light exposures. A print which has, for example, an all-over excess of blue may be improved by increasing the relative proportion of blue light; this will build density in the blue-sensitive layer of Type C paper—density which builds up the relative amount of *yellow* dye produced by that layer. White light printing requires filter correction *complementary* to that through which the test print appears best. In the example given, a yellow color correction filter would have given the best visual appearance and indicated the need for a corresponding *blue* filter of the same density as the yellow selected in viewing to be added to the printing filter pack. As noted above, excess filter densities may be often avoided by removing filters of complementary colors instead of adding an additional filter when the final correction balance is achieved. [See notes with the chart of color correction filters in *Data and Formulas*.]

Black-and-white Prints from Color

PRINTS ON ordinary black-and-white projection paper from originals photographed on color films in the Nikon are often useful or necessary. There are several processes and several film materials which may be adapted to the particular problem at hand. The method productive of the highest quality is the preparation of an intermediate negative on panchromatic film material for subsequent printing.

Negatives from color transparencies

Excellent black-and-white negatives may be made from color transparencies (even from those which are somewhat too thin or dense or of poor color balance) in a manner similar to the production of separation negatives outlined above under dye transfer printing. Maximum image acuity is preserved if these are made by contact printing with the transparency emulsion pressed firmly against that of the film. (The negative must be inserted in the enlarger emulsion side up when enlarging to keep correct left-to-right relationships.) Contact printing requires immaculate surface cleanliness of transparency and film, however, as dust spots will become very evident on subsequent projection of the negative.

Any fully panchromatic film may be used. The fine-grain emulsions have obvious advantages and such films as Kodak Panatomic X, Super-XX (sheet film) and Plus-X (35mm), Ilford Pan F, Ansco Isopan (sheet film), and other films with similar characteristics may be used. If a strip-printer is available, a short succession of slightly varying exposures may be made on black-and-white 35mm film as a test-strip, one frame of which will probably serve as the final negative. If exposures must be singly made, it is more convenient to work with one of the smaller sizes of sheet film and to develop in a small tray.

Most color transparencies are quite contrasty, so negatives made from them require a shorter than normal development time to reduce this contrast to the limits which will correctly print on a No. 2 grade photographic paper or with the "medium contrast" filter in use with variable grade papers. It is impossible to assign an exact development factor, but a two-thirds normal time may be taken as a starting point.

The black-and-white interpretation of the colors in the transparency may be controlled with even greater precision than when facing the original scene with black-and-white film in the Nikon. The usual range of filters employed in conventional black-and-white photography may be used to modify the exposure light (usually the enlarger with lens stopped down). As an example of this greater precision of control, with a landscape for which a Nikon Y (K2) filter would be used with the Nikon in order to separate the image densities of blue sky and white clouds, the color transparency of the subject may be printed onto black-and-white film with light modified by any one of the yellow or red color correction (CC) filters for a more exact modification of the blue light reaching the film. Filters and combinations may be freely employed to alter the emphasis and interpretation of the colors as represented in monochrome.

8.1 F. B. Grunzweig
Marcel Marceau in rehearsal

Nikon S2, 50mm f/1.4 Nikkor
Tri-X, 1/30, f/2

8

Available Light and the Nikon

The recent increases in film sensitivity and the exceptional light-gathering power of Nikkor lenses have moved back the shadows for 35mm photography. It is now easily possible to work under illumination which only a few years ago tested the technical ingenuity of a photographer. When it is required, we can push a long way into the "available darkness" toward the picture of the black cat, pouncing on his midnight supper. In very many cases, it is now possible to use the existing light as it is encountered for Nikon negatives which are equal in quality with those made under sunlight conditions and which have only the contrast, graininess and blur which the photographer chooses for pictorial effectiveness.

At any level of illumination, the photographer must be concerned with the direction and the contrast of his light. The direction will determine not only the local illumination on his important subject, but the recording of its form and texture. There may not always be opportunity to alter this in any way, but a flexibility in the choice of viewpoint and moment makes the work of some photographers outstanding, even in dim light. (It is probably no accident, either, that many of these have had an apprenticeship in "studio" lighting or have trained their perception of lighting effects by other means.)

In editorial illustration, working under existing light helps keep picture subjects less camera conscious, permits maintenance of ordinary routine and often results in more truthful-appearing pictures than those in which a subject is brightly illuminated by flash against a dark background which the light failed to penetrate. Available-light techniques also make possible the inconspicuous photography from a more distant vantage point which is valuable for photojournalism and other work.

The necessity of photographing without auxiliary lighting under poor illumination using the less sensitive film emulsions previously available and slower lenses than present-day Nikkors, has had a considerable effect on photographic "style" and toward educating the public to appreciate as well

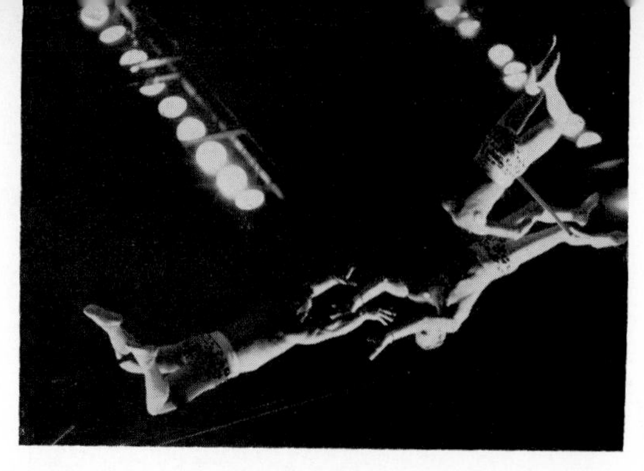

8.2 RAY SHORR

Nikon S2
105mm f/2.5 Nikkor

circus

Tri-X, 1/250, f/2.5

as to accept certain image "distortions." Forcing film to higher speeds formerly necessitated a grainy and high-contrast negative and often some blur of subject movement as well. During World War II, photographs of great impact and with emotional significance to a wide audience were exposed and developed in circumstances which emphasized these "surface" qualities. They became, in fact, associated with pictures of dramatic content, so grain, blur and poor contrast became a fad imposed on photographs made even under optimum conditions when perfect negative quality was easily possible. This phase has fortunately passed, but it has left a visual method which has significance for many people who see photographs. It is a means for more lucid communication when used creatively.

There are two kinds of "available light" photography, although the exact boundary between them may be sometimes hard to define precisely. Perhaps the best division is the point beyond which the "medium speed," general purpose films cannot be used without exceeding their latitude and necessitating processing which produces graininess, loss of acutance, or fog and unpleasant contrast. These general purpose films [see table, *Data and Formulas*] are sufficient in speed, today, for use indoors under average lighting conditions, unless it is necessary to photograph action or to use a small aperture for depth-of-field with moving subjects. Exposure Indexes up to 320-400 with these general purpose films and Nikkor apertures of f/1.4 and faster combine to make the Nikon inconspicuously useful under conditions which would have called for forced development only ten years ago.

Among professionals, there are two schools of thought about picture results, and two technical approaches. One group welcomed the rapid emul-

8.3 DAVID LINTON

Nikon S2
50mm f/1.4 Nikkor

near Resolute Bay, Canadian Arctic

Tri-X, 1/30, f/2.8

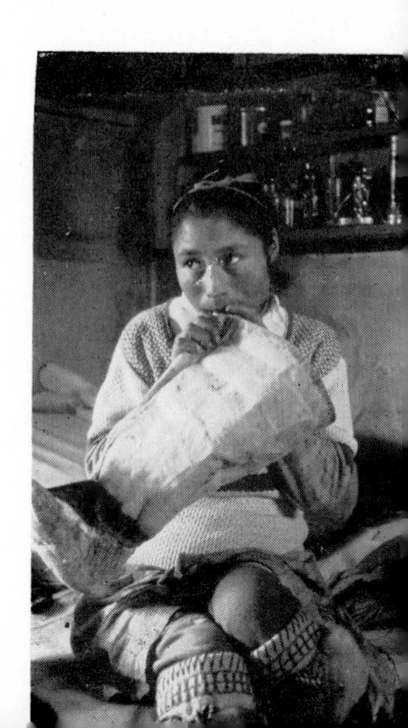

8.4 TED RUSSELL

Nikon S2, 50mm f/1.1
Plus-X, 1/60, f/1.1

sions such as Kodak Tri-X and Ilford HPS and uses them in almost every situation, except the brightest sunlight, taking advantage of their enormous latitude to expose them at "normal" ratings from 400-650 (320-500 tungsten) and forcing them when required to 1600 or more. Other professionals standardize on the medium speed Kodak Plus-X, Perutz Peromnia 21, Ilford FP3 and similar films which they use for both outdoor and moderately low level illumination, and reserve the faster films for more difficult lighting. Both groups can document their argument with excellent negatives, but the second approach is considerably safer and makes quality easier to maintain. [See Chapter 5.]

This technical division is paralleled by a "stylistic" one. Some photographers prefer to work with selective focus, to isolate the important portions of the field at maximum sharpness and allow the rest to fall off into deliberate softness. This is a more "traditional" approach, and is challenged by those who prefer a maximum sharpness throughout the total depth of the picture. This reinstates the picture organization problem of the beginner who may find that the background detail becomes too important and overwhelms his intended center of interest. In the hands of a skillful and sensitive photographer, however, this integration of all visible elements may convey more meaning and more impact than a background obscured by soft focus. Both camps, for opposite reasons, have welcomed the very rapid wide-angle Nikkors. Used at wide apertures, they not only gather light so efficiently that exposures may be made under very low illumination, but their depth-of-field is necessarily relatively shallow at these openings and selective focus may be very precisely controlled. Yet with existing light as it is commonly encountered, they produce a considerably greater depth-of-field than do the "normal" 50mm Nikkors at comparable apertures, as well as an "expanded perspective" [see Chapter 4] which many photojournalists consider desirable. In fact, this latter group is now tending to consider the 35mm Nikkor as the most satisfactory "normal" focal length. [See also Chapter 10.]

Exposure and development

The general purpose films may be quite safely used from three to six times the tungsten E.I. (1½-2½ stops) suggested by the manufacturer depending on the contrast of the subject and on the developer. A soft-working developer like D-23 will not build the highest contrast (gradient) of which these films are inherently capable, but does permit the use of film on the same cartridge under varying lighting conditions (daylight and low-level) with uniform development if exposures were reasonably adequate. Exposed two stops faster than the manufacturer's E.I., they may be developed in Clayton P-60, Ethol UFG or

8.5 Jacques Lowe

Nikon S2
25mm f/4 Nikkor

woman praying, Haiti
Tri-X, 1/30, f/4

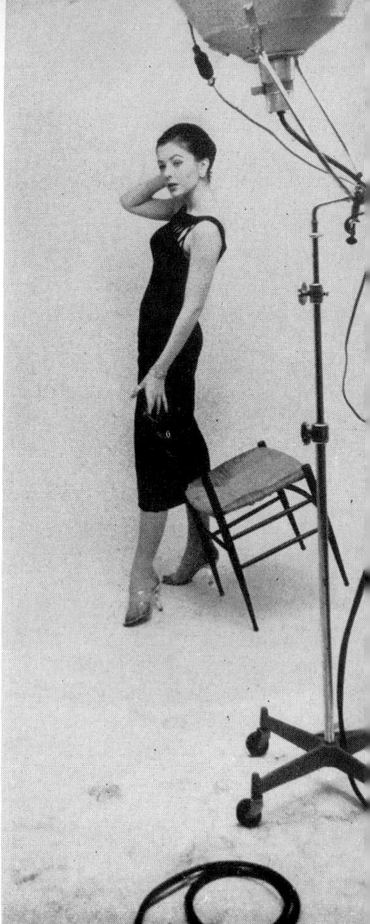

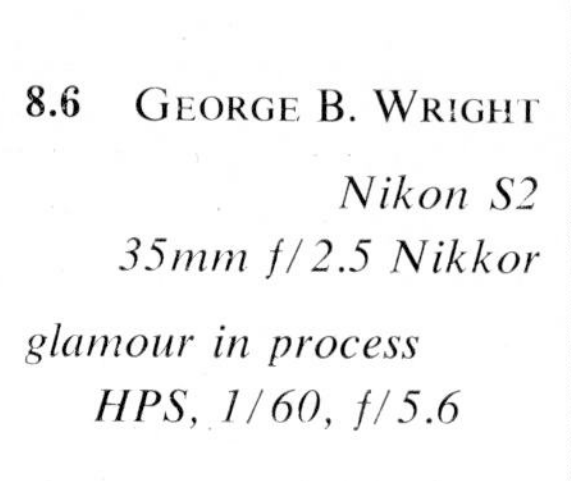

8.6 George B. Wright

Nikon S2
35mm f/2.5 Nikkor

glamour in process
HPS, 1/60, f/5.6

Kodak D-76 with excellent results. These film speeds are more than fast enough for 90 percent of the low-intensity illumination normally encountered.

With dimmer light or with the Nikkor stopped down for greater depth-of-field, the rapid emulsions may be given much faster ratings. Kodak Tri-X, for example, may be exposed at a (tungsten) E.I. of 6-800 for excellent negatives with Microphen, D-23 and Ethol UFG. Speeds up to 16-3200 are possible with Microphen or DK-50 without complete loss of quality.

When these extra speeds are required from either film group, it is best to develop by inspection [see Chapter 5] for complete control and protection against over-development. The Phenidone-based "compensating" developers now common [see *Data and Formulas*] are also very useful, for they tend to decrease the rate of highlight development gradually without simultaneously slowing down their action in the shadow areas, thus bringing up the contrast of the latter without seriously increasing over-all contrast or blocking highlight detail.

Probably the chief enemy of good quality in processing the medium speed films is *over-development* to force an extreme measure of speed beyond the 320-400 E.I. limit. The substitution of one of the higher energy developers named above for the standard D-76 or UFG or an extended processing time to obtain an E.I. of 800-1200 may lead to building grain and losing acutance. These films have good basic contrast and energetic or prolonged development may increase this to an undesirable point, at least until further development exceeds the "gamma infinity" point and the over-all fog level rises so gradient begins to decrease as negative tones block up and fine detail is destroyed.

On the other hand, the negative quality of the rapid film group is easily destroyed by *over-exposure.* These emulsions have an extraordinary latitude for under-exposure and a negative of good quality may be forced at an E.I. of at least 1200. Given too much light, the irradiation (light-scatter) through the emulsion and the halation (reflection from the base) will produce a latent image which spreads out through the sensitive halide crystals to destroy the possible acutance, already lower than that of the general purpose films, and to induce conspicuous graininess. These consequences may not be remedied by reducing development. The rapid group has inherently low contrast, a valuable characteristic for many available light conditions, and this will be further lowered by restricting development. Printing on a more contrasty paper to compensate will further emphasize the grain and lack of image contour sharpness.

There are times when quality must be abandoned and fairly heroic efforts made to secure any kind of a printable image at all on a severely under-exposed film. If recommended developers [*Data and Formulas*] are inadequate, very strong developers may be used, such as D-11 [*not* ID11], D-72 (or Dektol) or D-82. Developers intended for X-ray films have even been employed. All these, of course, result in large grain, poor acutance and distorted image tones. They are last-resort measures when an image which will print must be obtained at any cost. It is also possible to intensify the developed negative, although all intensifiers will build grain size. The printing strength of negatives will be improved, too, by the change in color imparted by one of the sepia toners intended for prints. This will produce a stronger effect on the paper which is primarily sensitive to blue and ultraviolet. All three measures may be used in turn.

Subject and illumination contrast

As light levels decrease, the contrast generally increases. (This may be a problem at higher intensities as well. A person seated near a window, for example, may have bright sunshine as a back or side light and very little useful illumination on the shadow side.) It is possible to record detail throughout a very considerable contrast range, particularly with the rapid films, but under extreme conditions (a large interior with little reflectivity and harsh lighting on faces) the range may be far beyond the capacities of the film. Formerly, and for many years, photographers were taught to "expose for the shadows and develop for the highlights." With earlier films this was excellent advice, but it is rarely applicable today. It might, indeed, produce a good negative but it would preclude available light photography at all lower illumination levels, except for the most static subjects. It is based on the assumption that the only "acceptable" negative is one which has a full range of tone gradation and an over-all density comparable to those made under "normal" lighting.

Professional photographers must neglect this advice in order to make pictures at all under many circumstances. They have demonstrated that it is frequently sufficient to record a range of proper values in the significant highlight areas and to let the shadows go black, if necessary. The brighter tones in the scene are recorded along the extended "toe" of the film curve [see Chapter 5] and this is developed (Microphen is a frequent choice) to reasonable contrast and the shadows are left to shift for themselves. (As noted, the compensating developers assist in bringing up the more weakly exposed portions without blocking highlights. Clayton P-60, for example, seems to increase shadow contrast while retaining an over-all soft effect with a desirable gradient.) The most useful general advice today seems to be to expose for the most important subject areas and to develop for them also. The resulting negatives may not satisfy the formal requirements of the sensitometrist who knows the optimum possibilities of the emulsion, but it provides a satisfactory picture under working conditions. This, it would seem, is the real object of photographic techniques.

The photographer following events or interested in the subtle fluctuations of human inter-relationships develops a sense of the precise instant and point-of-view which will give him a film image revealing the significance of what he sees. At times the lighting may be unfortunate but to modify it would alter the situation and defeat his primary purpose. These exacting conditions do not always exist. It is possible in many instances to change one's point-of-view or to wait for some occasion when the lighting on the subject is easier to handle on film. Photographing a home interior or working with children, it may alter the truthfulness of the resulting pictures in no way if the prevailing light level is raised (and contrast thereby lowered) by means of a photoflood or two directed against a ceiling or wall for indirect illumination. When only a few exposures are made, this indirect light may be provided by flashbulbs or electronic flash, although these sources tend to make many subjects aware of the photographer and self-conscious.

Reflecting surfaces are also an aid in reducing contrast or to raise the illumination level slightly. Moving a subject toward a light-colored wall, throwing a sheet over a near-by chair, or even an expedient like wearing a white shirt, a white smock or apron may make a considerable difference in contrast. Waiting for a subject to move, or changing his position when that is possible, may bring the tone range within film limits. Moving three or four feet away from a window will lower the illumination level surprisingly but will also reduce the effective contrast of the lighting even more. Shifting a desk lamp by a foot when making an available light portrait of an executive, may cut contrast in half without altering the truthfulness of the picture or interfering with the subject's activities.

Utilizing natural reflectors or awaiting a change in subject position will also affect modeling and textures. As outlined in the following chapter, lighting angle and shadows create our impressions of three-dimensional form and surface. It may be necessary to ignore these to capture an elusive significant instant, but regretfully so, for effective lighting might add considerably to the content of the photograph.

Color film and available light

Color films have now reached the speed, but not the latitude, of black-and-white films which were regarded as "fast" not so many years ago. The current Super Anscochrome is rated at E.I. 100 and may be safely exposed at twice that with proper processing. Ektachrome, too, may be doubled in rating, often without losing agreeable color or useful shadow detail [see Chapter 7]. Neither of these, nor regular Anscochrome, approaches the latitude of general purpose or rapid black-and-white films (although they are nearly comparable to some of the thin-emulsion fine grain films when these latter are exposed for maximum quality). In poor lighting situations, color films should be exposed as accurately as possible for the range of important highlight detail. Dense and even off-color shadows may be tolerated, in fact, scarcely noticed, yet blocked-up highlights annoy all but the most insensitive observers.

Boosting light levels and reducing contrast by adding bounce flood or flash is more often essential for color than for black-and-white, although the combination of the faster color films and processing for speed, together with the Nikkors with apertures of f/1.4 and faster, now make color photography possible in circumstances impossible only a year or two ago. Probably the next significant (and long) step will come with the development of color negative films which are inherently capable of considerably more latitude than positive (reversal) films.

These negative color films will also aid in solving the other major problem with current materials under existing light: the color temperature of the illumination. This varies through extreme limits everywhere, in the home, outdoors with illuminated signs, in the circus with its wild mixture of sources. Negative color films may be corrected in printing for a quite wide range of light sources (although not for mixtures, of course) but when the Nikon is loaded with the presently available reversal films, all too often, we can only abandon all attempts for "true" color and accept whatever results. Filtering becomes not only complicated, but reduces the film speed to impossible levels.

In fact, color photography under existing light now seems to be at the point where black-and-white was some years ago, when it was only possible to make a virtue out of the necessity for blur, grain and a restricted depth-of-field. With color films, a parallel set of distortions peculiar to them is necessary if we are to have any image with dim and contrasty illumination or with many kinds of lighting sources.

Pushing back the boundaries in this way and following through with the experiments it entails, however, may well contribute as much to creative vision in photography as did the earlier black-and-white experiments with existing light. The Nikon and the Nikkor lenses provide an instrument of excellent design and construction, obedient to those amateurs and professionals who prefer creative exploration to placid imitation. Photography still provides the stimulus to find new and better means of visual expression beyond any easy routine.

8.7 MORRIS JAFFE

Nikon S2
35mm f/2.5 Nikkor

Dutch interior
Plus-X, 1/8, f/3.5

9

Flash and other Artificial Lighting

AMATEUR OR PROFESSIONAL, THE PHOTOGRAPHER'S PENCIL is his Nikon, and his grammar is his command of light. Many whose pictorial statements are effective and memorable went through the "grammatical" drill of studio lighting. Although their pictures now speak a much less stilted language, this training strengthened their awareness and skill to exploit available light or to introduce flash or floods when conditions require. The serious Nikon user will find that working with flash and floods will not only make possible many pictures he could not otherwise take, but will sharpen his perception of light effects to improve even pictures made in bright sunshine.

General Lighting Principles

THE WAY to learn lighting is to become aware of shadows. Ordinarily, our perception of objects and people censors out much of the effect of cast shadows and we ignore what the camera will see all too clearly. Setting up lights, flash, photofloods or studio light sources, is largely a matter of noting the kind of shadows created and where they fall. Shadows are of two kinds: *cast shadows* from projections or from a near-by object; and *modeling shadows* which result from the shape and texture of surfaces. Cast shadows all contain an inner, dark core and a lighter edge. A tiny light source such as a bare bulb (in unreflective surroundings) casts shadows with a hard edge and outer zone (penumbra) almost non-existent. Larger sources of illumination cast shadows with softer edges, and very large sources such as a large lamp reflector, a translucent screen over the light

---

9.1 DAVID LINTON *Nikon S2, 50mm f/1.4 Nikkor*
Editorial illustration *studio fluorescents, Tri-X, 1/60, f/5.6*

9.2 JACQUES LOWE *Nikon S2, 35mm f/2.5 Nikkor*
Bounce floods and window light, Tri-X, 1/60, f/8

source, or a large surface from which the light is "bouncing" will cause the dark shadow core (umbra) to vanish. If the source is very large, the shadow may be only a faintly darker area. The size of cast shadows depends in large part on the distance of the light source (and, of course, the relative size of the light and the object which blocks off the light rays). A small, near-by source such as a bare bulb will cast large shadows.

Modeling and texture effects are also dependent upon the type of source. A bare bulb (a flash with the reflector removed) will produce tiny, dense shadows from surface irregularities and will be rapidly reduced in intensity with distance around the form of an object, and the "drawing" will be strong and contrasty. If the bulb is at the focal point of a parabolic reflector or is in a spotlight behind a lens, the rays will emerge in a narrow, strongly directional beam and will weaken much less with distance than the "law" of illumination [below] indicates. Shallow reflectors such as those on most flash equipment act as diffuse sources, particularly since they "spill" light to reflect back from the surroundings into the areas of shadow. Larger light sources (a translucent screen or a flat reflecting surface may become the "source") cast low-contrast shadows with much weaker clues to form and texture.

Lighting "patterns"

There are several arrangements of one or more lamps which the amateur should learn to recognize. The last thought in his mind, however, should be that artificial lighting of any subject (except, perhaps, a flat document he proposes to copy) may become a matter of rote. These lighting patterns or arrangements, however, are "base points," and have definite contrast and exposure characteristics which are useful to understand.

Photographers need artificial lighting for controlled results in many circumstances, and there is no "creative" conflict between "building" lighting and the truthful and penetrating use of available light in the situations for which that is appropriate. The family or another indoor group in the evening, a baby portrait, the movement of the dance, a fashion illustration, a catalog or advertising illustration of a product, or the interpretive record of a sculpture, all require some measure of control, some forethought in the placing of the light sources. Photographic illumination involves much more than providing sufficient intensity for an adequate film exposure.

The number and arrangement of light sources for any purpose is simplified if we consider each of them primarily in terms of their *function.* The first (and sometimes only) lamp is placed to establish the drawing of form and textures of the picture subject and to establish the tone and "mood" by means of its direction and intensity. The height of this *key light* and its angle in relation to the imaginary line between the subject and the Nikon establish the possible strength of modeling, the visual impression of the subject as a real, three-dimensional object in space. The angle also establishes the possible maximum contrast of the lighting. Both of these factors may, of course, be modified when and if we add more light sources.

From the infinite possible locations for this key light, several may be isolated as *points of departure.* In Chapter 3, these were noted as positions of the sun outdoors, and the results considered in terms of modeling, contrast, exposure and latitude. Indoors, the principles are the same, although we have usually much greater control over the light position and the relative contrast. If we set an imaginary hemispheric dome over our whole picture area, we may think of the light source as hung from a wide choice of points over the subject. At or near the Nikon, it is *front lighting;* up the curve of the bowl somewhat it is *top front;* half way to the side and half way up it is the often-advised *angle light* or "double 45°"; and at the zenith, overhead or *top lighting.* It becomes *side lighting* at 90° and *back lighting* at positions beyond that. These positions blend into each other and the names are unimportant as long as we remember that these lighting angles produce increasingly contrasty illumination in the order given.

From a keylight location near the Nikon around to about 45° exposure will be "normal"; from there to about 60° (if there is little general reflected illumination or added light directed into the shadows) it requires a 1 stop increase; at 70° 2 stops; and at 90° 3 stops. Beyond that, light produces a bright edge and a silhouette. When the light reaches a position such as this, however, it may lose its prime function as a key light, unless we desire a silhouette or a softly-lit semi-silhouette when the level of illumination is sufficient for "non-directional" light from reflections or another light to permit some detail on the surfaces toward the Nikon to be recorded.

With a single light, we must think, too, of how evenly the illumination covers the subject. With smaller objects, the studio rule-of-thumb is a reflector equal in diameter to subject size for strong modeling (10-14 inches for a head-and-shoulders portrait), and larger sources (or a shallower reflector) for softer effects. With subjects much wider than any light source can be, such as a group of persons, in order to get reasonably equal (1.5 to 1) coverage across the front, the reflector should be back at least three-quarters of the subject width when a wide-angle Nikkor is used, or back a distance one and a half times subject width with a 50mm Nikkor on the Nikon, and correspondingly further as the focal length of the Nikkor is increased. This is theory, only, and is influenced by the shape and efficiency of the reflector. With black-and-white film, an intensity difference between center and sides of as much as 3:1 may be tolerated.

The same considerations apply to coverage in depth, which in illumination theory should place the reflector back 4 to 5 times the depth of the subject. This is not often possible with flash and informal shooting of interiors or groups, for example, and a standpoint so distant would lose most of the effective light intensity. Instead, the reflector should be aimed toward the most distant important subject area, with the weaker edges of the beam falling on the nearest points, as a practical way of securing even illumination.

Reflecting light from walls or ceiling is also efficient when the room is small and reasonably light-colored. A flash or flood reflector tilted upward so part of the light strikes directly and the rest is "bounced" will give some modeling and sparkle with lowered contrast and better coverage.

Placing additional lights

To supplement the key light, one or more additional light sources may be useful. Again, their position may be selected with greater assurance if their function is kept clearly in mind. The usual purpose of a second light is to increase illumination in the shadow areas (hence the usual label "fill light") and enable the photographer to modify the lighting contrast when the key light has been located at such an angle that it produces strong modeling and consequent deep shadows. (Obviously, if the key light is close to the Nikon there will be few, if any, such cast shadows and a second light, if one is added, will serve some different function than the one we are considering.) A fill light belongs in a position where it will not cast a second and conflicting group of shadows which are visible to the camera. This is somewhat flexible, but the "safe" location is at the front lighting position, as close to the Nikon as possible, so the shadows this "fill" light throws fall behind the subject and are invisible.

With the main light at any point except the back-lighting position, the second light will not only reach the shadow areas but also increase the illumination of the highlights. With two lights of equal strength (two photofloods in identical reflectors or two flashbulbs) their relative distance will govern the contrast. At the same light-to-subject distance this will be 2:1. Moving the key light in closer by 1/8 will change this to 3:1; to the half-way position, 4:1. At 1/3 the distance the contrast will be 5:1 and at 1/4, 10:1. This ignores the reflections from surroundings, and is a broad generalization.

With an immobile subject, we may use a single light in several positions. For example, with the Nikon S or S2 on a tripod, we may re-wind the shutter for multiple exposures, with flash or flood, or if the surroundings are dark, open the shutter of any Nikon on time exposure and fire as many flashbulbs from different positions as we choose.

If more than two lights are employed, the same caution is necessary to avoid conflicting and over-lapping shadow patterns. The problem of placement is much simplified, if the *function* of each additional source is kept clearly in mind. Then, a background light may be placed to control the tone and its distribution, or accent lights placed to illumine details, reveal form more strongly or to attract attention to a particular point. (Form is modified in a picture on the simple principle that lighter areas appear to advance, and darker areas to recede, from their surroundings.)

The relative intensities of these additional lights may be painlessly calculated by using the f/stop numerical scale as a footage guide. A light from 4 feet away is twice as bright as one (of the same strength) from 5.6 feet, or four times as bright as one 8 feet away. Other factors, such as the overlapping of the light beams will modify this neat scheme, but professionals have used it as a handy rule-of-thumb.

Selecting exposures

It is possible to train one's eye to make quite accurate estimations of exposure from a summary of clues in familiar situations, but vision adjusts rapidly to changes in the level of illumination and error is easily possible. Indoors, a No. 2 photoflood 4 feet from the subject gives an apparently intense light, but actually is only 1/12 that of summer sunshine (an exposure difference of 3 1/2 stops). It is always better to use the Nikon Exposure Meter for accuracy, particularly to find the minimum correct exposure recommended in

9.3 GERRY LOW *Nikon S2, 50mm f/1.4 Nikkor*
Studio floods, Tri-X, 1/125, f/4

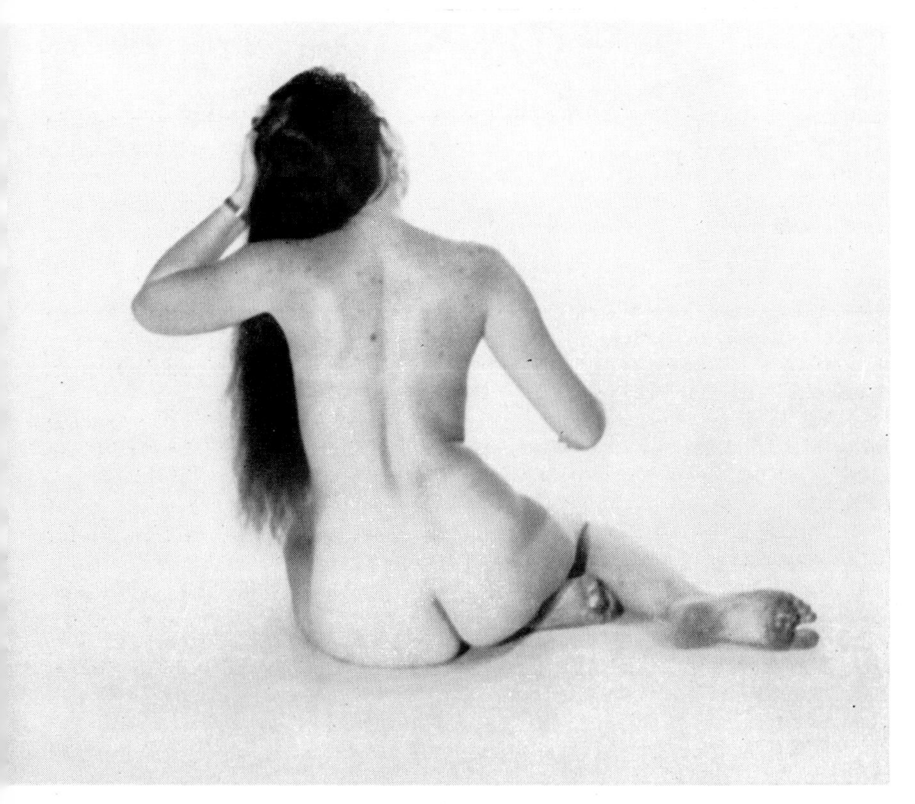

9.4 Gerry Low

Nikon S2
50mm f/1.4 Nikkor
Studio floods
Tri-X, 1/125, f/4

other parts of this Manual for quality negatives. Much of what was said in Chapter 3, applies here also. The meter may be used for a reflectance reading from camera position which will be quite accurate for an over-all scene, yet sometimes misleading when the important subject is against a background much different in illumination level. Then, it is better to take a close-up reading of the most important area or to measure the lightest and darkest important areas and determine the contrast range. From subject position, the Nikon Exposure Meter (with the opal plate inserted) may be used for an incident reading of the main light strength, although this, too, needs "interpretation" to avoid under-exposing important shadow areas or dark subject tones, particularly with color film.

While circumstances alter cases far beyond the limits of rules, the contrast of artificial lighting may usually be controlled fairly easily and kept within a 3-stop (8:1) range with color films and a 6-stop (64:1) range with black-and-white to compress reflectance values within the useful exposure tolerance of the films. Most often, contrast considerably less than this is preferable for quality work.

Photofloods and tungsten sources

The amateur will find that excellent portraits, interiors and still-life photography are possible with photoflood bulbs with inexpensive clamp-on attachments or folding portable stands. Aluminum reflectors in a variety of sizes are available. The No. 1 and No. 2 photofloods resemble household bulbs in size and are "over-rated" to burn at high intensities (equivalent to approximately

250 and 500 watts) with a correspondingly shorter life, one measured in hours. They are rated at 3400K, but this is somewhat misleading for their "color" temperature" alters considerably during their life. Similar bulbs of 3200K maintain their color somewhat better and are slightly more expensive. There are also blue floods (4800K) intended for movie color work, but these are of dubious assistance in still photography. "Projection" bulbs for studio lights are either in the 3150-3250K range (when new) or rated at 3350K. They are long-lived and much more consistent in color.

Household tungsten bulbs (in America) average around 28-3000K when new. Fluorescents have, properly, no color temperature because of their radiation of a set of narrow-band emissions which the eye blends into satisfactory illumination. Color films must be carefully filtered for reasonably good tones under these illuminants, although there have been many very excellent color photographs made with colors deliberately distorted for effect. Normally such off-color rendition may be made acceptable, if the illumination source is included or clearly evident in the picture.

Flashbulbs

THE INVENTION of flashbulbs, a photographic generation ago, brought convenience and safety to portable instantaneous lighting. At first the tool of the professional, the amateur has learned the simplicity of the flashbulb and uses the newer, midget bulbs by the millions each year. The professional is turning more and more to electronic flash, but the flashbulb remains a necessity and a convenience in many situations. They are especially valuable to the amateur Nikon owner, for his small investment of a Nikon BC Flash Unit is justified by better pictures when the larger cost of an infrequently-used electronic unit would not be.

Flashbulb types

Flashbulbs consist of a glass envelope containing a *primer* (a fast-burning substance) and, in most types, a filler of extremely thin wire-like, sheared aluminum (sometimes with a small percentage of magnesium). A weak (3-amp.) current ignites the primer and, in turn, the wire which burns very rapidly in the oxygen atmosphere of the bulb. The glass envelope is lacquered on both surfaces to provide strength against shattering under the intense sudden heat of this "bonfire in a bottle." There are several base sizes, including a medium screw base (like household bulbs) and the "single contact bayonet" which fits the sockets of the Nikon BC Flash Units.

These bulbs vary in other ways to suit different purposes. The two kinds most suitable for use with the Nikon are the *M-type* and *FP-type* flashbulbs. There is a small but measurable interval between the time current is applied to the primer and when the wire ignites. This is measured in milliseconds (1/1000 second). As illustrated in Figure 9.11, it requires about 20 milliseconds for M and FP bulbs to ignite and reach maximum light output. The peak of M-type bulbs is brief and intense; that of FP-type (of comparable size) weaker but longer lasting.

Light is measured in *lumens,* the intensity of an engineering "candle" point-source over a square foot area from a 1-foot distance. (A hundred-watt

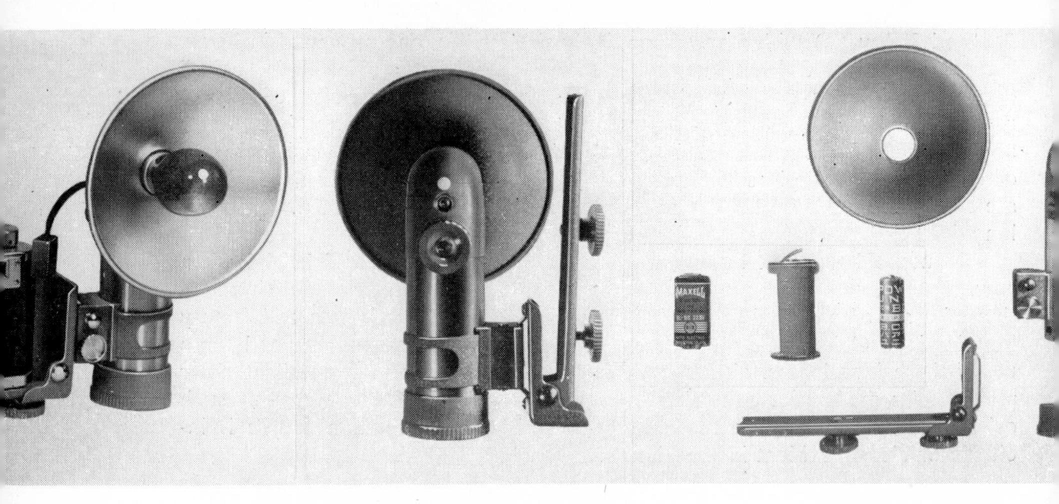

Nikon Model BC III Flash Unit

The Nikon BC III Flash Unit is a compact battery-capacitor flashgun of simple construction. Inserting a flashbulb in the socket causes the capacitor to charge rapidly to provide full power to the bulb. An angle bracket attaches to the Nikon body at the tripod screw and the unit is normally mounted at the left. This places the outlet (marked "Sh.") next to the synchronizer outlet on the Nikon. A short positive-lock cord connects the two, or a longer cord may be used when the gun itself is held away from the camera. (A tripod screw is provided in the bottom cap of the flash unit.) The other outlet on the case (marked "Ex.") may be used to connect an extension flash when this is desired.

When the bottom cap is removed (by a short counter-clockwise turn) the battery-capacitor unit itself will slide out. This contains the capacitor and a hearing aid type battery (22½ volt). Engraved marks indicate the proper side for each and the direction in which they should face. It is important that both "plus" ends should be toward the top of the unit.

---

household bulb produces approximately 13-1500 lumens.) Flashbulbs are rated in *lumen-seconds,* their total lumen output if they were to emit light for a full second instead of the 35-70 millisecond flash duration of the small bulbs we are considering. Not all of this emitted light is useful. The effective output is measured [see Figure 9.11] between the points where they emit half their maximum intensity, and the elapsed milliseconds to these two half-peak points is the basis for determining proper synchronization with the shutter opening of the Nikon. [See section on synchronization, following.]

Other bulb types include the fast (5 millisecond) peak *F* bulbs, comparatively weaker and with only primer material to burn, designed for simple amateur cameras; the *M-2* and smaller bulbs (with as-yet unstandardized base sizes) which are even weaker so simple camera users will not over-expose their pictures; and the larger *S-type* which is slower to reach peak and delivers a much greater lumen-second output. The lacquer coating of the glass envelope

Open the mounting bracket to a right-angle, slide the outside knob over and fasten it securely. Attach the bracket to the Nikon body by means of the tripod screw. The flash unit slides onto the bracket from below and is held in place by the knurled locking-knob on the front.

The connecting cord attaches to the flashgun socket with a short clockwise turn (push in gently when attaching or removing). The other end attaches to the synchronizer socket on the Nikon body.

When a flashbulb is inserted, the knob at the rear of the gun behind the reflector is extended and the bulb may be ejected by depressing this knob to its normal position.

Immediately below this ejector button is a transparent test button. The flashgun circuit may be tested (without a flashbulb) by holding this test button depressed for about 4 to 5 seconds, then pushing the shutter release button (on the S or S2 Nikon). If the battery, and capacitor are properly functioning, the test button will give a brief flicker of light. (See illustration below.) An alternate trial may be made with a test bulb inserted in the same way as the flashbulb. About 4 to 5 seconds after inserting, press the shutter release button (on the S or S2 Nikon) and the bulb will flash if battery, capacitor and circuit are correctly functioning. These tests should be made, of course, before winding the film and setting the shutter. The Model SP Nikon has a safety interlock which prevents closing the circuit through the camera when the shutter is unwound, so these tests will not be effective when the flash unit is used with that model.

The flashbulb itself may be tested (right below) by pressing the small lamp within the knurled knob on the back of the case about 4 to 5 seconds after the flashbulb has been inserted. If the flashbulb is sound, this lamp will briefly light.

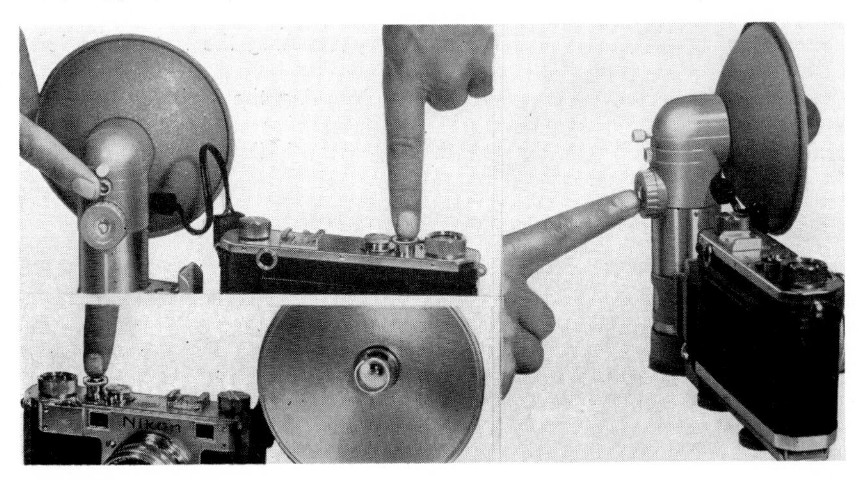

Nikon BC IV Flash Unit (for S2 and SP)

The Nikon BC Flash Unit slides into the accessory clip of the Nikon and eliminates all external connections. It features a folding reflector which makes the unit unusually compact.

When the back cover of the unit is removed (right) a tiny capacitor will be found under a metal cover. The plastic tape fastened to this, loops under a 22 ½-volt battery to facilitate its removal. Above the capacitor is a small test lamp, and the cover incorporates a dial exposure calculator (opposite page).

For use, slide the BC IV into the Nikon accessory clip as far as it will go; to remove, depress the release button at the bottom rear of the gun. Normally, perfect contact is automatic. However, the length of the contact pin may be adjusted by turning the tiny knurled adjustment wheel with a pointed tool (right below) but do not force the pin too tightly against the Nikon flash terminal.

The circuit (including battery and capacitor) may be checked before inserting a flashbulb by pushing the bulb ejector (top of unit) for a few seconds then pressing the Nikon shutter release while still holding the ejector button down. The small test bulb should glow briefly (visible through the translucent back cover). This method will work with the Nikon S2 before advancing the film and winding the shutter, but not for the Nikon SP. With the latter, wind the shutter, cap the lens and carefully wind back the film a frame after performing the test. (See left, below.)

The flashbulb itself may be checked by inserting the bulb, winding the shutter, then pushing the checking button in the side of the case (bottom center, this page). The test bulb will light if the bulb is good, permitting the capacitor to charge.

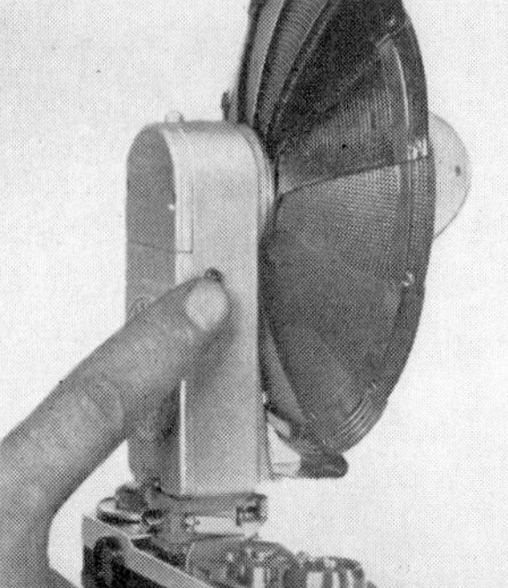

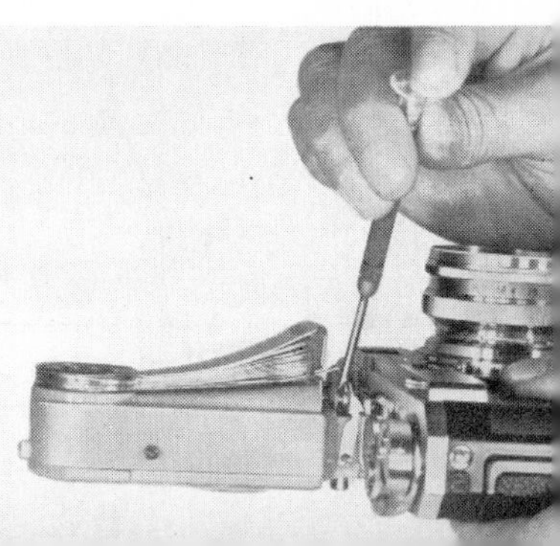

The dial exposure calculator is set by aligning the tungsten speed of the film in use against the shutter speed (top dial settings, right). The proper aperture for any subject distance when either M or FP bulbs are used may then be read directly from the bottom scales.

When F flashbulbs are used, set the film speed arrow against the dot just to the right of the 1/125 shutter speed mark on the upper scale and set the Nikon for 1/30 (or slower) shutter speed. The bottom dial may then be used in the same way to find the proper aperture for any subject distance.

For proper synchronization settings and other flash information, consult the tables in the Data and Formulas section at the end of this Manual.

---

is tinted blue in bulbs labeled *B* to change the normal 3800K color temperature to about 6000K (at some loss of lumen-second output) for use with daylight type color films. There are also *A* bulbs lacquer-tinted for a 3200K output. Less-frequently encountered kinds include those designed to filter out nearly all radiation except the invisible infrared for special application use with infra-red films.

Flash unit design

Self-contained light-weight power sources to attach to cameras quickly followed the introduction of flashbulbs. In their simplest form, these deliver current from small dry-cell batteries directly to the bulb to fire the primer and have a switch arranged to time this ignition with the opening of the camera shutter. At first, the battery current was also required to trip the shutter for this synchronization unless a special mechanical cable-release linkage was provided. Modern camera shutters (including the Nikon) now provide internal electrical contacts which close at the proper moment to connect the current to the flashbulb, with a consequent great improvement in reliability of action.

Quite as importantly, well-designed guns for the Nikon now employ even smaller, light-weight batteries which build a charge in a storage capacitor instead of firing the bulb directly. This *battery-capacitor* design has many advantages. As batteries weaken with use or age, the capacitor charge still builds to a constant level (only .01 amps provide peak charge in slightly under 2 seconds), and battery life is increased because the drain at any time is so considerably reduced over that necessary to fire the flashbulbs on direct connection. The surge from the capacitor is uniform throughout battery life and bulbs are dependably ignited without variations in delay time. The powerful surge burns the primer in about 1 millisecond and has only a 1-2 millisecond duration so current flow ceases before the shutter contacts re-open, thus reducing the cause of contact pitting and wear.

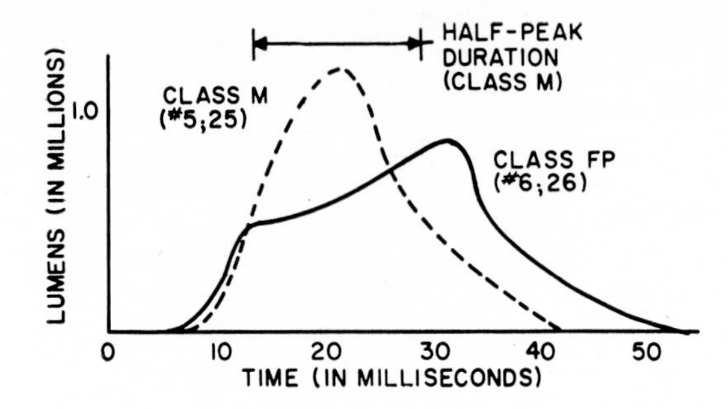

9.11 *Class M flashbulbs emit light for only a few milliseconds. The useful light from FP bulbs extends over a longer period (see text).*

Flashbulb synchronization with the Nikon

The open-time of the Nikon shutter must coincide with the instant when the flashbulb is burning at full brightness. Since the Nikon shutter is a (variable width) slit in a curtain, moving at high speed across the surface of the film, the flashbulb must either emit light at a fairly constant level for a long enough period so both ends of the film will receive light or, if a short-peak, high-intensity bulb is used, the shutter must be set for a slower speed so the slit in the curtain is wide-open to expose the whole surface of the film simultaneously when the bulb is at peak. As Figure 9.11 indicates, these two alternative conditions can be fulfilled with the small FP and M bulbs respectively.

A measure of shutter efficiency is the extent to which it approaches the ideal of uncovering and then covering again every point on the film, at full entering light intensity for the exact fractional second duration for which the shutter is set. Focal-plane shutters like that of the Nikon always approach this ideal more nearly than can the opening and closing blades of a between-the-lens shutter, and focal plane efficiency itself increases as shutter travel (traverse) is speeded up. Nikon design has improved in this respect from the 24-millisecond traverse (usual in 35mm camera design) of the S to the 17 milliseconds of the S2 and to the present 13-millisecond traverse of the SP. Consequently, there is some difference between these models in the way they are synchronized with the several classes of flashbulbs. A table of ranges of shutter settings for the three Nikon models with a table of characteristics of those bulbs which are designed to work most efficiently with the Nikon will be found in *Data and Formulas.*

Flashbulb guide numbers

The simplest way to determine exposures with flash is to establish a *guide number* for a particular film-bulb combination at a shutter speed which will admit most or all of the light between the half-peak points. The guide number provides a figure which may be divided by the distance *from flash to subject* to give the f/stop for proper exposure. A guide number of 160, for example, would indicate an f/stop of f/16 at 10 feet or f/11 at 15 feet or f/22 at 7 feet. (The latter two distances are rounded off within the acceptable limits.) This guide number is based on the fact that light intensity falls off at a rate proportional to the square of the distance. If we visualize the light from a point-source coming through a small opening to illuminate a surface 1-foot square at a distance of 1 foot and then the same "volume" of light spread over 4 square feet at a 2-foot distance [see Figure 9.12], we can see how it is weakened at this "distance squared" rate.

Guide numbers for their flashbulbs are provided by the manufacturers and listed in abbreviated form on each carton. These, of course, are averages and can serve only as general guides, not as universally applicable or rigid rules. It is always better to establish a personal guide number which automatically compensates for individual habits and interpretation. This may be done for any shutter speed and bulb combination at the cost of a half cartridge of film and a few flashbulbs. The most certain results will be obtained with Kodachrome because of its relatively limited latitude and sensitivity to exposure variation and the uniform processing it receives. The results from tests on color film may be interpreted for black-and-white film, but it is dangerous to interpret the results for color from black-and-white tests.

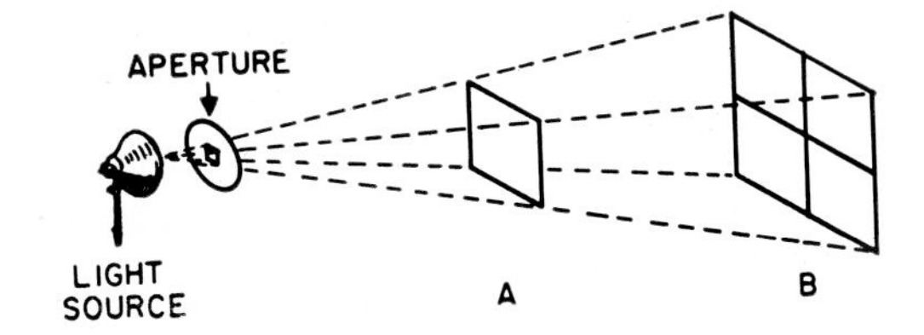

9.12 *Light from a small source covers a surface area which increases by the square of the distance from the source.*

Set up a test subject which includes a full range of tones and arrange to give an approximate 8:1 highlight-to-shadow range of illumination. Determine this by meter readings while it is lighted by a photoflood set up ten feet away in the *exact* position which the flashbulb will occupy. Make a series of exposures at half-stop intervals each way from the rated guide number of the flashbulb you are using and extending over at least two stops either way. Request that the film be returned after processing as a single strip for better comparison of the results and identification of the exact exposure from your records. Select the f/stop which gives the best density and the best color rendition of both highlight and shadow areas and multiply this number by 10 for your subsequent guide number at this shutter speed. A table of half- and third-stop f/numbers is included in *Data and Formulas.* The guide number for black-and-white films (at the same shutter speed) may be found by counting down the table from the whole or fractional stop best for Kodachrome: each f/stop (or equivalent in fractions, of course) represents a doubling of film speed. This new f/number, multiplied by 10, will be the proper black-and-white guide number.

Remember, however, that it still remains a guide, although a more reliable one. In light-colored, reflective surroundings you may decrease exposure by as much as a half to full stop; in dark surroundings or out-of-doors at night increase exposure by an even greater amount. It is best to make separate tests for other shutter-speeds. Computation is difficult because faster speeds may not utilize as much of the flash output between the half-peak points.

"Bounce light" exposures are figured by taking the flash-to-reflecting-surface-to-subject distance to divide into the guide number for the f/stop, then opening up a full stop for the light absorption of a white ceiling.

9.13 JACQUES LOWE

Nikon S2
50mm f/1.4 Nikkor
Bounce electronic flash
Plus-X, f/16

Multiple flash from another unit connected with the Nikon BC III Flash Unit or more elaborate set-ups may require only a slight correction for added over-all "bounce" from surroundings. If more than one flash is directed at the same area, however, an exposure correction from that indicated by the one-flash guide number is required. This includes cases where two reflectors are adjacent and throw approximately parallel beams, as well as when two or more light beams converge from different positions (as a key and fill lamp in one of the "patterns" considered previously). In the latter instance, the beams will usually overlap so the highlight areas are illuminated by both bulbs.

There is an exact formula for finding photographic effectiveness of the combined intensities of overlapping beams (when both photographer and subject have the leisure for calculation). The combined intensities of the lights equal the square root of their number: 2=1.4; 3=1.7; 4=2, etc. This assumes that the lights are equal in output and in their distance to the subject. If they are not, instead of adding "1" for each light to arrive at the sum, add their relative intensities. That is, a key light (or the one for which the guide number of the flash would apply if it were used alone) is taken as 1, and a fill-light moved back to a greater distance for half-intensity at subject position, is taken as 0.5. The square root of their sum (1.5) is close to 1.25. This is equivalent to closing down 1/3 f/stop for correct exposure of the highlight area. This correction depends, of course, on the actual importance of full gradation in the highlights. Lighting experience, gained at greater or lesser expense, usually substitutes for a scratch-paper solution of square roots.

Elaborate multiple flash set-ups employing several synchronized flashbulbs (or electronic flash units) arranged around the subject, may be calculated from readings with the Nikon Exposure Meter. Set up (matched) photofloods in reflectors at the same positions occupied by all the flash reflectors which will illuminate the surfaces of the subject facing the Nikon, that is, all except back-light or background sources. (This is also useful for a direct, visual check of relative intensities to eliminate clairvoyance about the lighting results with flash). Then, from the distance of the key light and the flash guide number, calculate the single-bulb f/stop at the chosen shutter speed. *Next,* turn on the photoflood at this key light position and make a meter reading. Set the meter at a *purely arbitrary* high film speed index to bring together the guide number f/stop and shutter speed on the calculator dial at the indicated needle reading. (If the needle reading makes this inconvenient, another *arbitrary* shutter setting may be used on the meter, but use only the f/stop calculated from the guide number.) *Next,* turn on the other photofloods and take a second meter reading from the same position as used before. *Then,* reset the meter calculator dial for the new light reading, and determine where this change places the shutter speed which you had previously set against the guide number f/stop. This *new* f/stop opposite the shutter speed on the dial will be correct for the multiple-flash exposure. Up until this last step, the f/stop used in these calculations must be that determined for the one-flash guide number. All other values on the calculator dial may be arbitrary; the dial is being used here only as a slide-rule.

As indicated in the earlier part of the chapter, the *relative* photographic effect of individual lights may be quickly determined from the f/stop series on the Nikkor barrel. The relative strength of a light is doubled, for example, when it is moved in toward the subject from 11 to 8 feet, and doubled again when brought in to 5.6 feet.

A multiplied light intensity may be improvised when photographing with the Nikon BC Flash Gun: fasten one or two extra bulbs with a rubber band or Scotch tape to the one properly in the reflector socket. The ignition heat of this synchronized bulb will usually fire the others, although there will be a few milliseconds delay and a slow (1/8 or more) shutter speed should be used to take full advantage of the longer combined duration when the subject movement permits.

Synchro-sunlight flash exposures

With side lighting, back lighting or other contrasty situations out-of-doors, the shadows may be illuminated to a more useful level with synchronized flash. Naturally, this technique works as well indoors, although the flash more often becomes the main light rather than a balance for the existing illumination.

The basic rule is simple: determine the exposure for daylight or existing illumination anywhere; take the selected f/stop number for this exposure and divide it into the flash guide number for the daylight shutter speed setting to find the correct flash-to-subject distance. This will usually provide a 2:1 highlight-shadow ratio.

The relative strength of the flash may be reduced to about one-half by covering it with one thickness of handkerchief, by moving back to a greater distance without altering the f/setting, or even by removing the reflector from the flash gun (or closing the Nikon BC IV reflector). Note, however, with the latter method the position of the bulb when the gun is on a hand-held camera. Flashbulb ignition heat and the slight percentage chance of its shattering add a certain touch of Russian roulette with no reflector.

Open flash

The total effective light output of the flash may be utilized if the Nikon shutter is set for a relatively slow speed, and such settings may also be used when the photograph will gain in effectiveness if the (usually low level) existing light is allowed to build image density on the film in addition to that created by the flash. This often gives a feeling of natural light and realism to scenes or slow-moving subjects which permit exposures of 1/8 to a full second with a synchronized bulb. Or we may place the Nikon on a tripod with the shutter set on Time and use multiple flash either from the camera position or from (several) other vantage points.

Electronic Flash

ELECTRONIC FLASH units consist of a power source (or a means of tapping external current) which is used to charge a capacitor. A trigger circuit, synchronized with the camera shutter, discharges the stored energy through a gas-filled tube in a nearly instantaneous surge which produces a brilliant flash.

These units may be designed in several forms, depending on the requirements of the service for which they are intended. The simplest circuit is a *direct battery* system which employs a high-voltage dry battery (or two in series) to deliver about 450-500 volts (dc) directly to the capacitor. Its simple design makes this arrangement light, rugged and efficient. Recycling time is shorter than with any other battery-powered units and the batteries will deliver from 500 to 3000 flashes at 0.5-4.0 cents apiece.

Another type uses a single dry *battery plus vibrator*. This latter splits the current from the battery and delivers it alternately to two capacitors connected in series to bring the voltage up to the approximately 500 volts required. This too, is an efficient system and may be designed around several battery sizes, including small, low-voltage cells. The recycling time is increased with this circuit, and various units deliver from 50 to 1500 flashes during battery life, but at about the same cost per flash as direct battery circuits.

Heavier and somewhat more complicated systems are designed around a dry battery and vibrator which charges the capacitor through a *transformer and rectifier*. The additional components involve higher energy loss, especially with the small transformers needed if portability is important to the unit design. However, this circuit permits a transformer wound for alternative use with the unit plugged into an a-c line. Inexpensive short-lived low-voltage batteries for these units may produce variation in capacitor charge and effective light output if not replaced promptly. Recycling time (on battery) is longer than with the previous types and cost per flash slightly higher. On ac, recycle time is very rapid and cost per flash negligible.

Similar designs employ small *lead-acid storage batteries* and are generally heavier, more complex and expensive. Recycling time is moderately long, but these units can be designed to deliver a much brighter flash than those from dry battery units. The cost per flash varies widely, depending on many factors, but again is negligible from a-c current if the unit is convertible.

Lead-acid cells require attention and may produce corrosion. They require a re-charging unit (working on ac). Battery capacity is usually in the range of 6-12 ampere hours which may be insufficient for a heavy drain of frequent flashes during a short period. (Stand-by current alone when the set is switched on frequently reaches 1 amp.) Most of these disadvantages are removed when *nickel-cadmium storage batteries* which deliver about twice the energy per pound are employed. There is no corrosion danger from their potassium hydroxide electrolyte; they may be used in any position and require little attention. They retain their charge for 6-12 months of storage, may be safely recharged in about 2 hours (at 3 amps) or briefly "boosted" at up to 5 amps, and recharged several thousand times. They deliver a very constant voltage and cost per flash is considerably lower than with lead-acid cells.

Larger studio electronic flash units work from ac only. The initial investment is high, but light output is considerable and cost per flash very low.

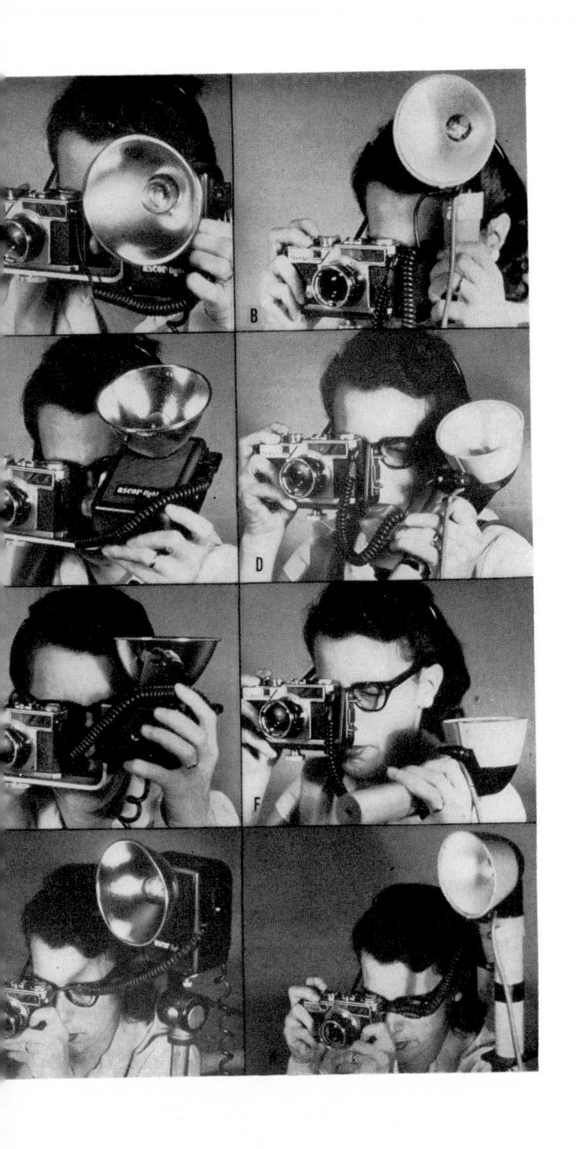

9.14 *The electronic flash may be used with the Nikon for direct light (A, B); for "partial bounce" (C, D); for full bounce (E, F); or mounted on a tripod so the camera may be moved around for the correct viewpoint. Units illustrated are the Ascor 201 and the Heiland Strobonar 71A. The Ascor unit has the reflector mounted directly on the capacitor case.*

Dry batteries have a shelf life, a period during which they retain a useful charge without use. This will vary considerably depending on storage conditions. If they are kept cold, about 45F, this may be considerably prolonged. (Allow them about 6-8 hours to come to room temperature before use.) They also have a variable useful life in the unit. They are more quickly exhausted by rapid-sequence flashing than by moderate use a few hours each day. Rapid firing also produces an output loss of about 25 percent after 50 flashes (one-half stop exposure difference) but this remains constant and batteries recover somewhat with rest. With moderate use, output drops about 15 percent after a month and then remains constant. Output varies also with temperature, at 100F it is about 40 percent more than at 70F. About 30 percent is lost at 40F and over 95 percent at 6F.

Capacitors

Early flash-tubes required up to 4,000 volts but capacitors (sometimes called "condensers") could produce only about 500 volts and had to be connected in series. Portability and efficient battery operation have arrived with tubes manufactured for the 4-500 voltage range and improved capacitor output.

Portable unit designs vary in positioning the capacitor. Some place it at the flash-tube [see Figures 9.14 and 11.10] and others in the same case with the batteries. Close to the tube there is minimum resistance and maximum efficiency at the cost of an additional hand-held weight greater than that of the Nikon. This design, however, easily permits use of the capacitor-tube as a "slave" remote light with a photo-tube to activate the tripper circuit. In completely flexible unit design, the capacitor (with tube removed) will also function as a booster for another capacitor to double (approximately) light output from a single flash-tube. (Tubes used on portable lights will usually take capacitor doubling without failing or curtailing useful life.) Some units also permit tapping two flash-tubes into a single capacitor. Light output from each tube will be approximately halved and flash duration lengthened slightly.

Capacitors which have been idle for a month or more require "reforming" which may seriously drain a battery. Units using ac should be switched to this circuit and the flash discharged several times to reform the capacitor before use with battery. Circuits of well-designed units maintain a "trickle" charge" to keep the capacitor formed without battery drain.

Unit *recycling time* is calculated from the interval required for the capacitor to reach 90 percent of peak voltage [see Figure 9.15]. Tubes may be flashed as a level of about 60 percent is reached, but exact output will be uncertain. Recycle times for portable units may range up to 15 seconds,

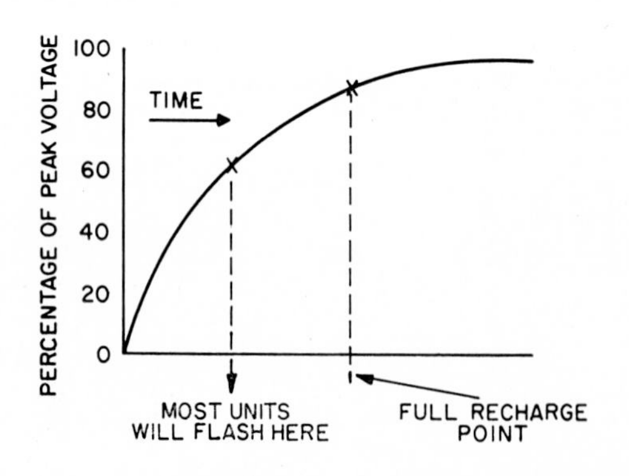

9.15 *For full output, electronic capacitors should be charged to at least 90% of capacity. Most units will fire, however, when capacitors reach about 60% charge.*

although many recycle in 3 or 4. Larger a-c units may be designed to recharge up to the 120-times-per-second cycle of regular (U.S.) alternating current which is used to time the trigger circuit for "continuous light" applications, and special 10,000 per second flashing rates have been produced.

Note: Charged capacitors contain high-voltage and must be handled with respect. Do not open the unit (and thereby nullify its safety design) unless you know what to expect.

9.16 Gene Cook
Nikon S
35mm f/3.5 Nikkor
Dancer Iva Kitchell
two electronic flash units
Plus-X, f/16

Flash Tubes

Tubes are generally formed as a helix, U or loop of glass or quartz and filled with xenon gas at a pressure such that it will not spontaneously flash at the rated capacitor voltage. A trigger element, fine wire around the tube or electrically-conducting glass in newer designs, conducts a high-voltage ionizing pulse to the gas. The gas becomes conductive, discharges the capacitor in a surge accompanied by the brilliant flash. American flash tubes range from 400 to 4000 volts for portable units; some European tubes are rated as low as 180 volts. Tubes may range in output from 8 w/s (watt-seconds) to 24,000 and in conversion efficiency between 35-45 lumens per watt. The color of this light varies between 64-7000K. This color temperature rating is not strictly accurate for the tube emission spectrum is not directly comparable to that of a "black-body." The illumination is of daylight "quality," however, and daylight type color films are used sometimes with a weak minus-blue filter such as the 81A usually recommended for Kodachrome which has a strong response to bluish light. The inner surface color of reflectors may vary from unit to unit or as they age, and this is usually as important to exact color film response as the color of the light emitted at the tube envelope.

Effective light output

The simplest and often misleading method of measuring the effectiveness of units is their power output. (Input is an even less useful measure.) This is rated in watt-seconds (joules), found by multiplying the capacity of the capacitors (in microfarads) by the square of the voltage and dividing by two. Watt-seconds loading times 35 is a very rough guide to lumen-seconds output. This neglects the rest of the system and is at best a very rough approximation of efficiency in use.

The measure of *BCPS* (beam candle power seconds) was first substituted for the w/s rating. This is the light strength along the axis of the beam from the reflector as measured by an integrating light meter such as the one produced by General Radio. This, too, is not completely an accurate evaluation. for reflectors differ considerably in the fall-off of illumination at greater angles out from the axis.

To include this important factor, readings out to a 20° half-angle are weighted (for method see American Standard PH2.4-1953) for the *ECPS* (effective candle power seconds) and manufacturers are beginning to rate their units by this scale.

Reflectors are an important component of the light system: their shape influences the distribution of the light and their inner surface its color and its

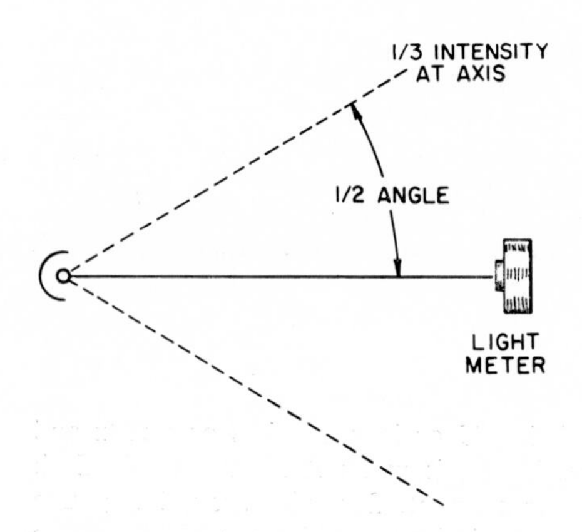

9.17 *Reflector coverage for electronic flash units is measured from the points where the intensity of the beam falls off to 1/3 that at the central axis. The proper angle of coverage should be slightly larger than that of the Nikkor in use (see also Chapter 4).*

brilliance. Any reflector will distribute less light at increasing angles from the axis and the coverage of a reflector is properly established from the half-angle where the illumination drops to 1/3 that at the beam. [See Figure 9.17.] This angle should be somewhat larger than the viewing angle of whichever Nikkor is used, e.g., 50° for a 50mm Nikkor.

Synchronization

The trigger circuit of the flash tube must be activated when the shutter is fully open, and this is accomplished by built-in contacts on the Nikon shutter which close the circuit through the tripper cord [see Chapter 2]. The current through the Nikon shutter should be a weak one, of course, and is in all well-designed units.

A flashbulb, as previously noted, requires an appreciable time (small FP and M types about 20 milliseconds) to ignite and come to peak output. The electronic flash-tube delay is so small that it may be taken as zero in all calculations. (Some electronic flash models have a built-in (3-10ms) delay in their trigger circuits) Flash duration, however, will vary. This is measured between the times when the illumination is at 1/3 peak output [see Figure 9.18]. Many portable units are in the 1/750 to 1/1500 second range, a duration somewhat longer than studio units. Very accurate measurement of the lumen-second distribution requires a microsecond (1/1,000,000) scale.

The focal-plane shutter of the Nikon travels across the film at a constant rate, with the width of the open slit which admits light to the film varied with

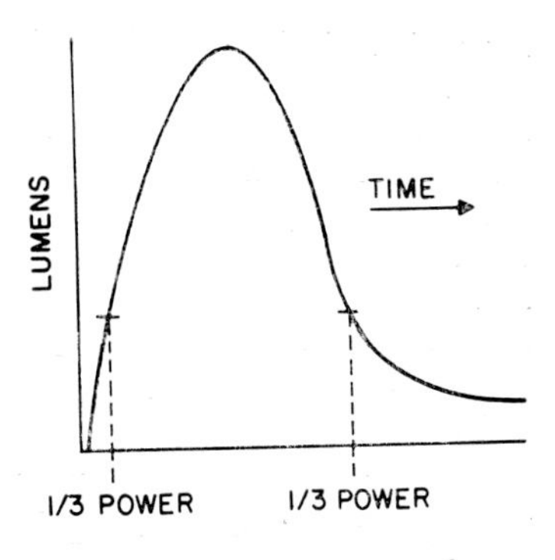

9.18 *The effective duration of electronic flash is measured between the points when the illumination reaches 1/3 of its greatest intensity. This is a much briefer duration than that of any flashbulb.*

the shutter-speed setting. At slower speeds, this slit is fully opened to expose the whole film area simultaneously and an electronic flash must be fired to synchronize with this brief instant of full opening if the whole film area is to receive the flash illumination as reflected from the subject. The fastest speed (full slit opening) at which the model S may be synchronized is 1/30; the S2 at the "X" (1/50); and the SP at 1/60 [see chart, *Data and Formulas,* page 275]. Even at these shutter speeds, the actual film *exposure* time is that of the flash duration, unless there is enough bright ambient light present at the scene to cause a "ghost image" or double exposure while the shutter curtain is open, as discussed below. During this time, some tubes emit up to a maximum level, of 25,000,000 lumens, compared to the 320,000 lumens of a 6B flashbulb.

Synchronization of the Nikon and an electronic flash unit may be tested by removing the camera back and connecting the tripper cord. Point the reflector away from the Nikon to reduce its brilliance and look into the back of the camera. When the unit is fired, the flash should disclose the shutter at the fully opened position.

Guide numbers for electronic flash

Some manufacturers have waged a battle of guide number claims, sometimes based on watt-second *in*put and optimism. Actually, guide numbers are flexible and depend on many circumstances. Excellent results may be obtained with guide numbers apparently 2–2 1/2 stops apart, depending upon exposure and processing methods.

The guide numbers are used like those for flashbulbs [above] and also control effective exposure by modifying the f/stop with distance. One guide number is correct for all speeds at which the shutter curtain is fully open, since the flash duration is usually briefer than any of these shutter speeds.

An extremely conservative guide number may be computed from the ECPS rating and this formula:

$$\sqrt{.063 \text{ x ECPS x film Exposure Index (ASA)}}$$

This is more useful as mental exercise than in practice, for it will produce overexposure and neglects many important factors. It is comparatively easy to determine a guide number which is based on individual conditions. Kodachrome (with an 81A filter) should be used. It receives standardized processing and a black-and-white guide may be determined from this but not vice versa. Set up a subject with a range of colors and contrast (determined by meter reading with a photoflood bulb at the intended position of the flash reflector) between shadow and highlight of about three f/stops. Place the flash reflector exactly ten feet from the subject and make a series of exposures at 1/2 or 1/3 stop intervals all the way from f/2.8 to f/8. (Have the developed film returned as a strip rather than as individually mounted slides for better identification of the exact exposure setting for each frame. The f/stop which produced the most acceptable result in terms of color rendition in both shadow and highlight areas, multiplied by 10, will be the proper guide number for subsequent work with that flash unit. [See *How to use guide numbers* earlier in this chapter.]

Black-and-white guide numbers may be derived from this one for Kodachrome, but it is better to make an independent test. Start at the f/stop you would use for a slow-speed flash with a No. 6 flashbulb and make a series of exposures of a subject like that described above from a 10-foot distance. Proceed by 1/2 stops at least two stops each way. If no starting point is known, cover the full range of f/stops on the Nikkor used. Develop this test the *normal time* for the film-developer combination. From the negatives (or

9.19 GEORGE B. WRIGHT — *Nikon S2, 105mm f/2.5 Nikkor*
"Mathew Brady" — *electronic flash, Ilford FP3, f/16*

test prints) determine the best f/stop and multiply by 10 for the guide number The full strip will also indicate the full extent of film latitude for subjects of moderate contrast range.

There are several variables which keep this number a "guide" and not a rule. In addition to such factors as subject color and the reflectivity of the surroundings, the *focal length* of the Nikkor employed will influence the results. Reflectors all produce a center beam of illumination stronger than that toward the edges. The longer focal length Nikkors have an angle of view narrower than do Nikkors of shorter focal length and thus image only the area covered by the brightest beam of a (properly aimed) reflector. The guide number may therefore be increased somewhat to compensate in part. Film reciprocity failure may sometimes become a factor, but not usually with portable units. There is some slow-down in response at exposures briefer than 1/500 but it remains slight to 1/5000 (and will, of course, have been included automatically as a factor in the tests suggested).

Exposure and development with electronic flash

The principal enemy of good negative quality with electronic flash seems to be over-exposure, over-development or both simultaneously. The usual advice to increase development appreciably with electronic flash is well-intentioned but unnecessary. The conditions for producing an "ideal" negative in the sensitometric laboratory are different from those of practical work. The bluish electronic flash may produce a slightly soft and "flat" negative (higher color temperatures usually tend toward lower gradients), but in common practice no more than a 10 percent increase of exposure is required. It may even be better, when negatives are slightly too low in contrast, to *reduce* exposures slightly and keep development constant.

It is a wise practice to make some additional test exposures at a range of f/stops and to give these a longer development time to derive a separate guide number for maximum possible film speed consistent with personal standards of acceptable negative quality. Sheet films are often forced by a 50 percent extra developing time (the Associated Press is reported to recommend a normal 1/3 increase) but this processing is very drastic for 35mm. Results may be adequate for photos reproduced by coarse-screen newspaper printing, but for little else.

The rapid films are often necessary with electronic flash only when a smaller aperture is required for extra depth-of-field or when covering a large area with little reflectivity. Not all rapid films retain their full relative speed advantages with electronic flash. (The latitude and reciprocity of this film group extends toward latent image building under weaker illumination.) One of the best rapid films seems to be Kodak Tri-X, developed in either D-76 or Ethol UFG. The electronic flash speed response of Ilford HP3 is about a half-stop slower than Tri-X, but HPS does not respond quite as satisfactorily as Tri-X.

Many of the medium speed film group respond well and are very sensitive to the brief flash. Excellent speed without graininess is possible with Ilford FP3 or Kodak Plus-X, developed in either D-76, UFG or in Ethol 90 (diluted 1:10). The slower, fine-grain emulsions also respond well, especially Kodak Panatomic-X with normal development in D-76 (*never* Microdol) to preserve grain structure and acutance.

10

Professional Photography with the Nikon

COMPACT SIZE AND SIMPLICITY OF HANDLING make the Nikon an excellent camera for the amateur. These same characteristics impress the professional, who must handle his camera semi-automatically with his full attention directed to his subject. Nikon design not only permits rapid exposures, quick re-loading and one-hand operation, it also provides precision construction and sturdiness under the conditions of steady use. Nikkor lenses and Nikon bodies are completely interchangeable. A new Nikkor lens "off the shelf" will attach to any model Nikon body (which has not been mistreated) without front- or back-focus errors. Unfortunately, this precision is not universally encountered even among well-known and expensive camera lines. The serious amateur will find he has, in his Nikon, a sturdy, accurate instrument which will answer all his requirements and which he will continue to use and admire if he goes on into free-lance photography and then into professional work.

Photojournalism

The extremely quick growth in popularity of the Nikon line in the United States stems directly from the experience of photojournalists and news photographers covering the war in Korea. The successful photojournalist is an inveterate experimenter, constantly searching for better tools which will translate to film the succession of significant glimpses of reality which form his stories. To see a lens is to try it, and in the case of the Nikkors to include it in the working kit. The professional grapevine soon transmitted their enthusiasm to America.

The basis for it is the method of photojournalism. To cover a story, an unfolding event or a personality "in depth," the photojournalist must work

---

10.1 TED RUSSELL
General Dean repatriated

Nikon S, 50mm f/1.4 Nikkor
Super-XX, 1/20, f/2

10.2 Arthur Rickerby
Nikon S2
28mm f/3.5 Nikkor
Old age home, N.Y.C.
(United Press Photo)
Tri-X, 1/30, f/3.5

rapidly, yet often spend many days and many cartridges of film in the search for a picture series which will present a full and truthful story. All the while, he must search for variety and freshness: in angle and point-of-view, in working distance, in perspective. Most often, he must follow through in the existing light, from sunshine to candle-light.

His "tool-kit" depends upon the nature of his assignment and his own style of work. It might well consist of two Nikon bodies (with a third as spare) and two Nikkors of different focal lengths in use on the Nikons and alternate Nikkors for interchange or special shots. Two Nikons on neck straps and ready for instant use are enough to handle and the rapid bayonet introduces little delay when conditions change. The professional, however, would feel himself handicapped with only one Nikon with one focal-length Nikkor at hand. No matter how fast a lens interchange is possible, pictures do not wait.

The particular Nikkor combination in use will vary with the assignment: an f/1.8 (or f/2.5) 35mm and the f/1.5 85mm; the f/1.4 50mm and the f/2.5 105mm; the f/4 25mm and the 50mm; or some other pair of focal lengths which will provide an instant change in perspective, depth of field and angle of coverage. With the combination immediately at hand and an occasional substitution of a different Nikkor on one of the Nikons, he can isolate his subject even from a little distance away, relate the subject and background with a lens of wider angle, or compress or expand perspective [see Chapter 4] as required.

A 50mm Nikkor is often considered "normal" for 35mm work. More and more, photojournalists seem to be shifting to the 35mm focal length as the basic Nikon lens. For their purposes, the 63° angle of view offers advantages over the 46° of the 50mm, as does the deeper zone of sharp focus at comparable f/stops, or the ability to open up a little for speed without losing too much depth.

When maximum speed is required, there is now the extraordinary speed-plus-acutance of the f/1.1 50mm Nikkor. At the expense of depth-of-field which is very shallow at f/1.1 (a consequence of optical laws, not lens design) he can isolate his subject in comparative darkness and at a reasonable shutter

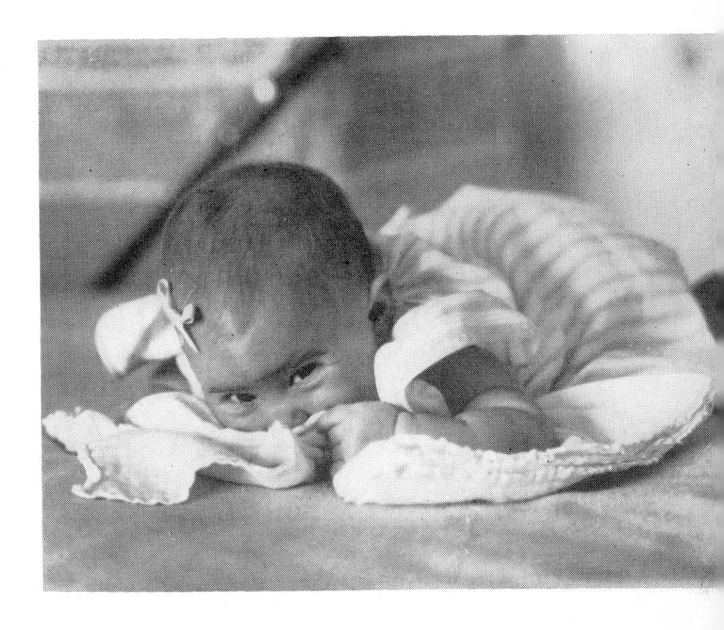

10.3 Gene Cook
Nikon S2
50mm f/1.4 Nikkor
Eddie Fisher's baby
Available light;
Plus-X, 1/60, f/4

speed. The f/1.8 35mm, of course, will give considerably greater depth at comparable f/stops. With those two and the f/1.5 85mm Nikkor (which is the same basic improvement in design as the f/1.4 50mm), the professional will have three matched lenses of very useful focal lengths, all of which give him freedom under poor lighting conditions yet produce an image acutance beyond that of any film he can find to use.

With the Nikon S or S2, the auxiliary Varifocal, Variframe or a matched individual finder is used on the Nikon when Nikkors other than 50mm are attached. The extraordinary finder system of the SP offers a combined range-finder and view-finder which indicates the field of coverage of six different focal-lengths and is parallax-corrected for four of them. This not only speeds up the already rapid process of focusing, then framing, with lenses other than 50mm, it presents to the photojournalist the instant comparison of the fields of view of the lenses he is using and eliminates wasted movement in selecting the Nikkor for a particular exposure.

News photography

The news photographer, generally seeking one picture to illustrate one event, is a much more conservative fellow than the photojournalist. With many conspicuous exceptions, he prefers a proven approach and this attitude is more solidly crystalized, if anything, in the mind of his picture editor or the city desk. For many years, a routine has been built around the 4x5-inch sheet film camera with a (sometimes very firmly) attached flashgun. Processing on larger newspapers places a still-damp print on the editor's desk only a few minutes after the photographer totes in his holders. It has been necessary to prove beyond doubt that the Nikon can compete in dependability and speed from exposure to finished print, as well as enable easier and more extended picture-coverage, before photo departments would accept it and then begin to include it in official equipment provided.

10.4 GENE COOK
Nikon S2
28mm f/3.5 Nikkor
Walter Winchell
(for "Colliers")
Tri-X, 1/15, f/4
forced development

10.5 *(right)* BURT OWEN
50mm f/1.4 Nikkor
Story illustration
(for "Modern Romances")
Plus-X, 1/100, f/4

The lead was taken in this by the more adventurous and pioneering photo staffs of the midwestern newspapers, whose news photo coverage often puts newspapers published elsewhere in the shade. The *Milwaukee Journal,* for example, had Nikons before photographers on *The New York Times* or the *Herald Tribune* began to use them in their work.

The news photographer uses a Nikon somewhat differently than does the photojournalist. Normally, he is in a hurry and one Nikon body and one Nikkor is enough to have in hand, although there may be other Nikkor lenses in his car. It is different when he is assigned to feature work or to an event, such as a ball-game lasting several hours. At the latter, he can make crowd shots with the 28mm or 25mm Nikkor, cover near-by action with a 50mm Nikkor, and action in the field (or an interesting face in the crowd) with either the 250mm f/4 or the 500mm f/5 Nikkor. The latter, mounted on a light tripod, will give him the advantage of bringing in distant action which was formerly the monopoly of the ponderous, custom-built "Big Berthas" fixed in some lofty overlook.

The motor-drive of the new SP Nikon will be especially effecive in news work. The rapid sequence exposures, for example, can cover the slide into home plate or the ring knock-down with a series which will more certainly provide the most effective picture than will even the extraordinary timing and anticipation of the peak moment which so many news photographers acquire. This motor drive has another advantage when it is set for single-exposure use. The design of the S2 and SP, even without the motor drive, provides a very fast film advance lever. With this, while the press camera user is reversing a sheet film holder (and the news photographer is very dextrous at this feat!), the Nikon user can make a half-dozen different exposures, even on the move. The Nikon SP camera, with electric motor drive set for single exposures, will cut down this interval even further. If a bystander blocks the lens at the instant of exposure, a second trip of the shutter release, as fast as human reflex

permits, repeats the shot before the subject has shifted or the action is over.

The fast Nikkor lenses have brought existing light into news photography. Without the bulky press camera and the inevitable flashgun, the news man can become as inconspicuous as the photojournalist if he chooses, or may select a more distant viewpoint and the 105mm f/2.5 or a longer Nikkor. Night action and foreground detail at a fire scene become possible with the f/1.1 or the f/1.4 50mm Nikkor, the f/1.5 85mm and the f/1.8 35mm Nikkors. And these are useful, too, for interior action when flashbulbs are forbidden or inconvenient.

News photographers have depended upon the processing speed of a single sheet film and the "advantage" that coarse grain from harsh processing will not show in the newspaper engraving. Fast processing techniques are now available which permit retaining the necessarily finer grain required by 35mm, yet meeting the speed requirements of news work. Developers such as Ethol UFG and a number of others bring up image density at the fastest rate possible to control with useful accuracy in most newspaper darkrooms, although the news-picture syndicates seem to have developed private formulas, witch-brews to retain a semblance of reasonable grain at nearly dip-and-drain speeds.

The 35mm camera gained considerable new respect at the 1956 Democratic convention in Chicago, where it was used by several newspapers and news syndicates, most notably United Press Newspictures. News and picture magazine photographers covered the convention floor and caucus rooms with 35mm, 28mm and 25mm lenses for proper picture angles in the crowded surroundings and a few much longer ones for distant close-ups. Both UP and International News Photos used (approximately) 4-minute development by inspection in UFG (with deep tanks to eliminate reel-loading time) for fast films like Tri-X exposed at E.I. 500. This resulted in a negative matched to the low-contrast prints required for wire transmission, with a margin of safety for the inevitable over-exposures under changing light conditions. A further reduction in ex-

10.6 PHILIP O. STEARNS
Nikon S
50mm f/1.4 Nikkor
Winston Churchill
Plus-X, 1/8, f/1.4

posure-to-wire-transmitter elapsed time was used by UP's picture editor, Harold Blumenfeld who received the 35mm negatives (3-minute force-dried) at his desk in 6-exposure strips in cellophane sleeves. These were edited in a small colorslide magnifying viewer which gave an image approximately 4x6 inches, large enough to appraise their subject content and their quality. Many front-page pictures were used across the country, including sequence strips, and produced the decision to exploit 35mm coverage of such events more intensively in the future.

Illustration work

The fields of advertising and editorial illustration overlap in some areas where the ultimate use of the picture seems to be the only distinction. In very large part, of course, advertising photographs are born on a drawing board in an advertising agency and executed as projects of technical ingenuity with elaborate lighting and studio cameras. A glacier-like but steady progress away from this has become more evident in recent years.

The necessity for being "different" to compete for attention, combined with the developing education of the public to the natural, truthful photograph made by a perceptive photographer, has opened a window to the atmosphere of life, if only by a crack. Institutional advertising by insurance companies and some others, for example, is employing excellent single prints originally made in the course of the photographer's own visual exploration of the world around him, often with no expectation of an immediate market. Many art directors apparently either first became aware of this vast area of photography at the "Family of Man" exhibit, or aware that there was a public appeal in such pictures awaiting exploitation. In any event, some superior pictures have been widely published, many of them made on 35mm film. It seems safe to predict that a quite large fraction of institutional and even some product advertising will be made on 35mm in the next years, capitalizing on its "realistic" appearances.

Editorial illustration on the other pages of the magazines has long anticipated this. The general interest and women's field magazines commission photography which is, at times, indistinguishable in standards from photojournalism at its best. Many of the same photographers are employed and they bring their 35mm-oriented approach, the frank, sharp-eyed appraisal of life seasoned by their individual emotional reactions to what they observe.

Alongside the "editorial look" of contemporary illustration is the contrasting approach of deliberate distortion. Ironically, a Nikon was used by one photographer in a way its designers could never have anticipated. A tiny area from a 35mm negative was enlarged to 16x20 on contrasty paper and copied from a distance (for a tiny negative image within the 35mm frame) and this film carefully developed for *maximum* grain, emphasized by the necessarily great enlargement ratio to bring the tiny image up to 11x14. Color films, too, are intentionally misdeveloped, utilizing the "errors" which manufacturers warn against, to produce over-all color casts or reversals for their attention-compelling value. A new version of these techniques appears almost daily and the current magazines provide a text-book for any photographer anxious to eliminate the fine-grain, long gradation negative of excellent acutance his Nikon and Nikkor lenses make possible.

Industrial publication photography

A not too distant cousin of the previous photographers is employed by many corporations. This is not the "service photographer," a few of whose working techniques are mentioned in Chapter 11, but rather the staff member (and sometimes editor as well) of the company publication. This may be circulated among employees or directed to stockholders and to the mailing-list maintained by the public relations director. In either case, the photographer generally finds himself assigned to make what are called feature pictures by news photographers, industrial process shots (either descriptive or pictorial), informal portraits of executives who are not notably informal in the presence of a camera, a picture story of a pension-supported employee or of a new company cafeteria, the action-moments of an employee sand-lot baseball team, and even the "mug shot" of the department safety-award winner. He is a versatile fellow.

There is none of these assignments which may not be adequately handled with a Nikon. Even the industrial-process photograph is almost always one which may be successfully made with the proper choice of Nikkor, often the f/1.8 or f/2.5 35mm which permits a deep zone of focus under either existing light or with some general boost in over-all intensity. In some companies, the visit of the photographer becomes a full-dress project. He appears with a heavy 8x10 camera, and will require (or bring along) at least one assistant equipped with a strong back. A carpentry crew may be needed to erect a platform. The plant electrician must be assigned to tap lines for powerful lights, wires will be strung about and the working crew in the plant distracted. Even a minor slowdown in any manufacturing operation will show up in the bookkeeping department as a red-ink entry, and the memory of these earlier photographers on safari lingers in some industries to haunt those who follow them.

One photographer with one Nikon can often accomplish as much or more than the view-camera man accompanied by his bands and out-riders. He may ask the plant electrician to substitute brighter bulbs, and the plant manager will send around a painter to "neaten up." The safety engineer will scout to see which protective devices visible to the Nikon have been sabotaged by machine operators in their battle of wits against his booby-traps. After this brief diversion, the photographer's approach will seem casual compared to the old-time one. The Nikon may be set-up for coverage in depth over a large area, moved in (or a longer Nikkor substituted) for middle distance shots, and close-ups of individuals at work made without disturbing the routine and often without making workers conscious of the continuing operation of the camera.

Portraiture and people

The formal studio portrait is a stylized ritual, an event which progresses by stages from appointment to sitting to proof presentation to the framed "likeness" on the mantel. The customer expects to be not only beautiful in the photograph, but expects to resemble the image she has mentally projected into her mirror for many years. The studio photographer accordingly employs tricks of lighting and camera angle and uses a negative large enough to be rebuilt with pencil and etching knife to supply a product engineered to specification. There would probably be little purpose in using the Nikon for this work. The clean, sharp Nikkor image would prove a handicap.

If we enlarge the definition of "portrait" to include the informal and casual, the interpretive study of an individual, the close-up of a person in action against his normal background, and the quickly-seen laughter of a child held on film for others to enjoy, we open a world of pictures for which the Nikon is designed. It includes the work of many magazine photographers as well as the amateurs who are interested in and respond to people around them and to their activities and curious interrelationships.

The Nikon with the f/2 50mm Nikkor is sufficient equipment for the amateur to set down his perceptions of the people in his environment. The f/2 is the "slowest" of the 50mm Nikkor lenses, but there will be few occasions when he will ever feel the need for more light-gathering power in portraiture. Certainly, the gallery of memorable photographic portraits contains few made with faster lenses. Out-of-doors, even children at play, or other action, will require far less than maximum aperture; indoors, under moderate illumination, f/2 will permit selective focus for the semi-formal, "planned casual" seated figure. A photoflood or two, or flash reflected from a white ceiling, will provide enough light even with medium speed films for a picture of a child or baby.

At a professional level, a 50mm Nikkor used at the common working distance of 5-8 feet will give too small a head-and-shoulders image on the 35mm negative. At these distances, good perspective and image size are both obtained with an f/1.5 or f/2 85mm Nikkor or at these or slightly greater distances, with the f/2.5 105mm Nikkor. In fact, anyone interested in portraiture will find this 105mm, with its image 2.1X that of the 50mm Nikkors from the same distance, an excellent choice as the second lens acquired. It will give an image size comparable to that of the 50mm at a slightly greater working distance.

Perspective is slightly "compressed" in an interesting and frequently useful way [see Chapter 4] at normal print enlargements and viewing distances. Changes in aperture size will easily shift the depth of field boundaries for either selective focus with an indistinct background for a portrait or a more sharply-

10.7 JACQUES LOWE
Nikon S2, 105mm f/2.5 Nikkor
Mike Wallace
(from "Argosy")
Tri-X, 1/8, f/2.5

recorded environment "brought in" somewhat by the perspective of this focal length when this space rendering is useful to the photograph.

Magazine photographers seem to choose the 85mm Nikkor more often, perhaps because it is a satisfactory compromise length for either portraits at medium distances or for small groups of two or three persons photographed from a somewhat closer distance than the angle of view of the 105mm permits. From any given standpoint, there is, of course, a somewhat greater depth of field with the 85mm than with the 105mm at identical f/stops. This extension of sharpness may be used to link together the subject and his environment-in-depth, a practice of great value for expressive pictures.

Prints for publication

Producing optimum contrast, gradation and image color on photographs intended for engraving is widely regarded as one of the black arts. Variations of reproduction accuracy among magazines has even been known to incite the suspicion of some lack of good faith on the part of the editor who purchased the prints. Matching the print to the engraving process, and the necessary allowances for the printing method, paper and ink used by the magazine are not matters of indifference to the photographer. Many who are recognized as great contemporary camera workers secure optimum reproduction of their prints in any publication, through no more mysterious means than providing suitably printed originals to be sent to the engraver.

These prints do not resemble those intended for exhibition which come out of the same darkroom. Prints for engraving function as the basis for a photographic copying process which, like any copying, tends to build contrast and to merge tones, particularly at the high and low ends of the scale. For letter-press printing, the most common kind, a photograph should have full detail throughout. The tone range of average subjects should be slightly restricted, that is, the print will appear *slightly* flat, as if printed on paper a "half grade" too soft, but *not* dull, muddy and dead. This lack of full, brilliant

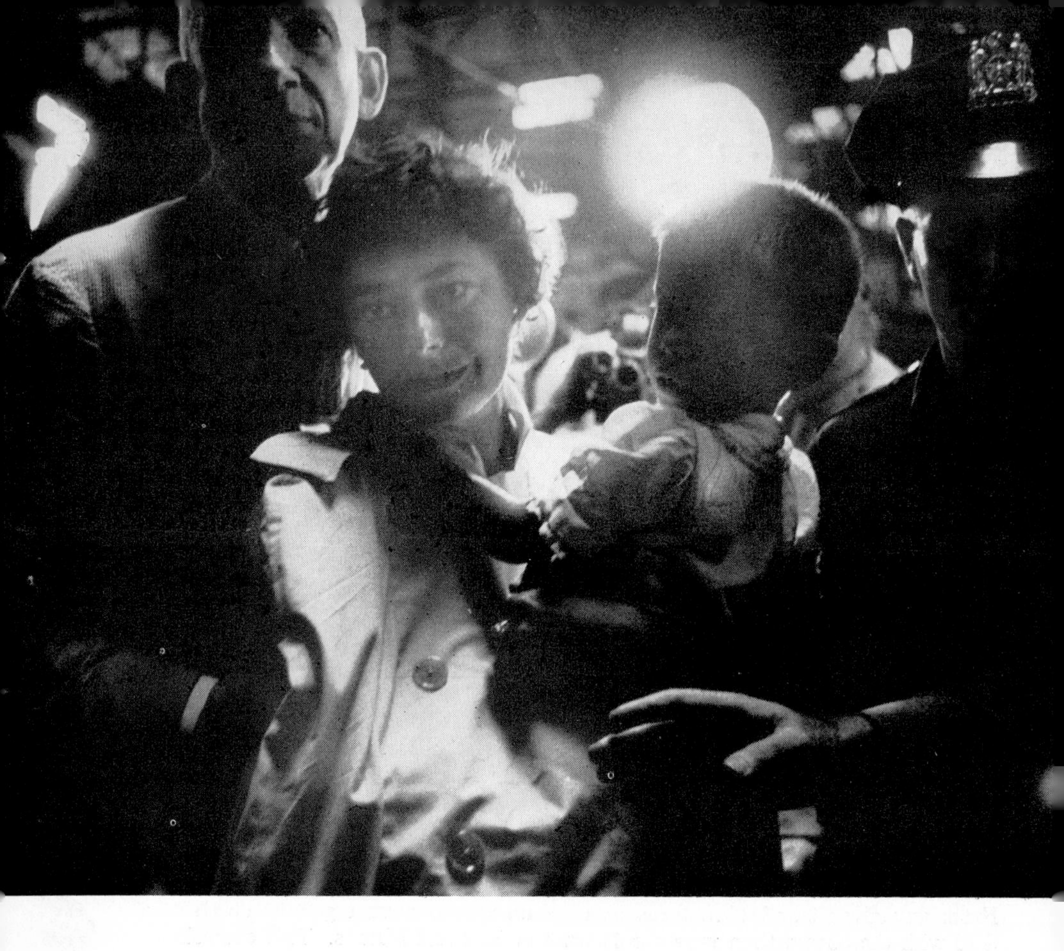

contrast (which will be restored in engraving) should not result in tone mergers, a lack of distinction between adjacent areas which are nearly the same image density. Hold the print close to a strong light and look through the back. If there are many details visible which are not apparent from the front with normal viewing, the negative has more in it than is being transferred to the paper.

Glossy papers have better tone separation, even at less than maximum contrast, than do other surfaces of the same emulsion. A badly-ferrotyped glossy may give trouble, and an excellent compromise which will keep both photographer and engraver happy is the unferrotyped glossy print, dried as if it were a matte surface. It will retain excellent tone separation with a uniform surface smoothness. Other surfaces also reproduce well, among them the Kodak *A,* Du Pont *BT,* Ansco *B* and Ilford's Smooth Lustre. Smaller engraving shops or those in sections of the country which are not publication centers succeed in convincing many customers that anything but a perfectly-ferrotyped full glossy is an affront to an honest tradesman. Obviously a textured paper surface, one embossed to resemble linen, canvas or bathmat, offers a difficult problem. Any reasonably smooth surface which is printed for the proper tone separation without full contrast is accepted by engraving plants accustomed to publication work as the basis for a perfectly satisfactory result.

In general, cold-tone prints tend to favor slightly the rendering of shadow details in the subsequent engraving and warm-toned images, the reproduction of highlights. It is the firm conviction of engravers that sepia-toned prints never

10.8 *(left)* TED RUSSELL
Nikon S2, 50mm f/1.4 Nikkor
Andrea Doria survivors
Ruth Roman and child
Plus-X, 1/30, f/1.4

10.9 *(right)* TED RUSSELL
Nikon S2, 50mm f/1.4 Nikkor
Andrea Doria survivors
Plus-X, 1/125, f/5.6

produce good engravings. Some years ago, tests demonstrated that sepia prints actually aided in fine detail separation in the engraver's camera, but until the men in the shop alter their opinion, only black-and-white prints should be offered.

Prints should be well-fixed and well washed. Most plants illumine the copy with strongly ultraviolet light which will discolor an improperly fixed photograph with visible rapidity.

In making prints for offset lithography, it should be kept in mind that all except the most expensive quality offset tends to reproduce black as a dark gray. Originals with large areas of shadow or with delicate shadow detail are poor choices. Prints with full shadow contrast are more satisfactory. Properly executed, offset can reproduce photography better than any other process except sheet-fed gravure, but is used largely for short-runs and economy printing.

Photogravure will accept full scale originals, printed for maximum detail and delicate gradation throughout the whole range of paper tones. Some slight restriction of contrast is advisable, however for best results. Rotogravure is printed on high-speed web presses and is not capable of the beautiful reproduction which the slower sheet-fed gravure can deliver.

Color for publication

Engravers have only reluctantly accepted the 35mm transparency as a proper engraving subject, and this has naturally interfered with sales to editors and to advertising agencies. There has been a change of climate recently in this, although the market is by no means completely open. One of the most influential pioneers has been *The National Geographic* magazine which has used 35mm originals since the introduction of Kodachrome and run many of them as double spreads (nearly 11x14 inches). *Life* magazine and many, many others have demonstrated that 35mm originals are perfectly usable for full-page illustration.

There has been some legitimate basis for past reluctance to make large engravings from 35mm color. Only Kodachrome provides a fine-grain image structure although recently the user-processed films have been considerably improved. Also, it is necessary to enlarge them by a two-stage process, first making continuous-tone separation negatives, then continuous tone positives before ending with (the normal first step of) screened negatives of the proper size. This also introduces registration problems not present with larger originals. Final plates for printing always require some hand-engraving for better detail and color and these craftsmen find it difficult to study the original as they work. A surcharge of $150 for plates from 35mm was sometimes required, in the not-too distant past, to restore the engraver's trust in the essential goodness of humanity.

The obvious photographic advantages of 35mm and the persistence of photographers is effecting an obvious change of attitude, and engravers are accepting the inevitable and working out methods to produce plates in a mood not so heavily charged with reluctant martyrdom.

There is no doubt that 35mm color will eventually become as important in the magazine illustration field as 35mm black-and-white is today. The current problem seems to revolve around devising methods of presentation of 35mm originals to editors and other buyers. There have been several strategies to avoid scattering a double handful of slides on an editor's desk. When circumstances have justified, photographers have made enlarged duplicate transparencies, up to 8x10 inches, which have paid off many times in sales. A good art director or picture editor can visualize the transparency in the proper size and translated into printer's ink colors. The agency client and most word-editors cannot. The large transparency impresses them (and there are editors at large who would be quite surprised to learn that cover transparencies they had bought were originally 35mm). It is also much more than mere suspicion that many agency clients, if not editors, feel that they are getting much more for their money with an 8x10-inch color film than they would with a tiny

10.10 ARTHUR RICKERBY

Nikon S2
50mm f/2 Nikkor
Don Larsen after perfect World Series game.
(United Press Photo)
(Newsreel lights) Plus-X, 1/30, f/5.6

10.11 Ted Russell *Nikon S2, 50mm f/1.4 Nikkor*
Lumberyard blaze, Brooklyn *Plus-X, 1/60, f/4*

transparency which has nothing to recommend it except excellence for their purpose. It is not the photographers who are entirely responsible for the bitter advice, "If you can't make it good, make it large, or red, or both."

A few photographers carry a slide projector with them when they visit (friendly) picture editors and others a large-screen table viewer and this latter seems a successful compromise very often.

With improvements in color papers, it is now possible to make a color print on Ansco Printon or Kodak Type R Color Print Material [see Chapter 7] which will serve for display and sales, with the transparency itself used for the engraving original for optimum color reproduction. A Type C print was used for a cover by *Modern Photography* in mid-1957 with excellent results, and perhaps is a forecast of future reality. We are probably on the threshold of more important changes as soon as 35mm color negative materials are perfected and become generally available. Then, either large duplicate transparencies or color prints may be more easily made and both sales and these reproduction problems will be the subject of pleasant reminiscence, rather than immediate economic considerations for the professional, who knows that a large fraction, at least, of his good color photographs are either made on 35mm, or should have been.

11

Copying and Close-up Photography

A GREAT MANY USERS OF THE NIKON, both amateur and professional, employ it for photography at close distances, either to record small objects or details, or to make copy negatives of documents or other flat originals. The actual applications are too numerous for listing. Every amateur encounters them occasionally and they occur regularly in commercial, industrial, medical and scientific practice. Present-day 35mm film emulsions and, even more particularly, the excellent acutance of Nikkor lenses and their freedom from residual aberrations at close working distances [see Chapter 4], enable the Nikon to be used for many types of photography formerly considered the province of large cameras. Nikon negatives of these subjects are equal or superior in many characteristics, as well as more convenient and less expensive to make, use and file.

Individual problems may differ a great deal, and some demand considerable ingenuity before the most effective solution is found. However, close-up working procedures may be grouped together because all involve certain techniques and control variables to a greater or lesser extent, as they progress from subjects photographed with the Nikon at or near the closest working distance of the particular Nikkor lens employed, through same-size (1:1) images of the subject and on to direct magnification on the negative (macrophotography).

The Nikon and Its Accessory Equipment

IN THIS CHAPTER, we first describe the Nikon accessory equipment for close-up work, and then a series of practical applications which includes many of the exposure, lighting and image-size control problems which will be encountered, no matter what the subject or its direct magnification on the negative. The relevant tables of field-size, exposure compensation formulas, etc. will be found in the *Data and Formulas* section at the end of the Manual.

The Nikon, fitted with one of the Nikkor lenses, may be used alone for many close-up and copying projects. The 50mm f/3.5 Micro-Nikkor is especially constructed for the greatest acutance at these short working distances and image reductions in the 1:20-1:1 range of much copy and small object work, but any of the Nikkors from 50mm to 135mm may be used at the full lens-mount extension of the Nikon with assurance of sharpness as great as the film itself will record.

The SP range-finder—view-finder automatically adjusts for the *parallax* (the slight separation between the viewpoints of lens and range-finder which becomes important at these short working distances) for all Nikkors between 50mm and 135mm. The accessory finders [see Chapter 2] may also be adjusted for this parallax on the S2 Nikon, but require an estimated correction for the slight lateral (displacement to the left) separation between lens axis and accessory shoe on the earlier Nikon S models. Nikkors of focal lengths longer than 135mm are used with the Prism Reflex Housing [see Chapter 4] which permits direct viewing through the lens and eliminates all problems of image placement and depth-of-field calculations.

It is often more convenient to use Nikkors of focal lengths longer than 50mm in order to secure a greater working distance and allow more space for the placement of artificial lighting when the Nikon is used alone for small-object photography, but the 50mm is "standard" and most commonly used.

For close-up work, vibration must be avoided and a tripod is always recommended. Slight evidences of camera-shake may be demonstrated at extremely high magnifications of the negative when any camera is hand-held at even the fastest speeds. This is negligible in ordinary photography, but becomes important with negative images approaching 1:1 or larger and where high resolution and acutance are important. Subject-movement must also be avoided. Electronic-flash illumination is a common choice for close-up work not only to eliminate all movement but because of other advantages which will be obvious in the later sections.

The Nikon Close Focusing Device

This accessory consists of two pieces: a range-finder attachment, in three models designed for the S, S2 or SP Nikon, which slips into the accessory shoe and places correcting optical elements over the range-finder windows; and a supplementary lens which screws into the front of the lens. Two models of the latter are available to fit either the f/1.4 or f/2 50mm Nikkor. With either lens, the Nikon may be used at distances of 2.6 to 1.5 feet (as measured from the film-plane mark on the top of the body) with a full life-size (in the S2 and SP) parallax-corrected image in the range-finder—view-finder for accurate framing. This single accessory will considerably extend the useful range of the Nikon for both amateur and professional work. No exposure correction is required with the *Nikon Close Focusing Device*. Depth-of-field and area tables for the 50mm Nikkors at the close distances this accessory makes possible, will be found in *Data and Formulas*.

Several manufacturers offer lines of supplementary lenses of various strengths (diopters) for use in front of camera lenses. These may often degrade the excellent image acutance of Nikkor lenses and usually require stopping down to very small apertures for best results, particularly to extend the depth-of-field which is very shallow when these are used. They do not provide the range-finder correction of the *Nikon Close Focusing Device* and the

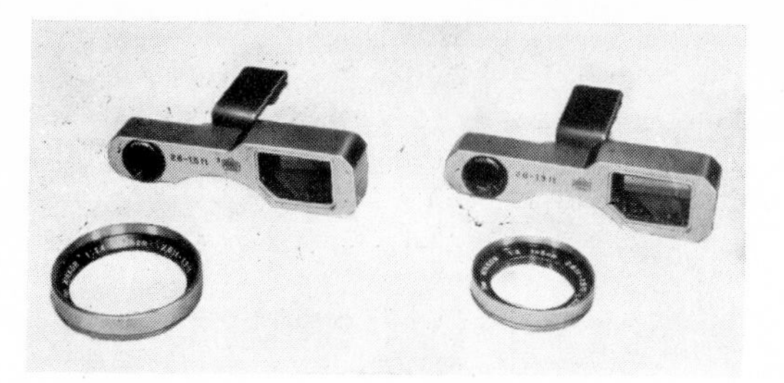

11.1 *The Nikon Precision Close Focusing Device (described on page 229.*

camera-to-subject separation must be set up by accurate measurement. These supplementary lenses should be considered only as expedients to substitute for the proper equipment in an emergency or when close-ups are so seldom made that efficient devices are uneconomic.

The Nikon Bellows Focusing Device

An auxiliary bellows on a bi-post focusing track which fits between the *Nikon Prism Reflex Housing* attached to the Nikon and one of the Nikkor lenses, provides a further flexible range of separation between the Nikkor and the film plane. This additional distance permits a direct image magnification on the Nikon negative from .8X to 4.8X, the exact range depending on the Nikkor used.

Two adapter rings are available to permit either the 50mm f/1.4 or f/2 Nikkors to be mounted on the front of the *Nikon Bellows Focusing Device.* These 50mm lenses are used in reverse position. Their design is intended for maximum correction for a short lens-to-film (rear conjugate) distance as compared to the lens-to-subject (front conjugate) distance. In direct image magnification, the lens-to-film separation becomes greater than the lens-to-subject distance, so acutance is best preserved by this reversal of mounting position.

With the 50mm Nikkor, image magnification extends from 2.2—4.8X. Longer focal length Nikkors are mounted on the front bayonet of the bellows in the usual position and permit direct magnifications of 1.3—3X with the 85mm Nikkor, 1.05—2.4X with the 105mm Nikkor, and 0.8—1.9X with the 135mm Nikkor. A full range of focus from infinity to same-size

11.2 *The Nikon Bellows Focusing Device (described above). Also see Figure 11.11.*

image (∞ to 1:1) is possible with the specially designed 135mm short-mount Nikkor now in preparation and the focusing track is engraved with magnification ratios for this lens.

It is possible to use the Nikon with its *Bellows Focusing Device* hand-held, but a tripod mounting is preferable in practice, especially at direct image magnification, to minimize camera shake and preserve the excellent image-drawing of the Nikkor lenses. Focusing is accomplished by a knob on either side of the front support of the *Nikon Bellows Focusing Device* and the exact framing and depth of field is visible at all times in the *Nikon Prism Reflex Housing*.

The Nikon Repro Copy Outfit, Model S

This accessory kit was originally supplied as a stand to hold the Nikon body with a set of extension tubes to alter the lens-to-film distance by the proper amounts for a fixed series of image-object ratios, from same-size to a negative image one-quarter that of the subject. The newer *Nikon Repro Copy Outfit, Model S,* now available, incorporates a focusing bellows for a greater flexibility of image-object size ratios between 1:1 and 1:5 (a negative image one-fifth the dimensions of the original) plus a supplementary lens which extends this image-object ratio to 1:20. Directions for the older model follow those below for the one in current supply.

The **Nikon Repro Copy Outfit, Model S,** [see Figures 11.3, 10] is contained in a small, portable instrument case. It is assembled for use in the 1:1 to 1:5 reduction range, as follows:

1. Screw the upright post into the frame base.
2. Slide the bellows bracket and stage unit onto the post; center bracket over the frame base and tighten locking screw.
3. Insert f/1.4 or f/2 50mm Nikkor (for image-object ratios of 1:1 to 1:20) or the f/3.5 50mm Micro-Nikkor with the barrel in collapsed position (for ratios of 1:1 to 1:5) into the bayonet mount under the bellows, lining up the red dots and pushing the lens in with slight pressure while turning counter-clockwise, exactly as when mounting in the Nikon body. (Steps 2 and 3 may be performed in reverse order, if this is more convenient.)
4. Place the focusing finder on the stage; remove magnifying eye-piece.
5. Place subject in frame base; center by aligning with white dots in the middle of each edge of frame opening. Illuminate for focusing.
6. If an exact reproduction ratio is desired, loosen focusing lock knob, turn focusing knob so index dot under locking knob aligns with proper reduction figure. Lock bellows at this extension and loosen bracket locking knob. Move the whole bracket unit up or down the post until image seems sharp on ground-glass. Check the subject positioning within ground-glass frame. Replace the magnifying eye-piece and re-check focus. If exact magnification ratio is important, focus by slight re-adjustment of height of bracket unit above base. Changing the bellows extension, particularly as image-object ratio approaches 1:1, will change

11.3 *The Nikon Repro Copy Outfit, Model S (described on these pages). Also see Figure 11.10.*

magnification but not focus. [See section, **Focus, Illumination and Exposure,** following]. Tighten bracket locking knob.

7. If exact magnification ratio is not important, adjust height of bellows bracket until the image comfortably fills the ground-glass at reasonably sharp focus, replace magnifying eye-piece and focus precisely by either moving the whole unit up or down if image and object are in nearly 1:1 ratio or by changing bellows extension if reductions are nearer the 1:5 ratio.
8. If selected reduction is 1:2 or less (red index dots on bellows mounting) insert the diaphragm ring supplied with kit inside the lens mount of the Nikon body to eliminate internal reflections.
9. Dismount the focusing finder and replace with the Nikon body. Align red dots on Nikon and bellows stage, open locking lever and press body down gently while turning clockwise until it clicks into place. Use a cable release for exposure to eliminate vibration.

When photographing objects at greater reductions (1:5 to 1:20):

1. Assemble as above. Base plate may be swung out of position or removed; the handle supplied may be screwed into position for hand-held use, or the whole unit mounted on a tripod.
2. Screw attachment lens supplied onto the front of the f/1.4 or f/2 Nikkor, using the special adapter collar for the former.
3. Adjust image size and position in focusing finder visually or consult tables for **Nikon Repro Copy Outfit, Model S, in Data and Formulas** to determine proper distance from the film plane (engraved mark on the Nikon body) to the subject for exact reductions of image.
4. Insert magnifying eye-piece and focus precisely. At these reductions, use the focusing knob to change bellows extension slightly.
5. Replace the focusing finder with the Nikon body, as above. The anti-reflection diaphragm ring is not necessary for this range of image reductions.

In general, it is best to work with the Nikkor set at an aperture of f/5.6 or smaller to increase the depth-of-field sufficiently for small object photography, particularly as the image approaches 1:1. At these Nikkor-to-film extensions, it is necessary to increase exposure times or to re-calculate effective lens aperture (which will differ from the marked relative aperture on the lens barrel). Tables and a formula for this calculation are given in *Data and Formulas.*

The older **Nikon Repro Copy Outfit, Model S,** now out of production, is a useful device for many applications, if not so flexible as the newer model.

1. Clamp the two upright supports on the base and insert the proper plastic frame into the base plate to locate and outline the field covered at the chosen reduction (1:1 to 1:4).
2. Select the corresponding extension tube; assemble tube and lens holder; insert 50mm f/1.4 or f/2 Nikkor or 50mm f/3.5 Micro-Nikkor (mount collapsed); screw assembly into bracket.
3. Insert the correct rod for chosen reduction between the two uprights to support bracket at correct Nikkor-to-subject distance.
4. Insert focusing finder on the bracket stage and focus precisely by adjusting the length of the positioning rod with the screw provided. Once established, the exact length of the rod will enable the set-up to be repeated later with any subject of exactly the same thickness without the need for re-focusing.
5. Substitute the Nikon body for the focusing finder.

The older model may also be used horizontally, or mounted on a tripod or hand-held with the handle provided. Exposure corrections for the various reductions are the same as for the newer model. [See Tables, *Data and Formulas.*]

The Nikon Prism Reflex Housing provides an additional Nikkor-to-film separation of 74mm and a corresponding increase of image size (greater than 1:1) on the negative. It is inserted between the top of the bracket and the Nikon body. The image, right-side up, not reversed from left to right and of correct size, showing precise focus and depth-of-field may be seen directly through the image-erecting eye-piece of the Housing.

The Nikon Repro Copy Outfit, Model P

This equipment provides a bracket, sliding on an upright post, carrying both the Nikon body and a focusing ground-glass with magnifier in an auto-positioning carrier for instant interchangeability. The bracket may be positioned for either vertical or horizontal use. The upright post may be clamped either to the lid of the specially-designed wooden carrying case or to the edge of a table or other support.

As supplied, the *Nikon Repro Copy Outfit, Model P,* accepts either the f/1.4 or f/2 50mm Nikkors for the 1:1 to 1:17 range of image reductions, or the f/3.5 50mm Micro-Nikkor for the range between 1:1 and 1:4.6.

The design of the *Model P* offers some advantages over the Model S [above] for those who require a permanent or semi-permanent installation for close-up work at quickly variable degrees of magnification. (Unlike the Model S, it cannot be used hand-held nor mounted on a tripod.) It should be noted, also, that for industrial and laboratory work which requires especially-con-

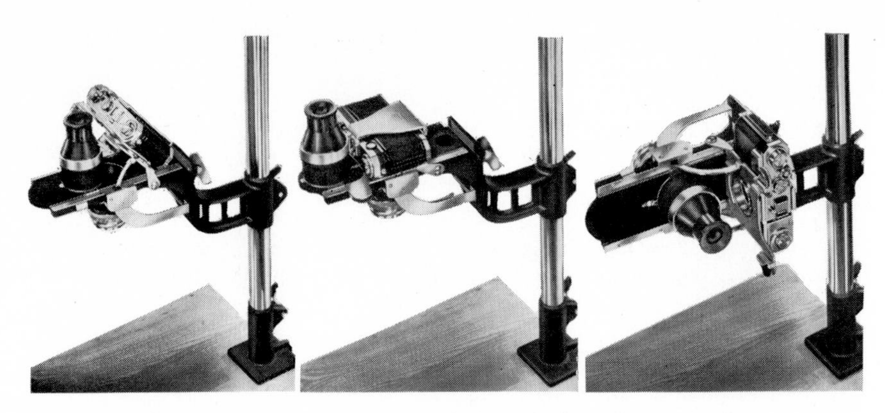

11.4 *The Nikon Repro Outfit, Model P (described on these pages).*

structed equipment for unusual problems of precision close-up photography, relatively simple and inexpensive modifications may be individually designed to adapt the *Model P* for these exceptional requirements. As supplied, the *Model P* offers laboratory precision and a design adapted to a wide range of working conditions.

Directions for using the **Nikon Repro Copy Outfit, Model P:**

1. Remove the two sections of the tubular upright from the case and screw them together; fix the base clamp to the lid of the case (which may be off-set on its hinges as shown in Figure 11.4) or to the edge of a table, shelf or other firm support.
2. Slide the bracket member over the upright post; tighten the clamping screw and attach the arm with auto-positioning carrier.
3. Loosen set-screw of camera-body clamp, remove plate and set Nikon body firmly into the light-trapped opening; replace plate and tighten set-screw with firm but not excessive pressure.
4. Rotate the two rings of the Micrometer Lens-Focusing Mount [element "**H**" in the reduction-ratio tables] so the focusing helix is extended forward; match the red dot on the retaining spring to the dot on the Nikkor and press Nikkor in with light pressure, turning counter-clockwise until retaining spring locks into place. (To remove Nikkor, again screw out focusing helix, depress spring and turn Nikkor clockwise gently until it releases.)
5. Screw Micrometer Lens-Focusing Mount directly into threads under carrier arm or select proper intermediate extension tube or tubes **(A,B,C)** from reduction-ratio table and screw Micrometer Lens-Focusing Mount into tube threads and then attach the tube assembly under carrier arm.
6. Open small catch-locks on camera clamp base-plate and raise clamp with Nikon body to position focusing ground-glass automatically over the Nikkor lens.
7. Center subject below Nikkor and illuminate for focusing. Adjust height of bracket and rotate lower knurled ring of Micrometer Lens-Focusing Mount to extend helix for focus while viewing on the ground-glass.

8. Insert focusing magnifier into bayonet mount above ground-glass and establish precision focus. [**Note:** at very large relative image sizes (near 1:1) as Nikkor-to-film and Nikkor-to-subject distances become nearly equal, movements of the focusing helix may change magnifications slightly without actually sharpening focus. The most accurate focus will be obtained at these image magnifications by very slight changes in the height of the bracket above the copy table (film-to-copy distances). The **Model P** ground-glass has a central clear circle and an etched cross for precision "parallax focusing" explained later in the section **Focus Illumination and Exposure.**
9. Pull down camera clamp and position firmly so the small catch-locks hold down clamp. Use the cable-release supplied to avoid all possible vibration when exposing film.

When the Model P is used in a permanent or semi-permanent set-up, the clamp at the base of the tubular post may be fastened to a block in the wall at waist-height or lower and centered above a flat shelf or table which is aligned exactly plane-parallel to the top surface of the bracket and consequently with the film-plane. This height will place the ground-glass of the focusing finder below eye-level for many frequently employed image-object ratios. The separation between the film-plane and the surface of the copy-table should be checked in advance to be sure it will permit the image magnifications required in practice. (Minimum useful separation [200mm] occurs at a 1:1 ratio.)

When the A, B or C extension tubes are added to increase the separation between Nikkor and film-plane, a corresponding increase in exposure is necessary [see the next section]. However, the addition of the accessory lens to enable a larger field to be covered at smaller image-object ratios does not require any additional exposure. [See tables, *Data and Formulas.*]

Focus, Illumination and Exposure

The following sections describe a number of close-up and copying applications with suggestions as specific as possible for setting up convenient and efficient working procedure. To some extent, all of these situations involve accurate focusing of the Nikkor, proper choice and placement of the illumination, and the calculation of accurate exposures. Some general remarks on these factors will lay the groundwork for later recommendations.

Focusing for close-ups

While accurate focusing is important in all photography, it is especially critical at close working distances. As the subject approaches the camera, the depth-of-field rapidly decreases, particularly when the Nikkor-to-subject distance is *shorter* than the Nikkor-to-film separation with direct magnifications (macrophotography). Even more importantly, the larger image magnifications are used when fine detail and structure are needed in the photograph or color slide and the great maximum acutance of the Nikkor at exact focus is required.

For some applications and with some Nikon equipment a wide choice of focal-lengths is possible. It was noted previously [Chapter 4] that at the same Nikkor-to-subject distances the shorter focal lengths had a somewhat greater depth-of-field than longer lenses, but at the same image magnification (the actual size on the negative) all focal lengths will produce the same depth-of-field. When working at very close distances, the 50mm Nikkors may have some advantages with small object photography because of this greater depth-of-field; longer Nikkors may provide the same image size with more convenience in handling the subject and placing the lighting.

The sharp resolution and absence of residual aberrations of both the f/1.4 and f/2 50mm Nikkors permits their use at all extensions of the Nikon or with the Repro Copy Outfits, Model S or P. With the Nikon Bellows Focusing Device, these 50mm f/1.4 and f/2 Nikkors may be attached in reversed position for direct magnification [see above].

Usually, the aperture of the Nikkor is closed down for the greatest depth-of-field with small-object work and for maximum sharpness. [See *Aperture and Critical Sharpness,* Chapter 4.] With all Nikkors, however, it is possible to focus at the largest aperture for a bright image and accurate placing of the plane of sharp focus and to stop down without changing the focus. (Many other lenses have sufficient uncorrected spherical aberration to produce a slightly different focal-length at various apertures and must be focused at the aperture to be used in order to retain a sharp image.)

Some Nikon copying equipment has a tiny clear circle on the ground-glass, enclosing an etched cross. This is very useful for checking accuracy of focus. With the magnifier focused precisely on this cross, move the head very slightly. If the image moves in the same direction, in relation to the cross, the actual plane of focus is below the ground-glass and the Nikkor must be racked back very slightly; if the image is displaced in the opposite direction, the plane of focus is above the ground-glass and the Nikkor should be racked very slightly forward. This effect is termed *parallax focusing.* The reference mark may be added to any ground-glass with India ink (on the ground side) and covered with a tiny piece of very thin glass held in place by Canada balsam.

When an optical system is very close to unit magnification (1:1), with the lens close to the mid-point between film and subject, it may not be possible to bring the system into focus by small movements of the lens. (Greater lens movement may establish a sharp focus but at a magnification other than the one desired.) When working at image-object ratios close to 1:1, it is most convenient to set the lens-to-film extension for the exact magnification desired [see Repro Copy Outfit tables, *Data and Formulas*] and with this extension fixed to move the whole apparatus toward the subject until the exact point of sharpest focus is discovered. No point of sharp focus, of course, can be found at film-to-subject separations closer than four times the focal length of the lens employed.

Illumination for close-ups

Lighting small objects involves many of the considerations previously encountered [Chapter 9] when form and texture must be displayed. Usually, however, since all-over detail is important, the lighting is held to very low levels of contrast with shadow-highlight illumination differences no greater than 1:2. For color photography, the lighting may be completely "flat." The

11.5 Philip O. Stearns *Nikon S2*
50mm f/1.4 Nikkor

Stunt cars, California
(Made for DeSoto)
Plus-X, 1/500, f/16

differences in local color are frequently sufficient to delineate the form and structure of the subject. With flat subjects (e.g., documents), evenness of illumination over the surface is most important.

Lighting from the front of the subject is most often employed but there are times when lighting from the back (for example, resting the subject on a sheet of white opal glass illuminated from underneath) will produce the best results. Combinations of this trans-illumination and direct lighting are also sometimes effective. [See data on specific close-up applications, below.]

The actual intensity of the light is especially important in close-up work. This must be balanced between the dangers to certain subjects from the heat or photochemical effects of prolonged or intense lighting, and the inevitable loss of exposure speed with increase of relative image-size [see next section]. Often, the most efficient solution seems to be electronic flash.

It will be found that when any light-source is brought close to the subject that the effective illumination intensity does not increase by the anticipated amount at distances closer than approximately 10X the diameter of the reflector. At very close distances, the effective intensity approximates that of a bare bulb. If the lighting is measured directly by an exposure meter at the subject, this loss of reflector efficiency will be automatically registered by the meter reading. If exposures are calculated, however, as they must be with flash (unless an "integrating" light meter like the General Radio model is used) this reflector factor must be considered and guide numbers revised accordingly.

Exposure for close-ups

The exposure for close-ups is more difficult to calculate than that for normal Nikkor-to-film extensions because of three factors which enter to varying degrees. In addition to the loss of reflector efficiency, mentioned above, it is necessary to determine the *effective* aperture for the Nikkor-to-film separation which will differ from the *relative* aperture as engraved on the lens barrel. At relatively large extensions, also, the light reaching the film rapidly falls off in intensity. With color film and sometimes even with black-and-white film, this fall off may so reduce the illumination on the film that reciprocity failure may occur. [See Chapters 5, 7 and 9.]

At comparatively great reductions, as when a document is copied with the Nikon and 50mm Nikkor used at a three-foot or greater distance, none of these factors may play any great role in determining exposure. When the Nikkor, however, is brought within about ten times its own focal length of the subject, the necessary Nikkor-to-film extension begins to reduce effective illumination on the film to a point beyond which normal film latitude is exceeded. For convenience in reference, the necessary exposure compensations for close-up work are summarized in *Data and Formulas* and included in several of the close-up tables also found there. They are based on the obvious fact that relative apertures, as marked on the lens barrel, represent a measured fraction of the aperture diameter over the lens-to-film distance when the lens is focused at infinity. For close-up photography, these must be recalculated by placing the aperture diameter over the actual Nikkor-to-film separation. The convenient formula is:

$$Ef = \frac{Rf \times V}{F}$$

$$\text{Effective aperture} = \frac{\text{relative (marked) aperture x lens-to-film distance}}{\text{focal length}}$$

This effective (or actual) aperture must be used in meter reading or guide number calculations. [See also *Data and Formulas,* p. 266.]

These exposure corrections may multiply surprisingly. A small machine part or biological specimen, for example, photographed on color film (E.I. 32) and illuminated for an apparent 5-second exposure may require about 7 seconds, instead, to compensate for reciprocity failure (plus filter correction). Calculating decreasing effective apertures and increasing reciprocity failure in this case: at a 2X direct enlargement on the film this will become about 18 seconds; at 4X, 45 seconds; at 5X, 1 minute; and at 8X, about 2 minutes. If measured illumination were to indicate a 1-minute exposure at normal lens-to-film extension, reciprocity failure immediately would bring this up to about 3 1/2 minutes; extended by the exposure factor to 7 minutes at 2X; 23 minutes at 4X; 31 minutes at 5X; and to 50 minutes at 8X. (These figures, of course, are intended to be indicative of the extent of the exposure corrections sometimes necessary in macrophotography, rather than as an actual guide. Reciprocity and reflector efficiency failures must be calculated for a particular set-up on the basis of actual tests.)

Flat Copy Subjects

SATISFACTORY NIKON negatives or color transparencies of flat originals are easily made if simple principles are followed. Large subjects (documents, photographs, drawings, paintings, etc.) may be copied without any supplementary equipment for the Nikon except a tripod or other firm support and the necessary lights. For more frequent work or a semi-permanent set-up, the Nikon Repro Copy Outfit, Model S or P, will increase convenience and speed; for location work (for example, photographing small paintings hung in a gallery), the Repro Copy Outfit, Model S, mounted on a tripod, may prove advantageous, as will the Bellows Focusing Device with the specially-designed short mount 135mm Nikkor.

Flat copy subjects which may be handled by the photographer can be set up in front of the Nikon either vertically or horizontally. Figures 11.7 A, B, C illustrate three such arrangements. It is usually easier to support the original on a horizontal surface where it may be centered with the axis of the Nikkor and, if necessary, covered by a heavy sheet of glass to assure flatness. Glass, however, is best avoided whenever possible to minimize the possibility of reflections from the lights or mirroring the Nikon itself in the glass. It will help, if this latter difficulty is encountered, to use as long a focal-length Nikkor as is practical under the circumstances and to shield the Nikon from direct illumination from the lights or from reflected illumination from surfaces in the room. Figure 11.7B shows the Nikon protected in this manner.

Damage to originals suspended vertically may be avoided by using drafting tape rather than push-pins, or by using small pieces of cardboard at each corner so the pins will not actually penetrate the original. [See arrangement in Figure 11.7A.]

Great care must be taken to assure that the film plane and the original are exactly plane-parallel. This is, of course, no problem with either of the Repro Copy Outfits except in the case of books or other bound material [see *Small-volume microfilming,* below.] When the Nikon is set up on a tripod a small level is useful. Any misalignment will show up as "keystoneing," a convergence of parallel lines which distorts the appearance of the copy.

Illuminating the copy subject

An even, overall lighting is required for flat originals. This is best secured by either two or four lights of equal intensity [see Figures 11.6, 7A, B, C]. Check the arrangement by covering the original subject (or the surface on which it is to be supported) by a white card and making meter readings at the center and the four corners. A rough but effective check may also be made by touching a pencil to each of these points and comparing the density of the shadows cast on either side.

Light is reflected from a surface at an equal (and opposite) direction from that at which it strikes. The illumination should reach any original particularly one with a smooth or glossy surface, at such an angle that specular reflections will not strike back into the lens to create opaque spots or to degrade contrast. [See diagram, Figure 11.6.] Check this carefully from the lens position or on the ground-glass of the Repro Copy Outfit or the Prism Reflex Housing, if they are used.

In the case of oil paintings, it may be desirable to indicate the surface texture. One light may be placed to skim the surface from a shallow angle to bring out small cast shadows from the brush strokes and the light from the other side adjusted to illuminate detail within these shadows without eliminating them.

Oil paintings and many other originals (including pencil lines and many types of art work) show strong specular reflections which may be eliminated, at least in large part, by copying with polarized light. Large polarizing screens are used over the light sources and a regular polarizing filter over the Nikkor. The planes of polarization of the lamp screens should all be at the same angle. Some or all of the specular reflections are removed as the polarizing filter on the Nikkor is rotated toward 90° in respect to the lamp plane of polarization. The effect may be observed through the lens filter itself or on the ground-glass of the copying apparatus. (Exposure reading for this polarized light may be made from a white card in subject position with the lens filter held over the end of the meter at the same angle it will be used on the Nikkor.)

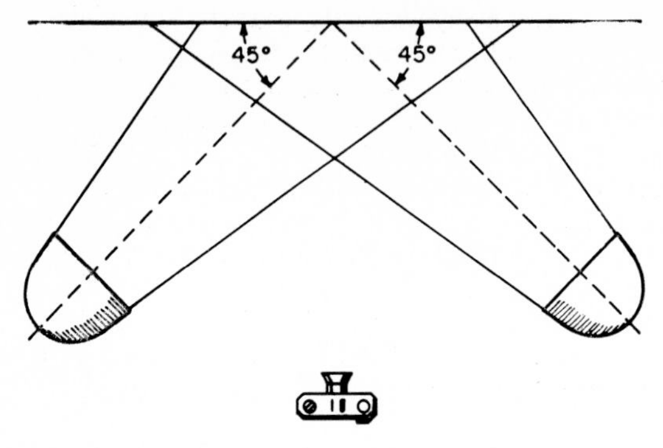

11.6 *Copy lights should illuminate the copy-board from an angle of 45 degrees or less to prevent reflections (see text).*

The color temperature of the illumination is important, of course, with color films in the Nikon and the proper conversion or color balancing filter should be employed. Color compensating filters may be used, also, to control the exact rendition of the original colors, either to preserve or to distort them. The full range of stronger filters may be employed with black-and-white film to improve contrast or modify color emphasis or even to eliminate elements of the original. A Nikon R or the Wratten 25 or 29 red tri-color separation filters, for example, will prevent red pencil annotations on a document from recording on the copy, or the contrast of a yellowed original will be improved if it is copied on black-and-white film through a Nikon Y filter.

Filtering becomes especially important for such phases of copy work as document investigation. Erasures, alterations and additions may be photographically demonstrated or the lettering on charred documents restored by use of infrared and ultraviolet illumination and suitable filters over the Nikkor. The "expertizing" of paintings has also developed an elaborate technique based on photographic copying and narrow-band radiation.

Films for copying flat originals

Originals may be loosely divided into *line* and *half-tone* subjects. Line subjects (documents, drawings, some maps and charts, etc.) require a more contrasty copy negative than do half-tone subjects (photographs, paintings, etchings, etc.). Films should be chosen for their basic inherent contrast, but great differences of gradient are possible within the limits of many common films. Kodak Panatomic-X, for example, is a valuable copying material because of its fine-grain characteristics and may be an excellent choice for half-tone copies when developed to a gradient of from 0.5—0.7 in D-76 (diluted 1:1; 7 to 11 minutes at 68F). However, at some cost in graininess, it may be brought to a gradient of about 1.1 after 22 minutes of development in D-76, to 1.4 after 16 minutes in DK-50 or to 1.6 after 16 minutes development in DK-60a. Other high-acutance, thin-emulsion films listed in *Data and Formulas* may also be used, although some do not have the flexibility indicated here for Kodak Panatomic-X. Medium-speed films may also be used for casual work and personal notes [see the following section] and may also be boosted in contrast, but their graininess will be thereby increased, often to the point of serious degradation of acutance and fine-line resolution. If image reductions

11.7 *Three common copying situations are illustrated at right. From top: copying a flat original fastened to a board; copying a framed painting, with the Nikon film plane at the same angle as the painting surface and with a long-focus Nikkor to minimize the chance of reflecting the Nikon in the glass; and copying book pages.*

are small, this will not prevent their use for personal records. With normal development, of course, they are suitable for many half-tone copies.

For line-copies, the ideal materials are Kodak Micro-File Film, Ilford Micro-neg Pan Film or Fuji Minicopy Film. Kodagraph Micro-File Film may be brought to a gradient of 4.0 by 9-minute development in D-11. For half-tone copy subjects, excellent results will be had with films such as the Kodak and Ilford Fine Grain Positive emulsions.

In emergencies or when making one or two copies quickly is required, almost any black-and-white film which is in the Nikon may be used for line copies. Make several exposures, bracketing by a stop each, from the meter reading and develop normally with the rest of the cartridge or, if possible, slightly longer than normal. Select the frame which has the strongest highlight density without blocking up the finest lines of the original and reduce this frame in a cutting (subtractive) reducer (R-4a) until all lines are completely free of silver deposit; wash carefully; then intensify to maximum possible density. [See *Data and Formulas.*] If all silver has been removed from the lines, they will remain clear as the background is built up to greater opaqueness.

It is easy to increase contrast in making copies. Negatives of half-tone subjects normally should be developed to a fairly low gradient (0.5 to 0.7). Some contrast may be restored, if necessary, by printing on a No. 3 grade paper or its variable grade filtered equivalent. This extra contrast is useful in line copies and brilliant prints are desirable. An excellent material is Kodagraph Projection or Fast Projection Paper, available in several weights.

While any 35mm color film may be used for copying, Kodachrome has the finest grain structure of any material currently on the market. Daylight Kodachrome is a usual choice for work with electronic flash and Professional (Type A) Kodachrome for tungsten illumination. Anscochrome is somewhat coarser in grain but useful for many applications, and Ektachrome is now considerably improved in grain structure but still a less desirable choice for copy work. For occasional copies of black-and-white originals, Kodachrome is a convenient material if projection copies are desired. It eliminates developing a black-and-white negative and then printing for a diapositive for projection, or the purchase of Direct Positive Film and the special developing materials it requires. [See also the text on copies and diapositives in the latter part of Chapter 7.]

When copying on color film, it is very useful to include a gray scale and color patches [see Figure 11.8] if there is room to accommodate them in the Nikon frame. (They may be masked off if the copy is a slide for projection.) Even a quick visual inspection of these will reveal tone or color distortions from the original if these are picked up in the copying. Gray scale and color patches are especially useful if a copy on color film is to serve as the basis for color printing.

Exposure calculation for copying

The most accurate method of measuring the reflected light from the copy surface is to cover a line original with a white card (such as the Kodak Neutral Test Card which has a 90 percent reflectance) and to hold the photoelectric exposure meter pointed toward it from approximately a distance equal to the diagonal measurement of the card. Be careful that no shadow is cast on the card from the meter or hand. For these white-card measurements, set the meter for *one-fifth* the usual rated speed of the film used. Half-tone subjects may also be measured by this method or the meter reading may be made directly from the original or from the gray (18 percent reflectance) side of the Kodak Neutral Test Card. Use the *normal* rated film speed. As before, hold the meter away from the original or from the card at about a distance equivalent to the diagonal dimension of the surface being measured. With black-and-white films, modify this reading as indicated in the

Subject:	Reduce meter reading by:
Good quality printing or typing; India ink drawings; glossy photographs	0
Hand-written manuscript; light typing; fine-line originals	—5%
Pencil drawings and manuscript; faded printing; thin-line or colored graphs; Diazo positives	—15%
Weak pencil lines; poor or faded printing	—20%
Diazo negatives; blue-prints; photographic paper negatives	—70%

11.8 *Indian artifacts, photographed to include a strip of Kodak color patches (left) and a Kodak Gray Scale (right) for subsequent guidance in making color prints and duplicate slides.*

table on page 242. Some slight compensation from this meter measurement are also required for photographing originals which are predominantly light or dark on color films. Increase the exposure by about 1/2 stop for very dark subjects or decrease by the same amount for unusually light subjects. [See also suggested exposure-development modifications for Ektachrome when used in copying, Chapter 7.] Some types of paper take on a bluish tinge when copied on color film and a Skylight filter or one of the 81-series of light balancing filters will correct this. The meter reading may require a slight compensation, determined by practical tests of individual set-ups.

Many originals are of such size that copying them onto 35mm film will require little if any exposure compensation for additional Nikkor-to-film extension. Directions for this correction were noted in the previous section and are summarized in *Data and Formulas.*

Flat copy requires careful focusing to place the sharpest plane of the Nikkor accurately at the surface of the original and the lens should be focused at its widest aperture when a Repro Copy Outfit or the Bellows Focusing Device and Prism Reflex Housing are used.

Copy negatives of half-tone material are usually printed on any enlarging paper of suitable contrast to produce a gradation approximating that of the original. Copy (microfilm) negatives of line originals may be printed on a contrasty grade of ordinary enlarging paper or on a special material such as Kodagraph or Kodagraph Rapid Projection Paper which is available in several weights or, if dimensional stability is important, on Kodagraph Projection Cloth. Other print materials of very high contrast (such as the Ilford Document Papers) are also available from manufacturers here and abroad. Copy which is much reduced, as a full double-page spread of a newspaper, may be printed on Kodagraph Microprint Paper, available in 75x125mm sheets, which has sufficient resolution to accept detail (such as type) 1/20 original size.

The final print may also be on film such as Kodagraph Print Film or Kodak or Ilford Fine Grain Positive Films. In this form, they may be mounted for projection or left in strips for microfilm enlarging readers.

Archival permanence

While photographic films and papers are perishable, they are sometimes less so than originals such as newspaper stock. Copy negatives and microfilms designed for permanence should be carefully processed to remove all traces of chemicals which would discolor or fade the image. Only fresh fixing baths should be used, and washing should be thorough enough so residual hypo should not exceed 0.005 milligram per square inch. A final treatment in HE-1 is recommended. Precise standards for processing films and papers for maximum image stability may be obtained from the National Bureau of Standards and the American Standards Association, or the equivalent organizations abroad.

Films and paper should be stored under conditions which minimize the dangers of heat, fire, water, mold or chemical damage. Moderate care will assure a life of at least 25 years; storage conditions meeting the highest archival standards will permit image survival for many times this period of years.

Small Volume Microfilming

DOCUMENT COPYING on 35mm film began early in the 1920's with relatively crude individually-constructed equipment, but a little over ten years later had reached full mechanization. Current microfilm equipment can copy over 10,000 frames in a working day. The public came into direct contact with this technique during World War II when "V-mail" letters were microfilmed for overseas delivery. Business, industry and government now have extensive microfilming programs designed not only to reduce expensive filing space but to provide duplicate records for efficiency and as "insurance copying." Microfilm records kept British business structure functioning after the destructive fire-raids on London wiped out offices and original documents. Microfilming is multiplying scholarly and technical information as well. Copies of scientific papers and other publications are now circulated in this form and libraries are multiplied. Vast collections of the Vatican library, for example, are now available as microfilm in this country.

Nikon equipment makes microfilm and its advantages available to individuals and smaller business organizations and libraries efficiently and inexpensively. The Nikon and a 50mm Nikkor (preferably the especially-designed f/3.5 Micro-Nikkor) alone will serve as a recording device. However, the Nikon Repro Copy Outfit, Model P, offers great advantages when a permanently-available set-up is required, and the Nikon Repro Copy Outfit, Model S, provides considerable flexibility, particularly for field use. The Model P will copy originals up to 17x25 1/2 inches in size and the Model S up to 20x30 inches. When the Nikon is used alone or with the Model S, the addition of the motor-drive back [see Chapter 2] will add speed to repetitive copying at the same magnification.

Microfilming techniques

Small-volume microfilming does not differ essentially from the copying methods outlined in the previous section. Illumination and exposure techniques remain the same. When books or other bound materials are copied, one or two small wooden wedges will be found useful to level the two facing book pages. The pages may be flattened with a sheet of plate glass, but this may produce annoying reflections and will show finger-prints after short use. It is better to hold the page edges flat with two pieces of strong fish-line with lead weights at the ends. A foot-switch (a common dark-room accessory) connected with the lights will prove a convenience and reduce the heat from photoflood illumination in small rooms or during the summer.

The Nikon Repro Copy Outfit, Model S, makes an ideal tool for the researcher of either laboratory or ivory-tower variety. It is conveniently portable, easily assembled and may be used to copy documents, charts or illustrations in the field. For many purposes, it is not even necessary to set up artificial lighting: copies which are legible, if not up to completely professional standards, may be made on any of the medium speed films by the existing light on location or the sunlight on a wide window-sill. When used in this fashion, it is most convenient to set up a fixed magnification ratio and to compute the exposure for this and expose all of the material rapidly. If the originals classify easily into several sizes, more than one ratio can be used, working with one group at a time. Kodak Microfile or Ilford Micro-neg Pan or their Fine Grain Positive films, or one of the fine-grain thin-emulsion films are better choices for good image quality than any of the medium speed film group [see *Data and Formulas*] but require a more exact exposure. When artificial illumination is available, these high-acutance films are recommended. If it is permissable, then portable electronic flash may be employed.

Exposure times (apertures for 1/60 or slower shutter setting) for several magnification ratios with electronic flash may be worked out ahead of time for the film employed. *Note:* To keep pages in proper sequence along the film when photographing the two facing pages of a book or periodical simultaneously, the top of the publication should be toward the top edge of the Nikon.

With natural or existing light or with photoflood or fluorescent illumination, the correct exposure is best determined from a meter reading from a 5x7-inch white card placed at subject-position. Read as described in the previous section and compensate for the character of the subject-matter as indicated in the chart in that section. Appropriate films and development will also be the same.

X-ray filing

A variation of this microfilming procedure has gained currency in clinical work. Radiological films bulk large when filed and a considerable gain in convenience and efficiency of use will result from transferring them to 35mm form. A quarter-million such copies occupy no more volume than 2,000 14x17 X-rays in drawer storage. Complete hospital or clinical collections may be copied or only those of special interest. While the Nikon Repro Copy Outfit, Model P, is ideal for this work, particularly in large volume, the Model S may be easily set up for rapid and convenient copying and the Nikon alone, on tripod, and with one of the 50mm Nikkors is completely adequate for the recording of larger X-rays such as 14x17.

The original is placed on the surface of an X-ray view-box and trans-illuminated for the exposure. Two L-shaped pieces of black cardboard should be used to mask off any stray light from the edges and room lighting should be subdued, particularly any sources which might be mirrored on the surface of the X-ray itself. A suitable legend, typed on tissue paper and containing all necessary information (hospital, X-ray number, patient identification, date, age, sex, diagnosis and treatment), is placed over the corner or some unimportant area of the X-ray. This tissue need be no larger than about 2x3 inches and gains legibility if typed with a sheet of carbon paper "wrong side up" against the back of the tissue to give the letters greater density. If copies are made for projection as lecture illustrations, small cut-out arrows may be laid on the X-ray to point out the areas to be described.

Exposures may be measured by making a meter reading through a half-inch hole cut in heavy cardboard. Locate this hole over the most important area of the X-ray. Exposure corrections for magnification ratio and the color of the viewing-box light may be made as previously described and confirmed by test. These will remain constant throughout a run of similar-sized X-rays. One of the thin-emulsion films may be used and subsequently printed on film or paper [see previous section] or direct positive film or Professional (Type A) Kodachrome may be used for slides. If a black-and-white negative is made, small (4x5-inch) prints may be made for filing with case-history records or other use.

Interested readers will find relevant articles in *Radiology, Am. J. Roentgenol., Radiography and Clinical Photography*, and other professional journals.

Slide Films

SLIDE FILMS may be photographed from suitable original material directly in the Nikon. Lighting and exposure problems are identical with those treated above. The Nikon Repro Copy Outfits, Model P or S, will be found efficient for this work. The tripod-mounted Nikon alone, however, may be used if the originals are prepared to a larger size.

Slide *sets* for lectures or instruction are standard individually mounted 2x2-inch slides. Slide *films* are strips of 35mm film run vertically through a projector and each frame is 18x24mm or half the size of the image area of the S2 or SP Nikon models. Consequently, the slide films photographed in the Nikon are exposed as double frames and must be arranged in the proper sequence and facing in the correct direction.

A light metal or stiff cardboard template to fit over the copy board is an essential accessory. This should have two openings, each 13x18 inches (or some exact multiple of these dimensions), and separated by 1 1/4 inch (or the equivalent multiple if the openings are made larger). The bottom of the opening for the second frame in sequence should lie toward the film take-up spool of the Nikon. [See diagram, Figure 11.9.]

Originals may be black-and-white photographs, drawings or lettering, color prints or drawings. Half-tone material, particularly photographs, should be carefully matched in contrast and gradation. It is better to print these somewhat "soft" and with full detail throughout, especially in the highlights. Any of the medium-speed or fine-grain thin-emulsion films may be used to produce a black-and-white negative from which the actual slide films may be contact printed. When only one or a few projection prints are required, it is easier to photograph each in turn on a direct positive film or on Professional (Type A) Kodachrome. Panatomic-X and some other films may also be reversed in processing. An exposure error in any frame, of course, will spoil the whole strip.

Opaque color originals are photographed on Kodachrome or other color film with illumination arranged as above in the section on *Flat Copy Subjects*. Test to determine which, if any, filters are required for proper color rendition.

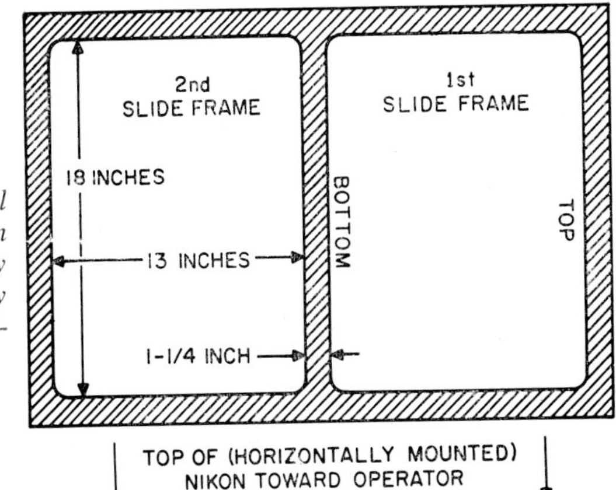

11.9 *Guide for material photographed for slide film use. The frames (of heavy cardboard or light metal) may be of a different size if all proportions are maintained.*

Color transparencies, if they are matched in size and proportion may be also copied, two at a time, for slide films. These color transparencies must match in color balance for separate filtering will become complicated. They are mounted over a light-table under a template and copied by the method outlined under *Duplicating Color Transparencies,* below.

Small Object Photography

CLOSE-UP AND SMALL OBJECT photography cuts across many fields of interest. In addition to its hobby values, it is an essential tool in botany and zoology, mineralogy, metallurgy and petrography, in archeology, numismatics and many other sciences. It is in constant use in dental, opthalmic and other clinical practice, as well as finding widening applications in industry and technical research. No metropolitan police department in the world is without equipment for this work.

Close-up photography begins at some arbitrary point approaching the near limit of focus with a 50mm Nikkor on the Nikon and extends through the larger images of the Nikon Close Focusing Attachment, the 1:1 or greater image-object ratios with Nikon supplementary equipment and on to the point where this macrophotography encounters practical difficulties and is replaced by the much greater image enlargements (photomicrography) through the microscope with the Nikon Microflex attachment.

Working with the Nikon alone or with the Nikon and its Close Focusing Attachment, lighting and exposure problems are little different from those outlined in Chapter 3. The amateur can, for example, make a close "portrait" of a single flower, an insect or other small object with no additional equipment, unless it be a small colored cardboard to serve as a combination background and windscreen. As the image is enlarged within the Nikon, these problems become identical with those previously outlined under *Flat Copy Subjects,* above, with the exception that sufficient depth-of-field must be arranged to cover the important parts of the object photographed. It may be necessary in some cases to work at a lower image magnification in order to secure this depth and to enlarge the negative considerably in printing.

Lighting for small-object photography

Flat originals are lighted primarily for even illumination, but many small objects require lighting which will establish their three-dimensional form, their texture and surface characteristics. The principles of such lighting follow those outlined in Chapter 9, complicated only by the necessity of working in the restricted space between the Nikkor and the subject. It is often advisable to elevate the subject on a small stage around which lights may be more closely placed. If tungsten lighting is used, small spotlights are useful if they throw a strong light. A magnifying lens such as a reading glass on a gooseneck may be used to concentrate light, if the subject is not affected by the heat of a concentrated beam. Reflectors may also be set up to confine the light. These may be white cardboard, board covered with crinkled aluminum foil, or a concave (magnifying) shaving mirror arranged to catch the spill light and reflect it back as a strong secondary lighting source.

This latter is especially useful when an electronic flash is used for illumination and provides a secondary source at least half as strong as the primary light source itself. It may be properly focused by placing an ordinary bulb at the point where the flash reflector will be . [See Figure 11.10.]

If diffused lighting is preferable, as it is with small, polished metal objects such as machine parts, a "tent" may be built around the subject. This may be of white paper which collects the light, or of opal glass. Large sheets of this latter are expensive and for bigger "sets" a tent may be made of heavy matte-surfaced, acetate sheeting. With such a translucent tent, some vestiges of lighting for form may be retained at very low highlight-shadow ratios. With non-reflective subjects, a "ring-light," an electronic flash bulb shaped to fit around the Nikkor, may be used.

Light from behind the subject will show the structure of a translucent small object or will provide an evenly-lit shadowless background for other small objects. The subject is placed on a light-table or a small stage topped by a sheet of opal glass with a tungsten or flash source placed beneath it. The subject may also be independently lighted from above to show form and texture. Exposure will depend on the light penetrating a translucent subject or on the front-lighting of a solid object, unless a silhouette is desired. [See exposure measurement, below.]

Films and exposure for small-object photography

Small objects photographed with the Nikon or with the Close Focusing Attachment on the camera may be recorded on any of the medium-speed or fine-grain films or any of the color films. With greater image enlargements, it is better to use the fine-grain materials.

Exposure calculations for additional Nikkor-to-film extensions (when they are used) follow the method previously outlined as to tests for reciprocity failure and loss of reflector efficiency. It is often difficult to confine a meter reading to the area of a tiny subject and it is more accurate to substitute a white or gray card in subject position and to take the reading from that, if possible. When lighting is arranged for displaying form and the light beams from several sources do not overlap on the subject itself, take the meter reading with all lights except the key light extinguished. A back light must always be turned off, unless the reading is for a silhouetted object, or is a measurement of the light penetrating a translucent object.

Whenever the subject permits, it is useful to include a gray scale and color patches, particularly if color prints or engravings will be made.

Industrial applications of close-up photography

As examples of the methods of small-object photography, we may take some industrial applications. These divide into two classes: the fast, informal photographs which may be made by men with no training in photography and which are intended for in-plant use, and the more carefully arranged photographs intended for research, training or circulation outside the plant.

For the first kind which demands a clear image without "fancy" manipulations an impatient employee may ignore, the Nikon fitted with a 50mm Nikkor and Nikon Flash Unit is ideal. A Nikon Close Focusing Attachment may also be provided and the camera shutter and aperture pre-set for a given working distance when it is signed out for use, or a card issued giving settings for a short series of predetermined working distances.

For pictures requiring more care and which will be made by better trained (or more patient) employees, the Nikon Repro Copy Outfit, Model S, may be set up, together with proper lighting and labeled with simple directions for use at a narrow range of image magnifications.

Photographic personnel, or those who will accept a minimum of training, may have the full range of Nikon equipment at their disposal to make parts photographs, exploded views, catalog and record pictures, training and inspection procedure series and other required photographs. Suitable working space should be provided, together with accessory equipment such as a 20x30-inch opal glass light table, portable backgrounds, reflectors, and lighting (including floods, flash and electronic flash), as well as proper darkroom facilities for fine-grain development and for printing.

Medical applications of close-up photography

Medical and dental photography also demands an excellent photographic image obtained with a minimum of time and attention. Close-up procedures may be simplified to a formula by the orthodontist who desires a clinical record, pictures displaying his professional competence or a before-and-after series as lawsuit insurance against patients who require nothing less than miracles. Similar procedures are available in opthalmic work and many other specialties.

In dental photography, as a typical case, two basic positions may be selected, a full head picture and a mouth close-up. For both of these the Nikon equipped with the Bellows Focusing Device and mounted on a tripod will prove an excellent choice. The head shot may be illuminated by an electronic flash with the reflector on the camera. A medium grey background of suitable heavy paper obtainable in art supply stores is desirable. Alternately, the illumination may be bounced from the ceiling or a white reflector for a softer and more evenly distributed illumination. Distance, background and camera settings may all be established by test and picture-taking may proceed very rapidly. Detail close-ups may be made with no change in equipment, al-

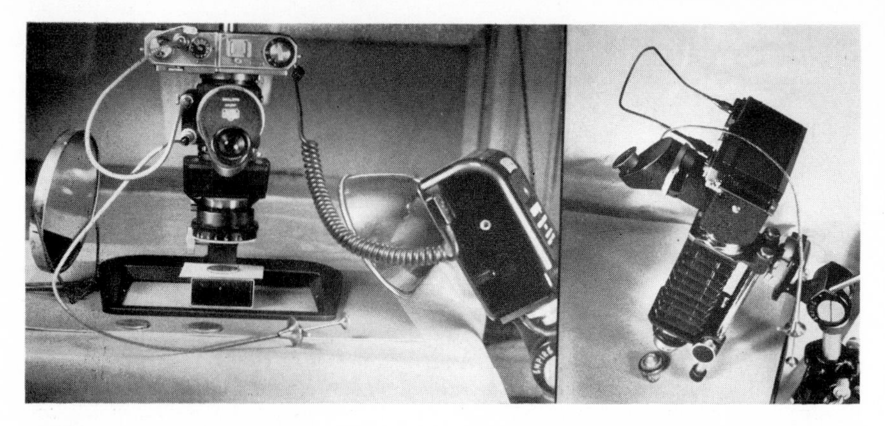

11.10 *Extreme close-up of coin, employing Nikon Repro Copy Outfit, Model S with Reflex Housing and Micro-Nikkor, and electronic flash and mirror reflector.* **11.11** *Nikon Bellows Focusing Attachment in use.*

though the substitution of a "ring-light" electronic flash reflector around the Nikkor will give the best oral illumination. No deviation from uniformity of procedure and identical relative scale for photographs, particularly time-lapse series, should be made without reason.

Duplicating Color Transparencies

THE NIKON COPYING and close-up equipment may also be used for making same-size duplicate transparencies or for enlarging a portion of a 35mm color transparency to fill the complete 24x36mm area. With the proper choice of filters, a very close match between these duplicates and the original may be secured, or changes in all-over color effected which actually improve the appearance of the duplicate over the original.

This method has also been used by professionals who have made color photographs under impossible lighting conditions where their best transparencies were several stops under-exposed, dense and off-color. By making corrected duplicates in the manner outlined here, transparencies of normal density with color rendition sufficiently corrected for publication (even if not "true" color) have been obtained.

The most convenient set-up for duplicating transparencies uses the Nikon Repro Copy Outfit, Model S. A very similar arrangement is possible with the model P or with the Bellows Focusing Attachment on the Nikon. Essentially, any alignment of equipment which will extend the Nikkor to a 1:1 (or greater) copying position, that is, to twice its focal length or more in front of the film plane, will serve. [Instructions for making duplicate transparencies with the enlarger are found in Chapter 7. Not all enlargers permit a 1:1 duplicate, and the weaker light may also lead to difficulties, particularly when heavy filtering is required.] The Nikon Repro Copy Outfit, Model S, is focused on the original transparency which lies on a sheet of opal glass. This, in turn, is supported by a box (to shield off stray light) within which is the reflector of an electronic flash unit, aimed directly at the transparency from underneath. The details of this set-up may be varied within quite wide limits to suit personal convenience, from a quickly-improvised arrangement to a permanent one for rapid and efficient work. The addition of the Nikon Prism Reflex Housing to the basic Model S Repro Copy Outfit, enables a direct enlargement of part of the transparency being copied, if required, as well as direct focusing without removing the Nikon body between originals.

The original may be mounted in either glass or cardboard. Focus should be checked carefully (and will be slightly different when the original is bound in glass). If the transparency is in a glass binder (or if an unmounted transparency is laid on the opal glass) watch for Newton rings, a pattern of striations caused by light interference when the surface of the transparency is separated from the glass by a very small distance. If trouble is encountered on this score, it is best to have several small pieces of anti-Newton-ring glass, available at larger camera stores from several suppliers.

The best position for corrective filters is between the light source and the transparency, rather than suspended in front of the Nikkor where they may interfere with the acutance of the image. One workable arrangement is to place the corrective filters on the opal glass and cover them with a sheet of heavy cardboard or 1/8-inch Masonite with a rectangular hole over which the original transparency may be placed.

This shield will also help to mask off stray light if the opal glass is larger than 2x2 inches. This is important, for no significant amount of illumination should reach the original transparency from the side to be reflected up into the lens, nor should any side light ever strike up into the Nikkor itself to reduce contrast and degrade colors. A cardboard tunnel, darkened inside, and placed around the bellows of the Repro Copy Outfit between the base and bracket arm will be effective for this.

It is also possible to use the Nikon Flash Unit and flashbulbs in a copying set-up such as this or even to use photoflood illumination. However, filter corrections are not so easily accomplished with these light sources, and the problem of heat control with photofloods (as well as the simultaneous control of stray light) becomes a difficult one. The heat from a strong bulb will quickly warp the original (or cause Newton rings in a glass-mounted slide). These light sources should be regarded as expedients, rather than as desirable arrangements. *Note:* Filter suggestions [below] do *not* apply to any illumination other than electronic flash.

Exposure calculation for duplicating transparencies

Every set-up such as the one outlined must be tested in operation to find the exact exposures necessary. There are many variables. The exposure factor for bellows extension [see section *Focus, Illumination and Exposure,* earlier in the chapter] will be a constant, of course, at a 1:1 copying ratio. However, the choice of color film on which to copy (and to a small extent the conditions of processing it, see Chapter 7), the color characteristics of the opal glass used and the slight variations between electronic flash units, and the actual separation between the flash-tube and the original transparency, all enter into exposure determination.

Any set-up similar to the one which has been described and which is so constructed that it may be re-assembled without significant alteration may be tested on a single cartridge of color film and the basic exposure determined. Thereafter, it will only be necessary to make very slight changes in exposure (f/stops) to accommodate differences in density of the original or for the

11.12 BURT OWEN

135mm f/3.5 Nikkor
Plus-X, 1/100, f/4

addition or subtraction of correction filters, at this 1:1 copying ratio. If an original is re-cropped and enlarged in copying, the appropriate correction for the change in bellows extension may be calculated from the Repro Copy Outfit tables in *Data and Formulas.*

When the copying equipment is tested for the first time, select an original transparency with a full range of colors and with good detail in both highlight and shadow areas. Load the Nikon with Daylight Type color film to match the electronic flash source. Use an 81A filter under the original transparency for either Kodachrome or Ektachrome in the Nikon (the film used for the original transparency is not important here) or a UV16 if the copy is to be made on Anscochrome. Run a series of exposures, 1/3 stop apart, over about a three-stop range. If your electronic flash unit has an 80 watt-second rating and the reflector is about 12 inches below the opal glass, the range should extend from about f/8 to f/16 for Ektachrome or Anscochrome, or from f/5.6 to f/11 for Kodachrome. (These are *relative apertures* as engraved on the Nikkor barrel, rather than true *effective apertures* as re-calculated for the bellows extension.) Keep a record of the range of exposures used. If you develop your own Anscochrome or Ektachrome, clip off the exposed strip and develop; if you use Kodachrome, ask to have the film returned unmounted, as a single strip for better comparison of the results.

Check original and duplicates over a good viewing box (4000K) and compare for color rendition and density. Note whether the duplicates are evenly illuminated from corner to corner. If they are not, it may be necessary to raise or lower the position of the flash reflector slightly. If the duplicates are all toward the side of over-exposure, increase the distance of the reflector from the glass or add a neutral density filter to the system. Locating the point of correct exposure at about f/8 for copying a normal original will give a good range of flexibility to accommodate difficult originals.

In comparing the original with the strip of duplicates, you will almost certainly find that there has been some shift in over-all color. Examine the duplicates through the series of color correction filters to find the one (or combination) which seems to match the original. (Hold these filters up between eye and transparency; do not place them on the face of the transparency which will double their visual effect.) This color correction filter or combination will then become a permanent addition to the copying set-up for normal transparencies. Open the Nikkor aperture to compensate for the filter factor of these added gelatin filters. (A new re-test strip for any important changes is desirable, of course, before proceeding with important duplicates.)

From this now-standardized set-up, it will be comparatively easy to modify exposures for correcting originals which are off-color, too thin or too dense. Small corrections for density variations in originals may be measured by meter. Secure a metal plate (about two or three inches square) or a piece of 1/8-inch Masonite or stiff cardboard and pierce the center with a 3/16-inch hole. Place this hole over the most important highlight area of the original which you used for your exposure tests, with the transparency over a light table. This may be the one used under the Nikon Repro Copy Outfit, Model S, described above, or some other light source which will remain constant from measurement to measurement whenever the occasion arises. Note the meter reading from this highlight detail and set the meter computer dial for the actual f/stop used for the best copy and for an (arbitrary) film speed which will place this f/stop against some particular speed mark such as 1/100. Now, place the mask and its 3/16-inch hole over the most important highlight area of another transparency and make a new reading. With the meter set for the arbitrarily chosen film speed, note the f/stop opposite the previously (and also arbitrarily) selected (1/100) shutter speed. The f/stop shown on the meter calculator dial will be correct for a normal density copy of the new original. (Keep a written record of this arbitrary film speed and shutter speed setting for the meter; they are easy to forget.) This metered f/stop plus compensation for whatever corrective filter is needed, will establish the correct exposure for almost any duplication at a 1:1 ratio. Other arbitrary film speeds or shutter settings may be established for other image reductions or enlargements commonly used.

For very elaborate corrections or for duplicating to very close matches or actual improvements over the originals, the full range of color correction filters and the 81-82 series [see *Data and Formulas*] may be used. In addition, the originals may be *masked,* following the suggestions in Chapter 7. A thin positive (black-and-white) mask, made by the laminated-mask method will reduce the contrast of the original and consequently of the duplicate. If this mask is made with a filter, as suggested in Chapter 7, it will also correct for a preponderance of a single color as well as for contrast.

NOTE

It is *illegal* to copy any of the following material:

- U. S. or foreign currency, bonds, notes or other obligations;
- Cancelled or uncancelled postage stamps *except* black-and-white copies less than 75 percent or more than 150 percent of the original size for philatelic purposes;
- U. S. government identification cards, badges, or insignia;
- Military, naval or other documents marked Secret, Confidential or Restricted;
- Certificates of citizenship, naturalization or arrival or their duplicates;
- Copyrighted material (without express permission of the copyright owner).

This list is, of course, merely a partial summary of pertinent laws and regulations and is not intended to substitute for proper legal advice.

12

Stereo with the Nikon

ESPECIALLY DESIGNED EQUIPMENT FOR STEREO photography is available for the Nikon. This includes a matched pair of 35mm Nikkor lenses, a pair of auxiliary prisms which alter the effective lens separation for correct stereo rendition of more distant subjects, and a special stereo view-finder which defines the exact field of view of the stereo frames. These items are furnished in a special leather case. Part of the kit also is a Nikon stereo hand-viewer which optically transposes the stereo frames for correct viewing and which has individually focused eye-pieces. The slides may be re-mounted and projected in any of several standard stereo projectors.

Stereo photography is not only a popular amateur hobby, it has important professional and scientific applications, as well. One of its most extensive uses today is for salesmen, who employ slides to present their line to customers in three-dimensional color, rather than carrying actual samples. This has proven itself, also, in heavy-goods lines and for construction firms, architects and even interior decorators, whose "samples" are far from portable.

Professional photographers specializing in candid wedding work find stereo color coverage a saleable item. This is often offered in conjunction with black-and-white album sales, rather than as a substitute, and substantially increases the size of the total order. Some of these professionals use an inexpensive, custom-made frame of light aluminum stock, tapped to hold two Nikon bodies and the reflector of their electronic flash unit. With one Nikon loaded with color film and equipped with the Nikon Stereo-Nikkor and the other loaded with black-and-white, the Nikons may be used either singly or simultaneously during the ceremony and reception.

There is a growing use of stereo for medical and dental (orthodontal) records. Dermatologists, in particular, have found that the appearance-in-depth of skin conditions is a more valuable record than ordinary (planar) color.

The Stereo-Nikkor

This is a matched pair of 35mm f/3.5 Nikkor lenses, mounted together in a barrel. The angle of acceptance of each lens is 45° 30′ and the effective separation of the two optical centers is 18mm. A septum prevents image over-lap on the two stereo frames, 17x24mm each, which occupy the regular 24x36mm exposure frame area. Marked apertures on the Stereo-Nikkor are: f/3.5, 4.5, 5.6, 8, 11, and 16. The Stereo-Nikkor couples with the Nikon range-finder for all distances from 3 feet to infinity. A lens hood is furnished to fit the front bayonet-mount of the Stereo-Nikkor, as is a 40.5mm diameter ultraviolet screw-in filter.

To mount the Stereo-Nikkor, turn the knurled focusing ring on the lens barrel until the red dots on focusing ring and on the front ring of the lens align. Holding the focusing ring, place the lens into the bayonet mount of the Nikon so the red dot on the ring and on the camera body also align. Insert the Stereo-Nikkor and turn counter-clockwise until it snaps into place.

12.1 *Nikon stereo equipment (described on this page).*

The Nikon Stereo-Prism

A pair of matched prisms increases the effective lens separation of the Stereo-Nikkor lenses to 80mm. This wide inter-ocular prism device employs total internal reflection rather than mirrored surfaces for a bright, undistorted image. To attach the Nikon Stereo-Prism, first loosen the small locking knob found on the bayonet ring, then align the red mark on prism with the red dot on the Nikon body. Insert into bayonet mount and turn counter-clockwise until the bottom of the prism is parallel with the bottom of the Nikon, then tighten the locking knob.

The Nikon Stereo-Finder

This finder slides into the accessory shoe on the top of the Nikon body and indicates the extent of the (vertical) field covered by the Stereo-Nikkor. The dotted line within the bright frame-line marks off the upper limit of the actual picture field when photographing at the nearest focusing distance of 3 feet, and indicates the necessary parallax compensation.

The Stereo-Nikkor in use

A correct effect of convergence in the stereo picture will be obtained if the Stereo-Nikkor is employed alone at distances from 3 feet to approximately 10 feet, and with the Nikon Stereo-Prism attached for distances beyond that. However, if the Stereo-Nikkor is used alone (without the Stereo-Prism) for portraits even beyond 10 feet, the results will often be superior pictorially, even though they are not actually correct (ortho-stereoscopic) in binocular perspective. The Stereo-Nikkor used alone at distances under 10 feet, or with the Nikon Stereo-Prism at greater distances will produce slides which keep the subject behind the picture-frame, rather than apparently extending forward toward the viewer.

The Nikon should always be accurately leveled for all stereo photography. It may be aimed up or down, of course, but a side-to-side twist off level will be disagreeable in viewing. In all record work, the Nikon should be used on a tripod.

While exceptions could certainly be cited, it is generally best to have stereo photographs in fairly sharp focus from front to back. "Differential focusing" is not necessary to separate image planes as it is in planar photography. A large object cut off near the frame edge may also be disturbing when the slide is viewed. Viewing will be more satisfactory, too, if the distance included is confined either to the 3 to 10 foot distance or to 10 feet and beyond.

Many processors will return stereo color slides properly mounted in pairs in 2x2-inch cardboard mounts for viewing in the Nikon (transposing) Stereo-Viewer. They may also be reproduced by standard duplicating methods. Kodachrome is recommended for color work with stereo; other color transparency films have more pronounced graininess. These grain patterns will not match in the two frames and are apt to give somewhat unpleasant "gauze-like" effects in the middle tones.

The stereo frames may be cut apart and re-mounted in special stereo mounts (such as those supplied by Emde) for projection in equipment designed for this size (such as American Standard projectors). Color film intended for this use should be very slightly over-exposed (by about 1/3 stop more than indicated by the Nikon Exposure Meter) to compensate for light-loss in projection. An aluminized screen is necessary for viewing.

Data and Formula

CONTENTS

Equipment Record

Nikon body serial number .... Date acquired ....

Nikon body serial number .... Date acquired ....

Nikkor lenses, focal lengths and serial numbers ....

....

Insured by ....

Policy number(s) .... Expiration date ....

....

....

Depth Of Field: Depth-of-field figures for distances not given on Nikkor depth-of-field tables may be computed from the following formulas. For scientific or other applications requiring extreme image acuity, use 0.01mm as the circle of confusion.

A—diameter of aperture;
U—lens-to-object distance
F—focal length
C—circle of confusion
D_n—near depth of field
D_f—far depth of field
R—relative lens aperture

$$A = \frac{F}{R} \qquad D_n = \frac{AUF}{(AF) + C(U-F)} \qquad D_f = \frac{AUF}{(AF) - C(U-F)}$$

Note: All measurements should be consistently in either metric system or in inches.

25MM NIKKOR

	3 ft.	3.5 ft.	4 ft.	4.5 ft.	5 ft.	5.5 ft.	6 ft.	6.5 ft.	7 ft.
f/4	2'7"-3'8"	2'11"-4'5"	3'3"-5'3"	3'7"-6'2"	3'10"-7'1"	4'2"-8'2"	4'5"-9'4"	4'8"-10'8"	4'11"-12'1"
f/5.6	2'5"-3'11"	2'9"-4'11"	3'-6'	3'3"-7'2"	3'7"-8'7"	3'9"-10'2"	4'-12'1"	4'3"-14'4"	4'5"-17'2"
f/8	2'3"-4'7"	2'6"-5'11"	2'9"-7'7"	2'11"-9'8"	3'2"-12'5"	3'4"-16'2"	3'6"-21'7"	3'8"-30'2"	3'10"-46'
f/11	2'1"-5'9"	2'3"-8'	2'5"-11'5"	2'7"-17'1"	2'9"-28'3"	2'1"-61'	3'1"-∞	3'2"-∞	3'3"-∞
f/16	1'10"-10'	1'11"-20'	2'1"-83'	2'2"-∞	2'4"-∞	2'5"-∞	2'6"-∞	2'7"-∞	2'8"-∞
f/22	1'7"-92'	1'8"-∞	1'9"-∞	1'10"-∞	1'11"-∞	2'-∞	2'⅝"-∞	2'1¼"-∞	2'1⅞"-∞

	8 ft.	9 ft.	10 ft.	12 ft.	15 ft.	20 ft.	30 ft.	50 ft.	∞
f/4	5'5"-15'6"	5'10"-19'10"	6'3"-25'6"	6'11"-45"	7'10"-188'	9'-∞	10'7"-∞	12'3"-∞	16'2"-∞
f/5.6	4'9"-24'11"	5'1"-38'6"	5'5"-68'	5'11"-∞	6'7"-∞	7'5"-∞	8'5"-∞	9'5"-∞	11'7"-∞
f/8	4'1"-288'	4'4"-∞	4'7"-∞	4'11"-∞	5'4"-∞	5'10"-∞	6'5"-∞	7'-∞	8'2"-∞
f/11	3'6"-∞	3'8"-∞	3'9"-∞	4'-∞	4'4"-∞	4'7"-∞	5'-∞	5'4"-∞	5'11"-∞
f/16	2'9"-∞	2'10"-∞	3'-∞	3'1"-∞	3'3"-∞	3'5"-∞	3'8"-∞	3'10"-∞	4'1"-∞
f/22	2'2¾"-∞	2'3½"-∞	2'4"-∞	2'5"-∞	2'6"-∞	2'8"-∞	2'9"-∞	2'10"-∞	3'-∞

28MM NIKKOR

	3 ft.	3.5 ft.	4 ft.	4.5 ft.	5 ft.	5.5 ft.	6 ft.	6.5 ft.	7 ft.
f/3.5	2'8¼"-3'5"	3'1"-4'1"	3'5"-4'9"	3'10"-5'6"	4'2"-6'3"	4'6"-7'1"	4'10"-8'	5'2"-8'11"	5'5"-9'11"
f/4	2'7¾"-3'6"	3'-4'2"	3'4⅝"-4'11"	3'9"-5'8"	4'1"-6'6"	4'5"-7'5"	4'8"-8'4"	5'-9'5"	5'3"-10"-6'
f/5.6	2'6"-3-8"	2'10"-4'6"	3'2"-5'5"	3'6"-6'4"	3'9"-7'5"	4'1"-8'8"	4'4"-10'	4'7"-11'5"	4'10"-13'2"
f/8	2'4"-4'1"	2'8"-5'2"	2'11"-6'4"	3'2"-7'9"	3'5"-9'5"	3'8"-11'5"	3'10"-13'11"	4'1"-17'1"	4'3"-21'2"
f/11	2'2"-4'9"	2'5"-6'3"	2'8"-8'2"	2'11"-10'8"	3'1"-14'3"	3'3"-19'5"	3'5"-28'	3'7"-44'7"	3'8"-91'
f/16	2'-6'7"	2'2"-9'11"	2'4"-15'10"	2'6"-29'7"	2'7"-94'	2'9"-∞	2'10"-∞	2'11"-∞	3'1"-∞
f/22	1'9"-12'4"	1'11"-33'5"	2'-∞	2'2"-∞	2'3"-∞	2'4"-∞	2'5"-∞	2'5"-∞	2'6"-∞

28MM NIKKOR (Con't.)

	8 ft.	9 ft.	10 ft.	12 ft.	15 ft.	20 ft.	30 ft.	50 ft.	∞
f/3.5	6'-12'	6'7"-14'6"	7'1"-17'3"	8'-24'5"	9'2"-41'	10'10"-137'	13'2"-∞	15'11"-∞	23'3"-∞
f/4	5'10"-12'11"	6'4"-15'10"	6'9"-19'3"	7'7"-28'7"	8'9"-55'	10'2"-∞	12'2"-∞	14'6"-∞	20'4"-∞
f/5.6	5'3"-17'3"	5'8"-22'11"	6'-30'10"	6'8"-65'	7'6"-∞	8'6"-∞	9'10"-∞	11'4"-∞	14'7"-∞
f/8	4'7"-34'6"	4'10"-68'	5'2"-∞	5'7"-∞	6'2"-∞	6'10"-∞	7'8"-∞	8'6"-∞	10'3"-∞
f/11	3'11"-∞	4'2"-∞	4'4"-∞	4'8"-∞	5'1"-∞	5'6"-∞	6'-∞	6'6"-∞	7'6"-∞
f/16	3'2"-∞	3'4"-∞	3'6"-∞	3'8"-∞	3'11"-∞	4'2"-∞	4'5"-∞	4'8"-∞	5'2"-∞
f/22	2'8"-∞	2'9"-∞	2'10"-∞	2'11"-∞	3'1"-∞	3'3"-∞	3'5"-∞	3'6"-∞	3'9"-∞

35MM NIKKOR

	3 ft.	3.5 ft.	4 ft.	4.5 ft.	5 ft.	5.5 ft.	6 ft.	6.5 ft.	7 ft.
f/1.8	2'10¾"-3'1⅜"	3'4¼"-3'7⅞"	3'9⅝"-4'2⅝"	4'3"-4'9"	4'8⅜"-5'4⅛"	5'2"-5'11"	5'7"-6'6"	6'-7'1"	6'5"-7'9"
f/2	2'10⅝"-3'1½"	3'4"-3'8⅛"	3'9½"-4'2⅞"	4'2¾"-4'9¾"	4'8"-5'5⅝"	5'1"-6'	5'6"-6'7"	5'11"-7'2"	6'4"-7'10"
f/2.5	2'10¼"-3'2"	3'3⅝"-3'8¾"	3'8⅞"-4'3⅝"	4'2"-4'10¾"	4'7"-5'6"	5'-6'1"	5'5"-6'9"	5'10"-7'5"	6'2"-8'
f/2.8	2'10"-3'2¼"	3'3¼"-3'9⅛"	3'8½"-4'4⅛"	4'1½"-4'11⅜"	4'6½"-5'6¾"	4'11½"-6'2¼"	5'4⅛"-6'10⅛"	5'8⅞"-7'6"	6'1½"-8'2¼"
f/3.5	2'9⅝"-3'2¾"	3'2¾"-3'10"	3'8"-4'5"	4'1"-5'1"	4'5"-5'9"	4'10"-6'5"	5'2"-7'1"	5'7"-7'10"	5'11"-8'7"
f/4	2'9¼"-3'3"	3'2¼"-3'11"	3'7"-4'6"	4'-5'2"	4'4"-5'10"	4'9"-6'7"	5'1"-7'3"	5'6"-8'	5'10"-8'10"
f/5.6	2'8"-3'5"	3'1"-4'1"	3'5"-4'9"	3'10"-5'6"	4'2"-6'3"	4'6"-7'1"	4'10"-8'	5'2"-8'11"	5'5"-9'10"
f/8	2'7"-3'7"	2'11"-4'4"	3'3"-5'2"	3'7"-6'1"	3'11"-7'1"	4'2"-8'1"	4'5"-9'3"	4'9"-10'7"	5'-11'11"
f/11	2'5"-3'11"	2'9"-4'10"	3'1"-5'10"	3'4"-7'	3'7"-8'4"	3'10"-9'11"	4'1"-11'8"	4'3"-13'10"	4'6"-16'4"
f/16	2'3"-4'6"	2'6"-5'10"	2'9"-7'5"	3'-10'	3'2"-12'	3'5"-15'7"	3'7"-20'8"	3'9"-28'8"	3'10"-43'
f/22	2'1"-5'7"	2'4"-7'9"	2'6"-10'11"	2'8"-16'1"	2'10"-26'	2'11"-52'	3'1"-∞	3'2"-∞	3'4"-∞

	8 ft.	9 ft.	10 ft.	12 ft.	15 ft.	20 ft.	30 ft.	50 ft.	∞
f/1.8	7'3"-8'11"	8'-10'3"	8'10"-11'7"	10'4"-14'4"	12'6"-18'10"	15'8"-27'7"	21'3"-51'	29'7"-163'	72'-∞
f/2	7'2"-9'1"	7'11"-10'5"	8'8"-11'9"	10'2"-14'8"	12'3"-19'5"	15'4"-28'9"	20'7"-56'	28'3"-218'	65'-∞
f/2.5	7'-9'5"	7'9"-10'10"	8'5"-12'4"	9'10"-15'6"	11'8"-21'	14'6"-32'4"	19'1"-71'	25'6"-∞	52'-∞
f/2.8	6'10"-9'7"	7'7"-11'1"	8'3"-12'8"	9'7"-16'1"	11'5"-22'	14'-34'11"	18'3"-85'	24'1"-∞	46'-∞
f/3.5	6'8"-10'1"	7'4"-11'9"	7'11"-13'7"	9'2"-17'7"	10'9"-24'11"	13'1"-43'	16'8"-155'	21'4"-∞	37'-∞
f/4	6'6"-10'6"	7'1"-12'4"	7'8"-14'3"	8'10"-18'10"	10'4"-27'7"	12'5"-51'	15'8"-∞	19'9"-∞	32'4"-∞
f/5.6	6'-12'	6'7"-14'5"	7'1"-17'3"	8'-24'5"	9'2"-42'	10'10"-140'	13'2"-∞	15'11"-∞	23'2"-∞
f/8	5'5"-15'4"	5'11"-19'7"	6'3"-25'2"	7'-44'	7'11"-176'	9'1"-∞	10'7"-∞	12'4"-∞	16'3"-∞
f/11	4'10"-23'5"	5'2"-35'3"	5'6"-59'	6'1"-∞	6'9"-∞	7'6"-∞	8'7"-∞	9'8"-∞	11'10"-∞
f/16	4'2"-∞	4'5"-∞	4'7"-∞	4'1"-∞	5'5"-∞	5'11"-∞	6'6"-∞	7'1"-∞	8'2"-∞
f/22	3'6"-∞	3'8"-∞	3'10"-∞	4'1"-∞	4'4"-∞	4'8"-∞	5'-∞	5'5"-∞	6'-∞

50MM NIKKOR

50mm Depth-of-field tables for distances from 1.5 - 2.75 ft. will be found on page 268.

	3 ft.	3.5 ft.	4 ft.	5 ft.	6 ft.	7 ft.	8 ft.	9 ft.
f/1.1	2'11⅝"-3'⅜"	3'5½"-3'6½"	3'11¼"-4'¾"	4'10⅞"-5'1⅛"	5'10½"-6'1¾"	6'10"-7'2"	7'9"-8'3"	8'8"-9'4"
f/1.4	2'11½"-3'½"	3'5⅜"-3'6⅝"	3'11⅛"-4'⅞"	4'10⅝"-5'1½"	5'10"-6'2"	6'9"-7'3"	7'8"-8'4"	8'7"-9'5"
f/2	2'11⅜"-3'¾"	3'5"-3'7"	3'10¾"-4'1⅜"	4'10"-5'2"	5'9"-6'3"	6'8"-7'4"	7'7"-8'6"	8'5"-9'8"
f/2.8	2'11"-3'1"	3'4¾"-3'7⅜"	3'10¼"-4'1⅞"	4'9"-5'3"	5'8"-6'5"	6'7"-7'6"	7'5"-8'8"	8'3"-9'11"
f/4	2'10¾"3'1½"	3'4⅛"-3'8"	3'9⅝"-4'3"	4'8"-5'4"	5'6"-6'7"	6'4"-7'9"	7'2"-9'	8'-10'4"
f/5.6	2'10¼"-3'2"	3'3½"-3'9"	3'8⅝"-4'4"	4'7"-5'6"	5'4"-6'10"	6'2"-8'2"	6'11"-9'6"	7'7"-11'
f/8	2'9½"-3'3"	3'2"-3'10"	3'7⅜"-4'6"	4'5"-5'10"	5'2"-7'3"	5'10"-8'9"	6'6"-10'5"	7'2"-12'2"
f/11	2'8⅝"-3'4"	3'1"-4'	3'6"-4'8"	4'3"-6'1"	4'11"-7'10"	5'6"-9'8"	6'1"-11'9"	6'8"-14'1"
f/16	2'7"-3'7"	3'-4'4"	3'4"-5'1"	3'11"-6'11"	4'6"-9'1"	5'-11'8"	5'6"-14'11"	5'11"-18'11"
f/22	2'6"-3'10"	2'10"-4'8"	3'1"-5'8"	3'8"-8'1"	4'1"-11'3"	4'7"-15'8"	4'11"-22'2"	5'3"-32'7"

	10 ft.	12 ft.	15 ft.	20 ft.	30 ft.	50 ft.	100 ft.	∞
f/1.1	9'7"-10'5"	11'5"-12'7"	14'2"-16'	18'6"-21'9"	26'8"-34'3"	41'-63'	71'-171'	238'-∞
f/1.4	9'6"-10'6"	11'4"-12'9"	13'11"-16'3"	18'1"-22'4"	25'11"-35'7"	39'7"-68'	65'-∞	187'-∞
f/2	9'4"-10'9"	11'-13'2"	13'6"-16'10"	17'5"-23'6"	24'6"-38'9"	36'4"-80'	57'-∞	131'-∞
f/2.8	9'1"-11'2"	10'8"-13'8"	13'-17'9"	16'7"-25'3"	22'10"-44'	32'9"-106'	49'-∞	94'-∞
f/4	8'9"-11'8"	10'3"-14'7"	12'3"-19'3"	15'5"-28'6"	20'8"-55'	28'6"-∞	39'9"-∞	66'-∞
f/5.6	8'4"-12'7"	9'8"-15'11"	11'6"-21'9"	14'2"-34'5"	18'5"-82'	24'4"-∞	32'1"-∞	47'-∞
f/8	7'9"-14'1"	8'11"-18'7"	10'5"-27'	12'7"-50'	15'10"-∞	20'-∞	24'10"-∞	32'11"-∞
f/11	7'2"-16'9"	8'1"-23'4"	9'4"-38'9"	11'-114'	13'5"-∞	16'4"-∞	19'5"-∞	24'-∞
f/16	6'4"-24'2"	7'1"-41'	8'-142'	9'2"-∞	10'9"-∞	12'6"-∞	14'3"-∞	16'6"-∞
f/22	5'7"-52'	6'2"∞	6'10"-∞	7'8"-∞	8'9"-∞	9'10"-∞	10'10"-∞	12'1"-∞

85MM NIKKOR

	3.5 ft.	4 ft.	5 ft.	6 ft.	7 ft.	8 ft.	9 ft.
f/1.5	3′5¾″-3′6¼″	3′11¾″-4′⅜″	4′11½″-5′½″	5′11¼″-6′¾″	6′11″-7′1″	7′11″-8′1½″	8′10″-9′2″
f/2	3′5⅝″-3′6⅜″	3′11⅝″-4′½″	4′11⅜″-5′¾″	5′11″-6′1″	6′10⅝″-7′1½″	7′10″8′2″	8′9⅝″-9′2½″
f/2.8	3′5½″-3′6½″	3′11⅜″-4′⅝″	4′11″-5′1″	5′10⅝″-6′1½″	6′10″-7′2″	7′9″-8′3″	8′8⅝″-9′4″
f/4	3′5⅜″-3′6⅝″	3′11⅛″-4′⅞″	4′10⅝″-5′1½″	5′10″-6′2″	6′9″-7′3″	7′8″-8′4″	8′7″-9′5″
f/5.6	3′5⅛″-3′6⅞″	3′10⅞″-4′1¼″	4′10⅛″-5′2″	5′9″-6′3″	6′8″-7′4″	7′7″-8′6″	8′6″-9′7″
f/8	3′4¾″-3′7¼″	3′10⅜″-4′1¾″	4′9″-5′3″	5′8″-6′4″	6′7″-7′6″	7′5″-8′8″	8′3″-9′11″
f/11	3′4⅜″-3′7¾″	3′9¾″-4′2½″	4′8″-5′4″	5′7″-6′6″	6′5″-7′9″	7′3″-9′	8′-10′4″
f/16	3′3⅝″-3′8⅝″	3′8⅞″-4′3⅝″	4′7″-5′6″	5′4″-6′9″	6′2″-8′2″	6′11″-9′7″	7′7″-11′
f/22	3′2⅞″-3′9¾″	3′7¾″-4′5″	4′5″-5′9″	5′2″-7′2″	5′11″-8′8″	6′7″-10′4″	7′2″-12′1″
f/32	3′1⅝″-3′11¾″	3′6″-4′8″	4′3″-6′2″	4′11″-7′10″	5′6″-9′9″	6′1″-11′10″	6′7″-14′4″

	10 ft.	12 ft.	15 ft.	20 ft.	30 ft.	50 ft.	100 ft.	∞
f/1.5	9′10″-10′2″	11′9″-12′3″	14′7″-15′6″	19′3″-20′10″	28′3″-32′	45′-56′	83′-126′	474′-∞
f/2	9′9″-10′3″	11′8″-12′5″	14′5″-15′7″	19′-21′2″	27′9″-32′8″	44′-58′	78′-139′	356′-∞
f/2.8	9′8″-10′4″	11′6″-12′7″	14′3″-15′11″	18′7″-21′8″	26′11″-33′11″	42′-62′	72′-164′	254′-∞
f/4	9′6″-10′7″	11′4″-12′10″	13′11″-16′4″	18′1″-22′5″	25′9″-35′11″	39′2″-69′	64′-∞	178′-∞
f/5.6	9′4″-10′9″	11′-13′2″	13′6″-16′11″	17′5″-23′7″	24′5″-39′	36′1″-82′	56′-∞	127′-∞
f/8	9′1″-11′2″	10′8″-13′9″	12′11″-17′10″	16′6″-25′6″	22′7″-45′	32′3″-112′	47′-∞	89′-∞
f/11	8′9″-11′8″	10′3″-14′6″	12′4″-19′3″	15′5″-28′6″	20′9″-55′	28′6″-∞	39′7″-∞	65′-∞
f/16	8′4″-12′7″	9′7″-16′1″	11′5″-22′1″	14′-35′4″	18′2″-88′	23′10″-∞	31′1″-∞	45′-∞
f/22	7′10″-14′	8′11″-18′5″	10′6″-26′10″	12′7″-50′	15′10″-∞	19′11″-∞	24′9″-∞	32′7″-∞
f/32	7′1″-17′2″	8′-24′5″	9′3″-42′	10′10″-157′	13′1″-∞	15′9″-∞	18′6″-∞	22′6″-∞

USEFUL LINEAR EQUIVALENTS

1 millimeter = 0.03937 inch
(millimeters divided by 2.54 = inches)

1 centimeter = 0.3937 inch

1 inch = 25.4 millimeters

1 foot = 0.3048 meter

1 meter = 39.3704 inches

1 meter = 3.2808 feet

1 meter = 1.0936 yards

INCH-CENTIMETER CONVERSION TABLE

Inches	Centimeters
1 =	2.54
2 =	5.08
3 =	7.62
4 =	10.16
5 =	12.70
6 =	15.24
7 =	17.78
8 =	20.32
9 =	22.86

Centimeters	Inches
1 =	0.3937
2 =	0.7874
3 =	1.1811
4 =	1.5748
5 =	1.9685
6 =	2.3622
7 =	2.7559
8 =	3.1496
9 =	3.5433

105MM NIKKOR

	4 ft.	4.5 ft.	5 ft.	5.5 ft.	6 ft.	7 ft.	8 ft.	9 ft.
f/2.5	3'11 11/16"-4'5/16"	4'5⅝"-4'6⅜"	4'11½"-5'½"	5'5⅜"-5'6⅝"	5'11¼"-6'13/16"	6'10⅞"-7'1⅛"	7'10½"-8'1½"	8'10⅛"-9'2"
f/2.8	3'11⅝"-4'⅜"	4'5½"-4'6½"	4'11⅜"-5'⅝"	5'5¼"-5'6¾"	5'11⅛"-6'⅞"	6'10¾"-7'1¼"	7'10⅜"-8'1¾"	8'9⅞"-9'2¼"
f/4	3'11½"-4'½"	4'5⅜"-4'6¾"	4'11⅛"-5'⅞"	5'5"-5'7⅛"	5'10¾"-6'1⅜"	6'10¼"-7'1⅞"	7'9⅝"-8'2½"	8'9"-9'3"
f/5.6	3'11¼"-4'¾"	4'5⅛"-4'7"	4'10⅞"-5'1¼"	5'4½"-5'7½"	5'10¼"-6'2"	6'9½"-7'3"	7'9"-8'4"	8'8"-9'5"
f/8	3'11"-4'1"	4'4⅝"-4'7⅜"	4'10⅜"-5'1¾"	5'3⅞"-5'8"	5'9½"-6'3"	6'8½"-7'4"	7'7"-8'5"	8'6"-9'7"
f/11	3'10⅝"-4'1½"	4'4¼"-4'8"	4'9¾"-5'2½"	5'3"-5'9"	5'9"-6'4"	6'7"-7'5"	7'6"-8'7"	8'4"-9'9"
f/16	3'10"-4'2⅛"	4'3⅜"-4'8⅞"	4'8¾"-5'3¾"	5'2"-5'11"	5'7"-6'6"	6'5"-7'8"	7'3"-8'11"	8'1"-10'2"
f/22	3'9⅜"-4'3"	4'2½"-4'10"	4'7⅝"-5'5¼"	5'1"-6'1"	5'6"-6'8"	6'3"-8'	7'-9'4"	7'9"-10'9"
f/32	3'8¼"-4'4⅝"	4'1⅛"-5'⅛"	4'5⅞"-5'8"	4'10"-6'4"	5'3"-7'	6'-8'6"	6'8"-10'1"	7'4"-11'9"

	10 ft.	12 ft.	15 ft.	20 ft.	30 ft.	50 ft.	100 ft.	∞
f/2.5	9'9⅝"-10'2½"	11'8½"-12'3¾"	14'6⅜"-15'6"	19'2"-20'11"	28'2"-32'2"	45'-56'	81'-130'	434'-∞
f/2.8	9'9¼"-10'2⅞"	11'8"-12'4"	14'5¾"-15'7"	19'1"-21'	27'11"-32'5"	44'-57'	80'-134'	388'-∞
f/4	9'8"-10'4"	11'6"-12'6"	14'3"-15'10"	18'8"-21'6"	27'1"-33'7"	42'-61'	73'-158'	272'-∞
f/5.6	9'7"-10'6"	11'4"-12'9"	14'-16'2"	18'3"-22'2"	26'1"-35'3"	39'11"-67'	66'-205'	194'-∞
f/8	9'5"-10'8"	11'1"-13'1"	13'7"-16'9"	17'7"-23'3"	24'9"-38'2"	36'9"-78'	58'-372'	136'-∞
f/11	9'2"-11'	10'10"-13'6"	13'2"-17'6"	16'9"-24'9"	23'3"-43'	33'6"-100'	50'-∞	99'-∞
f/16	8'10"-11'6"	10'4"-14'4"	12'5"-18'11"	15'8"-27'10"	21'1"-53'	29'1"-182'	41'-∞	68'-∞
f/22	8'6"-12'3"	9'10"-15'5"	11'9"-21'	14'6"-32'7"	19'-73'	25'2"-∞	33'5"-∞	50'-∞
f/32	7'11"-13'7"	9'1"-17'10"	10'8"-25'8"	12'11"-46'	16'3"-218'	20'7"-∞	25'9"-∞	34'3"-∞

135MM NIKKOR

	5 ft.	6 ft.	7 ft.	8 ft.	9 ft.	10 ft.
f/3.5	4'11⅝"-5'⅝"	5'11⅜"-6'⅝"	6'11⅛"-7'⅞"	7'11"-8'1¼"	8'10½"-9'1½"	9'10"-10'2"
f/4	4'11½"-5'½"	5'11¼"-6'¾"	6'11"-7'1"	7'10⅝"-8'1½"	8'10"-9'2"	9'9¾"-10'2⅜"
f/5.6	4'11¼"-5'¾"	5'11"-6'1"	6'10⅝"-7'1½"	7'10"-8'2"	8'9"-9'3"	9'8⅞"-10'3"
f/8	4'11"-5'1"	5'10⅝"-6'1½"	6'10"-7'2"	7'9"-8'3"	8'8"-9'4"	9'8"-10'5"
f/11	4'10¾"-5'1⅜"	5'10"-6'2"	6'9"-7'3"	7'8"-8'4"	8'7"-9'5"	9'6"-10'7"
f/16	4'10⅛"-5'2"	5'9"-6'3"	6'8"-7'4"	7'7"-8'6"	8'5"-9'8"	9'3"-10'10"
f/22	4'9½"-5'2⅞"	5'8"-6'4"	6'7"-7'6"	7'5"-8'9"	8'3"-9'11"	9'1"-11'2"
f/32	4'8"-5'4"	5'7"-6'7"	6'4"-7'9"	7'2"-9'1"	7'11"-10'5"	8'8"-11'10"

	12 ft.	15 ft.	20 ft.	30 ft.	50 ft.	100 ft.	∞
f/3.5	11'9⅛"-12'3"	14'7½"-15'5"	19'4"-20'9"	28'5"-31'9"	46'-55'	84'-124'	513'-∞
f/4	11'8⅝"-12'3½"	14'7"-15'6"	19'2"-20'10"	28'2"-32'1"	45'-56'	82'-128'	449'-∞
f/5.6	11'7"-12'5"	14'5"-15'8"	18'11"-21'3"	27'7"-32'11"	43'-59'	76'-145'	321'-∞
f/8	11'6"-12'7"	14'2"-16'	18'6"-21'10"	26'7"-34'5"	41'-64'	69'-179'	225'-∞
f/11	11'3"-12'10"	13'10"-16'4"	17'11"-22'7"	25'6"-36'5"	38'6"-71'	62'-∞	163'-∞
f/16	11'-13'3"	13'5"-17'1"	17'2"-24'	23'11"-40'	34'11"-89'	53'-∞	113'-∞
f/22	10'7"-13'10"	12'10"-18'	16'4"-26'	22'3"-46'	31'5"-125'	45'-∞	82'-∞
f/32	10'1"-14'10"	12'1"-19'10"	15'1"-30'1"	19'11"-62'	26'11"-∞	36'5"-∞	57'-∞

180MM NIKKOR

	7 ft.	8 ft.	9 ft.	10 ft.	11 ft.	12 ft.	13 ft.
f/2.5	6'11⅝"-7'1 11/32"	7'11½"-8'½"	8'11⅜"-9'⅝"	9'11¼"-10'¾"	10'11"-11'1"	11'10⅞"-12'1⅛"	12'10⅝"-13'1⅜"
f/2.8	6'11 19/32"-7'1 13/32"	7'11 15/32"-8' 17/32"	8'11¼"-9'¾"	9'11⅛"-10'⅞"	10'10⅞"-11'1⅛"	11'10¾"-12'1⅜"	12'10½"-13'1⅝"
f/4	6'11⅜"-7'⅝"	7'11¼"-8'¾"	8'11"-9'1"	9'10¾"-10'1¼"	10'10½"-11'1⅝"	11'10"-12'2"	12'10"-13'2"
f/5.6	6'11¼"-7'¾"	7'10⅞"-8'1⅛"	8'10⅝" 9'1⅜"	9'10"-10'2"	10'10"-11'2"	11'9"-12'3"	12'9"-13'3"
f/8	6'10⅞"-7'1⅛"	7'10½"-8'1⅝"	8'10⅛"-9'2"	9'10"-10'3"	10'9"-11'3"	11'8"-12'4"	12'8"-13'5"
f/11	6'10½"-7'1⅝"	7'10"-8'2"	8'9"-9'3"	9'9"-10'4"	10'8"-11'5"	11'7"-12'5"	12'6"-13'6"
f/16	6'10"-7'2"	7'9"-8'3"	8'8"-9'4"	9'7"-10'5"	10'6"-11'7"	11'5"-12'8"	12'4"-13'10"
f/22	6'9"-7'3"	7'8"-8'5"	8'7"-9'6"	9'6"-10'7"	10'4"-11'9"	11'2"-12'11"	12'1"-14'1"
f/32	6'8"-7'5"	7'6"-8'7"	8'5"-9'9"	9'3"-10'11"	10'1"-12'2"	10'10"-13'5"	11'8"-14'8"

	14 ft.	15 ft.	16 ft.	18 ft.	21 ft.	25 ft.	30 ft.	40 ft.
f/2.5	13'10⅜"-14'1⅝"	14'10⅛"-15'1⅞"	15'9⅞"-16'2¼"	17'9¼"-18'2⅞"	20'8¼"-21'3⅞"	24'6⅝"-25'5⅝"	29'4"-30'8"	38'10" 41'3"
f/2.8	13'10¼"-14'1⅞"	14'9⅞"-15'2⅛"	15'9⅝"-16'2½"	17'8⅞"-18'3⅛"	20'8"-21'4"	24'6"-25'6"	29'3"-30'9"	38'8"-41'5"
f/4	13'9"-14'3"	14'9"-15'3"	15'9"-16'4"	17'8"-18'5"	20'6"-21'6"	24'3"-25'9"	29'-31'1"	38'2"-42'
f/5.6	13'8"-14'4"	14'8"-15'4"	15'7"-16'5"	17'6"-18'6"	20'4"-21'9"	24'-26'1"	28'7"-31'7"	37'6"-42'11"
f/8	13'7"-14'5"	14'6"-15'6"	15'5"-16'7"	17'3"-18'9"	20'-22'1"	23'7"-26'7"	28'-32'	37'-44'
f/11	13'5"-14'8"	14'4"-15'9"	15'3"-16'10"	17'-19'1"	19'8"-22'6"	23'-27'	27'-33'	35'-46'
f/16	13'2"-14'11"	14'1"-16'1"	14'11"-17'3"	16'8"-19'7"	19'-23'	22'-28'	26'-35'	34'-50'
f/22	12'11"-15'4"	13'9"-16'6"	14'7"-17'9"	16'-20'	19'-24'	22'-30'	25'-37'	32'-55'
f/32	12'5"-16'	13'3"-17'4"	14'-18'9"	16'-22"	18'-26'	20'-33'	23'-42'	29'-65'

	50 ft.	70 ft.	100 ft.	200 ft.	300 ft.	600 ft.	900 ft.	∞
f/2.5	48'2"-52'	66'5"-74'	92'10"-108'4"	173'-237'	243'-392'	408'-1131'	528'-3048'	1276'-∞
f/2.8	48'-52'3"	66'-74'6"	92'1"-109'6"	170'-242'	238'-407'	393'-1265'	503'-4272'	1139'-∞
f/4	47'-53'	65'-77'	89'-114'	160'-266'	218'-480'	343'-2412'	423'-∞	798'-∞
f/5.6	46'-55'	63'-80'	85'-121'	148'-307'	197'-631'	293'-∞	349'-∞	570'-∞
f/8	45'-57'	60'-85'	80'-133'	134'-399'	172'-1199'	240'-∞	277'-∞	399'-∞
f/11	43'-60'	57'-92'	75'-152'	119'-636'	148'-∞	196'-∞	220'-∞	290'-∞
f/16	40'-66'	52'-107'	67'-198'	100'-∞	120'-∞	150'-∞	164'-∞	200'-∞
f/22	38'-75'	48'-133'	60'-314"	85'-∞	98'-∞	117'-∞	125'-∞	145'-∞
f/32	34'-98'	42'-226'	50'-∞	67'-∞	75'-∞	86'-∞	90'-∞	100'-∞

250MM NIKKOR

	10 ft.	11 ft.	12 ft.	13 ft.	14 ft.	15 ft.
f/4	9′11⅜″-10′⅝″	10′11¼″-11′¾″	11′11⅛″-12′⅞″	12′11″-13′1⅛″	13′-10¾″-14′-1¼″	14′10½″-15′-1½″
f/5.6	9′11¼″-10′⅞″	10′11″-11′1″	11′10¾″-12′1¼″	12′10½″-13′1½″	13′-10¼″-14′1¾″	14′10″-15′2⅛″
f/8	9′10⅞′-10′1⅛″	10′10⅝″-11′1½″	11′10¼″-12′1¾″	12′9⅞″-13′2⅛″	13′10″-14′3″	14′9″-15′3″
f/11	9′10⅜″-10′1⅝″	10′10″-11′2″	11′9⅝″-12′2½″	12′9⅛″-13′3″	13′9″-14′4″	14′8″-15′4″
f/16	9′9¾″-10′2⅜″	10′9″-11′3″	11′9″-12′4″	12′8″-13′4″	13′7″-14′5″	14′6″-15′6″
f/22	9′9″-10′3″	10′8″-11′4″	11′7″-12′5″	12′6″-13′6″	13′5″-14′7″	14′4″-15′8″
f/32	9′8″-10′5″	10′7″-11′6″	11′5″-12′7″	12′4″-13′9″	13′3″-14′11″	14′1″-16′1″

	16 ft.	18 ft.	21 ft.	25 ft.	30 ft.	40 ft.	50 ft.
f/4	15′10⅜″-16′1¾″	17′10″-18′2″	20′9″-21′3″	24′8″-25′5″	29′6″-30′7″	39′1″-41′	48′6″-51′7″
f/5.6	15′9⅝″-16′2⅜″	17′9″-18′3″	20′8″-21′4″	24′6″-25′6″	29′3″-30′9″	38′8″-41′5″	48′-52′
f/8	15′9″-16′3″	17′8″-18′5″	20′6″-21′6″	24′3″-25′9″	29′-31′1″	38′2″-42′1″	47′-53′
f/11	15′8″-16′5″	17′6″-18′6″	20′4″-21′9″	24′-26′1″	28′7″-31′7″	38′-43″	46′-55′
f/16	15′6″-16′7″	17′4″-18′9″	20′-22′1″	23′7″-26′7″	28′-32′	36′-44′	45′-57′
f/22	15′3″-16′10″	17′1″-19′1″	19′8″-22′6″	23′2″-27′2″	27′-33′	35′-46′	43′-60′
f/32	14′11″-17′3″	17′-20′	19′-23′	22′-28′	26′-35′	34′-50′	40′-67′

	70 ft.	100 ft.	200 ft.	300 ft.	600 ft.	900 ft.	∞
f/4	67′1″-73′3″	94′-107′	177′-230′	251′-372′	432′-982′	568′-2164′	1538′-∞
f/5.6	66′-75′	92′-110′	170′-244′	236′-412′	389′-1317′	495′-4943′	1099′-∞
f/8	64′-77′	89′-115′	159′-269′	216′-490′	338′-2705′	415′-∞	770′-∞
f/11	63′-80′	85′-121′	148′-309′	196′-642′	290′-∞	346′-∞	560′-∞
f/16	60′-85′	80′-134′	132′-412′	169′-1338′	235′-∞	270′-∞	385′-∞
f/22	56′-92′	74′-154′	117′-686′	146′-∞	192′-∞	214′-∞	280′-∞
f/32	52′-108′	66′-204′	99′-∞	118′-∞	147′-∞	159′-∞	193′-∞

SHUTTER SPEEDS NECESSARY TO STOP MOTION

Approximate speed in miles per hour	Subject types	Subject-to-camera distance	Direction of Motion		
			Toward or away	45°	Right angle
			Proper Shutter Speeds		
5-10	Pedestrians Children Boating	25 ft 50 ft 100 ft	1/125 1/60 1/30	1/250 1/125 1/60	1/500 1/250 1/125
20-30	Baseball Motorboats Diving	25 ft 50 ft 100 ft	1/250 1/125 1/60	1/500 1/250 1/125	1/1000 1/500 1/250
over 60	Auto races Airplanes Trains	25 ft 50 ft 100 ft	1/500 1/250 1/125	1/1000 1/500 1/250	(pan) 1/1000 1/500

500MM NIKKOR

	25 ft.	30 ft.	40 ft.	50 ft.	60 ft.	70 ft.	80 ft.
f/5	24'10¾"-25'1¼"	29'10⅛"-30'1⅞"	39'8⅝"-40'3½"	49'6½"-50'5½"	59'4"-60'8"	69'1"-70'11"	78'10"-81'3"
f/5.6	24'10⅝"-25'1⅜"	29'10"-30'2⅛"	39'8⅛"-40'3⅞"	49'6"-50'6"	59'3"-60'9"	69'-71'1"	78'8"-81'5"
f/8	24'10"-25'2"	29'9⅛"-30'3"	39'7"-40'6"	49'3"-50'9"	58'11"-61'1"	68'7"-71'6"	78'1"-82'
f/11	24'9⅜"-25'2¾"	29'8"-30'4"	39'5"-40'8"	49'-51'	58'7"-61'6"	68'-72'1"	77'5"-82'9"
f/16	24'8"-25'4"	29'6"-30'6"	39'1"-40'11"	48'7"-51'6"	57'11'-62'3"	67'-73'	76'-84'
f/22	24'7"-25'6"	29'4"-30'8"	38'9"-41'4"	48'1"-52'1"	57'-63'	66'-74'	75'-86'
f/32	24'4"-25'8"	29'1"-31'	38'3"-41'11"	47'-53'	56'-65'	65'-77'	73'-89'
f/45	24'1"-26'	28'8"-31'5"	37'7"-42'9"	46'-55'	55'-67'	63'-80'	70'-93'

	90 ft.	100 ft.	150 ft.	200 ft.	300 ft.	400 ft.	500 ft.
f/5	88'6"-90'7"	98'1"-102'	145'8"-154'7"	192'-208'	283'-319'	370'-435'	454-556'
f/5.6	88'3"-91'9"	97'11"-102'3"	145'-155'	192'-209'	281'-322'	367'-440'	449'-564'
f/8	87'7"-92'7"	97'-103'	143'-157'	188'-214'	274'-332'	354'-459'	431'-596'
f/11	87'-94'	96'-104'	141'-160'	184'-219'	265'-346'	340'-486'	409'-642'
f/16	85'-95'	94'-107'	137'-166'	177'-229'	252'-371'	318'-539'	378'-738'
f/22	84'-97'	92'-109'	133'-172'	170'-242'	237'-408'	296'-619'	347'-899'
f/32	81'-101'	89'-114'	126'-185'	160'-268'	217'-488'	264'-825'	304'-1411'
f/45	78'-107'	85'-121'	119'-205'	147'-312'	195'-655'	232'-1455'	263'-5471'

	600 ft.	800 ft.	1000 ft.	1500 ft.	2000 ft.	4000 ft.	6000 ft.	∞
f/5	535'-683'	689'-954'	832'-1254'	1150'-2155'	1423'-3365'	2208'-21321'	2705'-∞	4921'-∞
f/5.6	528'-694'	677'-977'	815'-1293'	1119'-2275'	1375'-3666'	2095'-44403'	2538'-∞	4394'-∞
f/8	503'-744'	636'-1079'	756'-1479'	1009'-2921'	1213'-5702'	1740'-∞	2035'-∞	3076'-∞
f/11	474'-818'	590'-1242'	692'-1803'	899'-4534'	1057'-18675'	1436'-∞	1631'-∞	2238'-∞
f/16	433'-980'	527'-1659'	607'-2841'	761'-56850'	871'-∞	1112'-∞	1226'-∞	1539'-∞
f/22	392'-1285'	468'-2780'	529'-9208'	642'-∞	719'-∞	876'-∞	944'-∞	1120'-∞
f/32	338'-2678'	394'-∞	436'-∞	510'-∞	557'-∞	647'-∞	683'-∞	770'-∞
f/45	288'-∞	326'-∞	355'-∞	402'-∞	431'-∞	483'-∞	503'-∞	548'-∞

CLOSE-UP CALCULATIONS

These formulas are useful for working distances closer than 8X the focal length of the lens.

Definition of terms

I—image size
O—object size
U—lens (diaphragm)-to-object distance
V—lens (diaphragm)-to-film distance
F—focal length
m—image-object ratio (magnification)

I. Formula for finding image-object ratio:

$$\frac{I}{O} = \frac{V-F}{F} = \frac{F}{U-F} = \frac{V}{U}$$

Example: V = 250mm; F = 50mm

$$\frac{I}{O} = \frac{250-50}{50} = \frac{4}{1} \text{ or } 4:1$$

II. Formulas for calculating U or V when one of two is known:

$$U = \frac{VF}{V-F} \qquad V = \frac{UF}{U-F}$$

Example: V = 250mm; F = 50mm

$$U = \frac{250 \times 50}{250-50} = \frac{12500}{200} = 62.5\text{mm}$$

III. Formulas for finding U or V if image-object ratio is known:

$$U = F\left(1+\frac{1}{m}\right);\ V = F(1+m). \text{ Example: } F = 50\text{mm};\ m = \frac{I}{O} = \frac{4}{1}$$

$$U = 50\ (1+\tfrac{1}{4}) = 62.5\text{mm}$$

IV. Close-up Exposure. The relative aperture (engraved on the Nikkor lens barrel) is not the actual aperture when working close-up. The effective, or actual, aperture on which exposure must be based can be calculated from this formula:

$$\text{Eff. f/number} = \frac{\text{rel.f/number} \times V}{F(\text{of Nikkor})}$$

Example: rel.f/number = 8; V = 200mm
F = 50mm

$$\text{Eff. f/number} = \frac{8 \times 200}{50} = \frac{1600}{50} = f/32$$

V. Close-up Exposure. If you prefer not to calculate the effective aperture, you may find the exposure factor (times by which exposure must be increased) from the following formula:

$$\text{Exposure factor} = \frac{V^2}{F^2}$$

Example: V = 200mm; F = 50mm

$$\text{Exposure factor} = \frac{40{,}000}{2{,}500} = 16$$

Multiply this figure times shutter speed to arrive at correct speed to use without changing the aperture setting. Examples:

2 sec. x 16 = 32 sec.; ½ sec. x 16 = 8 sec.

Note: For depth-of-field formulas see page 258.

Image Magnification with Nikon Bellows Focusing Device

50mm Nikkor	1:2.2—1:4.8
85mm Nikkor	1:1.3—1:3
105mm Nikkor	1:1.05—1:2.4
135mm Nikkor	1:0.8—1:1.9
Short-mount 135mm Nikkor	1:1—∞

Note: The Nikon Bellows Focusing Device is used with the Prism Reflex Housing.

50mm Nikkors are attached in reverse position with rings supplied.

Short-mount 135mm Nikkor is in preparation.

CLOSE-UP TABLES — NIKON REPRO COPY OUTFIT S

Range of Repro S	Attachment lens	Diaphragm ring	I:O	f/1.4	f/2	f/2.8	f/4	f/5.6	f/8	f/11	f/16	Subject area (in mm)	Subject distance* (in mm)	Exposure Factor**
				50mm Nikkor Depth of field (in mm)										
Range of new Repro S (used on stand)	With attachment lens	Without diaphragm ring	1:20	±20	+31 −30	+41 −37	+59 −52	+88 −74	+126 −102	+180 −135	+280 −190	720 x 480	1247	1.4X (with attachment lens)
Range of new Repro S (used on stand)	With attachment lens	Without diaphragm ring	1:15	±11	+17 −16	+24 −22	+33 −31	+47 −43	+70 −60	+97 −80	+170 −110	540 x 360	964	1.4X (with attachment lens)
Range of new Repro S (used on stand)	With attachment lens	Without diaphragm ring	1:12	±7	±10	+15 −14	+21 −20	+30 −28	+44 −39	+62 −54	+94 −75	432 x 288	794	1.4X (with attachment lens)
Range of new Repro S (used on stand)	With attachment lens	Without diaphragm ring	1:10	±5	+7 −6	+12 −10	+17 −13	+22 −19	+32 −27	+44 −36	+64 −53	360 x 240	681	1.5X (with attachment lens)
Range of new Repro S (used on stand)	With attachment lens	Without diaphragm ring	1:8	±4	±5	+8 −7	+10 −9	+14 −12	+21 −18	+28 −24	+42 −36	288 x 192	568	1.6X (with attachment lens)
Range of new Repro S (used on stand)	With attachment lens	Without diaphragm ring	1:6	±2	±3	±4	±6	±8	+12 −11	+16 −15	+23 −22	216 x 144	457	1.7X (with attachment lens)
Range of new Repro S (used on stand)	Without attachment lens	Without diaphragm ring	1:5	±1.4	±2.0	±2.8	±4.0	±5.6	±8.0	±11	±16	180 x 120	365	1.4X
Range of new Repro S (used on stand); Range of old Repro S (on stand)	Without attachment lens	Without diaphragm ring	1:4	±0.9	±1.3	±1.9	±2.6	±3.7	±5.3	±7.1	±10	144 x 96	315	1.6X
Range of new Repro S (used on stand); Range of old Repro S (on stand)	Without attachment lens	Use diaphragm ring	1:3	±0.6	±0.8	±1.1	±1.6	±2.3	±3.2	±4.3	±6.2	108 x 72	268	1.7X
Range of new Repro S (used on stand); Range of old Repro S (on stand)	Without attachment lens	Use diaphragm ring	1:2.5	±0.4	±0.6	±0.8	±1.2	±1.6	±2.3	±3.1	±4.5	90 x 60	246	2.0X
Range of new Repro S (used on stand); Range of old Repro S (on stand)	Without attachment lens	Use diaphragm ring	1:2	±0.3	±0.4	±0.6	±0.8	±1.1	±1.6	±2.2	±3.1	72 x 48	225	2.3X
Range of new Repro S (used on stand); Range of old Repro S (on stand)	Without attachment lens	Use diaphragm ring	1:1.5	±0.2	±0.3	±0.3	±0.5	±0.7	±1.0	±1.4	±2.0	54 x 36	208	2.8X
Range of new Repro S (used on stand); Range of old Repro S (on stand)	Without attachment lens	Use diaphragm ring	1:1	±0.1	±0.1	±0.2	±0.3	±0.4	±0.5	±0.7	±1.1	36 x 24	199	4X

* Distance from film plane stage to focused subject plane. Nikon Prism Reflex Housing added between S bellows stage and Nikon adds 74mm of extension.
** See exposure factor calculations, page 266.

COPY TABLES REPRO OUTFIT MODEL P

Use Extension Tubes:		Reduction Scale (I:O)	Subjcet area covered (mm) Maximum Field	Minimum Field
H	With Supplementary lens	1:17–1:5.9	580 x 410	200 x 140
H+A		1:5.9–1:3.5	200 x 140	185 x 112
H		1:4.6–1:3	155 x 110	100 x 70
H+A		1:3–1:2.2	100 x 70	75 x 52
H+B		1:2.2–1:1.75	75 x 52	59 x 41
H+C		1:1.75–1:1.45	59 x 41	49 x 34
H+A+C		1:1.45–1:1.23	49 x 34	42 x 29
H+B+C		1:1.23–1:1.09	42 x 29	37 x 26
H+A+B+C		1:1.09–1:1	37 x 26	34 x 24

H = micrometer focusing mount.

Tubes: A = 6mm, B = 12mm, C = 18mm

Note: This table is computed for 24 x 34mm field of Nikon S. When S2 and SP bodies are used, add 1/17th to horizontal dimension.

50mm NIKKOR CLOSE-UP DEPTH-OF-FIELD TABLE

Note: These distances apply to the Nikon Close Focusing Attachment as well as to other copying arrangements.

	1.5 ft.	1.75 ft.	2 ft.	2.25 ft.	2.5 ft.	2.75 ft.
f/1.4	1'5 29/32"–1'6 3/32"	1'8 7/8"–1'9 5/32"	1'11 13/16"–2' 3/16"	2'2 3/4"–2'3 1/4"	2'5 5/8"–2'6 3/8"	2'8 5/8"–2'9 3/8"
f/2	1'5 7/8"–1'6 1/8"	1'8 13/16"–1'9 3/16"	1'11 23/32"–2' 9/32"	2'2 5/8"–2'3 3/8"	2'5 1/2"–2'6 1/2"	2'8 1/2"–2'9 5/8"
f/2.8	1'5 13/16"–1'6 3/16"	1'8 23/32"–1'9 9/32"	1'11 5/8"–2' 3/8"	2'2 1/2"–2'3 1/2"	2'5 3/8"–2'6 5/8"	2'8 1/4"–2'9 7/8"
f/4	1'5 23/32"–1'6 9/32"	1'8 5/8"–1'9 3/8"	1'11 1/2"–2' 5/8"	2'2 1/4"–2'3 3/4"	2'5 1/8"–2'7"	2'7 7/8"–2'10 1/8"
f/5.6	1'5 5/8"–1'6 3/8"	1'8 1/2"–1'9 5/8"	1'11 1/4"–2' 3/4"	2'2"–2'4"	2'4 3/4"–2'7 3/8"	2'7 1/2"–2'10 5/8"
f/8	1'5 1/2"–1'6 5/8"	1'8 1/4"–1'9 7/8"	1'11"–2'1 1/8"	2'1 5/8"–2'4 1/2"	2'4 1/4"–2'8"	2'6 7/8"–2'11"
f/11	1'5 1/4"–1'6 3/4"	1'8"–1'10 1/8"	1'10 5/8"–2'1 5/8"	2'1"–2'5"	2'4"–2'9"	2'6"–3'
f/16	1'5"–1'7"	1'7 1/2"–1'11"	1'10"–2'2 1/2"	2'–2'6"	2'3"–2'10"	2'5"–3'2"
f/22	1'4 1/2"–1'7 1/2"	1'7"–1'11 1/2"	1'9 1/2"–2'3 1/2"	1'11 1/2"–2'8"	2'2"–3'	2'4"–3'5"

I:O	Image Reduction									
Scale	1:10	1:5	1:4	1:3	1:2	1:1.8	1:1.6	1:1.4	1:1.2	1:1
Exposure Factor	1.21	1.44	1.56	1.77	2.25	2.4	2.55	2.9	3.25	4

I:O	Image Magnification									
Scale	1.2:1	1.4:1	1.6:1	1.8:1	2:1	3:1	4:1	5:1	10:1	20:1
Exposure Factor	4.8	5.7	6.7	7.8	9	16	25	36	121	440

Exposure factors can be translated into usable terms in two simple ways: 1) divide the factor into the exposure index for your film and use this new figure as the film index; 2) multiply time of exposure by the filter factor to arrive at new exposure time to use. For the exposure factor–lens opening relationship of frequently used factors, see page 269.

FRACTIONAL F/STOPS

The figures on the right-hand side of the page are the full, ½, and ⅓ f/stops (rounded off to nearest useful values). In determining full or partial stops from the ⅓ and ½ stops given, bear in mind that the latter are fractional values of full stops. Hence: f/4.5–f/5 (for example) is ⅓ stop; f/4.5–f/5.6 is ⅔ of a stop; f/4.5–f/6.3 is a full stop; and f/4.8–f/5.6 is ½ stop. (See filter data here and on following pages.)

Filter Factor	1.2	1.5	1.7	2	2.5	3	4	5	6	8	12	16	25
Open up by (f/stop)	⅓	⅔	⅔	1	1⅓	1⅔	2	2⅓	2⅔	3	3⅓	4	4⅓

Nikon Filters

Filter Color or Type	Nikon Filters	Equivalent Kodak Wratten Filters**	Filter Factor		B & W Corrective	B & W Contrast	Color Separation
			Day.	Tung.			
U V	L38, L39, L40	2C, 2B, 2C	1	1			
Light Yellow	Y43, Y44, Y45	K1	1.5	1			
Light Yellow	Y47, Y48, Y49	—	1.7	1.2			
Medium Yellow	Y51, Y52, Y53	K2, K3, 12	2	1.5	X		
*Orange	O55, O56, O57	G	3	2.5		X	
*Light Red	R59, R60, R61	23A	6	3		X	
*Light Green	XO	—	2	1.7			
*Light Green	XI	—	—	2	X for tungsten		
Neutral Density	ND-4X	ND-2	4	4			
Neutral Density	ND-8X	ND-3	8	8			

* These filters are for use with panchromatic, but not orthochromatic film.
** Approximate match; for scientific use, check exact spectral absorbtions.

Other Filters For Black-And-White Film

Filter Color or Type	Kodak Wratten Designation	Filter Factor		B & W Corrective	B & W Contrast	Color Separation
		Day.	Tung.			
*Light Green	X1	4	3	X for tungsten		
*Medium Green	X2	5	4			
*Medium Red	25(A)	8	6		X	X
*Green	58(B)	8	8		X	X
*Blue	47(CS) 47B	8	16		X	X
*Deep Red	29(F)	25	12		X	X
*Green	61(N)	12	12		X	X

* These filters are for use with panchromatic, but not orthochromatic film.

½	full	⅓
	1.	
		1.1
1.2		
		1.3
	1.4	
		1.6
1.7		
		1.8
	2	
		2.2
2.4		
		2.5
	2.8	
		3.2
3.4		
		3.5
	4	
		4.5
4.8		
		5
	5.6	
		6.3
6.7		
		7
	8	
		9
9.6		
		10
	11	
		12.5
13.4		
		14
	16	
		18
19		
		20
	22	
		25
26		
		28
	32	
		36
38		
		40
	45	

FILTER and LENS ATTACHMENT SIZES FOR NIKKOR LENSES

Nikkors \ Filter Sizes		34.5mm	40.5mm	VI (41.3)	43mm	48mm	VII (50.8)	52mm	58mm	62mm	VIII (63.5)	IX (82.5)	(110mm)
25mm	f/4	L		L			N						
28mm	f/3.5	L			N		N						
35mm	f/1.8				NL								
35mm	f/2.5	L		L	N		N						
35mm	f/3.5	L		L	N		N						
50mm	f/1.1									NL			
50mm	f/1.4				NL		NL						
50mm	f/2		NL	NL									
50mm	f/3.5	NL		NL									
85mm	f/1.5								L		N		
85mm	f/2					NL	NL						
105mm	f/2.5						NL	NL					
135mm	f/3.5				NL		NL						
180mm	f/2.5											NL	
250mm	f/4											NL	
500mm	f/5												NL
(50mm	f/1.5)		NL	NL									
(135mm	f/4)		NL	NL									
L38, L39, L40		X	X	X	X	X	X	X		X			
Y43, Y44, Y45		X	X	X	X	X	X	X	X	X	X		
Y47, Y48, Y49		X	X	X	X	X	X	X		X			X
Y51, Y52, Y53		X	X	X	X	X	X	X	X	X	X	X	X
O55, O56, O57		X	X	X	X	X	X	X	X	X	X		
R59, R60, R61		X	X	X	X	X	X	X	X	X	X	X	X
XO		X	X	X	X	X	X	X		X			
XI		X	X	X	X	X	X	X		X			
ND-4X										X			
ND-8X										X			

N—Nikon mount
L—Leica mount
X—filter available

KODAK LIGHT BALANCING FILTERS

	Wratten Number	Exposure Increase in Stops*	Color Temperature of Source: Converted to 3200 K	Color Temperature of Source: Converted to 3400 K
Bluish	82C + 82C	1⅓	2490 K	2610 K
	82C + 82B	1⅓	2570 K	2700 K
	82C + 82A	1	2650 K	2780 K
	82C + 82	1	2720 K	2870 K
	82C	⅔	2800 K	2950 K
	82B	⅔	2900 K	3060 K
	82A	⅓	3000 K	3180 K
	82	⅓	3100 K	3290 K
No Filter Necessary			3200 K	3400 K
Yellowish	81	⅓	3300 K	3510 K
	81A	⅓	3400 K	3630 K
	81B	⅓	3500 K	3740 K
	81C	⅓	3600 K	3850 K
	81D	⅔	3700 K	3970 K
	81EF	⅔	3850 K	4140 K

* These values are approximate. For critical work, they should be checked by practical test, especially if more than one filter is used.

Note: Using the No. 82 (bluish) series is equivalent to raising the temperature of tungsten illumination; using filters in the No. 81 (yellowish) series is equivalent to lowering it. The color temperatures opposite the filters indicate the color temperature of the light source before a filter is added to convert to 3400K or 3200K.

KODAK COLOR COMPENSATING FILTERS

	Peak Density	Yellow (Absorbs Blue)	Exposure Increase in Stops*	Magenta (Absorbs Green)	Exposure Increase in Stops*	Cyan (Absorbs Red)	Exposure Increase in Stops*
Subtractive Colors	.05	CC-05Y	—	CC-05M	⅓	CC-05C	⅓
	.10	CC-10Y	⅓	CC-10M	⅓	CC-10C	⅓
	.20	CC-20Y	⅓	CC-20M	⅓	CC-20C	⅓
	.30	CC-30Y	⅓	CC-30M	⅔	CC-30C	⅔
	.40	CC-40Y	⅓	CC-40M	⅔	CC-40C	⅔
	.50	CC-50Y	⅔	CC-50M	⅔	CC-50C	1
	Peak Density	**Red (Absorbs Blue and Green)**	**Exposure Increase in Stops***	**Green (Absorbs Blue and Red)**	**Exposure Increase in Stops***	**Blue (Absorbs Red and Green)**	**Exposure Increase in Stops***
Primary Colors	.05	CC-05R	⅓	CC-05G	⅓	CC-05B	⅓
	.10	CC-10R	⅓	CC-10G	⅓	CC-10B	⅓
	.20	CC-20R	⅓	CC-20G	⅓	CC-20B	⅔
	.30	CC-30R	⅔	CC-30G	⅔	CC-30B	⅔
	.40	CC-40R	⅔	CC-40G	⅔	CC-40B	1
	.50	CC-50R	1	CC-50G	1	CC-50B	1⅓

To determine the minimum number of filters for the desired color correction, or to reduce combinations to their simplest form:

First, convert any primary colored CC filters to their equivalent subtractive colors. From the chart above we can see that because a red filter absorbs blue and green, it is equivalent to a yellow filter (which absorbs blue) plus a magenta filter (which absorbs green). In this manner green = yellow + cyan; blue = magenta + cyan. Next add like filters together: for instance 20Y + 10Y = 30Y, but eliminate any filters, such as 10Y + 10M + 10C which combine to produce only a neutral density. Finally, if the remainder includes two subtractive filters of equal density, replace them with a single filter of primary color, but note that 10Y + 10M = 10R (not 20R).

FILTERS FOR DAYLIGHT-TYPE COLOR FILMS

(E. I. stands for exposure index)

Daylight, clear or hazy sun	No filter needed for Kodachrome (E.I. 10), Ektachrome (E.I. 32), Anscochrome (E.I. 32) or Super Anscochrome E.I. 100).
Daylight, open shade, or bluish daylight, or overcast weather; no shadows.	Use Skylight filter with Kodachrome, Ektachrome, Anscochrome or Super Anscochrome. No exposure increase is required.
Daylight; distant scenes and aerial shots	Use Skylight filter with Kodachrome, Ektachrome, Anscochrome or Super Anscochrome. No exposure increase is required.
Daylight; to darken blue skies without affecting the color of other objects; also for subduing non-metallic reflections	Use a polarizing screen or filter and follow the exposure recommendations given by the filter manufacturer.
Blue flash lamps used indoors or outdoors	No filters required. Use guide numbers given for blue bulbs.
Clear flashbulbs, wire filled; used indoors at night or in similar situations	Use an 80C filter with Kodachrome, Ektachrome, Anscochrome and Super Anscochrome. Guide number for blue bulbs of equivalent numbers should be used.
Clear flashbulbs, wire-filled, when used for flash-fill-in by daylight	Though blue flashbulbs are generally recommended for synchro-sun, many professionals like the warmer effect of clear bulbs, and no filter over lens, for outdoor fill-in flash.
Photofloods; new 3400K bulbs.	Use an 80B filter for Kodachrome (at E.I. 5), or Ektachrome (at E.I. 12); use an 80A filter with Ansocochrome (at E.I. 8), or Super Anscochrome (at E.I. 25).
Electronic flash	The color of electronic flash is approximately balanced to daylight color film. If pictures are too bluish use a filter which warms up tones slightly like the 81A.

FILM SPEED CONVERSION TABLE

Use these conversion tables only as an approximate guide, since different methods are used to arrive at the systems.

ASA-BSA* arithmetic (used in U.S.)	ASA-BSA* logarithmic (in degrees)	General Electric†	Weston†	European Scheiner	American Scheiner	Din**
1	11	1	0.75	—	8	1/10
1.2	12	1.5	1	—	9	2/10
1.6	13	2	1.3	—	10	3/10
2	14	—	1.5	—	11	4/10
2.5	15	3	2	—	12	5/10
3	16	4	2.5	—	13	6/10
4	17	4.5	3	18	14	7/10
5	18	—	4	19	15	8/10
6	19	7.5	5	20	16	9/10
8	20	9	6	21	17	10/10
10	21	12	8	22	18	11/10
12	22	15	10	23	19	12/10
16	23	18	12	24	20	13/10
20	24	24	16	25	21	14/10
25	25	30	20	26	22	15/10
32	26	36	24	27	23	16/10
40	27	48	32	28	24	17/10
50	28	60	40	29	25	18/10
64	29	75	50	30	26	19/10
80	30	100	64	31	27	20/10
100	31	120	80	32	28	21/10
125	32	150	100	—	29	22/10
160	33	200	125	—	30	23/10
200	34	250	160	—	31	24/10
250	35	300	200	—	32	25/10
320	36	400	250	—	33	26/10
400	37	500	320	—	34	27/10
500	38	600	400	—	35	28/10
650	39	800	500	—	36	29/10
800	40	900	650	—	37	30/10
1000	41	1000	800	—	38	31/10

* American Standards Association and British Standards Association. ** German film speed system.
† Older meters; newer ones have ASA scale.

FILTERS FOR FLASH AND TUNGSTEN-TYPE COLOR FILMS

(E. I. stands for exposure index to use)

Daylight	Use an 85C filter with Kodachrome, Type F (at E.I. 10), or Ektachrome Type F (at E.I. 20), or Anscochrome, Type F (at E.I. 25), or Ektacolor SO1185 (at E.I. 25). With Kodachrome Professional Film, Type A use an 85 filter and E.I. 10.
Clear flashbulbs wire filled only; used indoors at night or in similar situations	No filter is required for Kodachrome, Type F; Ektachrome, Type F; Anscochrome, Type F; and Ektacolor SO1185. With Kodachrome Professional Film, Type A use an 81C filter and base guide numbers on an E.I. of 12.
Photofloods; new 3400K bulbs	Use an 82A filter with Kodachrome, Type F (at E.I. 12); or with Ektachrome, Type F (at E.I. 16); or with Anscochrome, Type F (at E.I. 20), or Ektacolor SO1185 (at E.I. 20, at 1/25 or faster only). No filter is required for Kodachrome Professional Film, Type A which has an E.I. of 16.
Tungsten Room Light	Use recommendations given above for photofloods. Pictures may have a "warm" cast. If this is displeasing try the following: 82C filter and Kodachrome, Type F (at E.I. 10); 82C filter and Ektachrome Type F (at E.I. 12); 82B filter with Anscochrome, Type F (at E.I. 16); Kodachrome Professional Film, Type A, use an 82A filter and E.I. 12. Ektacolor SO1185 is not recommended for speeds slower than 1/25 sec.
Electronic Flash used indoors or outdoors	Use an 85C filter with Kodachrome, Type F (base guide numbers on E.I. 10); or with Ektachrome, Type F (base guide numbers on E.I. 20); or with Anscochrome Type F (base guide numbers on E.I. 25), or with Ektacolor S01185 (base guide numbers on E.I. 12). With Kodachrome Professional Film, Type A use an 85 filter and base guide numbers on E.I. 10.

SAFELIGHT FILTERS

For	Safelight filter to use	Color
Regular U. S. contact and enlarging papers	Kodak Wratten OA, or equivalent	Greenish-Yellow
Ilford Bromide and Plastika papers	Ilford S, or equivalent	Light Brown
Du Pont Varigam	Du Pont S-55X, or equivalent	Orange-Brown
Kodak Polycontrast papers	Kodak Wratten OC, or equivalent	Light Amber
Ilford Multigrade	Ilford S, or equivalent	Light Brown
Panchromatic film (not desensitized)	Kodak Wratten 3, or equivalent. For brief inspections only. See Ch. 5.	Dark Green
Kodak Color Print Materials Type C and Type R	Kodak Wratten 10; for brief inspections only	Dark Amber

Note: Direct-illumination safelights usually call for 15-watt bulbs and should be no closer than 4 ft. to the sensitive material. For safelight tests to run, see Chapter 6.

Selected Flashbulbs For Nikon Flash Units

	Number	Manufacturer	Milli-Sec. to Peak	Flash Duration at ½ Peak (in millisecs)	Approx. Peak Lumens (in 1000's)	Approx. Total Lumen Sec. Output (in 1000's)	Approx. Color Temperature
Focal Plane	6	Dura, GE, Westinghouse	—	—	700	17.5	3800K
	6	Amplex	—	—	620	16	3800K
	FP-26	Sylvania	—	—	600	15	3800K
	6B	GE, Westinghouse	—	—	320	8	6000K
	6B	Amplex	—	—	280	7.5	6000K
	6B	Dura	—	—	300	8.5	6000K
	FP-26B	Sylvania	—	—	270	7.5	6000K
	6A	Dura	—	—	550	14.5	3200K
	5	GE	20	13	1,500	18.5	3800K
Class M	5	Westinghouse	20	—	1,500	20	3800K
	Press 25	Sylvania	20	14	1,250	20	3800K
	5B	GE, Westinghouse	20	13	720	8.8	6000K
	Press 25B	Sylvania	20	14	560	9	6000K
	5A	Dura	20	—	1,250	14	3200K
	8	GE	20	10	900	9	3800K
	8	Westinghouse	20	10	700	7	3800K
	Bantam 8	Sylvania	20	10	700	7	3800K
Class F	SM	GE	5	5	810	4.8	3300K
	SM	Westinghouse	5	—	900	5	3300K
	SF	Sylvania	6	5	800	5	3400K

Note: All bulbs listed above have a Single Contact (S.C.) Bayonet Base which fits the Nikon Flash Units. (B stands for blue bulbs.) Synchronization settings for Nikon cameras are in chart on opposite page.

Indoor Exposure From Foot-Candles of Illumination With No. 2 Photoflood or 500-Watt RFL-2	inches				feet			
lamp to subject distance	12	17	24	34	4	5½	8	11
single lamp, front light	4600	2600	1400	750	400	200	100	50
1 lamp each side, 45°	6400	3600	2000	1050	550	275	140	70

$$\text{Exposure (in sec.)} = \frac{25 \times (\text{Aperture number})^2}{\text{foot candles} \times \text{film speed}}$$

Synchronizing Flash with the Nikon

		S shutter traverse 24 milliseconds		**S2** Shutter traverse 17 milliseconds									**SP** Shutter traverse 13 millisecs
		Connecting Socket		Synchro-selector Dial settings									Synchro-selector window settings
Shutter Speeds		1/20—1/500	1-1/8	1/1000	1/500	1/250	1/125	1/60	X	1/30	1/15	1/8-B	Shutter speed dial figures color coded
Flashbulb type	FP	F		1000	500	250	125	60		60	X	X	Match color of dot in window
	M		S		1000	1000	500	125		60	X	X	Match dot (up to 1/125)
	F-SF		S							X	X	X	Match color of "F" in window
Electronic Flash	no delay	F (1/30 or slower)							X	X	X	X	FX (1/60 and slower)
	firing delay	F (1/20 or slower)		Click stops (+ and —) on synchro-selector dial alter delay 2 millisecs						X	X	X	FX (1/30 and slower)

Metric

weight: grams (gm.)

volume: cubic centimeters (cc)
1000 cc = 1 liter

To convert temperature scales:

$$C^\circ = \frac{5(F^\circ - 32)}{9}$$

$$F^\circ = \frac{9(C^\circ + 32)}{5}$$

Avoirdupois

Weight

1 dram = 27.343 grains (gr.)
16 drams = 1 ounce
1 ounce = 437.5 grains (gr.)
16 ounces = 1 pound

Fluid (U.S. Measure)

60 minims = 1 dram
8 drams = 1 ounce
480 minims = 1 ounce
32 ounces = 1 quart
4 quarts = 1 gallon (U.S.)
160 ounces = 1 gallon (Imp.)

Conversions

Weight

1 dram = 1.7718 grams (gm.)
1 gram = 15.4325 grains (gr.)
1 grain = 0.0648 grams
1 ounce = 28.3495 grams
1 gram = 0.03527 ounces
1 pound = 453.5924 grams
or 0.453592 kilograms
1 kilogram = 2.2046 pound

Fluid

1 minim = 0.06161 cubic centimeters
1 cubic = 0.2705 drams (fluid), or
centimeter 0.0338 fluid ounce
1 quart = 0.9463 liter
1 liter = 1.0567 quarts

Note: Calculations to one decimal place are sufficiently accurate for photographic chemicals.

SELECTED 35mm FILM-DEVELOPER COMBINATIONS

Rapid Black-and-White Films

Film	Manufacturer	Manufacturer's Exposure Index (ASA) Day.	Tung.	Preferred Rating for Normal Use* (ASA scale meters) Day.	Tung.	Developers*
Tri-X	Eastman Kodak	200	160	400-650	320-500	Normal use: Kodak D-76, Ethol UFG, D-23. For pushing film speed to 800-1200; Ethol UFG, Kodak D-76; D-23; up to 1600-3200: Ilford Microphen, DK-50. Softworking: Kodak D-23. Clayton P-60, Ilford Microphen.
HPS	Ilford	400	320	800-1200	640-800	Normal use: Kodak D-76 (same as Ilford ID-11), Ilford Microphen, Ethol UFG. For pushing film speed to 1600: Ilford Microphen.
HP3	Ilford	200	160	400-600	320-400	Normal use: Kodak D-76 (same as Ilford ID-11), Ethol UFG. For pushing film speed: Ilford Microphen.
Peromnia 25	Perutz	250	320	500-650	640-800	Normal use: Kodak D-76, Ethol UFG. For pushing film speed: Ilford Microphen.
Isopan Ultra	Agfa	200	320	400-650	640-800	Normal use: Kodak D-76, Ethol UFG. For pushing film speed: Ilford Microphen.

General Purpose Black-and-White Films

Film	Manufacturer	Manufacturer's Exposure Index (ASA) Day.	Tung.	Preferred Rating For Normal Use* (ASA Scale Meters) Day.	Tung.	Developers* General Use	Special Purposes
Plus-X	Eastman Kodak	80	64	160-200	200-400	For general use; Kodak D-76, Ethol UFG, Clayton P-60, Edwal Thermofine, Ilford Microphen.	For pushing to 800: Kodak D-76, Ilford Microphen, UFG.
FP-3	Ilford	64	50	125-180	150-200		For pushing to 320-400: Ilford Microphen. Fine grain: Ilford ID-48 (with 50% film speed loss), UFG.
Gevapan 33	Gevaert	64	40	125-180	125-200		Fine grain: Ethol UFG, Edwal Thermofine.
KB-21	Adox	80	64	160-200	150-200		
Peromnia 21	Perutz	100	80	200-300	200-320		For pushing to up to 800: Ethol UFG, Ilford Microphen, Kodak D-76.
Isopan ISS	Agfa	80	64	160-200	150-200		Fine grain: Ethol UFG, Edwal Thermofine.

Fine-Grain, Thin Emulsion Films

Film	Manufacturer	Manufacturer's Exposure Index (ASA) Day.	Tung.	Preferred Rating For Normal Use* (ASA Scale Meters) Day.	Tung.	Developers* General Purpose	Special Purposes
Panatomic-X	Eastman Kodak	25	20	50-64	32-40	Kodak D-76, Edwal Minicol, Edwal Fine-grain Concentrate No. 2.	Extra fine grain: Edwal Minicol Maximum film speed (up to 3X manufacturer's rating) and higher contrast: FR X-22.
Pan F	Ilford	25	16	40-50	25-32	Kodak D-76 (same as Ilford ID-11), May & Baker Prom-	Extra fine grain: Tetenal Neofin Blue, Ilford ID-48 (with 50% film speed loss).
KB-14	Adox	16	12	24-32	20-24	Edwal Minicol, May & Baker Promicrol.	Extra fine grain: Tetenal Neofin Blue. Maximum film speed (2-3X manufacturer's rating) and higher contrast: FR X-22.
KB-17	Adox	32	25	50-64	32-50	Kodak D-76, Edwal Minicol, Promicrol, Tetenal Neofin Blue.	Extra fine grain: Tetenal Neofin Blue. Maximum film speed and higher contrast: FRX-22. For increased contrast: Tetenal Neofin Red.

* Preferred ratings are for normal use, and provide reasonable starting points for film to be developed normally following time-temperature and agitation instructions given by the developer manufacturer. However, even within the limits of "minimum correct exposure" tastes and methods vary according to the individual and the type of subject matter. For example, low-contrast subjects outdoors, or available light material (where only detail in lighter tones is important) can be exposed at higher ratings than scenes where full shadow and highlight detail is required. To determine the exact film speed and development time that suits your subject matter and needs, run a test roll for each new developer-film combination. If results are slightly over "minimum correct exposure", increase the film index about 50% on your next test roll, but maintain same developing time; if results are somewhat under "minimum correct exposure," decrease the film index (without changing developing time), or increase developing time moderately (without changing the film rating). Note: When pushing film, develop by inspection.

MAJOR BLACK-AND-WHITE 35mm FILMS

Film	Manufacturer	Area of Origin				Film Type				Manufacturer's Rating (ASA)		Sizes available in U. S.		
		U. S.	England	Europe	Pacific	Rapid	Gen. Purpose	Fine Grain	Spec. Purpose	Daylight	Tungsten	20 — exp.	36 — exp.	Bulk loading
Tri-X	Eastman Kodak	X	X	F	A	X				200	160	X	X	X
Plus-X	Eastman Kodak	X	X	F			X			80	64	X	X	X
Panatomic-X	Eastman Kodak	X	X	F	A			X		25	20	X	X	X
Fine Grain Positive	Eastman Kodak	X	X	F					X	—	—	—	—	X
Direct Positive Panchromatic	Eastman Kodak	X							X	64	50	—	—	X
Micro-File	Eastman Kodak	X		F					X	—	16	—	X	X
Infrared	Eastman Kodak	X		F					X	—	20	X	—	X
High-Speed Infrared	Eastman Kodak	X							X	50	160	—	—	X
Quick-Finish*	Eastman Kodak		X						X	40	32	—	—	—
HPS	Ilford		X			X				400	320	—	X	X
HP3	Ilford		X			X				200	160	—	X	X
FP3	Ilford		X				X			64	50	—	X	X
Pan F	Ilford		X					X		25	16	—	X	X
Fine Grain Safety Positive	Ilford		X						X	—	—	—	—	X
Micro-neg	Ilford		X						X	—	—	—	—	X
KB-21	Adox			G			X			80	64	—	X	X
KB-17	Adox			G				X		32	25	X	X	X
KB-14	Adox			G				X		16	12	X	X	X
UKB-17* (direct positive)	Adox			G					X	40	—	—	—	—
Isopan U (Ultra)	Agfa			G		X				200	320	—	X	X
Isopan ISS	Agfa			G			X			80	64	X	X	X
Isopan F	Agfa			G				X		32	25	X	X	X
Isopan FF	Agfa			G				X		16	16	—	X	X
Gevapan 36	Gevaert			B		X				250	160	—	X	—
Gevapan 33	Gevaert			B			X			125	100	X	—	X
Gevapan 30	Gevaert			B			X			64	40	X	—	X
Gevapan 27 (Microgran)	Gevaert			B				X		32	20	X	—	—
Infrared	Gevaert			B					X	—	—	—	X	—
Duplo Ortho (microfilm)	Gevaert			B					X	—	—	—	—	X
Duplo Pan Rapid (microfilm)	Gevaert			B					X	—	—	—	—	X

* — Not available in U.S.; A — Australasia; B — Belgium; F — France; G — Germany

Note: Data for this chart was checked at publication time with manufacturers or importers of these materials. Film characteristics and availability are, of course, subject to change without notice.

(Continued on page 278)

B & W Films (Continued from page 277)

		Manufactured in Japan	(Rapid)	(Gen. Purpose)	(Fine Grain)	(Spec. Purpose)	Day.	Tung.	* Not available in U.S.
Neopan SSS*	Fuji		X				200	160	
Neopan SS*	"			X			100	80	
Neopan S*	"				X		50	40	
Minicopy*	"					X	—	25	
Konipan SSS*	Konishiroku		X				200	160	
Konipan SS*	"			X			100	80	
Konipan S*	"				X		50	40	

SELECTED PROPRIETARY DEVELOPERS

	Manufacturer	High energy	Gen'l purpose	Fine grain	Temp. tolerance	Replenisher	
Finex-L	Ansco		X	X		X	
BFi No. 80	Brown-Forman	X	X		X		Short devel. times
Clayton P-60*	Clayton	X	X		X	X	Phenidone; compensating
Clayton P-20	Clayton	X	X		X	X	Phenidone; compensating
Fine Grain Conc. #2*	Edwal			X	X		
Super 12	Edwal	X		X			High E.I., rapid films
Super 20	Edwal			X		X	
Minicol*	Edwal			X			For thin-emulsion films
Thermofine*	Edwal		X	X	X	X	
Microdol	Eastman Kodak			X		X	Use mfg's. E.I.
X-33B	FR Corp.			X		X	Soft working
X-22*	FR Corp.			X	X		
Microphen*	Ilford	X	X			X	Phenidone; compensating
ID 48*	Ilford			X			50% loss in film speed
Promicrol*	May & Baker	X		X		X	
Ethol UFG*	Plymouth	X	X	X	X	X	
Ethol 90	Plymouth	X			X	X	45-360 sec. times
Panthermic 777	Sussex Chem. Corp.		X	X	X	X	
Neofin Blue*	Tetenal			X			Soft-working; for thin emulsions
Neofin Red*	Tetenal		X	X			

* See page 276

MAJOR 35mm COLOR FILMS

Film	Manufacturer	Area of Origin				Film Type							Manu-facturer's Rating (ASA)		Sizes available in U.S.		
		U. S.	England	Europe	Pacific	Daylight Type	Flash Type	Type "A"	3200K	Reversal	Negative	User can process	Day.	Tung.	20 exp.	36 exp.	Bulk Loading
Ektachrome, Daylight Type	Eastman Kodak	X	X	F		X				X		X	32	—	X	—	X
Ektachrome, Type F	Eastman Kodak	X	X	F			X			X		X	See p. 273		X	—	X
Kodachrome, Daylight Type	Eastman Kodak	X	X	F	A	X				X			10	—	X	X	X
Kodachrome, Type F	Eastman Kodak	X		F			X			X			See p. 273		X	X	X
Kodachrome Professional Film, Type A	Eastman Kodak	X	X	F	A			X		X			—	16	—	X	X
Ektacolor SO1185	Eastman Kodak	X					X				X	X	See p. 273		—	—	X
Super Anscochrome	Ansco	X				X				X		X	100	—	X	—	—
Anscochrome (Daylight)	Ansco	X				X				X		X	32	—	X	—	X
Anscochrome Flash Type	Ansco	X					X			X		X	See p. 273		X	—	—
Anscochrome Tungsten	Ansco	X						X		X		X	—	32	—	—	X
Ansco Color Slide Dupli-cating Film, Type 538	Ansco	X								X		X	—	—	—	—	X
Agfacolor CUT 18	Agfa			G		X				X			40	—	Av. early in 1958		
Agfacolor CN 17	Agfa			G		Universal					X		32	25	Av. early in 1958		

A—Australasia, F—France, G—Germany

Note: 35mm color films not available in the U.S. include those made by Ilford (England), Dufay (England), Gevaert (Belgium), Ferrania (Italy), Fuji (Japan), and others.

Data for this chart was checked at publication time with manufacturers or importers of these materials. Film characteristics and availability are, of course, subject to change without notice.

IODINE THIOCARBAMIDE REDUCER. For local reduction of small dark areas (such as black spots, or lines) on dry prints.

Formula		Instructions
Solution A		Combine 1 part each of A and B, diluting with water when less reduction is desired. Apply to dark spot or line with nearly dry fine (00 or 000) sable brush; then swab quickly with methyl alcohol in tuft of cotton. Repeat process till desired effect is achieved. Absorb excess alcohol. Fix, and wash. If effect is too light, rebuild area with Spotone till tone is correct.
Iodine	40 gr.	
Methyl alcohol	2 oz.	
Shake until dissolved		
Solution B		
Thiocarbamide	80 gr.	
Water to make	2 oz.	

USEFUL DEVELOPER FORMULAS

Ingredients	Kodak DK60a		DK 50R		Kodak DK-50		Kodak D-23	
Water (125F-50C)	96 oz.	750. cc.	96 oz.	750. cc.	64 oz.	500. cc.	24 oz.	750. cc.
Elon (Metol)	145 gr.	2.5 gm.	290 gr.	5. gm.	145 gr.	2.5 gm.	¼ oz.	7.5 gm.
Sodium Sulfite, desic.	6¾ oz.	50. gm.	4 oz.	30. gm.	4 oz.	30. gm.	3 oz. 145 gr.	100. gm.
Hydroquinone	145 gr.	2.5 gm.	1 oz. 145 gr.	10. gm.	145 gr.	2.5 gm.	—	—
Kodalk	2 oz. 290 gr.	20. gm.	5¼ oz.	40. gm.	1 oz. 145 gr.	10. gm.	—	—
Potassium Bromide	30 gr.	0.5 gm.	—	—	30 gr.	0.5 gm.	—	—
Water, to make	1 gallon	1.0 liter	1 gallon	1.0 liter	1 gallon	1.0 liter	1 quart	1.0 liter

KODAK D-23

Simple to mix. Extremely suitable for contrasty available light situations because is soft-working and gives maximum exposure latitude, usually without blocking highlights. Moderate grain. Used by many professionals, and custom photo-finishers. DK-25R is the replenisher but will make D-23 unsuitable for 35mm work. Maintain level with D-23 instead. Useful life: until developing times reach twice normal. Normal developing times: Tri-X, 10 min.; Plus-X, 12 min.; 68F; agitation 5 sec. every 30 sec. small tank.

KODAK DK-50

In 35mm work, best used only for pushing film speed beyond the preferred rating. Moderate grain. DK-50R is replenisher formula. Develop by inspection.

KODAK DK-50R

KODAK DK-60a

General purpose, fairly high-energy developer. One of the emergency developers for underexposure, but not as strong as D-82. Develop by inspection.

Note: mix ingredients in order listed.

USEFUL DEVELOPER FORMULAS

Ingredients	Kodak D-82		Kodak DK-15		Kodak D-11		Ansco 17	
Water 120F, 50C	24 oz.	750. cc.	24 oz.	750. cc.	16 oz.	500. cc.	24 oz.	750. cc.
Wood alcohol	1½ oz.	48. cc.	—	—	—	—	—	—
Elon (Metol)	200 gr.	14. gm.	80 gr.	5.5 gm.	15 gr.	1. gm.	22 gr.	1.5 gm.
Sodium Sulfite desic.	1¾ oz.	52.5 gm.	3 oz.	90. gm.	2½ oz.	75. gm.	2½ oz. 80 gr. anhydrous	80. gm.
Hydroquinone	200 gr.	14. gm.	—	—	130 gr.	9. gm.	44 gr.	3. gm.
Kodalk	—	—	¾ oz.	22.5 gm.	—	—	—	—
Sodium Carbonate, mono.	—	—	—	—	1 oz.	30. gm.	—	—
Sodium Hydroxide	130 gr.	9. gm.	—	—	—	—	—	—
Borax	—	—	—	—	—	—	44 gr.	3. gm.
Potassium Bromide	130 gr.	9. gm.	30 gr.	2. gm.	75 gr.	5. gm.	7½ gr.	.5 gm.
Sodium Sulfate, desic.	—	—	1½ oz.	45. gm.	—	—	—	—
Water, to make	1 quart	1 liter	1 quart	1 liter	1 quart	1 liter	1 quart	1 liter

ANSCO 17

A general purpose, medium-fine grain developer. Normal development times, 10-15 min.; 68F; agitation 5-10 sec. every minute.

KODAK D-11

A high-contrast formula used for microfilm and copying work where high contrast is desired. For process photography use without dilution; for development of copies of continuous tone subjects, dilute 1:1. Develop by inspection. **Do not confuse with Ilford ID-11, which is identical with Kodak D-76**. See page 282.

KODAK DK-15

For tropical development of films. Following development, rinse: immerse 3 min. in Hardening Bath SB-4; omit water rinse if emulsion tends to soften. Develop test roll by inspection.

KODAK D-82

For extreme underexposure. Use only when underexposure is so great that high energy developers listed on page 276 are not likely to produce a printable image. **Do not expect good negative quality.** Develop by inspection.

Note: Mix ingredients in order listed.

KODAK D-76 General Purpose 35mm Developer

One of the most useful single developers for general 35mm use, first introduced in 1927. It produces high resolution and acutance combined with moderate grain, long scale gradation, good contrast, and permits using full speed of emulsions. Classified as a medium fine-grain developer, D-76 has a relatively high content of sodium sulfite which acts primarily as a preservative, but also functions as a silver solvent to prevent the formation of excessive grain. The common alkali, sodium carbonate, is omitted from the formula because it produces a heavy fog in the presence of excess sodium sulfite. The much weaker borax (sodium borate) is substituted in quantities to produce normal negative density within reasonable times. Potassium bromide is also omitted. Although restoring it will decrease grain, contrast is greatly reduced.

D-76 resembles, or is identical with, Ilford ID-11, Du Pont 6-D and Gevaert 206.

	D-76			D-76R	
	Avoirdupois — U. S. Liquid		Metric	Av.—U.S. Liquid	Metric
Water, about 125F	24 oz.	96 oz.	750. cc.	24 oz.	750. cc.
Elon (Metol)	30 gr.	115 oz.	2.0 gm.	45 gr.	3.0 gm.
Sodium Sulfite, desiccated	3 oz. 145 gr.	13¼ oz.	100.0 gm.	3 oz. 145 gr.	100.0 gm.
Hydroquinone	75 gr.	290 gr.	5.0 gm.	¼ oz.	7.5 gm.
Borax, granular	30 gr.	115 gr.	2.0 gm.	290 gr.	20.0 gm.
Water to make	1 qt.	1 gal.	1 liter	1 qt.	1 liter

Normal development times (in small tank, at 68F, with agitation for 5 sec. every 30 sec.): Tri-X, 11 min.; Plus-X, 8 min.; Panatomic-X, 7 min. (1:1 dilution).

D-76 and available light While other developers (listed on page 276) are more suitable for highly accelerated film indexes and forced development, reasonable speed rating increases may be secured by slight increases in D-76 developing times, without objectionable grain or contrast. These ratings include Tri-X at 800-1200, Plus-X at 500-800. Develop to normal times, then continue developing by inspection 2-4 min. more. Plus-X is particularly suited to this treatment because results show high acutance and resolution plus moderate fine grain. Results with Tri-X are acceptable on 11 x 14 enlargements made from most of the 35mm frame.

High energy D-76F Use 10× quantity of borax called for in the formulas above for forcing underexposed films. Grain will be increased in proportion to the extent of under-exposure. Normally exposed negatives require about half-time in D-76F; are slightly more grainy than in D-76.

D-76F is also excellent as a second developer when forcing underexposed film, and processing by inspection. If only a very faint image appears after a reasonable time in D-76 (or D-23), transfer the film to D-76F and continue developing by inspection.

Maximum energy D-76 Very short developing times are possible (with a loss of maximum quality) by substituting Kodalk for the borax in these proportions:

to cut time to:		D-76 per qt.	D-76 per liter	D-76R per qt.	D-76R per liter
50%	A	75 gr.	5 gm.	290 gr.	20 gm.
35%	B	145 gr.	10 gm.	1 oz. 45 gr.	40 gm.
25%	C	290 gr.	20 gm.	(Add double replenisher volume of B)	

Hot Weather D-76 Add sodium sulfate: for 75-80F, 1 oz., 290 gr./quart (50 gm./liter); 80-85F, 2½ oz./quart (75 gm./liter), 85-90F, 3 oz. 145 gr./quart (100 gm./liter). Development times increase with temperature; at 90F and over, they are about ⅓ more than normal.

Chemical-physical D-76 The addition of 1⅕ oz./quart (40 gm/liter) ammonium chloride causes D-76 to behave partly as a physical developer: silver dissolved from the emulsion by the sodium sulfite is redeposited on the developing image as exceedingly minute particles and the (medium-speed film) negative will be virtually grainless. Reduce preferred E.I. ratings on page 276 by 50%; increase development time to twice normal.

SHORT STOPS	**Gen. Purpose**	**Kodak SB-5**
Water	1 gal.	64 oz.
Acetic Acid, 28%	3 oz.	4 oz.
Sodium Sulfate, desiccated	—	6 oz.
Water to make	—	1 gal.

General Purpose—Films: immerse 1 min. Discard bath after single use. If any apparent increase of grain is noted in enlargements, substitute plain water rinse for stop bath. Papers: agititate 5-15 sec. before transferring to fixer. Renew stop bath frequently. **SB-5**—Use for hot weather processing of film to prevent swelling of gelatin and reticulation. Immerse 3 min., agitating at start. Capacity of bath: about 50 rolls per gallon.

To Make 28% Acetic Acid: To 8 parts water add 3 parts Glacial Acetic Acid. Warning: **Always add the acid to the water.**

HARDENING BATHS	**Kodak Hardening Bath SB-4**	**Kodak Special Hardener SH-1**
Water	32 oz.	16 oz.
Potassium Chrome Alum	1 oz.	—
Sodium Sulfate, desiccated	2 oz.	—
Formaldehyde, ab. 37% solution by weight	—	2½ drams
Sodium Carbonate, monohydrated	—	90 gr.
Water to make	—	32 oz.

SB-4—For use in conjunction with DK-15 when working above 75F. Use SB-4 at 75-90F. Immerse about 3 min., after development, before fixation, agitating 30-45 sec. If temperature is below 85F rinse 1-2 sec. in water before hardening. Fresh bath is violet-blue; discard when turns yellow-green. Hardening power of partially used bath decreases rapidly on standing a few days. **SH-1** — For after treatment of negatives which would be softened by further chemical treatment such as intensification or reduction. Immerse in bath 3 min.; rinse; immerse 5 min. in fresh acid fixing bath; wash thoroughly before giving further chemical treatment.

FIXING BATHS	**Kodak F-5**	**ATF-1 (Mallinckrodt)**
Water	80 oz. (ab. 125F)	3 qts.
Soduim Thiosulfate (Hypo)	2 lb.	—
Ammonium Thiosulfate, 60%	—	25⅝ fl. oz.
Sodium Sulfite	2 oz. (desiccated)	1⅝ oz. (anhydrous)
Acetic Acid	6 oz. (28%)	1$\frac{5}{32}$ fl. oz. (Glacial)
Boric Acid, crystals	1 oz.	1 oz.
Potassium Alum	2 oz.	—
Aluminum Chloride Hexahydrate	—	1$\frac{1}{16}$ oz.
Cold water to make	1 gal.	1 gal.

Note: Mix in order given

F-5 — Film fixing time: 5-10 min. Discard when time required is over 10 min. Prints: fix 5-10 min. If odor of sulfur dioxide given off by bath is objectionable or if more rapid washing time is desired, modify F-5 as follows to turn it into Kodak F-6: eliminate the Boric Acid, and substitute twice its weight in Kodalk Balanced Alkali.

ATF-1 — a moderately rapid fixer. Clearing time with films, 1-3 min. Films should fix properly in twice clearing time. Discard bath when clearing time exceeds 7-8 min. With paper: dilute with one part water, two parts bath. Print fixing time for most prints: less than 1 min. Do not leave prints in bath for more than 3 min. Note on mixing: dissolve Boric Acid in small amount of hot water before adding.

INTENSIFIER — Kodak Silver Intensifier In-5

A proportional intensifier which deposits additional silver on the grains of the negative image. Increases grain less than any other intensifier. Before intensifying, fix film, wash thoroughly and harden in SH-1.

A	Silver Nitrate, crystals	2 oz.
	Distilled water to make	32 oz.
B	Sodium Sulfite, desiccated	2 oz.
	Water to make	32 oz.
C	Sodium Thiosulfate (Hypo)	3½ oz.
	Water to make	32 oz.
D	Sodium Sulfite, desiccated	½ oz.
	Elon (Metol)	365 gr.
	Water to make	96 oz.

To Mix: Add 1 part solution B slowly to 1 part solution A. Mix thoroughly. White precipitate is dissolved by addition of 1 part of solution C. Let stand a few minutes till clear; then add, with stirring, 3 parts solution D. Use immediately; mixed intensifier solution is stable about 30 min. at 68F.

Remarks: Time of treatment (which should not exceed 25 min.) governs the degree of intensification. Use the intensifier in artificial light, since solution tends to form a precipitate of silver quite rapidly when exposed directly to sunlight. After intensifying, immerse film for 2 min., with agitation, in a plain 30% hypo solution. Wash thoroughly.

REDUCERS

Note: Before reduction film should be fixed, washed thoroughly, and hardened in Kodak SH-1.

		Kodak R-4b	Kodak R-4a
A	Potassium Ferricyanide	¼ oz.	1¼ oz.
	Water to make	1 qt.	16 oz.
B	Sodium Thiosulfate (Hypo)	6¾ oz.	16 oz.
	Water to make	1 qt.	64 oz.

R-4a: Just before use add 1 oz. A to 4 oz. B, then add water to make 32 oz. For less rapid action use ½ oz. A, but same amounts B and water.

Remarks: **R-4b,** a two-bath reducer, is proportional and lowers contrast. Agitate negative in A for 1-4 min., at 65-70F, depending on degree of reduction desired, then immerse in B for 5 min. Wash thoroughly. Process may be repeated. R-4a: One-bath cutting reducer for clearing shadow areas. Place negative in tray (preferably white), and pour mixed solution over negative. Watch action closely. When reduction is sufficient, wash film thoroughly, then dry.

DU PONT 3R: Super-proportional; lowers contrast

Water	32 oz.
Ammonium Persulfate	2 oz.
Sulfuric Acid (see warning below)	¾ dram

Add 1 part stock solution to 2 parts water. Just before desired reduction is obtained remove film and immerse in an acid fixing bath for a few min., then wash.

WARNING: Always add acids to water slowly; **never add water to acid.**

EDER'S HARMONIZING REDUCER: Reduces highlights; intensifies shadows

Bleaching Solution

Water	25 oz.
Hydrochloric Acid, Concentrated	1 oz.
(see warning above)	
Potassium Bichromate	146 gr.
Alum	1 oz., 292 gr.
Water to make	1 qt.

Bleach negative to completion. Wash until yellow stain discharged; (or after 2-3 min. wash, accelerate removal of stain by immersing in 2% solution sodium bisulfite for a few min., then return film to wash). Redevelop in MQ developer (like DK-50) diluted 1:5.

PAPER DEVELOPERS		Kodak D-72	Kodak D-52	
Stock solutions	Water, about 125F	16 oz.	16 oz.	Remarks: **D-72** is an all-purpose, cold-tone, paper developer. With enlarging paper, dilute stock solution 1:2; develop 1-2 min. at 68F. D-52 is designed for use with warm-tone papers. Dilute 1:1 and develop about 1-2 minutes at 68F. Note: Dissolve chemicals in order given.
	Elon (Metol)	45 gr.	22 gr.	
	Sodium Sulfite, desiccated	1½ oz.	¾ oz.	
	Hydroquinone	175 gr.	90 gr.	
	Sodium Carbonate, monohydrated	2 oz., 90 gr.	250 gr.	
	Potassium Bromide	30 gr.	22 gr.	
	Water to make	1 qt.	1 qt.	

Selected Proprietary Developers For Enlarging Papers

Developer	Manufacturer	Remarks	Packaged Form
Dektol	Eastman Kodak	Gen. purpose; cold tones; rec. for Kodak Polycontrast papers.	Single powder Mix
Selectol	Eastman Kodak	For warm tones.	Single Powder Mix
Ethol LPD	Plymouth	Gen. purpose; long life; also rec. for variable contrast papers.	Single Powder Mix
Velvet Developer Concentrate	Edwal	Phenidone type; gen. purpose; cold black tones; for use up to 80F.	Concentrated Liquid
P-20	Clayton	Phenidone type; gen. purpose; cold black tones.	Concentrated Liquid
Vividol	Ansco	Gen. purpose; cold tones.	Single Powder Mix
BFi: No. 84	Brown-Forman	For cold black tones; high processing capacity.	Concentrated Liquid

Kodak Gold Protective Solution GP-1: for print permanence

Water	24 oz.	1% gold chloride stock solution = 1 tube (15 grains) in 3¼ oz. water. Add gold chloride stock solution to 24 oz. water; dissolve sodium thiocyanate in 4 oz. water, then add slowly to gold chloride solution while stirring latter rapidly.
Gold Chloride (1% stock solution)	2½ drams	
Sodium Thiocyanate	145 gr.	
Water to make	1 qt.	

To use: immerse print (which has received HE-1 treatment below) for 10 min. at 68F, or until just perceptible change in image tone takes place. Wash 10 min. in running water; dry. Capacity: 30 8 x 10 prints per gallon. For best results, mix GP-1 immediately before use.

Kodak Hypo Eliminator HE-1

Water	16 oz.	Mix in order given. Ammonia solution = 1 part concentrated ammonia (28%) to 9 parts water. **Warning:** make solution just before use and keep in open container. Stoppered bottle may burst.
Hydrogen Peroxide (3% solution)	4 oz.	
Ammonia solution	3¼ oz.	
Water to make	1 qt.	

To use: Wash prints 30 min. in running water at 65-70F. Immerse print in HE-1 about 6 min. at 68F; then wash 10 min. before drying. Capacity: about 50 8 x 10 prints per gallon.

Index